Warfare in History

WAR AT SEA IN THE MIDDLE AGES AND THE RENAISSANCE

Warfare in History

General Editor: Matthew Bennett
ISSN 1358–779X

*Previously published volumes in the series
are listed at the back of this volume*

WAR AT SEA IN THE MIDDLE AGES
AND THE RENAISSANCE

Edited by
John B. Hattendorf and Richard W. Unger

THE BOYDELL PRESS

© Editors and Contributors 2003

All Rights Reserved. Except as permitted under current legislation
no part of this work may be photocopied, stored in a retrieval system,
published, performed in public, adapted, broadcast,
transmitted, recorded or reproduced in any form or by any means,
without the prior permission of the copyright owner

First published 2003
The Boydell Press, Woodbridge

ISBN 0 85115 903 6

The Boydell Press is an imprint of Boydell & Brewer Ltd
PO Box 9, Woodbridge, Suffolk IP12 3DF, UK
and of Boydell & Brewer Inc.
PO Box 41026, Rochester, NY 14604–4126, USA
website: www.boydell.co.uk

A catalogue record for this book is available
from the British Library

Library of Congress Cataloging-in-Publication Data
War at sea in the Middle Ages and the Renaissance / edited by
John B. Hattendorf and Richard W. Unger.
    p. cm. – (Warfare in history)
Includes bibliographical references and index.
ISBN 0–85115–903–6 (Hardback : alk. paper)
    1. Naval art and science – Europe – History – To 1500. 2. Naval
art and science – Europe – History – 16th century. 3. Naval history –
Europe – To 1500. 4. Naval history – Europe – 16th century.
5. Sea-power – History. I. Hattendorf, John B. II. Unger, Richard W.
III. Series.
V43.W37 2002
359'.0094'0902 – dc21   2002011117

This publication is printed on acid-free paper

Printed in Great Britain by
St Edmundsbury Press Ltd, Bury St Edmunds, Suffolk

CONTENTS

List of Illustrations	vii
List of Contributors	viii
Preface *John B. Hattendorf and Richard W. Unger*	xi
Acknowledgements	xiv
Introduction Theories of Naval Power: A. T. Mahan and the Naval History of Medieval and Renaissance Europe *John B. Hattendorf*	1

I: Northern Europe

Naval Force in the Viking Age and High Medieval Denmark *Niels Lund*	25
Scandinavian Warships and Naval Power in the Thirteenth and Fourteenth Centuries *Jan Bill*	35
Naval Power and Maritime Technology during the Hundred Years War *Timothy J. Runyan*	53
Oars, Sails and Guns: The English and War at Sea, *c.*1200–*c.*1500 *Ian Friel*	69

II: Southern Europe

Byzantium and the Sea: Byzantine Fleets and the History of the Empire in the Age of the Macedonian Emperors, *c.*900–1025 CE *John H. Pryor*	83
Iberian Naval Power, 1000–1650 *Lawrence V. Mott*	105
Venice, Genoa and Control of the Seas in the Thirteenth and Fourteenth Centuries *John Dotson*	119

Genoese Naval Forces in the Mediterranean during the Fifteenth 137
and Sixteenth Centuries
   Michel Balard

An Exemplary Maritime Republic: Venice at the End of the Middle Ages   151
   Bernard Doumerc

III: Sixteenth and Early-Seventeenth-Century Europe

The Navies of the Medici: The Florentine Navy and the Navy of the Sacred 169
Military Order of St Stephen, 1547–1648
   Marco Gemignani

The State of Portuguese Naval Forces in the Sixteenth Century   187
   Francisco Contente Domingues

Naval Power in the Netherlands before the Dutch Revolt   199
   Louis Sicking

Naval Power and Control of the Sea in the Baltic in the Sixteenth Century   217
   Jan Glete

The New Atlantic: Naval Warfare in the Sixteenth Century   233
   N. A. M. Rodger

Conclusion: Toward a History of Medieval Sea Power   249
   Richard W. Unger

Index   263

ILLUSTRATIONS

Scandinavian Warships and Naval Power in the Thirteenth and Fourteenth Centuries
1	Engelborg at Nakskov in south-eastern Denmark	36
2	The Helgeandsholmen V shipfind, as reconstructed from archaeological remains	38
3	Fourteenth-century mural from Skamstrup parish church, Denmark, showing the legend of St Olav	40
4	The Kollerup cog	42
5	Ship depictions from the parish churches of Himmelev and Skrøbelev	44

Byzantium and the Sea
1	Longitudinal section of a tenth-century bireme dromon	86
2	Oarage system of a tenth-century bireme dromon	88
3	Stowage of barrels or amphorae	91

Iberian Naval Power, 1000–1650
Map 1	The Western Mediterranean	116

Venice, Genoa and Control of the Seas in the Thirteenth and Fourteenth Centuries
Map 1	The Mediterranean: selected naval actions, 1250–1380	132

Genoese Naval Forces in the Mediterranean during the Fifteenth and Sixteenth Centuries
1	The Genoese Fleet and the Arsenal of Genoa	144

The Navies of the Medici
Map 1	The Grand Duchy of Tuscany and the Tyrrhenian Sea	170

Naval Power in the Netherlands before the Dutch Revolt
Map 1	The Netherlands in 1543	200
1	Seal of the Admiralty under Maximilian of Burgundy (1540–1558)	210
2	Detail from a map of the Netherlands by Hieronimous Cock (1557)	215

Naval Power and Control of the Sea in the Baltic in the Sixteenth Century
Map 1	The Baltic region	218

The New Atlantic: Naval Warfare in the Sixteenth Century
Map 1	The European Atlantic Coast	234

CONTRIBUTORS

Michel Balard is professor of Medieval History at the University of Paris I. Among his principal works are the two-volume *Gênes et l'Outre-mer* (1973–1980), the two volume *La Romanie génoise (XIIe–début du XVe siècle)* (1978), the three-volume *Genova e l'Oltremare* (1983–1988), *Les Croisades* (1988), *Le Journal de bord de Christophe Colomb* (1992), *Autour de la Première Croisade* (1996), *Le Partage du monde* (1998), and *Les Pays d'Islam et le monde latin (Xe–XIIIe siècles). Textes et documents* (2000), *Croisades et Orient latin XIe–XIVe siècle* (2001).

Jan Bill is senior researcher at the Centre for Maritime Archaeology at the National Museum of Denmark, a post he has held since 1998. Born in 1961 in Birkerød, Denmark, he earned a Cand. Phil. degree in archaeology from the University of Copenhagen 1993, and his doctorate from the same university in 1998, with a dissertation on local and regional seafaring in Denmark in the Middle Ages. He has contributed to several Danish and internationally published books on seafaring, including the authoritative *Dansk søfarts historie* ('History of Danish Seafaring') published in 1997.

Francisco Domingues lectures on Portuguese naval history and the history of expansion at the University of Lisbon. He has published a number of books and articles on those subjects, including the volume *A carreira da Índia / The India Run* (1998) and was coordinator of the two-volume *Dicionário de história dos descobrimentos portugueses* (Dictionary for the History of Portuguese Discoveries) (1994). He is a member of the board of directors of the International Committee for the History of Nautical Science and Hydrography.

John Dotson is professor of history at Southern Illinois University, Carbondale. He was editor and translator of *Merchant Culture in Fourteenth-Century Venice: The Zibaldone da Canal* (1994) and, with Aldo Agosto, *Christopher Columbus and His Family* (1998). He has also written a number of articles and chapters on Italian maritime trade and naval affairs during the late Middle Ages and the early Renaissance.

Bernard Doumerc is professor of medieval history at the University of Toulouse, France. A specialist in the history of the Mediterranean world, he has collaborated on a number of works, including the ten-volume *La storia di Venezia*, and has published *Venise et l'émirat hafside de Tunis 1235–1535* (1999).

Ian Friel is curator of the Chichester District Museum, West Sussex. From 1977 to 1988, he worked as a medieval historian at the National Maritime

Museum, Greenwich, serving as research coordinator of the museum's Armada exhibit and was a co-editor of the exhibition catalogue, *Armada 1588–1988*. From 1988 to 1992, he was exhibition manager for the Mary Rose Trust at Portsmouth. He is the author of *The Good Ship: Ships, Shipbuilding and Technology in England, 1200–1520* (1995).

Marco Gemignani currently teaches naval history at the Naval Academy of the Italian Navy. Born in 1966, he gained a first-class degree at the University of Pisa and successfully completed a doctorate in military history at the University of Padua and postdoctoral studies in historical and philosophical sciences at the University of Pisa. He has published a book about the life of one of the most significant admirals of the navy of the Order of St Stephen, *Il cavaliere Iacopo Inghirami al servizio dei granduchi di Toscana* (1996), and has written several articles and essays for specialist magazines about naval history from the sixteenth century to the present. A member of the Società di storia militare, he has been for many years a voluntary research assistant in military history.

Jan Glete is professor of history at Stockholm University, Sweden. Born in 1947, he earned his doctorate at Stockholm in 1975. His main areas of research are Swedish industrial and financial history, technology and complex organisations and early modern naval history and state formation. His recent published work includes *Navies and Nations: Warships, Navies and State Building in Europe and America (1500–1860)* (1993) and *Warfare at Sea, 1500–1650: Maritime Conflicts and the Transformation of Europe* (2000).

John B. Hattendorf is the Ernest J. King Professor of Maritime History at the US Naval War College, Newport, Rhode Island. A graduate of Kenyon College, he earned his master's degree at Brown University and his doctorate at the University of Oxford. The author, co-author, editor, or co-editor of more than thirty books in the field of maritime history, he has received an honorary doctorate from Kenyon College and the Caird medal of the National Maritime Museum, Greenwich. In an adjunct position, he is a member of the faculty of the Munson Institute of American Maritime Studies, Mystic Seaport, Connecticut, and served as its director, 1996–2001. Among his current projects, he is editor-in-chief of the forthcoming *Oxford Encyclopedia of Maritime History*.

Niels Lund is professor of Medieval History at the University of Copenhagen. He received his degree in history and archaeology from the University of Aarhus in 1969 and was awarded the golden medal of the University of Copenhagen for a thesis on the Vikings in England 1968. Among his appointments, he has been British Council Research Fellow in the University of Leeds in 1973–5 and lecturer in history at Copenhagen University from 1975, where he was promoted to professor in 1998. His publications are mainly focused on Vikings in Scandinavia and in England; they include scholarly articles, popular books, and translations of original sources from Latin and Old English. Among them is a full study of Scandinavian medieval military organisation, published in 1996.

Lawrence Mott is at the Center for Maritime and Regional Studies, University of Southern Denmark. He earned his master's degree in nautical archaeology at Texas A&M University in 1992 and his doctorate in history at the University of Minnesota in 1999. He has published nine articles covering aspects of medieval Iberian naval and maritime history and a book, *The Development of the Rudder: A Technological Tale* (1996).

John H. Pryor is Associate Professor in the Centre for Medieval Studies and the Department of History of the University of Sydney, Australia. He is the author of many articles and of chapters contributed to books on medieval Mediterranean naval warfare, maritime commerce, and the logistics of crusading by sea. His major publication is *Geography, Technology and War: Studies in the Maritime History of the Mediterranean, 649–1571* (1987). For the past decade he has been working on a major study of the Byzantine navy to be entitled *The Dromon: Terminology and Reality*.

N. A. M. Rodger is Professor of Naval History at the University of Exeter. He was formerly Anderson Research Fellow of the National Maritime Museum, and before that an assistant keeper in the Public Record Office. *The Safeguard of the Sea*, the first volume of his naval history of Britain, was published in 1997.

Timothy Runyan is director of the Program in Maritime History and Nautical Archaeology at East Carolina University, Greenville, North Carolina. He served as editor of *The American Neptune, a Quarterly Journal of Maritime History*. His publications include *European Naval and Maritime History, 300–1500* (with A. R. Lewis).

Louis Sicking is an assistant professor in medieval history at Leiden University. Born in 1966, he studied history in Leiden and Aix-en-Provence and obtained the diploma of archivist, first class, at the National School of Archives in the Netherlands. His doctoral thesis, *Zeemacht en onmacht: maritieme politiek in de Nederlanden, 1488–1558*, was published in Amsterdam in 1998. He has been a visiting scholar at Columbia University in New York and a fellow of the Royal Netherlands Academy of Arts and Sciences at Leiden University. His research interests include maritime history, the history of discoveries and European expansion, and the Netherlands in the fifteenth and sixteenth centuries, topics on which he has recently published several articles.

Richard W. Unger is a professor in the history department of the University of British Columbia. He has published work on the history of medieval and early modern ships and shipping as well as on the history of technology in the Netherlands, especially the history of brewing.

PREFACE

This book aims to serve both as a corrective to the older English-language interpretations of sea power in the Middle Ages and the Renaissance and as a general work on naval and maritime history in the period. The objective here is to draw broad conclusions on the role and characteristics of armed force at sea before 1650, conclusions that exploit the best current understanding of the medieval period. While this volume does not claim to be a comprehensive attempt at understanding the naval history of Europe from the late Roman Empire to the mid-seventeenth century, it may serve as a guide to suggest why the period is both important and unique. In addition, since this volume is not an exhaustive study of those years, the editors hope that it will serve as a stimulus for further work on the general theme as well as on specific aspects of warfare at sea in the Middle Ages and the Renaissance that we were unable to include here.

The use of armed force at sea during the Middle Ages and the Renaissance in Europe needs reconsideration. New research and new thinking about the broad nature of sea warfare in these periods, as well as a new understanding about the ships used, has created the need for a more general scholarly reappraisal. The development of scuba gear made possible, from the 1950s on, investigations of shipwrecks under water, which rapidly expanded knowledge of the history of ship design. The growth in that knowledge brought even more clearly into focus the absence of the discussion of technology and its impact on naval history, at least for the centuries before the introduction of steam. Recent history has focused attention on the different ways of reading what governments said, on the sometimes ignored language of policy makers and the impact of that language on naval history. Without question, changes in ships had a significant effect on naval power in the years before 1650, in the era before permanent navies existed in nation-states such as France, Spain, England, and the Netherlands. It was examining the effects of the technical changes that opened a more general discussion of naval forces. The central question has long been the degree to which ideas and theories about command of the sea, derived from the study of a later period, can and ought to be applied to what people did, thought, and said in the years between the fall of the Roman Empire and the Anglo-Dutch naval wars beginning in the mid-seventeenth century.

This book grew out of testing ideas about medieval naval history, a process that has expanded in scope with every stage. The project began with discussion of the central issues in a session at the American Historical Association meeting in New York City in 1997, which received a very positive response. The papers and discussion led to publication of an article later in the same year based on the results of the session,[1] which in turn led to the organisation of a full-scale conference on the topic. The fact that a number of scholars on both sides of the Atlantic have independently become involved in the study of medieval and Renaissance maritime history in recent years created an opportunity to draw on a range of new work. Fortunately it was possible to enlist the help and cooperation of the prominent naval historian Francisco Contente Domingues of the University of Lisbon. Through his participation in the organisation of the conference and under the auspices of the Fondaçao Oriente, it became possible to hold the meeting at Arrabida, Portugal, in February 2000.

The precise nature of the central issue of the conference dictated a highly directed and concentrated effort on the part of participants. They were to focus on the issues and an understanding of the uses of armed force at sea in the Middle Ages and the Renaissance, taking the older literature as a starting point or a foil for a re-evaluation of the topics of force, power and the sea, the roots, functions, and the concept of naval power. Before the meeting participants received a preliminary outline of topics for discussion, enabling a more fruitful discussion; and further papers were commissioned to give a broader overview of the subject, and to provide a broader balance to the present volume.

This volume specifically aims to make a substantial contribution to historical knowledge in raising new questions about the origins, development and practice of naval warfare. Its purpose is to search for new and alternative interpretations of naval history through a multi-pronged approach that uses comparative history, tests theoretical propositions, and promotes new historical research. By comparing and contrasting naval activities in northern Europe with those in southern Europe in the light of naval theory, for example, there is opportunity to see well-known events in a new and different light. The broad aspects of current naval theory can suggest some alternative interpretations to historical questions, while a new look at the medieval and Renaissance periods provides a convenient opportunity to challenge and to modify theory. In the years from the tenth to the sixteenth century war at sea was not primarily a monopoly of states, but it saw the beginnings of the transition toward that development. Why and how this occurred, as well as the nature of war at sea both before and after this development, are fundamental features for consideration.

In asking whether or not there was any naval thought at all in medieval Western Europe, a recent writer concluded, 'the study of naval thought in the Middle Ages remains an ocean to discover'.[2] This volume does not by any means exhaust the subject. Among the many additional subjects that deserve more detailed treatment within a broad account of medieval and Renaissance naval history is the survival of Vegetius' *De Re Militari*, written in the fourth

---

[1] Richard W. Unger, 'Alfred Thayer Mahan, Ship Design, and the Evolution of Sea Power in the Late Middle Ages', *The International History Review*, 19, 3 (August, 1997), 505–21.
[2] Philippe Richardot, 'Y a-t-il une pensée navale dans l'Occident Médiéval?', in Hervé Coutau-Bégarie, ed., *L'Evolution de la pensée navale VII* (Paris: Economica, 1999), 13–23, quotation translated from 23.

century, with its single short chapter on naval tactics as part of a larger discussion of military manoeuvres. Although scholars knew about it, that work seems to have played a very small practical role for those who went to sea in Western Europe during most of the medieval period. The work did find a new audience by the seventeenth century, a reflection of the development of modern navies.[3] There are, of course, other aspects of naval warfare in the period not explored in this volume: the actions of the Hanseatic League;[4] the development of French armed force at sea;[5] the extensive naval activity undertaken by the Knights of St John at Malta against the corsairs of North Africa; and the use of armed vessels by the chartered trading companies. Despite these omissions from the detailed examinations presented in this volume, we believe that it is still possible to discern some patterns and draw some general conclusions about the nature of war at sea during the Middle Ages and the Renaissance.

John B. Hattendorf
Naval War College
Newport, Rhode Island, USA

Richard W. Unger
University of British Columbia
Vancouver, BC, Canada

---

[3] On this, see Philippe Richardot, 'L'Influence du *Re Militari* de Végèce sur la pensée militaire du XVIe siècle', *Stratégique*, 60 (1996), 7–28, and *Végèce et la culture militaire au Moyen Âge, Ve–XVe siècles* (Paris: Economica, 1998).
[4] Horst Wernicke, 'Die Hanse als Seemacht im europäischen Spätmittelalter' (unpublished and untranslated paper presented to the Arrabida conference) and *Die Städtehanse. 1280–1418. Genesis–Strukturen–Funktionen*. Abhandlungen zur Handels- und Sozialgeschichte 22 (Weimar, 1983). Also, Konrad Fritze and Günter Krause, *Seekrige der Hanse* (Berlin, 1989).
[5] Among other works, see for example A. Chazelas-Merlin, *Documents relatifs au clos des galées de Rouen et aux armées de la mer du roi de France de 1293 à 1418*, 2 vols (Paris, 1977–9).

ACKNOWLEDGEMENTS

On behalf of all the participants of the conference from which this volume initially derived, thanks are due to the Fondaço Oriente for offering a site for the meeting and for financial support, and to its staff at the Fondaço's Arrabida conference centre for ensuring that the practical arrangements ran smoothly and effectively. All involved in the project are deeply indebted to Francisco Domingues for his unfailing efforts throughout and for his work with the Fondaço Oriente, ensuring productive cooperation at all times.

The editors greatly appreciate the work of Jason M. Peters of the Graphic Arts Department, US Naval War College, in preparing the final versions of the maps for this volume. They are also indebted to Pat Cormier of the Naval War College and to Jocelyn Smith of the University of British Columbia for their help in preparing the final version of the text; and to the publishers of this volume for their patience and assistance in its production. Additionally, the editors acknowledge the gracious permission granted by several other institutions, artists, and publishers to include the illustrations used in this volume, which is noted as part of the illustration captions.

INTRODUCTION

THEORIES OF NAVAL POWER:
A. T. MAHAN AND THE NAVAL HISTORY OF MEDIEVAL AND RENAISSANCE EUROPE

John B. Hattendorf

ONE of the interesting phenomena in naval historical study during the twentieth century was the curious way in which ideas attributed to the American naval officer, Alfred Thayer Mahan, permeated, for a time, nearly every aspect of Anglo-American writing on naval history. His thought even influenced historical thinking about the medieval and Renaissance periods, eras that he never even considered in his own writing. Thus, in thinking about the previous literature on maritime and naval affairs in Europe between the tenth and seventeenth centuries, one needs to start with a clear understanding of Mahan's place in the development of naval thought, to see both its contributions and its limitations, while understanding that interpretations of Mahan's work have also changed.

Mahan was certainly the most widely influential naval writer and theorist of the past century. In the years between the mid-1880s and his death in 1914, he wrote the fundamental books and articles that clearly established a distinctly Anglo-American theory of naval power, or in the words that he popularised, 'sea power'. Over the past century, his work has had immense influence on naval scholarship around the globe. With Britain's Royal Navy and the United States Navy as the successive and dominant superpower navies of the twentieth century, it is not entirely surprising that scholars have used Mahan's writings as a benchmark in their understanding of naval power and maritime conflict. Many of his 20 books, 161 journal articles, and numerous other pieces have been reprinted.[1] His most famous book, *The Influence of Sea Power upon History, 1660–1783*, has had more than fifty printings and been translated into at least six languages. It has never gone out of print since it was first published in 1890. Some writers have considered it to be one of the most influential books in history. Certainly we can trace references to Mahan's thought as far a field as the development of the German navy before the First World War, in the imperial Japanese navy in the years up to and including the Second World War and in

---

[1] John B. Hattendorf and Lynn C. Hattendorf, compilers, *A Bibliography of the Works of Alfred Thayer Mahan* (Newport: Naval War College Press, 1986; reprinted 1990).

Latin American navies.[2] In the past thirty years we have made significant strides in establishing a research basis for understanding Mahan and his ideas more thoroughly. His correspondence has been published;[3] there is also a major biography,[4] a guide to an important collection of his manuscripts,[5] a full bibliography of his works,[6] and, most recently, a new analysis and interpretation of his thinking.[7]

In examining Mahan's influence, however, we face a number of analytical problems. In some circles, he has been treated as a kind of distant oracle, unfathomable, and too complex to approach directly. Many use his name and quote a line or two from him, but few among this group have read his work in any depth. Others have disregarded Mahan completely, dismissing him as a commentator on things irrelevant, long past, and now forgotten. A third group, in commenting on his work, has attributed to Mahan thoughts and ideas that distort his contribution. Some have selected and exaggerated his ideas, using him as a kind of bogeyman in naval affairs so that one completely misses the careful nuances by which he actually saw issues. Such misperceptions about his thought have gained so much currency that, today, we are faced with a false ghost as well as the nineteenth-century man and what he actually wrote.

One can find all of these approaches among those that have thought and written about the practical applications of naval strategy in the twentieth century. Yet, Mahan has had influence with another group and in another context: historians and historical literature. One can find among them the same categories as I have described among naval strategists, but with some additional ones. First, there are historians who have taken out of context Mahan's analysis of the Anglo-Dutch and the Anglo-French naval wars in the period 1660–1815 and applied it to regions and periods that he never studied or thought about in any depth. Thus, one can find questionable applications of Mahan's ideas in

---

2   See Roger Dingman, 'Japan and Mahan', Holger Herwig, 'The Influence of Mahan upon German Sea Power', and Guillermo J. Montenegro, 'The Character and Extent of Mahan's Influence in Latin America', in John B. Hattendorf, ed., *The Influence of History on Mahan* (Newport: Naval War College, 1991), 49–80, 87–98.

3   Robert Seager II and Doris Maguire, eds., *The Letters and Papers of Alfred Thayer Mahan* (Annapolis: Naval Institute Press, 1977).

4   Robert Seager II, *Alfred Thayer Mahan: The Man and His Letters* (Annapolis: Naval Institute Press, 1971) and the author's reflections nearly twenty years later, 'Alfred Thayer Mahan', in James C. Bradford, ed., *Admirals of the New Steel Navy: Makers of the American Naval Tradition, 1880–1930* (Annapolis: Naval Institute Press, 1990), 24–72.

5   John B. Hattendorf, compiler, *Register of the Alfred Thayer Mahan Papers*, Manuscript Register Series 15 (Newport: Naval War College Naval Historical Collection, 1987).

6   See note 2 above.

7   Jon Tetsuro Sumida, *Inventing Grand Strategy and Teaching Command: The Classic Works of Alfred Thayer Mahan Reconsidered* (Washington: The Woodrow Wilson Center, and Baltimore: The Johns Hopkins University Press, 1997). For the most important earlier analysis, see Herbert Rosinski, *Commentaire de Mahan*, préface de Hervé Coutau-Bégarie (Paris: Economica, 1997). Originally written during the 1940s and 1950s in English by a German, it has been published only in French. Rosinski's manuscript is in the Naval Historical Collection, Naval War College, Newport, Rhode Island.

interpretations of such periods as ancient and medieval European history, the early modern history of the Baltic and the Mediterranean states, or even Asian history. Second, there are historians increasingly in a position to challenge Mahan's understanding of seventeenth and eighteenth-century British and French history. With all the advances that have been made in historical scholarship over the past hundred years, the accuracy of Mahan's conceptions about the nature and the character of warfare at sea in the very period that he studied are open to question. Mahan wrote at a time when modern historical scholarship was very much in its early stages. His first sea power book on the period 1660–1783 was based largely on even earlier secondary works in both French and English. Although his later studies on the years 1793–1815 were increasingly based on manuscript sources, he nowhere matched the range and depth of monographic studies that others have since written. There has been a tremendous outpouring of new scholarship on naval warfare in the last half of the seventeenth century and over the full range of the long eighteenth century. Only now are scholars beginning to synthesise and to analyse it in terms of the questions that Mahan posed about naval warfare.[8] There is a continuing long and arduous research effort, to which many scholars are contributing directly and indirectly, to evaluate Mahan's interpretation of this period in history. As yet there is no full answer as to how much the new research changes Mahan's ultimate conclusion.

All of these problems and issues show that Mahan is still very much with us. Those of us working on naval history have a large research agenda lying before us that involves Mahan and we are only part of the way along its path. In order to understand Mahan, we first need to locate him properly within the context of his own time and to understand what he was trying to do. Second, we need a clear analysis and careful understanding of what Mahan has said and how he modified his views over his career. Third, we need to compare and contrast his understanding of the seventeenth and eighteenth centuries with modern scholarship and see how accurate are the conclusions that he drew. Closely related to this point, we need to ask whether or not any altered conclusions merit a fundamental change to strategic theory based on Mahan's original historical analysis. Fourth, when all this is done, one hopes that naval strategists will have a better understanding of naval power and historians can be more sensitive in showing the characteristics, differences, and similarities involved in maritime conflict in various historical periods, cultures, and geographical areas.

These are things that will come in the future, but, given the current state of our knowledge, what can we say about Mahan's theories today? How can we summarise the current state of our understanding of his thought and use it as an entering hypothesis and as a foil to set off, to complement, and to contrast a new

---

[8] The most recent study in English on the first portion of the period 1660–1815 is J. R. Jones, *The Anglo-Dutch Naval Wars of the Seventeenth Century* (London: Longmans, 1996). The author of this article is undertaking a study of the Anglo-French Naval Wars, 1688–1815.

understanding of Europe and the sea in the Middle Ages and in the Renaissance?

First, let us go back and read his work in a new light, looking at him as neither deity nor devil, but as a classic writer, working within the context of his own times. We read a variety of other old authors and find value in their work, even if newer writers expand our knowledge in other directions. In doing this, we appreciate classic writers by putting them in a larger context, understanding that they are not the only lights we cherish. To do this with Mahan, we need to develop a little patience with Victorian writers and attitudes. We need to have some grounding in the world in which they lived and the naval scene that lay around them. Most of all, we need to accept the fact that Mahan wanted his historical writings to have direct relevance in his own time. At the same time, we need to be sensitive to the fact that naval theory is not dogma, but rather a constantly evolving process by which broad understanding of historical events is constantly changed and interpreted in the light of new insights, new dimensions, and new evidence.

For a significant part of the nineteenth century, Britain's navy was without a rival, as the pre-eminent force afloat. By the time that the term *Pax Britannica* came into use after 1886, it was already becoming a thing of the past.[9] Great Britain had never forced this situation upon the world through the operations of a large navy. It was merely created by the fact that no other nation had yet developed the industrial and economic capacity to challenge Britain with a rival navy. For the moment, other nations accepted the situation and were willing to accept her ideas of free trade, peace, and prosperity. The situation could only exist while others did not challenge it. The age of the *Pax Britannica* was over when nations other than Britain began to industrialise, produce steam machinery, lay iron railroads, construct iron and steel ships from the products of their own factories, and develop their own technological applications.[10]

In Mahan's time, the technological basis of navies had already begun to change in the long-term conversion from wood to iron and steel, from sail to steam, from round shot to shells. These revolutions in naval affairs and in industrial production began to take place at the same time as there was a fundamental change occurring in both the structure of international relations and the way governments were managing their armed forces. All this combined to bring a new approach to naval tactics and to naval strategy.

These manifold changes struck directly at traditional thinking about navies. Previously, naval leaders developed their strategy and tactics in terms of common sense and long professional practice, evaluating the capabilities of their ships and equipment in the light of the goals they wished to achieve. Of course, they still do, but it is done in a quite different way. The rapidly changing nature

---

[9] Barry M. Gough, '*Pax Britannica*: Peace, Force and World Power', *The Round Table*, 314 (1990), 168.
[10] Gerald S. Graham, *The Politics of Naval Supremacy: Studies in British Maritime Ascendancy* (Cambridge: Cambridge University Press, 1965), 120–1.

of international politics and of naval technology in the late nineteenth century brought everything into question and seemed to sweep all previous thinking away. Up to this point in naval affairs, there had been no real need to intellectualise the subject. Little professional naval literature existed. Mahan, and the others who may be counted among the earliest leaders of the movement to promote the study of naval history, Sir John Knox Laughton and Vice-Admiral Sir Philip Colomb of the Royal Navy and Rear Admiral Stephen B. Luce of the US Navy, all looked for a means to find some enduring and steady guide amidst the flux that surrounded them. Like these others, Mahan turned to Britain's experience as the pre-eminent naval power and sought to find guidance in its rivalry with France. This was neither an antiquarian pursuit of remote and forgotten technical details nor an academic enterprise to understand an important dimension of human experience, but quite differently: it was a search for understanding about the nature and character of naval power for Mahan's own times.

Mahan, like so many others in his era, shared a broad interest in the period from 1660 to 1815 during which Britain had successfully acquired a global empire. Understandably, Mahan was particularly interested in the naval wars of 1793–1815. Not only did those years mark the culmination of naval warfare under sail, but also they were, for his generation, as the Second World War is for ours, those of the last great, sustained naval war.

We realise today that these historical examples, which Mahan found so interesting, do not have universal validity, but a century ago they did seem relevant to aspiring nations, such as the United States, in a new age of imperial rivalry. In choosing this subject, Mahan focused on maritime conflict between two highly organised, great-power navies, that had extensive naval infrastructure, a relatively large bureaucratic establishment to manage the industrial support, manpower, and financial resources involved. This period was one of a relatively stable level of technology in navies, not one of massive and dramatic change. At the same time, the naval wars between England and France involved the repeated employment of naval forces in successive wars in the context of geostrategic issues that remained largely the same from war to war. Mahan focused his thought on understanding some broad aspects in the strategic relationships and battles between modern, great-power navies, but he never attempted to come to grips with the impact of advanced industrialisation on naval power and its dependency on the successful management of technological change and financial resources. To many of us today, Mahan's ideas seem quite inappropriate to small- and medium-sized navies in the context of contemporary affairs, particularly in terms of the current concerns of coastal navies. Today, we are much more wary of drawing universal conclusions based on too small an analytical base.

To be fair, we must not forget that Mahan himself also looked at some other, very different contemporary naval actions in his own time. These included the American Civil War, the Spanish American War, and the Russo-Japanese War. It is worthwhile to re-read his thoughts on these wars to see how he understood them as a contemporary. Yet, the very contemporaneousness of his observations creates problems for us when we are evaluating his historical judgements. This is something that presents a further problem in understanding Mahan's contribution today.

This is not the only problem; in general, it is very difficult to grasp what Mahan said. There are several reasons for this. First, there was Mahan's own reluctance to summarise his thought in any abstract form, along with the large quantity of material he wrote that needs to be compared and collated to find out how his ideas changed over his career. At the end of his career, he did not hold entirely to all of the things he had said in his first book. Like all of us, his ideas evolved and grew over time, with further experience and insight.

Second, along with Mahan's immense production, it is difficult to grasp his complete argument due to the very methods that he used. He worked with two approaches in a manner that we might today think are the conflicting methods of the historian and the political scientist. On the one hand, he was interested in historical narratives that explained broad aspects of the past and, on the other, in concepts that could be applied to formulating strategies for future situations. Different as these two are, Mahan found them closely tied, in fact essential, to one another.

> Formulated principles, however excellent, are by themselves too abstract to sustain convinced allegiance. The reasons for them as manifested in concrete cases, are an imperative part of the process through which they enter the mind and possess the will. On this account the study of military history lies at the foundation of all sound military conclusions and practice.[11]

Later, he expanded on the reciprocal method of using statements of principles with detailed historical narratives.

> Each is a partial educator; combined, you have the perfect instructor. Of the two, History by itself is better than formulated principles by themselves; for in this connection, History, being the narrative of actions, takes the role which we commonly call practical. It is the story of practical experience.[12]

Noting the need for greater professional understanding in the naval service, Mahan went on to say,

> We all, I trust, have advanced beyond the habit of thought which rates the rule of thumb, mere practice, mere personal experience, above practice illuminated by principles, and reinforced by knowledge, developed by many men in many quarters. Master your principles, and then ram them home with illustrations, which History furnishes.[13]

---

[11] A. T. Mahan, 'The Naval War College', *Armaments and Arbitration* (Boston: Little Brown, 1912), reprinted in John B. Hattendorf, ed., *Mahan on Naval Strategy*. Classics of Sea Power series (Annapolis: Naval Institute Press, 1991), 350–1.
[12] A. T. Mahan, *Naval Strategy Compared and Contrasted with the Principles and Practices of Military Operations on Land* (Boston: Little Brown, 1911), 17.
[13] Ibid.

By and large, this duality of understanding is very wise advice and we can gain much from Mahan's pioneering efforts and ideals. However, the last sentence might give us pause. Our modern eyes see very differently from this; at least, we would express it differently. As historians, we certainly do not want to promote the idea that it is sensible to use arbitrary principles or that we should ravage history and take examples out of context to prove a political point. Today, I suspect many of us would probably prefer to proceed by inductive observation of many detailed instances to create a changing, general understanding rather than to deduce our understanding of a particular instance from a decreed principle.

Mahan was always careful to point out that there were only a very few leading considerations of importance. Using them in an extensive study of detailed cases, he believed, gave firmer grasp of the central points, deeper understanding, and allowed one to sort out the critical features in naval strategy from the less important details. Nevertheless, he was uneasy about emphasising principles, even when he used them.

Mahan dealt with several broad areas of interest. Sometimes, he was talking about the broad effect of navies in history with naval historians in mind. At other times, he was talking about the basic character of naval strategy with naval officers and future strategists in mind. Between the two areas, there are some differences in the principal considerations. Since we are considering Mahan in the context of his historical interpretations, it is important to emphasise that Mahan's purpose was to educate naval officers for the future. Here he was dealing with the problem of how human cognition and learning relate to purposeful action. He believed that those who conducted naval warfare needed to balance the conflicting propensities of art and science, with art as the dominant factor. As Jon Sumida put it, 'Mahan therefore insisted that the study of history serve as the primary agent of advanced education for those charged with the task of directing what was technologically and bureaucratically the most complex institution of his time, and ours'.[14]

Many readers of Mahan's work have tended to concentrate on the first chapter of *The Influence of Sea Power upon History* and the argument that Mahan made there for the political-economic basis of sea power.[15] In fact, this chapter was not an original one, but an afterthought, built partially from ideas that he obtained from other writers, most notably through an essay by a young officer, Ensign William G. David, in the US Naval Institute *Proceedings* in 1882.[16] Mahan's political-economic argument was fundamentally based on his basic assumption that 'Notwithstanding all the familiar and unfamiliar dangers

---

[14] Sumida, *Inventing Grand Strategy*, 117.
[15] A. T. Mahan, *The Influence of Sea Power upon History, 1660–1783* (Boston: Little Brown, 1918), chapter 1, 25–89.
[16] Ensign W. G. David, 'Our Merchant Marine: The Causes of Its Decline and the Means to Be Taken for Its Remedy', US Naval Institute *Proceedings*, VIII (1882), 151–86, quote from 157. William Glenn David (d. 1934) was appointed to the Naval Academy from New York

of the sea, travel and traffic by water have always been easier and cheaper than by land'.[17]

As Jon Sumida has summarised Mahan's arguments, they had three aspects.[18] First, there were the maritime economic elements, specifically production, shipping, and colonies, which Mahan saw as the key to prosperity and the prime motivators behind the policies of coastal states.

Second, he argued that supremacy in organised armed force at sea, in other words naval supremacy, was essential to the protection of the maritime economic elements. This was something that he believed was critically important in conflicts between major powers. Third, sea power was the combination of both the naval and maritime economic factors. In Mahan's view, the capacity to develop sea power was determined by six conditions: geographical position, physical conformation including natural resources and climate, extent of territory, size of population, national culture, and political structure.

Closely tied to Mahan's political-economic argument is his argument about the need for a government to pursue a strong maritime and naval policy. In all of this, Mahan's general line of reasoning has several presuppositions. The first results from Mahan's choice of historical period. In the years 1660–1815, it a maritime state, Britain, that dislodges a land-based power, France, as the world's leading power. It is this particular development that Mahan is trying to explain and which he uses as the basis for his generalisations. Second, Mahan represents the 'navalist' school of thinking that found its justification in selected aspects of the broad outline of post-sixteenth-century global economic and political developments. Here Mahan was thinking of the shift from the Mediterranean to the Atlantic and the great profits and empires that resulted from colonial and commercial enterprise across the world's oceans. As some of Mahan's critics have shown, this interpretation tends to overlook the importance of domestic production and to exaggerate the importance of overseas trade. In the specific case of Britain in the long eighteenth century, it tends to ignore the complementary economic, political, and military 'continental' dimensions of British power.[19] Third, Mahan's argument about the importance of government policy is specifically designed to be a lesson to the American government. In Britain's case, Mahan argued, her geographical and economic conditions required emphasis on naval power rather than on land power. France, however, with both her land and maritime power, had mistakenly failed to institute aggressive and effective policies that supported the national, maritime dimension.[20]

In addition to these insights into Mahan's thought, modern historians working

---

and graduated third in the class of 1877. He resigned his commission in August 1884, but served again briefly during the Spanish–American War, May–September 1898.
[17] Mahan, *The Influence of Sea Power upon History*, 25
[18] Sumida, *Inventing Grand Strategy*, 17
[19] Paul M. Kennedy, *The Rise and Fall of the Great Powers: Economic Change and Military Conflict from 1500 to 2000* (New York: Random House, 1987), 96–7.
[20] Sumida, *Inventing Grand Strategy*, 28–30.

on the 1660–1815 period have begun to sharpen and recast the distinctions in Mahan's list of six specific conditions. Daniel Baugh, for example, has drawn a clear distinction between the *elements of naval power*[21] and the *foundations of sea power*.[22] The elements of naval power, he argues, include all matters relating to warships including their design, construction, guns, timber, stores, and facilities for upkeep and repair. In addition, there are the matters of the physical sustenance of sailors: food, drink, and general health issues. On top of that, there are the issues of training sufficient numbers of seamen for wartime needs and to educate and train a competent set of officers. These factors were ones that required the development of specialised administrative structures to coordinate activities and to nurture a profession. In examining the foundations of sea power as something distinct from the elements of naval power, it is clear that state-operated armies and navies were the instruments that directly carried on the contest between the rivals for global supremacy. To provide for them, the fundamental issue was state revenue. A substantial part of the taxes that created state revenue derived from maritime trade and commerce. Through this link, the success of the commercial system affected armies and navies. Additionally, when the sources of revenue were insufficient to meet the immediate demands of the state, financial credit based on the capital that merchants accumulated and the system of financial administration became matters of fundamental importance to naval and military power. In the eighteenth century, the relative successes in these areas were among the determining factors that governed overall naval success between rivals.

Mahan's analysis completely missed understanding the fundamental economic and financial basis for the creation and maintenance of a state's naval power. In this, he reflected his own explicit advice to naval officers: with Nelson's phrase in mind, that 'An officer should have political courage', Mahan repeatedly told officer students at the Naval War College,

> Political courage, to be well based, requires political knowledge as well. That you may more effectively concentrate upon this necessary knowledge, avoid dissipating your energies upon questions interior to the country; questions financial, sociological, economical, or what not. The sphere of the navy is international solely. It is this, which allies it so closely to that of the statesman.[23]

Mahan's narrow outlook here is one that more recent historians have been working to correct through their considerations of the 'The Financial Revolu-

---

[21] Daniel A. Baugh, 'The Elements of Naval Power in the Eighteenth Century', in John B. Hattendorf, ed., *Maritime History: The Eighteenth Century* (Melbourne, FL: Krieger Publishing, 1997), 119–35.
[22] 'Trade and Colonies: Financial and Maritime Strength', in Hattendorf, *Maritime History*, 145–63.
[23] A. T. Mahan, *Naval Strategy . . . Lectures Delivered at the U.S. Naval War College, Newport, R.I., between 1887 and 1911* (Boston: Little Brown, 1911), 21.

tion', 'The Military Revolution', the rise of the bureaucratic state, and the broader commercial and imperial aspects that comprised the Atlantic world.

It is not just the dimension of broad historical explanation in Mahan's thought that has been subjected to extensive re-examination and elaboration. The explication of the elements of naval strategy and war at sea interested Mahan as much or more and that dimension has drawn scrutiny as well. Mahan's in-depth studies of naval strategy and the conduct of naval warfare lie in works other than his *Sea Power* series.[24] In this area, in particular, Mahan stressed the importance of the art of command rather than rigid principles. Here, in particular, Mahan's followers often did heed what Mahan said. Stressing oversimplified maxims and rigid application of principles, they contributed to much misunderstanding about Mahan. The writer himself, however, had clearly cautioned that,

> the maxim [of war], rooting itself in a principle, formulates a rule generally correct under the conditions; but the teacher must admit that each case has its own features, like the endless variety of the human face, which modify the application of the rule, and may even make it a times wholly inapplicable.[25]

In analysing naval strategy, Mahan emphasised three conditions on which the strategic value of any place depends: its geographical situation in relation to essential lines for trade and communication, its offensive and defensive military strength, and its resources for survival. When all three conditions are found in the same place, one normally has a place of primary importance. A crossing point for two or more lines of travel is always a central, strategic position, as it facilitates travel in several directions. Narrow places along a main route are particularly important. Thus, places like Gibraltar, Suez, and Panama are key positions. So also are those key places where various means of trade and communication converge to serve a large area. The second element in considering strategic value is offensive and defensive military strength. In this regard, it is possible to think of a place that is ideally situated strategically, yet, in practical terms, is indefensible. The main consideration here is in maintaining defences from attack that allow the offensive portion of one's military strength to act more freely. For example, a naval base may be defended by various kinds of forces, including coastal artillery and mines, while the fleet, operating from that base, plays the offensive role, intercepting enemy forces. The third element, resources for survival, involves the ability to maintain a stream of all the necessary supplies. It means the ability to attend to all the needs of a fleet in terms of its people, relieving them as necessary. It also means the ability to repair ships and equipment expeditiously. Here, a navy's industrial repair facilities and dry-docks are key factors in maintaining its offensive power.

Mahan added a fourth interrelated area in analysing naval strategy. He called it strategic lines, the routes that connect the various places of primary strategic

---

[24] Sumida, *Inventing Grand Strategy*, chapter 4, 57–79: 'Strategic and Professional Arguments in the Lesser Works'.
[25] Mahan, *Naval Strategy*, 300.

position. At sea, these are generally the shortest practicable routes between places. These fall into two categories: open sea routes and coastal routes. The shortest route is usually an open sea route, but maintaining this in wartime requires military command of the sea. Without it, one is forced to use open sea routes evasively or, alternatively, to use whatever protected or neutral coastal routes might be available.

When one extends this thought from the lines that connect the key positions within a particular theatre of operations to the strategic lines that connect key points on a world-wide scale, one moves to the heart of a great power's naval strategy. In this context, Mahan argued that the fleet was a kind of movable, key strategic position. Organised force at sea, he said, is the determining strategic feature. Finding the way to reduce an enemy's fleet to inactivity, temporarily or (preferably) permanently, dislocates the enemy's ability to protect and to maintain its strategic lines. This is the point Mahan was making about decisive battles at sea. The obvious way to dislocate an enemy fleet permanently was to destroy it in a battle. This was the reasoning behind his emphasis on the great fleet battles that had such an objective in mind.

The key to dislocating an enemy's naval power was through maritime superiority. Mahan wrote, 'the supreme essential condition to the assertion and maintenance of national power in external maritime regions is the possession of a fleet superior to that of any probable opponent'.[26] To maintain this fleet, it is necessary to have a certain number of bases, but their defence and maintenance should be balanced and not be allowed to reduce the offensive power and superiority of the fleet at sea. Most importantly, the maintenance of a system of protected, maritime stations depends ultimately upon the navy to maintain its superiority. The main threat to that superiority is an enemy naval force and, therefore, it should be the proper objective. As the enemy's fleet is essential to the enemy's own connections between its scattered strategic points, a blow at them is 'the surest blow of all'.[27]

All of these areas of consideration, strategic position, strength, resources, and strategic lines, were interconnected in Mahan's thinking. He summarised his argument this way:

> The service of the fleet and of the ports is reciprocal; but, except for the home ports, they have more need of it than it of them. Therefore the fleet should strike at the organised force of the enemy afloat, and so break up the communication between his ports.[28]

In moving on from this basic point to consider the issues involved in distant operations and maritime expeditions, Mahan emphasised that there were two fundamental prerequisites: a reasonably secure home frontier and a navy

---

[26] Mahan, *Naval Strategy*, chapter VIII. Reprinted in Hattendorf, ed., *Mahan on Naval Strategy*, 168.
[27] Ibid., 176.
[28] Ibid.

adequate to dispute control of the enemy at sea. With these established, one could move forward, choosing an appropriate advanced base of operations, an objective, and a line of operations.[29] Such overseas expeditions usually involve transporting a large body of troops. In putting them ashore, the navy must seize and maintain superiority at sea in order to ensure their safety and their ability to carry out their own mission to hold a land area. When such a joint operation has successfully won its position, naval forces shift from playing an offensive role to an offensive-defensive one. At this point, the navy should be released from the expedition and the army should maintain full defence and further prosecute the campaign ashore, while the fleet resumes its natural role in charge of sea communications. The navy functions in two prominent ways in defending against an attack on one's own coastline: it can drive or draw any enemy sea force away from the critical area by a battle that defeats an enemy threat, or it can attack other areas that force the enemy to divide and, therefore, to weaken his forces.[30]

When one strips away the baggage that Mahan's critics and commentators have surrounded him with, and goes back to his own words and writings, we find in the principles and key points that Mahan made when he analysed naval history much that is fundamental and valuable to understanding naval operations. Mahan will continue to deserve our attention as the most successful and most widely recognised of the early theorists of maritime warfare. His understanding, summarised and translated into more modern terms, can stimulate some new insights. We can no longer rely on Mahan's insights alone, however, to interpret naval warfare. The experience of the past century demonstrates vividly how they have been misunderstood, misapplied, and distorted.

In examining naval theory, Mahan is not enough. One must deepen the approach and look to other writers who have since widened our vision and deepened our understanding.[31] Among Mahan's predecessors, Sir John Knox Laughton's writings provide key understanding for the foundations of the Anglo-American historical tradition of strategic study.[32] Rear Admiral Stephen B. Luce was the guiding force directing Mahan. His ideas are essential in placing Mahan in a wider context.[33] Among Mahan's contemporaries,

[29] Ibid., Chapter IX, reprint 182.
[30] Ibid., 219–20.
[31] In general, see Hervé Coutau-Bégarie, ed., *L'Evolution de la Pensée Navale, I–VII* (Paris: FEDN and Economica, 1990–9). The works of ten key writers are included in the US Naval Institute's Classics of Sea Power series edited by John B. Hattendorf and Wayne P. Hughes, Jr. For an overview of a range of thinkers, see John B. Hattendorf, 'The Anglo-French Naval Wars (1689–1815) in Twentieth-Century Naval Thought: The Caird Lecture', *Journal of Maritime Research* (2001), http://www.jmr.nmm.ac.uk
[32] On this general point, see D. M. Schurman, *The Education of a Navy: The Development of British Naval Strategic Thought, 1867–1914* (Chicago: University of Chicago Press, 1965), and on Laughton, in particular, Andrew Lambert, *The Foundations of Naval History: John Knox Laughton, The Royal Navy and the Historical Profession* (London: Chatham, 1998).
[33] John D. Hayes and John B. Hattendorf, eds, *The Writings of Stephen B. Luce* (Newport: Naval Institute Press, 1975).

Vice-Admiral P. H. Colomb's 1890 work, *Naval Warfare: Its Ruling Principles and Practice Historically Treated*,[34] provides an independent and pioneering attempt to analyse naval history done at the same time that Mahan was writing. Colomb's work, in particular, influenced strategic thinking in Russia and the Soviet Union, while Rear Admiral Bradley Fiske's *The Navy as a Fighting Machine* provides a contrasting, but nevertheless an equally valuable, early-twentieth-century approach to naval thought that deals more explicitly with the context of new technology. Another who deserves to be read alongside Mahan is Charles Callwell of the British Army whose nearly forgotten classic on joint warfare written in 1905 has recently been rediscovered and is having some impact on current thinking on joint warfare.[35]

Most important of all, however, is the 1911 work of Sir Julian Corbett, *Some Principles of Maritime Strategy*,[36] which subsumes a great deal of Mahan's thought into a much more complete analytical framework and is based on more sophisticated historical research. Corbett clarified Mahan's concept of the command of the sea, pointing out its temporal nature. He directed attention to the capacity of naval power for limited warfare. He showed that there was a significant difference between warfare that centred around the struggle to use the sea and warfare when a power had won the use of the sea and so used that control for its own purposes. Most important among Corbett's contributions to the theory of naval power is his refined understanding that maritime warfare is typically characterised by being limited in its objectives, and that naval warfare involves three main categories of operations: first, securing command of the sea by preventing an enemy from posing a threat, either through obtaining a decision in a battle or through a blockade; second, disputing another power's command of the sea by maintaining a potential threat or conducting minor counterattacks; and third, exercising control of passage and communication by sea. The last category of operations is quite different from the first two and involves the spectrum of naval operations for a power that has command of the sea. In this category, one may find defence against invasion, attack and defence of commerce, attack, defence, and support of military operations.[37] Corbett understood war at sea as part of the general phenomenon and theory of warfare and argued that navies involve only one aspect of related maritime activities. Admiral Sir Herbert Richmond carried forward Corbett's work and modified it

---

34 Vice-Admiral P. H. Colomb, *Naval Warfare: Its Ruling Principles and Practice Historically Treated*. See the revised third edition, with an introduction by Barry M. Gough (Annapolis: Naval Institute Press, 1988).
35 Charles Callwell, *Military Operations and Maritime Preponderance: Their Relations and Interdependence*. With an Introduction by Colin Gray. Classics of Sea Power series (Annapolis: Naval Institute Press, 1996).
36 Sir Julian Corbett, *Some Principles of Maritime Strategy*. See the critical edition with appendices and an introduction by Eric Grove. Classics of Sea Power series (Annapolis: Naval Institute Press, 1988).
37 Ibid., 161–7.

with insight gained in his own studies of eighteenth-century naval warfare as well as in observing the conduct of the First World War.[38]

Beyond these key writers, students of the theory of naval power need to understand, too, the contributions of writers who view naval strategy from national viewpoints outside the Anglo-American great-power tradition. There are other writers, even from Mahan's period, that have yet to be revived for modern study.[39] After Mahan's time, the experiences of the world wars in the early and mid-twentieth century have provided many new insights. For this period, no one has yet convincingly analysed the experience of the Royal Navy and the US Navy during the Second World War, using the broad analytical terms that Mahan would have employed. We certainly have the historical perspective for someone to take up that task. Yet, one can benefit from reading the work of writers dealing with smaller navies and with different national outlooks: Germans Wolfgang Wegener[40] and Herbert Rosinski;[41] a Frenchman, Raoul Castex;[42] and an Italian, Romeo Bernotti.[43] Students of naval theory are well advised to read many more historians from other countries with complementary and differing naval experiences. To do so brings into focus the point that there are different types of naval powers, whose navies serve different purposes and strive to achieve different objectives. Reflecting on a general survey of world history, one historian has identified three types of powers that have used navies, and suggested theoretical types of naval strategies. First, there are nations in which navies have been the principal strategic arm for defence and usually maintain a naval force that is relatively larger than their opponents', and tend to take an offensive naval stance. Second, there are continental powers that rely on their armies for protection and use naval power in a defensive stance and in support of their armies, depending on allies for offensive capabilities. Third, there are small powers whose armies and navies can only perform local services or deal with similarly sized powers, depending on larger allies for both land and sea defence in the event of a conflict with a major power.[44]

Since the end of the Second World War, we have come to understand clearly that navies have an important role in peacetime, and a role that Mahan did not

---

[38] See James Goldrick and John B. Hattendorf, eds, *Mahan is Not Enough: The Proceedings of a Conference on the Writings of Sir Julian Corbett and Admiral Sir Herbert Richmond* (Newport: Naval War College Press, 1993).

[39] However, we can now readily obtain a recent edition of the Russian Admiral S. O. Makarov's *Discussions of Questions in Naval Tactics*, translated by J. B. Bernadou with an introduction by Robert B. Bathurst (Annapolis: Naval Institute Press, 1990).

[40] Wolfgang Wegener, *The Naval Strategy of the World War*, translated with an introduction by Holger H. Herwig. Classics of Sea Power series (Annapolis: Naval Institute Press, 1987).

[41] Herbert Rosinski, *The Development of Naval Thought*, ed. B. Mitchell Simpson III (Newport: Naval War College Press, 1977).

[42] Raoul Castex, *Strategic Theories*, translated with an introduction by Eugenia Kiesling. Classics of Sea Power series (Annapolis: Naval Institute Press, 1991).

[43] With an introduction by Brian Sullivan (forthcoming).

[44] Clark G. Reynolds, *Command of the Sea: The History and Strategy of Maritime Empires* (New York: William Morrow & Co., 1974), 'Strategic Applications of Naval Power', 12–16.

explore at all. There is a wide range of literature on this topic that has arisen in the last half-century, the most important of which have been Sir James Cable's books on gunboat diplomacy[45] and Ken Booth's *Navies and Foreign Policy*.[46] Using the methodology of a political scientist, Booth argued that:

> The functions of navies can be conceived as a trinity, the idea of three-in-one. The unity (the one-ness) of the trinity is provided by the idea of the use of the sea. . . . The character of the trinity is then defined by the three characteristic modes of action by which navies carry out their purposes: namely the military, the diplomatic, and the policing functions.[47]

Booth pointed out that states use the sea for several purposes and that navies exist to further those ends. These include the passage of goods and people, the passage of military force for diplomatic purposes or for use against targets on land and sea, and, finally, to obtain the resources in or under the sea. While military capability and character is the fundamental basis for a navy, the ability to threaten or to use force facilitates and gives meaning to its other modes of action. It is the latent capacity to fight that gives meaning to the use of naval force in connection with negotiations with other powers. This became a fairly common idea for the late twentieth century, but it has a long history in practice. Oddly, however, it came only into serious consideration as part of naval theory in recent years.

Booth identified a policing role for navies, which includes such functions as the extension of sovereignty, gaining and maintaining access to maritime resources in contiguous areas, and maintaining order. Within this category, Booth sees another function that he calls 'nation-building'. He points out that this is a role that has been particularly important to small powers and is most important in terms of internal development, while other functions tend to be involved with external affairs. It is characteristically important in periods of political turmoil when naval forces can contribute to internal stability and internal development. Booth makes an important point for us, as we attempt to widen the scope of historical investigation of navies, by emphasising that no navy will exercise all of its functions in equal measure, the proportions of military, diplomatic, and policing functions changing with the ebb and flow of development. Different powers have different purposes in providing naval forces and, therefore, they will each have different priorities, levels of capability, and strategies to achieve their purposes.[48]

In addition to what Booth and others have done to explore the foreign policy dimensions in the use of naval force there has been other work that expands our understanding of navies in wartime operations. In Mahan's day, the emphasis

---

[45] James Cable, *Gunboat Diplomacy, 1919–1979*, 2nd edn (New York: St Martin's Press, 1981); *Diplomacy at Sea* (London: Macmillan, 1985); *Navies in Violent Peace* (New York: St Martin's Press, 1989).
[46] Ken Booth, *Navies and Foreign Policy* (London: Croom Helm, 1977).
[47] Ibid., 15.
[48] Ibid., 24–5.

was on a navy as a separate instrument of state, but the experience of the Second World War drove home a different lesson. We understand now that navies and armies need to operate and interact much more closely than Mahan imagined. Each of us, in our own modern countries, sees this reflected today as ministries of defence have absorbed admiralties. In the 1950s, the key work of Rear Admiral J. C. Wylie was a very important extension of our understanding in this area. In attempting to find the fundamental common features in the strategic theories for continental, air, maritime, and revolutionary warfare, Wylie identified their common features in an effort to create a general theory of power control.[49] The concept behind his theoretical work involved his understanding that the entire purpose of military conflict is to gain some selected degree of control over an enemy in order to achieve one's own purpose. In illustrating his theory, he chose as his example the Carthaginian War.[50]

Turning from the general issues, Wylie made an important contribution when he identified different types of naval strategy. The traditional categorisation was based on offensive and defensive strategies, but Wylie suggested another way of thinking, based on operational patterns. For this he suggested the ideas of sequential strategy, 'visible, discrete steps each dependant on the one that preceded it' and 'the cumulative, the less perceptible minute accumulation of little items piling one on top of the other until at some unknown point the mass of actions may be large enough to be critical'.[51] While he had in mind the contrast between the American 'island hopping campaign' in the Pacific during the Second World War, and the simultaneous American submarine campaign against Japanese shipping, parallels can certainly be made with privateering and corsairing activities in the context of wars in much earlier periods.

Much more recently, an Indian naval officer, Raja Menon, has made a substantial contribution to naval thought in his study of *Maritime Strategy and Continental Wars*.[52] Elaborating on a distinction that Clark Reynolds earlier pointed out, Raja Menon shows, through his own investigation into some wars that have often been overlooked, how continental powers have used navies in quite a different manner from the maritime powers that Mahan examined. Here, he mentions as examples the Graeco-Persian wars of the fifth century BC, the Punic wars, the Islamic expansion into North Africa and Europe as well as the Crusades, and the Turko-Iranian wars that occurred in the sixteenth, seventeenth, and eighteenth centuries.[53] In wars involving continental powers he pointed out that operations involving blockade, economic warfare, and amphib-

---

[49] J. C. Wylie, *Military Strategy: A General Theory of Power Control*, with an introduction by John B. Hattendorf and a postscript by J. C. Wylie. Classics of Sea Power series (Annapolis: Naval Institute Press, 1989).
[50] Ibid., 77–8. He based his historical understanding on B. H. Liddell Hart, *A Greater than Napoleon: Scipio Africanus* (London, 1930).
[51] Wylie, *Military Strategy*, 119.
[52] Rear Admiral Raja Menon, *Maritime Strategy and Continental Wars* (London: Frank Cass & Co., 1998).
[53] Ibid., 173–8.

ious operations have played a much larger and more important role than in wars between maritime powers.

It is clear that, today, our understanding of naval theory is far wider than Mahan expressed.[54] In many countries and in many languages, over the past century historians have found Mahan's work to be stimulating. No one has yet done a thorough and comprehensive examination of his multi-cultural impact. In this area, Mahan's legacy is a complex one, confused by the elusiveness of his own thought as well as by the varied uses to which it was put. On the one hand, Mahan's work was a positive influence that opened the way for historians in many countries to write narratives about neglected aspects of history: the broad subject of maritime affairs, the role of shipping, overseas communication, the development of nautical sciences, the lives and contributions of mariners and seamen.[55] On the other hand and in other circles of discourse, Mahan's influence merged with professional and propagandistic literature to become a political tool to promote naval growth. In Germany, for example, historians have already pointed out that the social Darwinist features of Mahan's thought merged with the legacy of von Ranke's historicism and the influence of Treitschke's political realism in a way that provided naval writers with a basis for claiming the intrinsic supremacy of the navy over the army.[56] In this, some writers went back to medieval history, looking to the German Hanse as a forerunner of modern German naval power.

Historians have been working for some time to correct the negative side of Mahan's legacy. Fernand Braudel, for example, found an entirely different focus on maritime activity in the Mediterranean, and could even suggest that attacks on trade were an indicator of good economic conditions in that region.[57] After the appearance of Braudel's work, John Guilmartin directly attacked the Mahanian legacy in his book *Gunpowder and Galleys*[58] pointing out that its Anglo-American framework obscured more than it enlightened. In particular, Guilmartin found that the concepts of sea control and sea power, implying destruction of enemy fleets in battle and linked to the vital importance of maritime trade, were dubious ones for understanding naval affairs in the sixteenth-century Mediterranean.

---

[54] See John B. Hattendorf, 'Recent Thinking on the Development of Naval Theory', in John B. Hattendorf and Robert S. Jordan, eds., *Maritime Strategy and the Balance of Power: Britain and America in the Twentieth Century* (London: Macmillan Press, 1989), 131–61.
[55] See, for example, the work on early Swedish maritime history by Arnold Munthe, *Sjömaktens inflytande på Sveriges historia* (Stockholm, 1921), vol. I: *Från äldsta tider till omkring år 1640*.
[56] See the works listed in Keith Bird, comp., *German Naval History: A Guide to the Literature* (New York: Garland, 1985), 11–13, 230–1.
[57] Fernand Braudel, *The Mediterranean and the Mediterranean World in the Age of Philip II* (New York: Harper Row, 1973), vol. II, 886–7.
[58] John Francis Guilmartin, Jr, *Gunpowder and Galleys: Changing Technology and Mediterranean Warfare at Sea in the Sixteenth Century* (Cambridge: Cambridge University Press, 1974), 16–41.

In more recent work, there has been an effort to widen the perspective of naval historians and to move from the specialised view of the professional naval officer that Mahan represented and to see conflict at sea as a dimension of human activity within the broader context of general history. Therefore, the new work encourages examination of naval affairs at various different levels of approach and within a variety of different contexts, including economic history, social history, internal politics, technological history, and every other imaginable dimension.[59]

As new areas of research open that touch on naval issues, sometimes unexpectedly, scholars are beginning to widen our outlook through their investigations of them. For example, John R. McNeill and Carla Rahn Phillips have both touched on the influence of environmental and ecological issues on the formation and development of Mediterranean navies.[60] 'Given the varied and difficult ecological conditions of the Mediterranean region', Phillips suggests, 'political power depended upon the availability of natural resources. Without adequate timber supplies, a large navy could not be sustained. Without a rich agrarian base, neither land nor sea power could be sustained.'[61] Similarly, she suggested that only those with control of key bases and islands having essential resources could maintain effective control at sea. Because of this, sea battles were far less important than the control of the bases. Corsairing has always been a distinctive feature of the Mediterranean and Phillips argues that the ecological situation fostered its practice, while major powers encouraged, tolerated, or actively sponsored it, depending on their interests and their circumstances.

Examples such as these from the recent literature clearly suggest that some of the questions that Mahan asked about history are far more interesting and useful to us now than are the answers he reached or the model he created in his understanding of the period between 1660 and 1815:

> Why did conflict at sea occur?
> What were the conditions that facilitated and sustained the use of armed force at sea?
> What was its function and how did it achieve its ends?
> What was its nature, its characteristics, and its effects?
> How did it relate to and depend upon other factors in these periods?

In the first years of the twenty-first century, the ideas of Mahan have gained renewed value through our deeper understanding of his own intent and usage,

---

[59] See here, the variety of approaches suggested in John B. Hattendorf, ed., *Doing Naval History: Essays Toward Improvement* (Newport: Naval War College, 1995).
[60] Carla Rahn Phillips, 'Navies and the Mediterranean in the Early Modern Period', and J. R. McNeill, 'Ecology and Strategy in the Mediterranean: Points of Intersection', in John B. Hattendorf, ed., *Naval Strategy and Policy in the Mediterranean: Past, Present and Future* (London: Frank Cass, 2000), 3–29, 374–91.
[61] Ibid., 25.

along with our appreciation of the contributions and the limitations of his thought. While we are now clearly aware that Mahan's ideas have been inappropriately used in some quarters, particularly in regard to the naval history of Europe in the Middle Ages and the Renaissance, we also have broadened and deepened our understanding of navies in general, through new work on naval theory as well as from the results of new research in different periods, using new approaches to naval history. One can no longer merely dismiss Mahan, without understanding what he was attempting to do. One can, however, show that his thinking reflects the beginning of the mainstream in Anglo-American naval theory and comprises a reflection on Anglo-American naval experience as great powers. Over the course of the twentieth century, scholars have clarified what Mahan's ideas were while others have modified and extended his initial thoughts.

The broad aspects of current naval theory can suggest some alternative interpretations to historical questions. In addition recent developments in both theory and in historical research provide us with a new opportunity. A new look at the medieval and Renaissance periods, eras in history that were quite different from those Mahan studied, provides a convenient opportunity to challenge and to modify theory. The developments in the theory of naval power since Mahan's time may also suggest alternative interpretations of history as research uncovers new information. At the same time, since the theory of naval power has been derived largely from a study of a historical period in which war at sea was quite different from what it was like during the Middle Ages and the Renaissance, we may well discover that a new look at the historical evidence challenges theory as it presently stands and provides the basis for modifications to it. From the tenth to the sixteenth century war at sea was not primarily a monopoly of states, but it saw the beginnings of the transition toward that development. Why and how this occurred as well as the nature of war at sea both before and after this development are fundamental features for consideration. Scholars may well determine after examining the evidence that alternative theories are required as a sound basis for interpreting naval force in the period.

By comparing and contrasting naval activities in northern Europe with those in southern Europe in the light of naval theory, we have an opportunity to see well-known events in a new and different light. This conference volume has been designed specifically to be an opportunity to make a substantial contribution to historical knowledge in raising new questions about the origins, development, and practice of naval warfare. Our purpose here is to search for new and alternative interpretations of naval history through a multi-pronged approach that uses comparative history, tests theoretical propositions, and promotes new historical research.

Many of the chapters that follow provide a distinct contrast with the theoretical discussion in this introduction. This contrast and tension helps to illuminate, on the one hand, our understanding of the applicability and limitations of current naval theory and, and on the other, our appreciation of the historical development in the Middle Ages and the Renaissance. The juxtaposition of theory based on 350 years of naval experience from 1650 to 2000 with detailed studies of the earlier 650-year period from 1000 to 1650 underscores the fundamental fact that Mahan's naval theories, and their subsequent modification by Corbett and other writers, describe European great-power navies that operated within the context of a similar geostrategic framework. Within this context, war at sea was largely funded and nearly fully controlled by bureaucratic states, sometimes within the context of coalitions of states, for the purpose of achieving national, political aims in periods of declared warfare against states or coalitions of states with navies of similar characteristics. Taking a longer term and larger view of European history that stretches back to the year 1000, this type of naval warfare is a distinctive and dominant feature limited to the modern period.

Our exploration of the Middle Ages and Renaissance emphasises that Mahan's modern naval warfare was unusual during earlier periods, although there are some interesting similarities and a foreshadowing of later characteristics in naval warfare that emerged in the context of the Mediterranean wars between Genoa and Venice in the thirteenth and fourteenth centuries as well as in the naval wars in the Baltic in the sixteenth century. The broader vision of the period from 1000 to 1650 shows war at sea occurring more commonly with a much wider variety of characteristics and types than it does in the period after 1660. These include plundering raids and robbery at sea by individuals, small groups, or warlords who were independent of governmental authorities, local or regional naval defence forces in use in peacetime to maintain order and safety of seagoing activities against such raids and robberies, conflicts at sea between rival groups undertaking such activities, joint activities of merchants and governments using armed force at sea to control or to suppress attacks on peaceful commerce. By and large, seagoing forces that were not navies undertook most of such activities. It took the larger and parallel development of state formation in early modern Europe to create the entities that we now call navies, organisations fully financed and maintained by a government to fight at sea with specialised types of vessels. In this regard, it is necessary to understand war at sea in the broadest terms, not merely in terms of the strict definition of a navy. In early-seventeenth-century France, for example, the administrative language of the day made a great distinction between *marine* (navy) and *galères* (galleys). Although both were fighting at sea, the word 'navy', as used during that period, applied only to sailing ships operating in the open seas, not to galley warfare.[62] We have necessarily set aside that distinction here to come to a broader understanding of our subject. The distinction, like many medieval categorisations of naval forces, was abandoned as modern navies emerged after 1650.

A theoretical understanding of navies in the medieval and Renaissance

---

[62] G. Lacour-Gayet, *La Marine militaire de la France sous les règnes de Louis XIII et de Louis XIV*, vol. I: *Richelieu, Mazarin 1624–1661* (Paris, 1911), 19.

periods requires an appreciation of the historical context in which they operated in order to see that all aspects of warfare at sea were experiencing change and development. First, we see separate and independent developments in northern and southern Europe that gradually merge into a single general trend in European history, although not all European navies became great-power navies. In the conclusion to this volume, Richard Unger identifies three periods in this broad pattern in both northern and southern Europe. The first runs from the late tenth century to the thirteenth century and is characterised by naval activity carried on by militias and local figures, including individual ship owners and merchants. The second period runs from the thirteenth century to the seventeenth century and is characterised by entrepreneurial navies, the parallel development of states, and a gradually increasing governmental interest in controlling and using force at sea. The third and final stage in the middle of the seventeenth century is an era of transformation to the characteristics of large navies typical of the late seventeenth and early eighteenth centuries.

Several historians in this volume point out that the period from 1000 to 1650 was one of great technological change and development for navies and properly contrast it with the period from 1650 to 1815, during which there was little technological advance. The great technological changes for navies that followed in the late nineteenth and early twentieth centuries, and the uncertainty that they posed for naval thinkers of that time, are the reasons why Mahan and his intellectual godfather, Rear Admiral Stephen B. Luce, chose to look to that more stable period as providing a 'norm' for modern theory. They wrote at a time when great-power navies operated in a relatively similar geostrategic context to their eighteenth-century counterparts, and the realities of the world in the twenty-first century are now very different. Today's navies operate in an atmosphere of seemingly perpetual and ever-accelerating technological change, while the geostrategic context in which they operate today is also no longer comparable to the eighteenth century or even to the late nineteenth and early twentieth centuries when modern naval theory was written.

A new examination of the deeper origins of naval power and the broader nature of war at sea is now appropriate; scholars need to consider such issues as the impact of changing technology, the development of state bureaucratic systems for finance and administration, the domestic politics of interstate warfare, the interrelationship of war at sea with other forms of warfare, and the conduct of war by those beyond the immediate control of a state system. The following essays provide a starting point for this wider agenda and take steps toward a general history of medieval and Renaissance sea power. In addition, the following chapters clearly suggest that there were several alternative models for warfare at sea in the Middle Ages and the Renaissance: for example, the practice of piracy and its suppression, the protection and extension of commerce, and state and local employment of both private and publicly owned warships as an extension of and complement to military operations on land. The nature and extent of war at sea in the Middle Ages and the Renaissance is far more complex and varied than has heretofore been understood. If nothing else this volume shows that no one model, as that proposed by Mahan or as is explained by modern naval theory, is sufficient for understanding the nature and extent of sea power in medieval and Renaissance Europe.

Part I

NORTHERN EUROPE

NAVAL POWER IN THE VIKING AGE AND IN HIGH MEDIEVAL DENMARK

Niels Lund

THIRTEENTH-CENTURY Scandinavian law codes describe a levy that may be conceived of as a naval militia. Such levies existed in Denmark, Norway and Sweden in similar, though not identical, forms. On the basis of territorial subdivisions into *skipæn*, districts responsible for supplying a ship, and of these districts into *hafnæ* responsible for furnishing a member of the crew, the kings of Denmark had, in theory, a fleet of about one thousand ships at their disposal. They had sizeable naval forces but raised them in a unique way, very different from states in the seventeenth century and later.

The age of this organisation, called in Old Norse *leiðangr*, Danish *leding*, is disputed, as are the contents of the provincial laws in general. Older generations of scholars were prepared to seek the origins of the laws in a remote Tacitean past[1] while in recent scholarship it has been claimed that they were basically new rules, intended to change the law in Scandinavia, not to record or conserve ancient customary law.[2] It has recently been argued that the code of Jutland was meant to complete and supersede older legislation, like the code of Skåne, and that it was intended as a national law; only the death of Valdemar II in 1241 prevented its ratification at all provincial courts.[3]

Those believing that the laws were rooted in the Germanic past naturally assumed that the *leding* had to be much older than the writing down of the provincial laws. The cautious dated its origins in the late Viking period, the bolder took its beginnings to early in the Viking period and even into the eighth century. The older generation of Swedish scholars even adduced Tacitus' remark that the Suiones *praeter viros armaque classibus valent*.[4] The *leding* has therefore often served as an explanation for the successes of the Vikings in Europe and elsewhere. It justified Godfred's self-confidence *vis-à-vis* Charlemagne, it explained Horik's ability to send a fleet of six hundred ships against Saxony in

---

[1] For example Karl Wührer, 'Die dänischen Landschaftsrechte als Quelle für die ältesten dänischen Rechtsverhältnisse', *Medieval Scandinavia*, 1 (1968), 51–6.
[2] For example, Elsa Sjöholm, *Gesetze als Quellen mittelalterlicher Geschichte des Nordens*. Acta Universitatis Stockholmiensis 21 (1977).
[3] Michael Gelting, 'Skånske Lov og Jyske Lov. Danmarks første kommissionsbetænkning og Danmarks første retsplejelov', forthcoming.
[4] *Germania*, 'The Suiones . . . are strong not only in arms and men but also in fleets', trans. H. Matingley (Harmondsworth, 1998), 137.

845, the siege of Paris with even more ships in 885–6, and it explained why a small country like Denmark and its kings, Swein Forkbeard and Canute the Great, could finally conquer England in the early eleventh century. In the centuries following the Viking Age this system of naval levies still ensured Danish superiority in Baltic waters and provided the Danish kings with their successes against the Wends in the twelfth century.

It is striking, however, how inconspicuous is this system in the narrative sources reporting Danish naval warfare in the ninth to thirteenth centuries. When Godfred raised two hundred ships to oppose Charlemagne we may of course find it unlikely that they were all his own ships but even if this were true it does not imply that only a *leding* of the type described in the provincial laws could account for their mobilisation. Not even Horik's alleged six hundred ships attacking the Saxons in 845 will vouch for the existence of the *leding*, just because they probably were not all the king's own ships. Horik may have had more than a hand in the sack of Paris in the same year but that does not imply that he was in anything like comfortable control of the military resources of Denmark. There is in fact positive evidence that chieftains who disliked his rule, or were exiled by him, went abroad to live *piratico more*.[5]

When William of Normandy prepared to conquer England in 1066 he demanded ships from his vassals. A list of their contributions was long regarded as spurious but its authenticity has now been established by Elizabeth van Houts. It lists the following contributions: William fitz Osbern, his steward, sixty ships; Hugh, later count of Avranches, sixty ships; Hugh of Montfort, fifty ships and sixty knights; Remigius, almoner of Fecamp and later bishop of Lincoln, one ship and twenty knights; Nicholas, abbot of St Ouen, fifteen ships and one hundred knights; Robert, count of Eu, sixty ships; Fulk d' Aunou, forty ships; Gerold the steward, forty ships; William, count of Evreux, eighty ships; Roger of Montgomery, sixty ships; Roger of Beaumont, sixty ships; Odo, bishop of Bayeux, one hundred ships; Robert, count of Mortain, one hundred and twenty ships; Walter Giffard, thirty ships and one hundred knights.[6]

In addition to these ships, the duke had numerous others, from certain of his men, each according to their capacity. His queen, Matilda, fitted out an especially magnificent ship, for which she received the county of Kent. Many new ships had to be built before the invasion could take place, as we know from the Bayeux Tapestry, so the magnates of Normandy may not have had these numbers of ships at their disposal under normal circumstances. It is unlikely, though, that the whole invasion fleet was built from scratch. Danish kings could draw in a similar manner on the military resources of their magnates, to the extent, that is, that they could control them. We have no direct evidence of how Godfred collected the two hundred ships with which he threatened to visit Char-

---

[5] Annales Fuldenses 854. *Quellen zur karolingischen Reichsgeschichte*, part III, ed. Reinhold Rau. Ausgewählte Quellen zur deutschen Geschichte des Mittelalters, Freiherr vom Stein Gedächtnisausgabe, vol. VII (Fulda, 1960/1975).
[6] Elisabeth M. C. van Houts, 'The Ship List of William the Conqueror', *Anglo-Norman Studies*, 10 (1987), 159–83.

lemagne in Aachen but a permanent fleet presupposes a permanent state, and the beginning of the ninth century is far too early to talk about such a thing in a Danish context. Throughout the Viking period Denmark had powerful kings who could organise vast resources and wield very considerable power but they alternated with much less powerful kings with apparently very little control over the magnates. This situation, in fact, applied well into the twelfth century and some would say much longer than that.

It is possible to learn something about the recruiting of Swein Forkbeard's and Canute the Great's armies. It is also possible to see that they were not alone in the business. Competing armies were recruited in Sweden and probably Norway, and possibly even in Denmark. The forces led by chieftains like Thorkel the Tall, who gathered a fleet of some two hundred ships and attacked England in 1009, or by chieftains mentioned in Swedish runic inscriptions, were composed of their own forces, their household troops or *lið*, and such other forces as they could persuade to join them.[7] When Thorkel's fleet dispersed in 1012 he kept forty-five ships with him, with which he took service with the English king. They were presumably his own forces.

In taking service with his former enemy, Thorkel followed a precedent established by numerous chieftains in the ninth century. Many Viking leaders acted as naval *condottieri*, taking service with whoever appeared to offer the best prospects of pay and loot. Weland is a good example of this. In 860, he was active in the Somme area but made a deal with the West Frankish king, Charles the Bald, to attack and expel another group of Vikings active in the Seine basin. For this he was to receive three thousand pounds of silver. This deal was confirmed with hostages, and while the Franks were collecting the money Weland and his army went to England. They sacked Winchester, but were beaten by the English before they could reach their ships with the booty. Back on the Continent, Weland and his forces burnt Thérouanne and then went up the Seine and began a siege of the Seine Vikings encamped since 858 on the island of Oissel, a little upstream from Rouen. For this service, Charles agreed to pay Weland and his men the increased amount of five thousand pounds of silver as well as to supply them with livestock and corn, that so as to avoid their helping themselves.

Before Oissel Weland was joined by another force of sixty ships, and the Oissel Vikings then gave up. They surrendered, paid Weland six thousand pounds of gold and silver and were allowed to join him, and both groups now made for the sea. They decided, however, that it was too late in the year to put to sea, so they had to find winter quarters in Francia. The *Annals of St Bertin* describe the procedures like this: so they split up according to their *sodalitates* into groups allocated to various ports, from the sea-coast right up to Paris. Weland with his company came up the Seine to the fort of Melun. Former occupants of the besieged fort on Oissel, with Weland's son, now occupied the monastery of St-Maur-des-Fossés.

---

[7] Niels Lund, 'The Armies of Swein Forkbeard and Cnut: *leding* or *lið*?', *Anglo-Saxon England*, 15 (1986), 105–18.

We cannot tell how big these *sodalitates* were but probably they could be anything from a handful of ships to a fleet like that of Thorkel the Tall, numbering forty-five ships. The *Life of St Ansgar* has an account of the exiled Swedish king Anund, who wanted to reconquer his kingdom. He had eleven ships of his own and found another twenty-two among Danish friends.[8] The *Annals of Fontenelle* give the names of several chieftains active in the Seine area in the 850s and some of them turn up in other contexts as well. One was named Sidroc,[9] and he is probably the earl Sidroc, who is reported dead together with his son in the bloody year 871, when the Danes lost nine earls and one king.[10] When such people gathered together, whether willingly or unwillingly, a big Viking army could be formed but they clearly possessed no great permanence. When Spring came in 862, Weland and his forces split up into several fleets, albeit after an attempt on the part of the former Oissel Vikings to resume normal activities in the Seine area. Weland himself stayed and with his company took service with Charles the Bald. He was baptised together with his wife and son but was killed a year later in single combat, having been accused of faithlessness by other Danes in Charles's service. One group of the departing Vikings was employed as mercenaries by Salomon, Duke of Brittany, while another one went into the service of Robert of Anjou for a fresh six thousand pounds of silver.[11] Since Salomon and Robert were fighting each other intensely, the Vikings once more found themselves on opposite sides.

Viking fleets were clearly composed of the forces of magnates or chieftains. Some of these were big enough to go on ventures of their own, others had to join company with a big man or with a group their own size. Kings who could coerce these forces into their service could wield power over considerable empires, which would vanish when a less talented king took over. This situation applied long after the Viking period. When Knud the Holy, King of Denmark (1080–6), was planning his invasion of England together with his father-in-law, Robert the Frisian, count of Flanders, in 1085, he did not simply order the Danish levies to be ready to carry out his plans in the spring of 1085. He discussed his ideas with the princes and the magnates of the country. They obviously were the ones who could supply the forces necessary. Little had changed when, almost a hundred years later, and following a series of civil wars during which the fates of the pretenders had been decided by the forces their kin and friends were able to support them with, Valdemar the Great set out to conquer the Wends.[12] He held a council of the magnates and put his plans before them and had to suffer rejection

---

[8] *Vita Anskarii*, 19. *Quellen des 9. und 11. Jahrhunderts zur Geschichte der Hamburgischen Kirche und des Reiches*, ed. Werner Trillmich and Rudolf Buchner. Ausgewählte Quellen zur deutschen Geschichte des Mittelalters. Freiherr vom Stein-Gedächtnisausgabe, vol. XI (Darmstadt: Wissenschaftliche Buchgesellschaft 1978).
[9] *The Annals of St Bertin*, trans. Janet L. Nelson (Manchester 1991), 75 n. 9, 76 n. 2.
[10] *The Anglo-Saxon Chronicle*, trans. Dorothy Whitelock *et al.* (1965), 46–7.
[11] *Annals of St Bertin*, trans. Nelson, 94–9.
[12] The importance of personal relations and the power of the elite has recently been demonstrated by Lars Hermanson, *Släkt, vänner och makt. En studie av elitens politiska kultur i*

by them on several occasions. A major theme of his reign was securing control of the magnates and their forces, not restoring an ancient popular levy. His campaign to Norway in 1165 is particularly illustrative. At that time political conditions in Norway were such that a Danish effort to assert traditional claims to superiority or at least influence in southern Norway made sense, and Valdemar staged a campaign to Norway in 1165. After spending some weeks in idleness, parts of the fleet, the Jutlanders in particular, urged the abandonment of the campaign and a return home. They called a meeting of the leaders to decide the matter. The king, seconded by Absalon, bishop of Roskilde, being against, sent some of his men to beat up the participants of the meeting and simply had his way by means of terror. Much the same happened a fortnight later, but finally the Jutlanders achieved the abandonment of the campaign, much to the derision of the historian, Saxo Grammaticus. Some of the leaders of the Jutlanders may be identified as belonging to the very top echelons of society. One was even a relative of the king.

The military qualifications of this top layer of society were demonstrated also in 1187 when news of the fall of Jerusalem reached Denmark and was discussed at the Christmas party of King Knud VI in Odense. Fifteen participants vowed to take the cross. Only five actually fulfilled their promise, but they were able by their own means to equip and man five ships and take them all the way to the Holy Land. None of those who carried out their vows to go belonged to the very richest and politically most influential class in the country. There must have been a substantial layer of people with military resources, including ships of their own, with which they could either accompany the king in war, having agreed to do so after consultations, or with which they could go about their own business.

What, then, is the place in history of the *leding* organisation described in the provincial law codes of the thirteenth century? A closer look at this organisation reveals that it was never intended for foreign warfare, nor did it ever serve such purposes. It was a defensive organisation intended to provide a coastguard. The system described in the codes of Skåne and Jutland really consisted of three obligations, all of them called *leding* or some variant of this. The 'legal *leding*' occurs under the names *ræthær lething*, *qwærsæthæ*,[13] *expeditio*, *lethang withe*, etc. This obligation was a payment for non-service, whether non-service was on a regular basis or occasional. A second obligation described in the codes involved actual service in the ships, service *leding*. This is referred to in the code of Skåne as *wdgerds ledingh* while the code of Jutland calls it simply *lething*. The third obligation described is the obligation of the commended men of the king, or of dukes, bishops and other lords. That these different services

---

1100-talets Danmark. Avhandlingar från Historiska institutionen i Göteborg 24 (Göteborg 2000).
[13] Modern Danish *kværsæde*, Swedish *kvärsäte*, sitting back, or at home. This term says in one word what Knud the Holy's charter for St Lawrence in Lund of 1085 explained in two sentences: if someone neglects a call to *expeditio*, he shall make amends to the king.

are all referred to by the same term, a term that in itself means nothing more than 'armed expedition', has led to much confusion.

In the law of Skåne a distinction is made between two obligations. Basically there was what the law calls *ræthær lethingh*, that is legal *leding*. It consisted of the payment each year of the sum of three marks of money per *hafnæ*, a unit liable to furnish one man for the *leding* ship. In addition to this there was the *wdgerds ledingh*, actual service in the *leding* ship. This could be demanded only every four years and was called with some ceremony. The king's representative in Skåne would carry a shield and a sword to the provincial assembly and proclaim it. This involved an obligation on those *hafnæ* that had been detailed[14] to furnish a man armed and victualled for sixteen weeks, as well as the payment of certain dues to the leader, the steersman, of the district, or *skipæn*, who provided the ship. The victuals consisted of sixteen *skæpper* (bushels, 1 *skæppe* = *c*.17 litres) of sifted flour and the same weight in butter, pork and beef. It was disputed whether the meat should be weighed with or without bones! The steersman was entitled to one mark for his byrnie, one for the ship, and to one *ørtugh* (= 12 *skæpper*) of malt and the same quantity of oats. It was also incumbent on the *hafnæ* to furnish the steersman a shield and a spear. Although not recorded before the late fifteenth century these provisions are probably as old as the main law, that is, from the beginning of the thirteenth century.

The law of Jutland was promulgated in 1241 and contains the most elaborate rules for the *leding* in Denmark. Also it distinguishes clearly between *leding* which the *bønder* had to *gøræ uth*, 'perform', and the *qwærsæthæ*, which they would *rethæ*, 'pay'. The first six paragraphs of book III describe the obligations of the *ledingsbønder*, who could serve, how they should be armed, and other practical details. A legal procedure and fines for neglect are also specified. The ship, or the *skipæn*, formed a jurisdiction of its own in these matters, the fines going to the other members of the crew, the *skipperæ*, not to the king. Paragraphs 12–20 describe the distribution of the burdens involved in this service. They were distributed according to wealth as expressed in landownership or rented land.

The law also accounts for exemptions. Men in holy orders were exempt to a specified degree, but only if they were celibate, and another group of *bønder* were exempt from the *wdgerds ledingh* because they served when called. This group consisted of men commended to the king or to other lords, bishops or lay magnates. They are called *herræ mæn* and all their demesne lands were free from *leding* payments by their service. If they neglected their service, if, as the

---

[14] The expression used in the law is: *tha schal af hware haffnæ i schipæn liger*, 'then from each *haffnæ* that lies in *schipæn* shall . . .'. There are two possible interpretations of this. What happened at the assembly probably was that one ship district, *schipæn* – ship soke as the English would call it – was detailed to do this year's service. *Haffnæ i schipæn liger* would then be a reference to the *haffnæ* belonging to this *schipæn*. Alternatively, to lie in *schipæn* simply means to have been detailed for service that year. Those not detailed for service that particular year would then not be thought of as lying in *schipæn*, but rather paying their *ræther lethingh*, as lying in what the law of Jutland describes as *qwærsæthæ*.

law puts it, they sat at home without due cause or leave, they had to pay the equivalent of one third of a *hafnæ* to the king on each *gærth*, or *mansus*, they owned. Only if they refused to pay this would they lose their privileged status and be reduced to ordinary peasants and required to contribute to the *wdgerds ledingh*.

These *herræ mæn* are thus comparable to the lower English nobility who in much the same way were able to commute service into a payment. The Danish *herræ mæn* were paying the equivalent of the English scutage. Their payment was also the equivalent of the *ræthær lethingh* mentioned in the law of Skåne, three marks of money per *hafnæ* in those years when *wdgerds ledingh* was not asked of the *ledingsbønder*. It is clear, therefore, that *ræthær lethingh* is what is also called the *ledingsbøde*, or *lethang wite*, the *fyrdwite* of the English.

One group of the Danish population, then, served whenever the king called upon them and through this service liberated their demesne lands, but not their other possessions from royal demands relating to military service, although they might choose to pay rather than to serve. Another group was required to pay rather than serve three years out of four, while in the fourth year it was required to perform the *wdgerds ledingh*.

The obligation common to both groups is the *ræthær lethingh* or *lethang wite*. If we assume that this had originally been a common duty for all, we have several possible explanations. The traditional one is that free and equal smallholders had since time immemorial been sharing the burdens of defence of the nation. Alternatively there might have always been great social differences so that some had to pool their resources to fulfil the military obligations of one man while others could do so on their own. This would resemble the situation in Carolingian France where for offensive purposes normally only the latter category was employed, while for defensive purposes the resources of the former category were also exploited.[15] Finally, an originally uniform group of peasants able to serve on their own may have split up into one continuing to perform their service as *herræ mæn*, and another whose resources had dwindled through the subdivision of their original estates so that they were unable individually to keep up full service. Their service would then have been permanently commuted, appearing in the early thirteenth century as *ræthær lethingh*, except that they were required to perform the *wdgerds ledingh* every four years.

The first evidence that a payment in lieu of service was imposed on Danish *ledingsbønder* dates from 1085. In that year Knud the Holy endowed the church of St Lawrence in Lund with something like fifty-two *mansi* in Skåne and in Sjælland and part of his income from the town of Lund as well as from those of Lomma and Helsingborg. To this he added the royal dues pertaining to those lands, with the following exceptions: if somebody lost his peace, he had to buy it back from the king and his lands would be taken over by the provost and the

---

[15] Timothy Reuter, 'The End of Carolingian Military Expansion', in *Charlemagne's Heir. New Perspectives on the Reign of Louis the Pious (814–840)*, ed. Peter Godman and Roger Collins (1990), 391–405.

brethren. If someone neglected military service, he had to make amends to the king. They had to supply wagon horses only when the king himself came.[16] Knud's younger brother Niels (1104–34) similarly retained for himself the compensation for neglect of *expedicio*, that is military service, here simply called *lethang withe*, when he gave privileges to St Knud in Odense.[17] Clearly, the occupants of the lands that had been given to St Lawrence and those holding land of St Knud had the same obligations as the *herræ mæn* in the law of Jutland. If they neglected *expedicio* they would pay compensation to the king. We are, however, not told at what rate, nor how it was calculated. The system employed in the law of Jutland no doubt belongs to the thirteenth century.

If the service of the *herræ mæn* in the law of Jutland and their compensation to the king in case of neglect and the *ræthær lethingh* of the law of Skåne are possibly connected with the *expedicio* appearing in the royal diplomas, where does the cooperative *wdgerds ledingh* belong? Is it, as traditionally claimed, how lesser landowners always organised their contribution when the king called up the *leding*, or is it something else?

The Danish provincial laws do not permit any closer insight into the character and purpose of the *wdgerds ledingh*. Parallel organisations are, however, described in the Norwegian and Swedish provincial laws in much greater detail, and particularly the Swedish *ledung* was clearly not an organisation of the military forces of Sweden for anything like the purpose for which the Danish *leding* was supposedly created and most often used: attack on foreign enemies. It was an organisation designed for coastguard service and defence. The rules laid down for it positively reek with the boredom of peacetime service in domestic waters. They deal with such problems as may arise in harbours, like damaging your neighbour's ship, occupying the bishop's berth, or falling asleep on watch duty. The last was more expensive if the enemy came and managed to harry and burn than if the negligence had no consequences.[18]

In the same way as the Norwegian laws restrict royal use of the *leding* to domestic waters, not beyond the end of the land,[19] the Swedish laws lay down that the king cannot demand the service of the organisation described beyond certain limits. It is not for offensive warfare abroad. However, if the king wanted to undertake such warfare, the same people might be persuaded to participate, but that would be under different rules. For attacks on foreign countries the king would also call upon the chieftains of the land and their household troops.

The conditions in Norway, not presented in detail here, were very similar to the conditions in Sweden. The regime prevailing in Norway is described in a complex of laws which are clearly closely related to the Danish description of

[16] *Diplomatarium Danicum*. Udg. af Det Danske Sprog- og Litteraturselskab (Copenhagen, 1938–), 1. ser. vol. 2 (1053–1169), ed. L. Weibull and N. Skyum-Nielsen (1963), no. 21.
[17] Ibid., no. 32.
[18] Swedish *ledung* is described in *Upplandslagen*, *Västmannalagen*, *Södermannalagen* and *Hälsingelagen*; from Västergötland and Östergötland, no rules are extant.
[19] The Law of Gulathing, *Norges gamle Love indtil 1387*, ed. R. Keyser et al., 5 vols. (Chritiania, 1846–95), vol. 1, 295.

the *wdgerds ledingh*. If we take as a point of departure what is known about Norway and Sweden it is *a priori* likely that in Denmark we also have to distinguish between the forces of the magnates and a coastguard.

A coastguard was, according to Saxo, introduced in Denmark after the conquest of the Wends in 1169. In the previous ten years incessant campaigns had been waged against the peoples on the Baltic coasts opposite Denmark but in 1169 the main fortress of Rügen, Arkona, was conquered and the people were converted and submitted to the king of Denmark. Rügen became part of the diocese of Roskilde. The campaigns, then, had achieved the (alleged) goal of all war: peace. So rather than sending a fleet against the Wends every year, patrolling Wendish waters was now required. It was therefore decided to divide the Danish fleet into four parts taking duty in turns. Saxo does not describe this reform in much detail. He only informs us who were put in charge of this coastguard and that it was decided to pick young and unmarried men for the job. They were supposed to be less liable to home-sickness than married men.[20] Norwegian laws are concerned with the maintenance of work on the farms of those away on service and give rules of how those remaining at home should look after these farms.[21] The organisation described in the provincial laws was clearly not introduced immediately, and very soon the ships on guard duty were sent away into the Baltic on a good old-fashioned plundering expedition.[22] However, what happened in 1169 foreshadowed the later *wdgerds ledingh* in at least one respect: the *wdgerds ledingh* could be called upon every fourth year, and in 1169 the fleet was divided into four parts, probably implying that each part would be called upon only once every four years. The more detailed rules for the distribution of the burden are the result of later development.

In the light of this the jigsaw puzzle of Danish *leding* should probably be solved in the following manner. The *leding*, or *expedicio*, in Knud's charter of 1085 and later charters referred to the military service of magnates and chieftains. It expressed an attempt to bring these forces under a royal control comparable to the control William the Conqueror exercised over his vassals, and an attempt to enforce defined quotas on warlords of any kind, lay or ecclesiastical, based on an assessment of their resources. Knud was killed in his attempt to bring the magnates under such control, and their military independence loomed large among their grudges against the king. We should therefore beware of assuming that because *expedicio* is referred to in Knud's charter that this royal claim was now established in Denmark. Whether it could be enforced or not would always depend on the authority of the ruling king. He may have made the claim, as Erik Lam must have done when he gave away the *expedicio* belonging to the tenants of St Peter in Næstved. It previously belonged to the donor, Peder Bodilsen and his mother and brothers,[23] but this does not imply that Erik Lam

[20] Saxo, *Gesta Danorum*, ed. J. Olrik and H. Ræder (Copenhagen, 1931), 14, xxxix, para. 49.
[21] See, for example, the Law of Gulathing, 295
[22] Saxo, *Gesta Danorum*, 14, xl.
[23] *Diplomatarium Danicum*, 1. ser. vol. II, no. 78.

was able to enforce it when the lands were still in the hands of the Bodilsen family.

Effective royal control of the magnates was hardly established before the reigns of Valdemar I the Great (1157–82) and his sons, Knud VI (1182–1202) and Valdemar II the Victorious (1202–41). By the end of this period the men who could accept the commendation of others as their *herræ mæn* had been limited to the king himself, who could do so throughout the country,[24] the Duke of Slesvig, who could do so within his duchy, and the king's children or relatives who had been enfeoffed by him, who could do so within their fiefs. Bishops could also do so, but only in their dioceses.[25] The *herræ mæn* performed, in principle, full military service, putting their lives on the line for the king whenever he called upon them, although it was possible for them to pay compensation for the service if they had due cause or had been granted leave of absence. The compensation paid on such occasions corresponded to the payment asked of those who were not *herræ mæn*. They had apparently, technically speaking, been granted permanent permission to sit at home, except that they were required to participate in the *wdgerds ledingh* every four years. Assuming that these obligations all go back to a common source, the *expedicio*, the best explanation is that the group of men supporting the original *expedicio* had split in two, one of which was still capable of doing full service, while the other had given it up in favour of paying and doing coastguard service in the *wdgerds ledingh*. Apparently some of those originally liable to perform the *expedicio* were no longer able to do so.

A study of the narrative sources of Danish history before 1200 produces few or no traces of this organisation. Viking fleets and armies as well as the fleets and armies raised by Scandinavian kings in the two centuries immediately following the age of the Vikings were *ad hoc* phenomena and consisted of whatever forces a king or chieftain could persuade to follow him. References to *expedicio* in charters of this period are to knight service, also described in the codes.

This old-fashioned way of recruiting military forces sufficed as long as the purpose was occasional attacks on enemies. When the Wends had been conquered, however, by *c*.1170, a need arose for forces to patrol the home waters as well as the waters of subdued but not necessarily reliable former enemies. This is probably when the cooperative navy described in the law codes originated. It was meant to preserve peace rather than to conduct war and thus comes closer to the idea of a standing navy than generally thought. It presupposes a degree of control and an administrative capacity that Danish kings did not possess before the closing years of the twelfth century. It was far from the standing naval forces of the seventeenth or eighteenth century, but also far from the *ad hoc* naval forces of the Viking Age.

---

[24] Although there is evidence of an understanding with the bishops that he should not take men within their *skipæn*, *Diplomatarium Danicum*, 1. ser. vol. VI, no. 147.

[25] The Law of Jutland, iii, 8.

SCANDINAVIAN WARSHIPS AND NAVAL POWER IN THE THIRTEENTH AND FOURTEENTH CENTURIES

Jan Bill

AS for many other parts of Europe, the thirteenth and fourteenth centuries were for Denmark a time characterised by internal and external wars. Thanks to its geography, and to the geography of the North Sea and Baltic area in general, seafaring always held an important position in the economics and politics of the country. Ships were needed to tie together the various parts of the country and when wars were fought, naval operations were mandatory. At the same time, Denmark during the eleventh to fourteenth centuries, thanks to its fertile lands and short distances to large north European urban centres, became much more influenced by continental social, economic and political developments than the likewise markedly maritime Scandinavian countries Norway and Sweden. It is therefore of interest to know whether the Danish situation, combining a Scandinavian maritime society with continentally coloured economic and social development, led to the early creation of structures that might foretell the formation of permanent navies like those known from the sixteenth century on.

In investigating this question it has to be admitted that neither the archaeological nor the literary sources provide ample information on maritime warfare and we have to extrapolate from scarce source material when we want to discuss high medieval naval organisation in Denmark. It is possible to attack at least three questions concerning the general issue because of the existence of relevant sources. These are: What were the ships like that were used for war in Scandinavian waters during the thirteenth and fourteenth centuries? What kind of military operations were they involved in? What kind of organisation was established in order to provide ships, crews and provisions for these naval forces?

The reason for asking what ships used for military purposes in high medieval Scandinavia looked like is that they may themselves reflect the organisation behind their existence. Specialised warships have a long history in Scandinavia before the twelfth century, their existence being archaeologically documented from at least the fourth century BC and the third, fourth, eighth, ninth, tenth and eleventh centuries AD.[1] The late medieval production and use of specialised

---

[1] The examples referred to are the Hjortspring boat, the Nydam boats, the larger of the Kvalsund boats, the Gokstad and Oseberg ships along with the Ladby, the Hedeby 1, the Roskilde 6 and the Skuldelev 2 and 5 vessels.

1. View from north-west of the royal shipyard Engelborg on the island Slotø outside Nakskov, south-eastern Denmark. The ships were being built in the triangular area between the two walls stretching from the tower to the coast.
Photo Hans Stiesdahl, National Museum of Denmark

warships is also well documented in Scandinavia, most markedly by the construction of a strongly fortified naval shipyard in 1509 by the Danish king Hans outside the town Nakskov in south-eastern Denmark (see Illustration 1).[2] The ships produced there and in the royal shipyard in Copenhagen were specialised men-of-war, equipped with cannon that could sink an enemy ship. Both the longships of the preceding centuries, and the heavily armed warships of the late medieval and early modern period represented specifically military investments closely associated with the power structures of their times. Is it possible to identify a similar situation in the High Middle Ages?

In order to discuss this question, we have the widest array of sources available, although they are far short of what we would like to have. The written sources from thirteenth and fourteenth-century Scandinavia do frequently mention ships, but generally without revealing much, if anything, about their

---

[2] I. Ericsson, 'Engelborg på Slotø – skibsværft, fæstning og lensmandssæde fra kong Hans' tid', *Hikuin*, 14 (1988), 261–74.

construction and characteristics. Names for ship-types are frequently reported, especially *navis/schep*, *skute*, *cogge*, *snekke* and, more seldom, *holc*. This type of information, however, is problematic, as we have no guarantee that medieval writers were consistent in their use of the names of ship types. From around 1400, there are examples in north European sources that the same ship alternately is called a cog and a hulk.[3] Nor can we be sure that we are able to identify the meaning of these terms today. In this context the problem is especially evident for the term *cogge* as this frequently appears in military contexts. There are, however, indications that cogs, as archaeologically defined today, were not as dominant in north European seafaring in the thirteenth and fourteenth centuries as previously thought. For this reason, it is necessary to distinguish between the literary and the archaeological cogs, a discussion that we will return to later. What is clear from the written sources is that fleets very often consisted of ships of different types and sizes. The examples mostly come from the fourteenth century, probably because the number of written sources from this century is much larger than from earlier years. A Danish fleet of 1316 is said to have included forty-five cogs and 'many other ships', and in 1360, monasteries and towns were required to provide 'cogs and fast ships' for the king.[4] The dualism in the last source is especially interesting as it may reflect that ship types other than cogs were not only available but also necessary.

Another type of information which can be extracted from the historical sources is about the size of vessels. In a military context, this was normally given as the number of armed men the ships carried, more seldom in the dead-weight tonnage, or cargo capacity. Most frequent, though, is the use of vague terms like 'large' and 'small'.

Iconographic sources can be more specific and can convey fairly detailed information on both ship construction and ship use. Detailed ship pictures from the High Middle Ages, however, are fairly rare in Scandinavia, as has been demonstrated in a recent study of Scandinavian ship depictions from 800 to 1400. While not claiming to be complete, the study was able to register only fifty-three images from the Gothic period (1275–1400), including a high percentage of very simple renderings providing little detailed information. The situation is not much different for the Romanesque period (1080–1275), although the number of images was substantially larger, namely one hundred and ninety-three. This is due to the even higher proportion of graffiti and the poor state of preservation for many of the ship pictures of this period.[5] Furthermore, the artists producing images of ships may have had other concerns than

---

[3] S. Fliedner, ' "Kogge" und "Holk" ', in K. Löbe et al., *Die Bremer Hanse-kogge. Ein Schlüssel zur Schiffahrtsgeschichte. Fund. Konservierung. Forschung.* Monographien der Wittheit zu Bremen 8 (Bremer, 1969), 67 n. 152.
[4] N. Lund, *Lid, leding og landeværn* (Roskilde, 1996), 284. *Annales Danici Medii Ævi*, ed. Ellen Jørgensen (Selskabet for Udgivelse af Kilder til dansk Historie, 1920), 187.
[5] M. Felbo, 'Skibsbilleder i Skandinavien 800–1400. Kontekst og funktion, indhold og kildeværdi' (unpublished MA thesis, University of Copenhagen, 1999), 10.

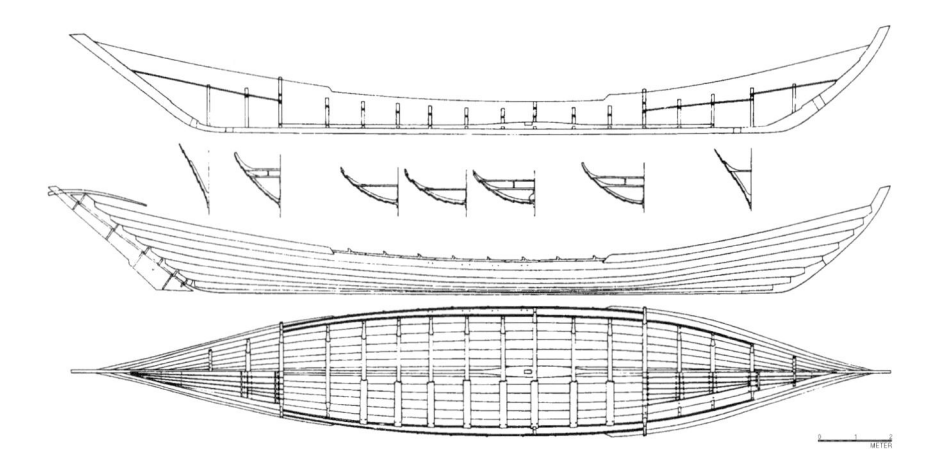

2. The Helgeandsholmen V ship find, as reconstructed from the archaeological remains. The vessel is a rare example of a combined rowing and sailing vessel from the fourteenth century. It may be suggested that it was used for military purposes in the narrow waterways leading through the archipelago to Stockholm. After Varenius 1989

accurately depicting contemporary vessels. Illustrations may show old or exotic ship types because they more efficiently conveyed the message of the image, or simply because artists relied on model books or convention.[6]

Finally, archaeological sources present us with hard-core data on ship construction, and here is a field in which Scandinavia – especially southern Scandinavia – can present a quite rich and detailed record. This does not solve the problem of weak sources, however, as the archaeological finds may not be easily identified as being military or non-military vessels, or tell us much about their use and ownership.

A common problem is that very often only small portions of a hull, and then often only the bottom, is preserved. Of a total of some fifty finds from thirteenth and fourteenth-century Scandinavia, only two to my eyes offer some evidence that they may have been used for military purposes. This does not mean, of course, that the rest were not. We just do not have any indication that they were. By chance it appears that the two archaeological finds to some extent represent what appear to be the two main categories of warships of their time, the big ship and the galley, and certainly the two contemporary, dominant ship-building traditions that can be attested in the archaeological material, the clinker-built or all-clinker-built tradition and the cog tradition.

---

[6] See ibid., 26–7, C. Villain-Gandossi, 'Illustrations of Ships: Iconography and Interpretation', in *Cogs, Caravels and Galleons. The Sailing Ship 1000–1650*, ed. R. W. Unger (London, 1994), 169–74, and R. W. Unger, *The Art of Medieval Technology. Images of Noah the Shipbuilder* (New Brunswick, 1991), 9–14 for discussion.

The first example is the unusually well preserved, *c.*19 m long, all-clinker-built Boat V from Helgeandsholmen in Stockholm (see Illustration 2).[7] The construction of the vessel is dated to between 1316 and 1350 and it is made for propulsion with oars and sail. It is very slim and lightly built, and is obviously constructed for personnel transport. Due to its restricted cargo capacity, it is unlikely to have had an economic function, like fishing or transportation of bulk goods. With its eight pairs of oars and available space for standing personnel on slightly raised decks in the stem and stern, it may have been efficient for guard and control purposes in the narrow waters of the Stockholm archipelago and in Lake Mälaren. It is certainly not to be regarded as a true galley or longship, and it may also simply have been the transport vessel for a magnate or an official of some kind. In its construction it shows some traditional features – for example the use of short, flush scarfs in the plank joints of the underwater hull – that had fallen out of use in cargo carriers by the beginning of the fourteenth century.[8] Thus it is not only in its propulsion and function, but also in its construction details that it is related to the longships known from ninth, tenth and eleventh century finds from Denmark, Norway and Germany.

The second example is a cog, built around 1390, and recently excavated outside Skanör.[9] The vessel is in terms of construction quite similar to the Bremen cog from 1380, which serves as a model for the archaeological cog.[10] Defining features are the combination of flush-laid bottom and clinker-built sides, the straight stem and stern posts connected to the keel plank with large, knee-shaped timbers, and the luting of moss, kept in place with laths and characteristic staples called 'sintels' in the literature. The Skanör cog was somewhat larger than the medium-sized Bremen cog, but the only reason for claiming it to have been in military use is the fact that fourteen stone cannon balls, of two different sizes, were found in the wreck. Only preliminary drawings have so far been published of the ship, but they do provide a clear impression of the poor and unfortunately all too common state of preservation.

One of the few Scandinavian ship depictions relevant to the discussion of high medieval maritime warfare is the beautiful but heavily restored mural found in the village church of Skamstrup in central Sjælland, Denmark (see Illustration 3). The motif, found in one of the vaults and dated to *c.*1380, shows the legend of a sailing contest between the Norwegian saint, Olav, and his heathen brother. St Olav, defending the honour of the Christian faith, was sailing a large, slow vessel, called *The Ox*, while his brother was using his speedy vessel

[7] Björn Varenius, *Båterna från Helgeandsholmen* (Stockholm, 1989), 38–45, 88–9.
[8] J. Bill, 'Getting into Business – Reflections of a Market Economy in Medieval Scandinavian Shipbuilding', in *Shipshape. Essays for Ole Crumlin-Pedersen on the Occasion of his 60th Anniversary, February 24th 1995*, ed. O. Olsen, J. Skamby Madsen, and F. Rieck (Roskilde, 1995), 195–202.
[9] A. Bunse and B. M. Jakobsen, 'Skanörskoggen. Forundersökning. Rapport från år 1992 och 1993', *Marinarkeologisk tidskrift*, 1995:1, 13–15.
[10] W. Lahn, *Die Kogge von Bremen, Band 1. Bauteile und Bauablauf* (Bremerhaven/Hamburg, 1992).

3. Late 14th century mural from the parish church of Skamstrup, Denmark. The scene illustrates the legend of St Olav, who with the help of God, wins a sailing contest against a much faster ship in his large, slow vessel.
Photo: Werner Karrasch, the Viking Ship Museum in Roskilde

named *The Snake*. Miraculously St Olav won the contest, and, according to legend, his ship was sailing so fast that an arrow fired forward fell behind the ship.

The artist of the Skamstrup mural very deliberately stressed the differences between *The Ox* and *The Snake*. He is showing us the former as a huge ship with castles fore and aft and even with a rudimentary top castle – perhaps only a wicker basket – while the latter appears as a smaller vessel with no castles, and crowded with soldiers. Although the story the artist wanted to tell was an old one, he obviously chose to illustrate it with contemporary ship types. The two ships in the depiction could very well represent the two main warships of the thirteenth century, the small but fast and the large but slow – or, to speak in the language of a 1360 chronicle, the *liburna* and the cog.

Although none of the remaining ship finds can be identified as fighting ships, and thus give us no direct information on the character of warships, they still help us to map the general technical development of shipbuilding in the period. An analysis carried out on all the known ship finds from the area of medieval Denmark, and dated independently between 1000 and 1600, demonstrates the presence of two significant periods of change in ship construction in this area.[11] One of these was during the thirteenth century, where many of the building techniques so characteristic of the ships of the Viking age gave way to new methods that were being commonly used all over northern Europe. The change is so dramatic that it is justified to speak about the end of a specifically Nordic shipbuilding tradition, and although the archaeological material is somewhat biased towards smaller vessels, it is unthinkable that this change was not also significant for the construction of ships used in war.

The archaeological finds show that by the middle of the twelfth century, the first cog-like vessels had appeared in Scandinavian waters.[12] Thirteenth-century cog finds are fairly few, but during the fourteenth century cogs form a significant proportion of the biggest vessels found, and they must have played an important role, in peace as well as war, at that time. On the basis of historical evidence, some researchers have strongly emphasised the military role of the cog, but the archaeological finds, apart from documenting the presence of the cogs, also give reason to be critical of this attitude.[13]

The putative military qualities of the cog are, especially, its large dimensions and high sides together with its sturdy construction. Comparison is often made with the longships of Scandinavian type, which are known from Viking-age finds in Norway and Denmark. Such a comparison, however, is anachronistic, because although literary sources indicate that vessels called cogs existed at the same time as the Viking ships, the known archaeological examples of cogs are all much later. Furthermore, the oldest example of the archaeological cog – the Kollerup cog from the middle of the twelfth century – does not have the qualities that should have made it superior to ships of Scandinavian type. Although very massively built, it is rather narrow, not especially high-sided, and certainly not impressive when compared to the largest, all-clinker-built ships of the twelfth century (see Illustration 4).[14] Remains of such a ship, known as the 'Big Ship from Bryggen' in the literature, was found as reused timbers in foundations in the Norwegian town of Bergen.[15] A reconstruction of the vessel has demonstrated that it had a cargo capacity of at least 120 tons, which can be compared to the 35 tons of the Kollerup cog.[16] Recent dendrochronological analyses of the

---

[11] J. Bill, 'Small Scale Seafaring in Danish Waters AD 1000–1600' (unpublished dissertation, University of Copenhagen, 1997).

[12] A new dendrochronological dating of the Kollerup cog places it in the mid-twelfth century, with a provenance in southern Jutland – possibly in the north Frisian area. See A. Daly, E. H. Eriksen and A. Englert, 'New Dendro Dates for Danish Medieval Ships from Eltang and Kollerup', *Maritime Archaeology Newsletter from Roskilde, Denmark*, 14 (2001), 61.

[13] See e.g. T. J. Runyan, 'The Cog as Warship', in *Cogs, Caravels and Galleons*, 47–58, and P. Heinsius, *Das Schiff der Hansischen Frühzeit* (Weimar, 1956).

[14] P. Kohrtz Andersen, *Kollerupkoggen* (Thisted, 1983).

[15] A. E. Christensen, 'Boat Finds from Bryggen', in *The Archaeological Excavations at Bryggen, 'The German Wharf', in Bergen 1955–68*, vol. I, ed. A. E. Herteig (Bergen, 1985), 47–278.

[16] A. E. Christensen, 'Hanseatic and Nordic Ships in Medieval Trade. Were the Cogs Better Vessels?', in *Medieval Ships and the Birth of Technological Societies. Volume I: Northern Europe*, ed. C. Villain-Gandossi, S. Busuttil, and P. Adam (Malta, 1989), 18–19. For the cargo

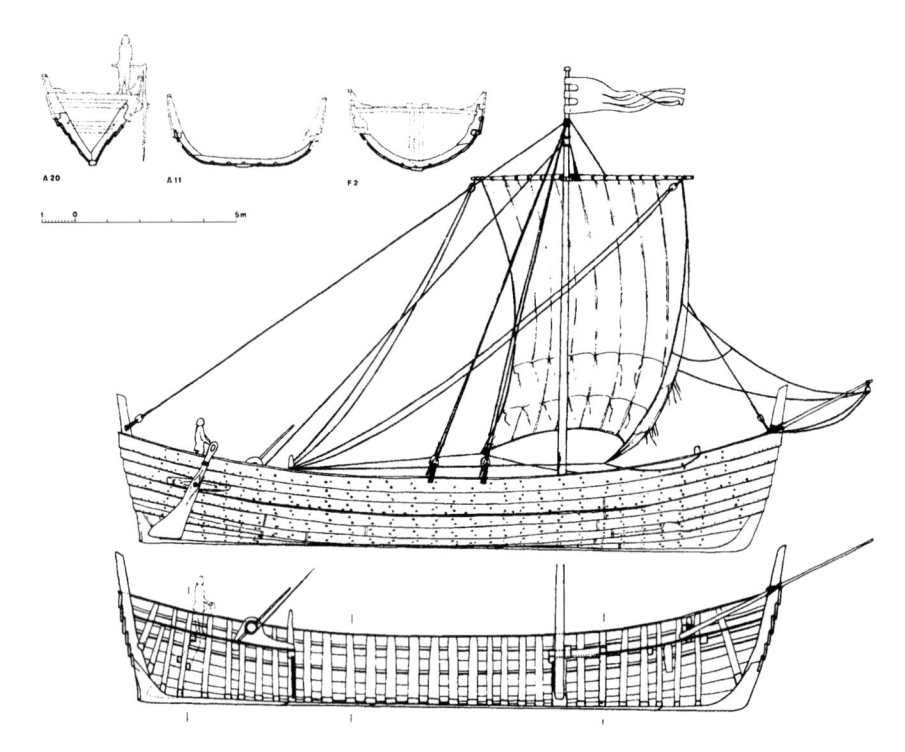

4. The Kollerup cog, wrecked on the northweast coast of Jutland, as reconstructed by Kohrtz Andersen (1983). No indications of upper structures were found, and indeed the hull shape, with its restricted stability, does not invite the construction of extensive upper works. That does not exclude, though, other 12th century cogs from having castles. Drawing by Per Kohrtz Andersen

timbers show that it was constructed locally as early as in 1187, and that some protruding beams, found elsewhere in the excavation, belonged to this ship. This makes it the earliest known example of this technique.[17] Comparing the Bergen ship with tonnage data preserved in the written sources it was clearly in the absolute top-size class in north European shipbuilding of the time,[18] and demonstrates beyond doubt that, although cogs may have been built much larger than the examples which have been accidentally preserved for us to investigate, they

---

capacity of the Kollerup cog, see e.g. O. Crumlin-Pedersen, 'Ships as Indicators of Trade in Northern Europe 600–1200', in *Maritime Topography and the Medieval Town*, ed. J. Bill and B. Clausen (Copenhagen, 1999), 9–18.

[17] T. S. Bartholin and A. Englert, 'Dendro-dating of the "Big Ship" from Bergen', *Maritime Archaeology Newsletter from Roskilde, Denmark*, 13 (2000), 48.

[18] J. Bill, 'The Cargo Vessels', in *Cogs, Cargoes, and Commerce: Maritime Bulk Trade in Northern Europe, 1150 to 1400'*, ed. L. Berggren, A. Landen and N. Hybel (Toronto, 2002), 92–112.

can hardly have had an advantage in terms of size potential in the twelfth century. Clinker-built ships could be made just as large. The recent finding and excavation of two large fourteenth-century ships of a hitherto completely unknown type on the Mecklenburg coast provide further evidence for this. The ships, which are both clinker-built from very massive pine planks, measured around 8 metres in width and 25–30 metres in length.[19] The two finds are a reminder of how limited our knowledge of the shipbuilding of this period still is.

However, cogs are frequently mentioned as being used for military purposes in the written sources, for example in England, where Runyan has extrapolated that they constituted 57 per cent of about 1300 ships that were arrested for military service during the years 1337–60.[20] However, cog finds are extremely rare in England, where so far only remains of one possible cog have been found, in spite of the quite large number of high-medieval ship finds that have been excavated, for example in London.[21]

The same situation appears to exist in the Scandinavian countries. In Denmark, as already mentioned, there are several cog finds, but they present a very different find distribution from that of clinker-built vessels. While the latter – or remains of them – can be found virtually everywhere, including as reused timbers in wells and other constructions, the cogs are found almost solely as wrecks. Also the evidence for cog-building within the Danish area, with the exception of the twelfth-century finds probably from north Frisian areas, is very meagre. Three of four fourteenth-century wrecks of cogs found within the borders of medieval Denmark have been dendrochronologically analysed and they have all proved to be built from German and Polish oak, indicating that local production of this vessel type in Denmark was probably not common at that time.[22] Also remarkable is that the extensive excavations in the harbour of Bergen, which was a very important port and trade station for Lübeck, have

---

[19] See F. Lüth and T. Förster, 'Schiff, Wrack, "baltische Kogge"', *Archäologie in Deutschland* (1999, no. 4), 8–13, for a preliminary description of the Gellen wreck. A second wreck was excavated at the island of Poel in the Bay of Wismar in 1999.
[20] Runyan, 'The Cog as Warship', 49, T. J. Runyan, 'Ships and Fleets in Anglo-French Warfare, 1337–1360', *The American Neptune*, 46 (1986), 92–3. In fact, the type of only 325 of 1291 arrested ships could be identified, but of these no less than 187 were described as 'cogs'. The second most common description was as 'ships', of which there were 46.
[21] D. Goodburn, 'Reused Medieval Ship Planks from Westminster, England, Possibly Derived from a Vessel Built in the Cog Style', *International Journal of Nautical Archaeology*, 26 (1997), 26–38; P. Marsden, *Ships of the Port of London, Twelfth to Seventeenth Centuries AD* (London, 1996).
[22] The Vejby cog was built in 1372 in Gdansk/Elblag (N. Bonde and J. S. Jensen, 'The Dating of a Hanseatic Cog-Find in Denmark. What Coins and Tree Rings Can Reveal in Maritime Archaeology', in *Shipshape. Essays for Ole-Crumlin-Pedersen*, 112–14), the Lille Kregme cog *c*.1362 in Pommerania (F. Rieck, 'Ll. Kregme koggen. Et middelalderligt skibsforlis i Roskilde Fjord', in *Søfart, politik, identitet – tilegnet Ole Feldbæk*, ed. H. Jeppesen (Helsingør, 1996), 23), and the Skanör cog *c*.1390 in northern Germany ('hatte' (Anders Bunse), 'Rapport fra Skanörskoggen', *Marinerat*, 14: 9, 1997).

5. The ship depictions from the parish churches of Himmelev (left) and Skrøbelev (right), in Denmark. The depictions shows that in the thirteenth century the longship still had a strong position in the both formal and informal art. Photos: National Museum of Denmark

produced only one piece of planking possibly originating from a cog, although hundreds of ship fragments were found.[23]

These observations may lead us to ask whether the name 'cog', as used in the written sources, does not have a somewhat wider meaning than the archaeologically defined cog. As mentioned before, during the thirteenth century, Scandinavian shipbuilding and cog-building practices amalgamated to a large extent, and by the fourteenth century, it was virtually only the choice of building material that distinguished the two vessel types from each other to the casual observer. Broader, sawn planks were preferred for cogs, while narrower, split planks were used for the clinker-built vessels. Other differences, such as in the bottom construction, the choice of luting method and material, and the choice of nails, were not visible from the outside. Thus it may have been other, more visible characteristics, for example the use of castles, an especially boxy hull shape or just a mere size criterion, that in some areas and periods made for the use of the term cog. In the present state of research, it is important to avoid rigidly translating the cog of the documentary sources into a vessel belonging to the building tradition that we archaeologically characterise as the cog. The cogs mentioned

---

[23] Christensen, 'The Boat Finds from Bryggen', 203. Christensen believes the plank, the deposition of which is dated from context to the early fifteenth century, originates from an early carvel-built ship.

over the next pages are all from the literary sources and should thus not be confused with the archaeological cogs, of which we have far fewer examples.

The development of military vessels in Scandinavia may well have followed the same pattern as in other parts of northern Europe, although based on local ship types. The growth in size has already been touched upon but it may be worth mentioning that Norwegian contemporary sagas, written between the late twelfth and the mid-thirteenth century, attest to a strong competition among Norwegian nobles in building the largest warships. Those appear still to have been equipped with oars, but it is also clear that speed was being sacrificed for the advantages of height and of carrying more men on board. They were fighting platforms, not troop-carriers like the earlier longships.[24] A Norwegian *Speculum Regale*, which was written down between 1240 and 1263, mentions that warships had castles in the stem and stern, as well as in the mast top.[25] This is about half a century later than the Dunwich seal, the oldest known north European representation of the same feature, but this may well be a coincidence. It is noticeable that castles do not occur on the few thirteenth-century ship depictions that we have in Scandinavia, but they are, as demonstrated by the examples from Skrøbelev and Himmelev, not very detailed ship representations (see Illustration 5).

The waters that the ships were intended to be used in could have set limits on their size. According to the historian Saxo Grammaticus, writing around 1200, the Norwegian king in about 1160 gave a large warship, 'built with the greatest of art in the fashion of a dragon', to the Danish king. The ship, however, was so big that it could not be used in the shallow coastal waters and rivers south of the Baltic, where the Danish king was operating.[26] Fast, manoeuvrable troop transports were of course always of importance for naval operations in a time when war at sea still was very much hand-to-hand combat, and therefore there still existed a need for rowed vessels, although the large ships were becoming floating fighting platforms. This is probably the background for the 1360 report of towns and monasteries in Denmark that provided ships for the king. The source states that the king demanded cogs (*coggones*), as well as ships called *liburnae*.[27] The word *liburna* is an ancient Latin term describing a Roman type of low, fast warship, and it is supposed to mean longship or fast ship in its medieval, north European usage.

The word 'cog' is being used to describe some of the vessels in military use in Denmark from 1249 on, and in 1304 it is this term the Danish king used when

---

[24] R. Malmros, 'Leding og skjaldekvad. Det elvte århundredes nordiske krigsflåder, deres teknologi og organisation og deres placering i samfundet belyst ud fra den samtidige fyrstedigtning', *Aarbøger for Nordisk Oldkyndighed og Historie*, 1985 (1986), 95–6.
[25] *Konungs skuggsiá*, ed. Ludvig Holm-Olsen (Oslo, 1945), 60, l.4–32.
[26] *Saxo Grammaticus Danmarks Krønike*, ed. F. Winkel Horn (Copenhagen, 1898/1975), 169–74.
[27] *Annales Danici Medii Ævi*, 187.

he wanted a new type of warship at his disposal other than those the *leding* organisation traditionally provided him with. The king, Erik Menved (1286–1319), in general was eager to modernise his military apparatus, and certainly large, high warships with castles must have operated in Danish waters on several occasions already before his time. Among the things preserved in the written sources are, for example, records of the Hansards' attack on Copenhagen in 1249 and, in cooperation with the Danes, their successful blockade of Norway in 1284. The close interaction with the Hanseatic towns, partly as allies, partly as enemies, during the thirteenth and fourteenth centuries must have ensured a balance of power, and therefore probably also a degree of similarity in naval organisation on both sides of the south-west Baltic during that time. The types of military operations in which ships and the fleets were involved were just as varied as those of land forces. Ships could be used for terrorising waters and coasts or for scouting, they could carry invasion armies or blockade individual towns or entire countries, and they could be used in large fleets for fierce sea battles or in smaller groups to protect convoys. However, it seems that the role of the individual ship can be described in two simple categories: as a means for transporting land troops in amphibious operations or as a platform for fighting other ships. Although ships certainly were used for attacks on coastal towns and castles, they were little suited for direct engagement against soldiers protected by any substantial fortification. Considering that with their tarred wood, ropes and sails ships are quite inflammable and considering that, due to stability requirements, ships could not be built very high nor carry heavy catapults, they were easily outmatched by land-based defences. An example is the failed invasion of Norway by the Danish king Waldemar I in 1168, where the defenders, according to Saxo, successfully blocked a strategically important strait by means of catapults.[28] The ships' role in such operations was therefore first and foremost to function as troop transports and to cut off the enemy from the seaward side.

The ships used for transportation and landing of forces in southern Scandinavia and the Baltic had to change during the High Middle Ages as a result of changes in how battles were fought on land. In the eleventh and twelfth centuries, mainly rather lightly equipped infantry were used, and in the protected, shallow waters of southern Scandinavia, such forces could be transported very efficiently in combined rowing and sailing vessels with shallow draft and built for high speed. The Roskilde 6 longship, dated by dendrochronology to 1025 or later, is an outstanding example of such a vessel. A preliminary reconstruction indicates that it measured 36 metres in length, with a beam of only 3.5 metres and a draught of about 1 metre, and that it carried about 100 men, 78 of whom could row the vessel.[29] A slightly older, but more thoroughly researched

---

[28] *Saxo Grammaticus*, 214–15.
[29] J. Bill, M. Gøthche, and H. M. Myrhøj, 'Nordeuropas største skibsfund. Skibskirkegård under museumsøen i Roskilde', *Nationalmuseets arbejdsmark*, 1998, 140–3.

example is the late-tenth-century longship from Hedeby, which measured *c.*30 metres and transported around 60 soldiers.[30] In spite of a relatively high number of ship finds from the twelfth and thirteenth centuries, finds of this type are lacking. Numerous passages in Saxo Grammaticus' *Gesta Danorum* demonstrate, however, that it was still in use in Baltic waters during the reign of Waldemar I the Great (1157–82).[31]

However, the increased use of heavy cavalry from the twelfth century on must have led to an increasing portion of the vessels used for amphibious operations being sturdy cargo vessels capable of transporting the large, specially trained war-horses and heavy equipment. Urbanisation and the construction of coastal fortresses to protect land and cities had a similar effect, as they made it necessary to bring along siege machines and provisions that would make it possible to besiege the enemy for weeks or months. The invasion fleet Lübeck sent in 1362, heading for Copenhagen and Helsingborg, is a good example of such an enterprise. The fleet consisted of 27 cogs, 25 smaller ships and 2740 armed men. With them they brought three *Werke*, a type of over-sized crossbow, and five catapults. After plundering Copenhagen, the fleet continued to Helsingborg, where it was supposed to meet allies from Sweden and Norway. These, however, never turned up, and the whole expedition was brought to a devastating end for the Hansards when the Danish king, Waldemar IV Atterdag, succeeded in capturing twelve of their cogs with a sudden fleet attack while the Hansards were besieging Helsingborg castle. It is reported that the seized cogs were full of provisions and weapons for the besieging army.[32]

Fighting at sea was basically infantry fighting from movable platforms, and major advantages were those of height and of manoeuvrability. As these two are contradictory, it is not strange that both galley-type vessels that could be rowed and massive vessels that could be built very high were favoured. Ability to fight at sea was the tool for one of the most powerful naval campaigns that could be launched: the isolating of whole countries or areas. It was to be a common naval practice from the seventeenth century on. In the High Middle Ages this concept, which was so much more realistic in the narrow, south Scandinavian waters than in the Channel, was probably realised in Scandinavia much earlier than elsewhere in Europe. The most impressive example is the fleet blockade of Norway that the Hanseatic towns and the Danish king established in 1284. Norway had at this time become dependent on grain imports, and the blockade was therefore a very powerful weapon. Perhaps the embargo established at the same time by the Hanseatic towns was even more efficient. Within a year the Norwegians had to negotiate a humiliating peace with the Hanseatic towns. Unfortunately the treaty did not include Denmark, and in the following years Norwegian ships,

---

[30] O. Crumlin-Pedersen, *Viking-Age Ships and Shipbuilding in Hedeby/Haithabu and Schleswig* (Schleswig and Roskilde, 1997).
[31] *Saxo Grammaticus*, 150–286.
[32] K. Fritze and G. Krause, *Seekriege der Hanse* (Berlin, 1989), 118–23; J. Barfod, *Flådens fødsel* (Copenhagen, 1990), 14–15.

assisted by Danish outlaws who had settled at a small, Danish island, Hjelm, in reality took control of Danish waters. Another example of a blockade comes from the civil wars in Denmark, where in 1326 the king was caught with his army on the island of Falster which was being guarded by a fleet collected by his enemies.

As to organisation, the sources from the thirteenth and fourteenth centuries mention several different ways of raising and provisioning fleets. The *leding*, which probably formed the backbone of naval organisation in the thirteenth and the first half of the fourteenth century, is described in an appendix to the Law of Skåne (*c*.1200) and, in some more detail, in the Law of Jutland from 1241.[33] The organisation described in these texts appears to be a coastguard, manned and provisioned by the farmers on the basis of land taxation. Each *hafnæ* (the unit in this system, which was to present and provision one man) could only be called upon for service for sixteen weeks every fourth year, but in the years in between a fee had to be paid.[34] Ships for the coastguard were normally, according to the Law of Jutland, paid for by the *skiben* (a group of *hafnæ*, responsible for equipping and manning one ship) but built by the *styresman* who was also in charge of the ship. If, however, the farmers of the *skiben* found that the *styresman*'s building was going to be too expensive, they could build the ship themselves. In the Law of Skåne it is not the *skiben* but the king who is responsible for providing ships for the *leding*, and, for using his own ship, the king could pay the *styresman*.

There are few sources to inform us how this system functioned in practice when it came to the building, manning and provisioning of ships. Possibly a royal confirmation of rights to the monastery of St Peter in Næstved, dating to 1249, does give some indication. The text, which is only preserved in summary, states that no one should embarrass the peasants and bailiffs of the monastery by 'the construction of cogs or moats or felling of timbers for donjons'.[35] This may indicate a direct peasant involvement in the construction of vessels for military use, but could also simply reflect the intensive consumption of timber that such constructions required. However, the source seems to document that cogs or cog-like vessels were used as warships in the middle of the thirteenth century.

Half a century later, in 1304, King Erik Menved attempted to introduce the use of cogs in a *leding* system. Together with his most prominent supporters, he issued a law that is today only known in its Jutland edition. On the basis of a new land assessment, the farmers would be organised in groups, each of which would be taxed 10,000 marks. Every group would in this way finance the buying of a cog of fifty lasts and its manning and equipping for an expedition of sixteen weeks duration every year.

It is uncertain both to what extent this *coggeleding* replaced or simply

---

[33] The most comprehensive discussion of the *leding* in the thirteenth and fourteenth centuries are found in N. Lund, *Lid, leding og landeværn* (Roskilde, 1996).
[34] See Lund, chapter 1 in this volume.
[35] *Diplomatarium Danicum*, 1:7, 326.

supplemented the existing *leding* organisation, and to what extent the reform succeeded.[36] The *coggeleding* is not mentioned in other sources, and it is unlikely that it survived the collapse of the Danish kingdom in 1332–40. The fact that it was possible for Erik Menved to send a fleet of forty-five cogs and many other ships against Stralsund in 1316 indicates at least a temporary success for the *coggeleding* and demonstrates perhaps also that it was thought of as an offensive, rather than a defensive weapon.[37]

Along with the coastal defence system of the *leding*, the maritime power presented by church and lay magnates undoubtedly played a very important if not dominant role. In 1208, the powerful Hvide family, for example, was able to transport their own army to western Sweden to help a member of the family in his efforts to take the Swedish throne.[38] From the middle of the fourteenth century onwards, however, the towns came much more into focus as economic bases for naval activities. In 1358 King Valdemar IV Atterdag ordered bread, drinks, herrings, peas and beans to be sent from the towns as provisions for his ships, and on an expedition into Slien he forced the people there to give him, among other things, ships. Although not specifically stated, this must refer to the town of Slesvig rather than to the farmers living along the fiord. The already mentioned report from the Sealand Chronicle from 1360 perhaps in one source combines the last example of the *leding* principle being applied, in this case to the monasteries, and pointing to the towns as the major future lay provider of maritime power.

Towards the end of the fourteenth century, towns and the nobility were the dominant sources for ships and men for naval actions. In 1384, Queen Margaret sent nine ships to fight pirates in Danish waters and of these seven were put at her disposal by the country's seneschal, Henning Podebusk, and three other noblemen. Those ships were, by the way, quite small as they carried only ten to twelve armed men each.[39]

In 1396, Queen Margaret decreed that those holding royal offices and townsmen should present ships for the defence of the kingdom, and that they should equip them with men and provisions when necessary.[40] The decree, which also regulated a number of other matters, is known from versions written for Jutland and for Fyn but probably covered the entire country and in this sense is general. It is important to note, however, that the section of the text dealing with defence makes several references to the 'Vitalie Brothers'. Those were privateers who originally had been invited to the Baltic in 1391 by Mecklenburg nobles and the Hanseatic towns of Ribnitz, Golwitz, Rostock and Wismar to fight Queen Margaret and prevent her taking power in Sweden. It is thus clear

---

[36] Lund, *Lid, leding og landeværn*, 282–4.
[37] See the Sealand Chronicle 1316 in *Annales Danici Medii Ævi*.
[38] Lund, *Lid, leding og landeværn*, 241.
[39] *Hanserecesse: Die Recesse und andere Akten der Hansetage*, series 1, 1256–1430, ed. K. Koppmann, vols I–VIII (Leipzig, 1870–97), II, no. 276, 4; IV, no. 154, 4 and 185, 8.
[40] *Aarsberetninger fra Det Kongelige Geheimearchiv*, 5, ed. C. F. Wegener (Copenhagen, 1852–83), 55–6.

that the 1396 decree certainly represented a way of creating a maritime force to be used against a very real and present threat, but it is not certain that it actually was thought to be a way of creating a new, permanent organisation.

The Vitalie Brothers soon became a threat to the seafaring of the other Hanseatic towns, and as early as 1394 Lübeck and Stralsund had to send out armed ships to protect their trade against them.[41] In 1398 the problems were great enough to make the Danish queen and the Hanseatic towns cooperate. Margaret promised to send three large ships with two hundred armed men on board and guns, the first written evidence of shipboard use of guns in Denmark. Lübeck promised a large cog with fifty men, Hamburg a small ship with fifteen men, other Hanseatic towns a large ship with seventy men, Prussia a large ship with seventy-five men and Livonia a small ship with thirty-five men.[42] The source gives a good impression of the size of vessels used for fighting at sea at the end of the fourteenth century. The term cog was no longer used to distinguish the largest class of ships. The pattern shown by the scarce and mixed source material illustrates that maritime warfare in southern Scandinavia seemingly was organised and financed in a variety of ways during the thirteenth and fourteenth centuries. The kings' and the loyal magnates' own contributions undoubtedly always played a major role by providing the largest and best-manned vessels, perhaps apart from vessels and troops that were simply hired for specific campaigns. There are no signs of these big ships being specialised warships, and they could therefore be used for other purposes in times of peace. As warships, however, they had their limitations due to draught and restricted manoeuvrability, and it was important to supplement them with other types of vessels. Galleys were essential because they could operate in shallow waters and were less dependent on wind direction, but they were of little use apart from their military function. It appears that this type of vessel was provided by the *leding*, a coastal defence system where farmers paid for, manned, and equipped galleys under the direction of local officials. This organisation apparently had its heyday in the twelfth and thirteenth centuries. Its earliest history is very vague but the system appears to have declined slowly towards the end of that period. However, in 1360 monasteries and towns could still be required to supply galleys.

The initiative of Erik Menved in 1304 to make the farmers finance an expedition force of cogs is important as it was seemingly not based on their serving on the vessels themselves as in the traditional *leding*, but instead on their paying for the hire of professional soldiers for the ships. Because of the continued need for galleys, the new organisation may have supplemented rather than replaced the traditional *leding* and perhaps its greatest importance was that it made the king less dependent on the magnates for providing offensive maritime power.

Erik Menved's initiative pointed to the future in the sense that it provided a more professional navy, but its economic basis did not last. The crisis and

[41] *Hanserecesse*, vol. III, no. 411; vol. IV, no. 192.
[42] Ibid., vol. IV, no. 482.

changes in the structure of the agricultural sector in the course of the fourteenth century and the pawning of land deprived the naval forces of resources. The towns, instead, turned out to be of more and more importance. This is consistent with what can be seen in other parts of northern Europe, for example in England, and it was a logical development since the towns not only represented a financial resource but they also had ships and seamen and could provide them even if they did not have money. The first time this new approach appeared in full scale was in the decree of Queen Margaret of 1396, but the presentation and context provided does not allow us to decide whether it was thought of as a permanent reorganisation of Denmark's naval affairs or simply an action made to deal with what was considered a temporary threat. Thinking of the size of medieval Danish towns, which were numerous but very small, it is also clear that they would not be the providers of any larger ships. Their role would rather mirror that of the earlier *leding*, although their vessels would be of merchant rather than military types.

It appears that in the thirteenth and fourteenth centuries in Denmark there were few signs of the development of a permanent navy. The most significant change was the disappearance of the *leding* as a coastal defence system, which was partly a result of the changing character of naval warfare, partly of societal changes. The attempt by Erik Menved to create a cog fleet on a tax basis in the long run proved abortive and Queen Margaret was just as dependent on her magnates as any monarch before her. The dissolution of the *leding*, however, may be seen as a step towards professionalisation, in the sense that the resources thereby released could be invested in the ships of the nobility and their hired soldiers. It set the stage for the emergence of state navies in Scandinavia in the sixteenth century.

NAVAL POWER AND MARITIME TECHNOLOGY DURING THE HUNDRED YEARS WAR

Timothy J. Runyan

King Edward III of England issued instructions in 1356 to fourteen sheriffs, whose authority encompassed nineteen counties, to supply arms for an expedition to the Continent. The purpose was to carry the war to France in the first phase of the Hundred Years War, a conflict whose roots included dynastic claims, the control of Gascony, and an ongoing undeclared battle at sea between French and English privateers, pirates and merchants.[1] The request was one step in what became the usual practice in preparation for an overseas expedition requiring naval forces. Men were recruited for the army, supplies and equipment purveyed for the expedition, a port was selected to stage the operation and provide a place of embarkation, ships were requisitioned or arrested, mariners were hired or impressed, the king's ships, meaning those purpose-built for war or converted for such use, were ordered to the staging port, and the whole assemblage of victuals, armaments, including horses, men and ships was coordinated to arrive for transport abroad by the assembled ships and their crews. Thousands of men flooded port towns such as Plymouth, Southampton and Sandwich where they taxed the local capacity to address their needs for food and space to work and rest and supply items they needed.[2]

The sheriffs, who received Edward III's command in January 1356, were ordered to produce 9900 sheaves of arrows and 5600 white bows, as opposed to painted ones.[3] Horses required feed and ships had to be modified to accommodate them for transport. Stalls were constructed by the use of hurdles to separate the animals and to keep them secure aboard the ships during the passage, which could be rough. Victuals included carcasses of salted beef, mutton or pork, quarters of oats, peas and beans, quarters of wheat ground into flour before shipment, weyes of cheese and dried fish, and of course, drink. Ale was provided in generous amounts as in 1340 when thirty ships were allotted supplies for forty

---

[1] H. J. Hewitt, *The Black Prince's Expedition of 1355–1357* (Manchester, 1958), 30.
[2] The records of the English Exchequer, housed in the Public Record Office in London, provide much information concerning war preparations. For war preparations based upon these sources, see Timothy J. Runyan, 'Naval Logistics in the Late Middle Ages: The Example of the Hundred Years' War', in J. A. Lynn, ed., *Feeding Mars. Logistics in Western Warfare from the Middle Ages to the Present* (Boulder, 1993), 79–100.
[3] Hewitt, *Black Prince's Expedition*, 38.

days. The 1510 men aboard were allotted 60,400 gallons of ale, one gallon per man per day.[4]

The preparations for a military campaign included the provision of a considerable store of weapons in addition to bows and arrows. Castles around the country were emptied of their arms, especially the Tower of London where the main cache of royal arms was stored. Arms were manufactured or purchased, stored and shipped from the Tower or elsewhere to the port of embarkation. Fletchers, bowyers, smiths, carpenters and other fabricators performed work. Crossbows and arbalests were in plentiful supply with winches to ratchet back the bowstrings. Crossbows were used aboard ships as well as in land battles, a subject to which we will later return.[5]

Engines for war constitute the category of weapons we know the least about based on information from the primary accounts drawn from exchequer records. Little description is given to explain the purpose and operation of engines of war. Principal among them were catapults to hurl stones, springalds, and arbalests to fire large arrows by torsion. Chemical weapons existed in the form of fire and gunpowder. This *artilleria* also included the recently introduced cannons. Ribalds (*ribaldi*), small cannon grouped together on a single mounting or carriage, are found in accounts of 1345.[6] Their first meaningful use in battle took place at Beversholdsveld in May, 1382, when men of Ghent overpowered the forces of Bruges. The use of the lowly and small ribald, firing stones or metal balls of perhaps one inch in diameter, made a difference on that occasion. Such devices could be used at sea as anti-personnel weapons. The development of large cannon capable of 'ship killing' required not only careful placement aboard ship, but a carriage adequate to provide for aiming and recoil. That development, however, would take time.[7]

When all was prepared for the expedition, the men, their horses, military supplies and victuals were boarded for the crossing. Delays were frequent and

---

[4] Public Record Office, London, Exchequer, PRO, E 101/22/25. H. J. Hewitt, *The Organization of War under Edward III, 1338–62* (Manchester, 1966), 52.

[5] Frederic C. Lane, 'The Crossbow in the Nautical Revolution of the Middle Ages', in D. Herlihy *et al.*, eds., *Economy, Society and Government in Medieval Italy, Essays in Memory of Robert L. Reynolds* (Kent, 1969), 161–72.

[6] For recent works on engines of war and gunpowder weapons, see Bert Hall, *Weapons and Warfare in Renaissance Europe* (Baltimore, 1988); Kelly DeVries, *Medieval Military Technology* (Peterborough, Canada, 1992), especially parts 2 and 4. For *ribaldi* see Hewitt, *Organization of War*, 72, and Hall, *Weapons and Warfare*, 49. Most early gunpowder weapons were anti-personnel weapons used to defend against boarding by an enemy.

[7] The use of shipboard gunpowder weapons to sink another vessel probably occurred first in 1513. Recent discussion of this subject includes: Kelly DeVries, 'The Effectiveness of Fifteenth-Century Shipboard Artillery', *The Mariner's Mirror*, 84 (November 1998), 389–99, a response to N. A. M. Rodger, 'The Dreadnought Revolution of Tudor England', *Mariner's Mirror*, 82 (1996), 269–301. See also K. DeVries, 'Catapults are Not Atomic Bombs: Towards a Redefinition of Effectiveness in Pre-Modern Military Technology', *War in History*, 4 (1997), 75–91, and R. A. Konstam, '16th Century Naval Tactics and Gunnery', *International Journal of Nautical Archaeology and Underwater Exploration*, 17 (1988), 17–23.

the consequences ranged from riotous and unruly behaviour in the port towns to food shortages leading to ravaging of the local countryside. The shortage of ships or their late arrival was a frequent problem. The Black Prince's expedition to France in 1355 was delayed because of lack of ships. Prince Edward was forced to spend more money to feed and pay his waiting army while awaiting the arrival of the seventy-three vessels requisitioned for the expedition.[8]

This experience preceded the start of most expeditions during the Hundred Years War and later. Indeed, little changed. The logistics of war began with foresters, farmers, bakers, brewers, craftsmen, labourers and the transporters who moved the goods by road, river and sea. The ship was the ultimate destination. Within its timber walls the knights, soldiers, horses, weapons and victuals were packed for the crossing. In some instances, as in the later Crusades, the transports became an amphibious operational force, releasing armed mounted knights from their decks down gangways to charge an awaiting enemy. Sometimes ships were positioned alongside defensive walls where ladders were mounted from the decks or from atop masts to allow the walls to be scaled.[9] The ship was both transport vessel and an assault weapon. The ship provided security from the sea itself as well as from sea-borne predators. If attacked by enemy forces the ship became a fighting platform.

That pride was taken in these vessels is evident from contemporary financial accounts. Flagships of fleets received special attention in preparation for sea duty. The accounts of the clerks of the ships detail expenses for paint and elaborate pennants flown from the mast and yards. Colourful vessels flying pennants of royal or noble warriors were an impressive display that was staged to discourage challenges and to deflate opponents. The exaggerated display illustrated in manuscripts of colourful vessels flying long streamers and pennants is perhaps less fanciful than we might imagine. Orders for red and gold paint and other bright colours illumine the mundane recitation of purchase orders in the accounts of the exchequer.[10] Appearances were important to medieval warriors of the knightly class. Accounts of shipboard recreation by nobles include music, dancing and stylish dress, complemented by boastful language either recorded or created by chroniclers such as Jean Froissart. Froissart also employed the

---

[8] Hewitt, *Black Prince's Expedition*, 40–2.
[9] For the amphibious assault on Damietta in the Sixth Crusade, see Jean de Joinville, *Chronicle*, in *Chronicle of the Crusades*, trans. F. Marzials. For the attack on Constantinople in the Fourth Crusade, see Geoffrey de Villehardouin, *Chronicle of the Fourth Crusade and the Conquest of Constantinople* in *Memoirs of the Crusades*, trans. F. Marzials (London, 1957), 59–62. For the nature of vessels employed see John H. Pryor, 'The Mediterranean Round Ship', in R. W. Unger, ed., *Cogs, Caravels and Galleons, The Sailing Ship 1000–1650* (London, 1994), 59–76, and 'The Transportation of Horses by Sea during the Era of the Crusades: Eighth Century to 1285 AD', *The Mariner's Mirror*, 68 (February 1982), 9–27, and (May 1982), 103–26; 'The Naval Architecture of Crusader Transport Ships and Horse Transports Revisited', *The Mariner's Mirror*, 76 (August 1990), 255–73, which continues the study in earlier issues of *Mariner's Mirror*, 70 (1984), 171–219 and 275–92.
[10] The purchase of paint, banners and streamers is included in the expenses of several expeditions, e.g. PRO, E. 101/392/1.

language of chivalric combat. 'King Edward III cried to the helmsman, "Steer at that ship straight ahead of us. I want to have a joust at it." '[11]

Beginning in the mid-fifteenth century medieval heraldic emblems such as banners and hereditary coats of arms were replaced with standards and ensigns bearing personal badges or *devises*.[12] Antoine de la Salle explained the significance of wearing arms in battle: 'When the coat of arms is on the armed knight or esquire, drawn up in *bataille*, upon so noble and perilous a day, let it be known that he cannot honourably be disarmed without great reproach to his honour except for one of these three reasons: victory . . . capture . . . or death. And he who does otherwise puts his life in the prince's mercy.'[13] The military historian Philippe Contamine argues that the change in dress is linked to the decision by the French crown that military command no longer depended on social status or blood, that professional commanders were the equal of nobles in the military forces. The social and practical world of noble warfare began to change in the fourteenth century. A uniform insignia unrelated to social status now identified armies, for the first time since the Roman legions. Standards and ensigns provided a recognisable focus for a new disciplinary centre to combat.[14]

Accounts of fighting aboard ship parallel the practices ashore, although the melee was rarely as chaotic at sea as on land. Froissart rejoiced at the English victory at L'Espagnols sur Mer in 1350:

> The King's ship was stoutly built and timbered, otherwise it would have been split in two, for it and the Spanish ship, which was tall and heavy, collided with a crash like thunder and as they rebounded, the castle of the King's ship caught the castle of the Spaniard with such force that the mast on which it was fixed broke and it was flung into the sea. The men in it were killed or drowned. The King's ship was so shattered water began to pour in. . . .
>
> Then the King looking at the ship with which he had jousted said, 'Grapple my ship to that one. I want to have it.' 'Let that one go', his knights answered, 'You'll get a better one.' So that ship went on and another big one came up. The knights flung out hooks and chains and fastened their own ship to it. A fierce battle began between them, the English archers shooting and the Spanish defending themselves lustily. The advantage was by no means with them for, the Spanish ships being bigger and higher than theirs, they were able to shoot down at them and hurl the great iron bars which did considerable damage.
>
> The knights in the King of England's ship seeing that it was making so much water it was in danger of foundering, made desperate efforts to capture the ship to which they were grappled. The Spaniard was taken, and all the men

---

[11] Froissart, *Chronicle*, trans. G. Brereton (Harmondsworth, 1968), 118.
[12] Malcolm G. A. Vale, *War and Chivalry: Warfare and Aristocratic Culture in England, France and Burgundy at the End of the Middle Ages* (London, 1981), 97–8. Philippe Contamine, *Guerre, état et société à la fin du Moyen Âge: études sur les armées de rois de France, 1337–1494* (Paris, 1972), 696.
[13] Quoted in Vale, *War and Chivalry*, 94.
[14] Contamine, *Guerre*, 676; Vale, *War and Chivalry*, 147–8.

on board it thrown into the sea. Only then was the King told of the danger they were in of sinking and urged to move into the ship they had just captured. This he did. But finally the day was with the English. The Spaniards lost fourteen ships, while the rest sailed on and escaped.[15]

Such paeans to victory and honour are reflected, perhaps most poignantly, a century later in Jean de Bueil's *Le Jouvencel*, written about 1466:

> What a joyous thing is war, for many fine deeds are seen and heard in its course, and many good lessons learnt from it. When war is fought in a good cause it is fought for justice and the defence of right. I believe that God favours those who risk their lives by their readiness to make war to bring the wicked, the oppressors, the conquerors, the proud and all who deny true equity, to justice. War is a proper and useful career for young men, for which they are respected by both God and man. You love your comrade so much in war. When you see that your quarrel is just and your word is fighting well, tears rise to your eyes. A great sweet feeling of loyalty and pity fills your heart on seeing your friend so valiantly exposing his body to execute and accomplish the command of the Creator. And then you prepare to go and live or die with him, and for love not to abandon him. And out of that there arises such a delectation, that he who has not tasted it is not fit to say what a delight it is. Do you think that a man who does that fears death? Not at all; for he feels so strengthened, he is so elated, that he does not know where he is. Truly he is afraid of nothing.[16]

Johan Huizinga in *The Waning of the Middle Ages* (1919) provided a social context for the era by his skilful look at literary and artistic sources of northern France and the Low Countries.[17] One of these, Jean de Bueil, author of *Le Jouvencel* and a veteran of the Hundred Years War, provided important though often anachronistic advice on the conduct of the warrior in an age now termed one of military revolution.[18] The march toward modern professional armies is interrupted by the life of the tournament and joust, activities that thrived in an age struggling to accommodate the new military technology, while chivalric codes may have become more flexible. This did not mean the practice of chivalry was less dangerous: recall the death of Henry II of France in a joust in 1559,

---

15 Froissart, *Chronicle*, 118–19.
16 Jean de Bueil, *Le Jouvencel*, translated by Vale in *War and Chivalry*, 30.
17 Johan Huizinga, *The Waning of the Middle Ages*, trans. F. Hopman (Harmondsworth, 1965; orig. pub. 1919).
18 For a summary analysis see Clifford J. Rogers, ed., *The Military Revolution Debate: Readings on the Transformation of Early Modern Europe* (Boulder, 1995). This interpretation originated with Michael Roberts's lecture printed in 1956, 'The Military Revolution, 1550–1650', reprinted in his *Essays in Swedish History* (Minneapolis, 1967), and Rogers, *Military Revolution Debate*, 13–36. Although C. W. C. Oman in *The Art of War in the Middle Ages*, rev. and ed. J. H. Beeler (Ithaca, 1953), 162, referred to 'the military revolution of the sixteenth century' during the European wars against the Ottomans. Rogers, *Military Revolution Debate*, 79 n. 2. The debate accelerated following publication of Geoffrey Parker's *The Military Revolution: Military Innovation and the Rise of the West* (Cambridge, 1988).

or Pierre de Bueil who died jousting at the court of Charles VII in 1445, or the triage necessary to save Philippe de Poitiers, Lord of La Ferte, whose arm was torn off in a joust during Anglo-Burgundian marriage celebrations at Bruges in 1468.

The development of gunpowder weaponry continued with the support of states capable of funding the range of materials and talent necessary to advance these machines of war, silently condemned by those participating in the chivalric tournament. Neither condemnations nor prescriptions would alter the drive for advantage in weapons technology. In the late twelfth century the Byzantine Anna Comnena in her *Alexiad* condemned the crossbow as truly a diabolical machine. The papacy agreed and at the Second Lateran Council of 1191 anathematised all who used the crossbow, and the bow. The council did see some advantages to the devilish instruments of war, however, and perhaps with some delight denied use only between warring Christians, who could use them with impunity against infidels. The Venetian Commune ordered 20,000 crossbow bolts in 1304. A decade later an inventory of the Arsenal recorded 1131 crossbows.[19] Ships carried them in abundance, as noted.

Tournaments and battles on land and sea had one quality in common: the sound of the drum. The evidence from underwater archaeology is scant, but drums and other instruments are among the artefacts found in Henry VIII's *Mary Rose*, lost off Portsmouth while engaging a French invasion fleet in 1545. Froissart describes the music aboard the ships of Edward III and his son the Black Prince, including the drum. The tabor (*tabour* or *tabourin*) was usually accompanied by the pipe (also found on the *Mary Rose*). Trumpets were used for both music and announcements. In anticipation of battle or the later celebration of victory, music aboard ship was employed to entertain and refresh. Dancing accompanied playing before the sea battle at L'Espagnols sur Mer in 1350. As late as the sixteenth century little had changed. Musicians included trumpeters and those playing drum, fife and shawm. The trumpeter sounded the going and coming of the commander, hailed ships, and sounded the charge to board an enemy vessel.[20]

For England the sources for examining a case study of the logistical work that preceded the launching of a fleet to transport an army abroad are found in numerous places. The key sources include financial accounts from the Exchequer and the Wardrobe account books. Fortunately, a Wardrobe account book has been edited for the early years of Edward III's reign, 1338–40.[21] As his

---

[19] P. Contamine, *War in the Middle Ages*, trans. M. Jones (Oxford, 1984), 72.
[20] For the *Mary Rose* artefacts see Margaret Rule, *The Mary Rose* (London, 1982), 199. Jean Froissart describes the musical accompaniment aboard Edward III's ship. Jean Froissart, *Chronicles of England, France, Spain and the Adjoining Countries from the latter part of the Reign of Edward II to the Coronation of Henry V*, trans. Thomas Johnes (London: George Routledge, 1868), I, 197–9.
[21] Bryce and Mary Lyon, eds, *The Wardrobe Book of William de Norwell, 12 July 1338 to 27 May 1340* (Brussels, 1983). There is also an edition of a book from the reign of Edward I,

personal financial account, the king could and did finance many of his campaigns from the Wardrobe. The personnel costs of soldiers and sailors, the numbers and types of vessels with their masters and homeports, the horses carried, are all recorded in the account book.

Edward prepared a campaign to the Low Countries in 1338 that was to last for over two years. It cost £382,000. Over 291 ships were utilised to transport his forces to Antwerp. Another 80 ships assisted in the operation. Manning the fleet required 12,263 masters, constables, sailors, pages and carpenters who were paid wages of £4797 11s. 6d. The fleet carried 2720 earls, bannerettes, knights, squires, men-at-arms and hobelars, 5550 mounted and unmounted archers, 4614 horses, and the 500 members of the king's and queen's household.[22] This was the largest logistical effort made for an overseas military campaign by an English king up to the time. The preparations were predictably delayed because of the difficulty in assembling the ships, men and supplies. Once they were in place at Orwell and Great Yarmouth the crossing of the North Sea took place from 16 to 22 July 1338. The 370 ships required 370 masters, but only 282 constables to govern the men as smaller vessels did not have constables, 11,325 sailors, 585 pages, 5 clerks and 4 carpenters. The ports providing most of the ships were Great Yarmouth (61) and Melcombe in Dorset (52). Hythe, Rye, Ipswich, Ravenscar and Plymouth provided another 179 ships. An interesting note is that 17 ships were arrested for service while in Brabant and Flanders. The men received higher pay. Perhaps ships arrested abroad commanded higher fees.[23]

One item of particular interest in the Wardrobe account book is the payment of £97 for 291 pilots to guide the ships from Orwell to Antwerp. Each pilot received one half mark (6s. 8d.) as wages. Pilots were also employed for return voyages. Their wages were good. Mariners earned only 3d. per day.[24]

Information is sketchy on the ships used in the expedition. The ship's type is not always given. The major vessel used was the cog, as fifty-two are noted. The balance included hulks, spinaces, busses and barges. Galleys were used by the king, but were not well suited for bulk transport of men, horses or *matériel*. Italians or other foreigners manned and operated galleys in most instances in both England and France. Ships and supplies came from at least sixty-four ports to carry the men and supplies about 220 kilometres (135 miles) across the North Sea to Antwerp.[25] But the nerve centre for naval and military operations was the Wardrobe, which served as the war treasury. The variety of sturdy vessels

Liber Quotidianus Contrarotulatoris Garderobe Anno Regni Regis Edwardi Primi Vicesimo Octavo, A.D. 1299 and 1300, ed. John Topham (London, 1787).
[22] Bryce Lyon, 'The Infrastructure and Purpose of an English Medieval Fleet in the First Phase of the Hundred Years' War (1338–1340)', *Maatschappij voor geschiedenis en oudheidkunde te Gent*, new series 51 (1997), 61–76.
[23] Lyon, 'Infrastructure', 67.
[24] Ibid., 74.
[25] Ibid., 67. For the cogs of this era see chapters 2 and 3 by Detlev Ellmers, 'The Cog as Cargo Carrier', and T. J. Runyan, 'The Cog as Warship', in Unger, *Cogs, Caravels and Galleons*. For the preponderance of cogs, see T. J. Runyan, 'Ships and Fleets in Anglo-French

manned by mariners transported the men, horses, supplies and victuals to their overseas destinations. The wardrobe accounts and other exchequer records detail the expenses of building, outfitting, repairing and provisioning ships for service. Busses, flunes, gabots, hulks, doggers, lodships, crayers, spinaces, galleys, carracks, barges, nefs, tarites, boats, ships and cogs are named in the records of English vessels active in the early phase of the Hundred Years War from 1337 to 1360.[26] Some were small sailing craft, others oared vessels and others large sailing ships capable of carrying several hundred tons of cargo, where each ton equates to the wine ton with a capacity of 264 gallons. Galleys, balingers and other oared vessels were useful in war because of their ability to manoeuvre in calms or against currents, tides, or the direction of the wind. Vessels dependent solely on the wind for propulsion had to tack to make headway against the wind. While two-masted vessels had long plied the Mediterranean, the appearance of two and three-masted ships in the northern seas did not occur until the early fifteenth century.

What changes made possible the creation of sailing ships and fleets that within a century dominated the seas of Western Europe while reaching south along the African coast and Indian Ocean and west to the New World?[27] Ship construction and design underwent substantial changes in the period from about 1300 to 1500. Part of that change may be explained as the continuous search for efficiency of sea-borne transport under sail. Another explanation is the merger of two distinct maritime traditions, that of the Mediterranean and that of the northern seas.[28] Florentine chronicler Giovanni Villani reported in the summer of 1304 that sailors from Bayonne on the Bay of Biscay sailed cogs into the Mediterranean. Their successful raids impressed the Genoese, Venetians and Catalans who began to build cogs. In fact, *coches* or cogs were known in the Mediterranean before that date. The literary and iconographic evidence is sketchy until the mid-fourteenth century when artists produced illustrations of *coches* in harbour and at sea.

Warfare, 1337–60', *The American Neptune*, 46 (1986), 91–9, and 'The Organization of Royal Fleets in Medieval England', in *Ships, Seafaring and Society: Essays in Maritime History* (Detroit, 1987), 37–52.

[26] Runyan, 'Ships and Fleets', 91–9.

[27] On ships of this era see Unger, *Cogs, Caravels and Galleons*, Ian Friel, *The Good Ship: Ships, Shipbuilding and Technology in England, 1200–1520* (London, 1995), R. W. Unger, *The Ship in the Medieval Economy* (London, 1980), and A. R. Lewis and T. J. Runyan, *European Naval and Maritime History, 300–1500* (Bloomington, 1985). For a study based on archaeological remains of ships, see Gillian Hutchinson, *Medieval Ships and Shipping* (Leicester, 1994).

[28] One approach to this subject is T. J. Runyan, 'The Relationship of Northern and Southern Seafaring Traditions in Late Medieval Europe', in C. Villain-Gandossi, S. Busuttil and P. Adam, eds, *Medieval Ships and the Birth of Technological Societies: The Mediterranean Area and European Integration* (Malta, 1991), 197–209. For ship construction, see J. Richard Steffy, 'The Mediterranean Shell to Skeleton Transition: A Northwest European Parallel', in Reinder Reinders and Kees Paul, eds, *Caravel Construction Technique: Fifth International Symposium on Boat and Ship Archaeology* (Oxford, 1991), 1–9.

Why did the Mediterranean shipwrights adopt the architectural form of the cog?[29] The answer is rooted in the pragmatism of ship construction and seafaring, coupled with the cost effectiveness of ships needed for trade and commerce in the age some describe as the commercial revolution.[30] While this commercial revolution ended about 1348 with the Black Death, the nautical revolution was just under way.[31] The cog was a key element in the impulse for Mediterranean shipwrights to build a new type of vessel, as Villani noted. Clinker-building, perhaps most dramatically illustrated in the Viking ships of the eighth to tenth centuries, marked northern European shipbuilding. The shipbuilding method practised in the northern seas was to fashion the hull from the keel up by overlapping the planking and fastening the planks or strakes with clinch-bolts, thus clinker construction. Frames were then inserted inside the hull. Shell-first construction required skilled craftsmen capable of fashioning the lines of vessels over twenty-five metres in length into marvellously fluid shapes that could withstand the cold and rough waters of northern Europe while providing enough durability and integrity to survive lengthy voyages to Greenland, Iceland, the Hebrides, Ireland, across the Baltic, the inland waterways of eastern Europe, and to the Mediterranean. Controlled by a side steering-oar, or quarter rudder, and driven by a square sail supported from a yard on a single mast, the vessel was clearly effective as a carrier of persons and a limited amount of cargo. The successor vessel that stands out among the many types

[29] Ships built frame-first include the Sefe Limani vessel of *c.*1025 and the Contarina ship of *c.*1300. George Bass, Sheila Matthews, J. Richard Steffy and Frederick H. Von Doorninck, eds, *Serçe Limani: An Eleventh-Century Shipwreck* (College Station: Texas A&M University Press, forthcoming). For the round ship and its replacement by the cog see John H. Pryor, 'The Mediterranean Round Ship', in Unger, *Cogs, Caravels and Galleons*, ch. 4; Hutchinson, *Medieval Ships*, 35–46.

[30] Raymond de Roover, 'The Commercial Revolution of the Thirteenth Century', *Bulletin of the Business Historical Society*, 16 (1942), 34–9, and the *Cambridge Economic History of Europe*, vol. III (Cambridge, 1963). Robert S. Lopez, *The Commercial Revolution of the Middle Ages, 950–1350* (Englewood Cliffs, 1971), 72: 'The Commercial Revolution of Italy and the western Mediterranean put to work every kind of ship, from the tiny rowboats to broad, roomy sailing 'nefs', but tied its fortune especially to the galley and its many relatives.' Frederic C. Lane, 'Venetian Shipping during the Commercial Revolution', *American Historical Review*, 38 (1933), 219–39, focuses on the fifteenth and sixteenth centuries.

[31] Frederic C. Lane identified the nautical revolution as innovations in navigation and shipping about 1300. 'While the Venetian aristocracy was consolidating its position domestically, reaffirming Venice's lordship of the gulf, and recovering from the defeat received in the Second Genoese War, it had to adjust its maritime and commercial institutions to profound changes in both the nautical arts and in business methods. If one may apply the term revolution to changes which went on over a period of a hundred years, one may properly call the changes about 1300 in the methods of navigation and in the construction, rigging and armament of ships the Nautical Revolution of the Middle Ages. It was a necessary preliminary to the more celebrated nautical revolution of the Renaissance which accompanied the oceanic discoveries about two hundred years later.' F. C. Lane, *Venice: A Maritime Republic* (Baltimore, 1973), 119. For a discussion of his views, see Michael Balard, 'La Révolution nautique à Gênes (fin du XIIIe – début au XIVe s.)', in Villain-Gandossi *et al.*, *Medieval Ships*, 113–23.

already noted is the cog. While its roots extend to the Carolingian era the cog arrived as a ship of major significance at the start of the fourteenth century.[32]

The fruits of underwater archaeology have provided much information about this vessel type since 1962 when a nearly complete cog was found at the harbour in Bremen. Dating to about 1380 with a capacity of about 78–80 tons, the vessel, though impressive, is not a large cog. As early as 1241, a cog is recorded with a capacity of 240 tons. These larger vessels became the mainstay of shipping in northern Europe.[33] They also were among the first to employ the significant advantage in navigation provided by the sternpost-mounted rudder affixed by pintles and gudgeons. The sternpost-mounted pintle-and-gudgeon rudder was in use in Western Europe by the late twelfth century. The most frequently cited evidence is the carved baptismal font at Winchester Cathedral dating to 1150–80. The seal of Ipswich of about 1200 also depicts a sternpost rudder. We can assume that this new rudder was in use for some decades since it is unlikely artists working in such varied media and locations immediately recorded its appearance on ships.[34] The adoption of the sternpost rudder in the northern seas was not a straight-line evolution of an improved technology. Dual quarter rudders were employed on large Roman vessels and later Mediterranean galleys, crusader ships and even those vessels that faced one another at Lepanto in 1571. They were efficient and seaworthy quarter rudders. The advantages of a sternpost rudder included convenient placement so that a tiller could control its movement, its protection from weather and attack, as well as when docking on the starboard or steering board side, and with pintle-and-gudgeon mounting, reliability. A disadvantage was that it was more difficult to replace or repair.[35]

A paradox in the history of the adoption of the sternpost rudder is that examples of it are found in Egyptian funerary boats and it was in use three millennia later by the Arabs in the Red Sea and Persian Gulf. Iconographic evidence from Arab manuscripts from the early twelfth century includes a sternpost rudder, in this instance assisted by two quarter rudders. If this is an advanced technology, then why was it not adopted throughout the Mediterranean? The answer is that there were no iron fasteners on these Arab vessels. The rudder was lashed to the stern of the vessel providing a weak connecting point. The use of iron pintles and gudgeons made the difference. Also, the Arabs used controlling lines to turn

---

[32] For ship construction techniques, see J. Richard Steffy, *Wooden Ship Building and the Intrepretation of Shipwrecks* (College Station, 1994), especially part II; Unger, *Cogs, Caravels and Galleys*, 29–58.

[33] Klaus-Peter Kiedel and Uwe Schnall, eds., *The Hanse Cog of 1380* (Bremerhaven, 1985); Detlev Ellmers, 'The Cog as Cargo Ship', *Cogs, Caravels and Galleys*, 29–46; Paul Heinsius, *Das Schiff der Hansischen Frühzeit* (Weimar, 1956) which identified the cog as a new type vessel of the twelfth century, a view not shared by Ole Crumlin-Pedersen, 'Danish Cog Finds', in Sean McGrail, ed., *Medieval Ships and Harbours in Northern Europe* (Oxford, 1979), 17–34.

[34] Lawrence V. Mott, *The Development of the Rudder: A Technological Tale* (College Station, 1997), 123.

[35] Ibid., 41–99.

the rudder. These lines were attached directly to the rudder so that by pulling on the port or starboard line the rudder would turn. This was not effective on larger vessels. The tiller is not found on larger Arab ships until introduced by the Portuguese in the fifteenth century.[36] The reintroduction to the Mediterranean of the sternpost rudder by northern mariners probably occurred in the mid-twelfth century, perhaps with the fleets carrying soldiers for the Second Crusade in 1147. The cog is closely associated with the sternpost rudder, which became one of its identifying characteristics. It appears the Catalan king Jaime I used cogs as part of his fleet to attack Mallorca in 1229. Cogs appear in graffiti on the bell tower of the cathedral of Palma de Mallorca, and the term *coca* appears in the Laws of Marseille of 1253.[37] We might predict that the rapid adoption of the pintle-and-gudgeon rudder in the early fourteenth century enabled the construction of larger and more seaworthy ships leading to the age of exploration and world trading empires, and that quarter rudders were doomed at the appearance of the new navigational technology. This was not so. Quarter rudders worked well and were used on ships of 400–500 tons as early as the fifth century BC on Roman grain ships, and large Mediterranean galleys and sailing ships used them successfully. Ships of the age of exploration were smaller and would not have required a pintle-and-gudgeon rudder as a precondition to Atlantic oceanic navigation. Columbus' ships were small though with more freeboard than galleys. The *Santa Maria* was rated at about 120 tons and galleons of the seventeenth century often were in the 300–600 ton range.[38]

War is cited as a major cause for change. Change may include the alteration of social structures, the realignment of political borders, the innovation of technologies and the creation of new institutions. Should it also be the catalyst for the rise of standing navies? The Hundred Years War of 1337–1453 largely dominated the fourteenth and fifteenth centuries in Western Europe. During this period, the English crown needed naval forces in order to address attacks from the sea, to protect shipping and to transport invading armies overseas. Ships were also necessary for victualling, blockades and to transport armies and goods back home. The French and their allies had similar uses for naval forces.

Privately owned shipping supplied the bulk of ships for royal expeditions through the process of obligation and arrest. The establishment of a more permanent fleet of king's ships with an administrative agent to supervise their care and maintenance emerged during this era. The office of admiral and clerk of king's ships in England was mirrored in France, though unevenly. The office of admiral was created and briefly there was a centralised navy with the *Clos*

---

[36] R. Bowen, 'Early Arab Ships and Rudders', *Mariner's Mirror*, 49 (1963), 303–4, and Mott, *Rudder*, 124–5.
[37] Mott, *Rudder*, 121–6.
[38] Ibid., 127. See also Ian Friel, 'The Carrack: The Advent of the Full Rigged Ship', in Unger, *Cogs, Caravels and Galleons*, 77–90; Martin Elbl and Carla Rahn Phillips, 'The Caravel and the Galleon', in Unger, *Cogs, Caravels and Galleons*, ch. 6; for tonnages, see 114.

des Galées established in 1293 at Rouen.[39] The Court of Admiralty developed in England in the fourteenth century, capable of adjudicating cases *in rem* to the dismay of the common-law courts.[40] The emergence of standing navies composed of purpose-built ships of war, carrying gunpowder weapons and capable of keeping the sea under the command of professional sailors occurred in the fourteenth century. The royal fleets did not always function well. The ships were sometimes more purpose-modified than purpose-built. There were gunpowder weapons aboard ship but they were not ship-killers. They were anti-personnel weapons. Sea-keeping was limited by the nature of the vessels and navigational knowledge, and mariners on the royal payroll under crown-appointed officers were effective for the length of individual expeditions, but did not constitute a standing navy.

Unlike admirals in the Mediterranean states and France, English admirals primarily served as administrators. Their responsibility was to arrest ships and men, get them to the chosen ports for assembly into fleets, and prepare them for the expedition. It was a big job. Once at sea, the admiral was active in directing the fleet, but often shared that responsibility. His flagship carried lanterns and flags, or streamers, to signal commands to the fleet. Nearly half of the admirals who served during the fifty-year reign of Edward III had served in the field as well as at sea.[41] Admirals outranked captains, masters, constables (responsible for marines), carpenters, clerks, and seamen. The admiralties were generally divided into a northern (Thames to Scotland), a southern (Thames to Bristol) and a western fleet (from Bristol to Carlisle including Ireland). The vice-admirals usually assumed duties for districts to which they were assigned, including coastal defence.[42]

Naval experience was doubtless applied to the development of strategy. Medieval knights at sea or ashore devised strategies and tactics. The French, who recruited Genoese naval commanders to prepare fleets to attack England, displayed strategic thinking as French diplomats also encouraged the Scots to raid northern England – a serious assault as well as a feint to divert English military resources from the Channel.[43]

---

[39] Anne Chazelas-Merlin, ed., *Documents relatifs au clos des galées de Rouen et aux armées de mer du roi de France de 1293 à 1418*, 2 vols (Paris, 1977–9), and for the carvel-built galley, Eric Rieth, 'Les Clos des galées de Rouen, lieu de construction navale à clin et à carvel (1293–1419)', in C. Villain-Gandossi, S. Busuttil and P. Adam, *Medieval Ships and the Birth of Technological Societies, Volume I: Northern Europe* (Malta, 1989).
[40] T. J. Runyan, 'The Laws of Oléron and the Admiralty Court in Fourteenth Century England', *American Journal of Legal History*, 19 (April 1975), 95–111; R. G. Marsden, ed., *Documents Relating to the Law and Custom of the Sea, I, 1205–1648* (London, 1915) and *Select Pleas in the Court of Admiralty* (London, 1894).
[41] N. A. M. Rodger, *The Safeguard of the Sea* (New York, 1997), 131–6.
[42] R. G. Marsden, 'The Vice-Admirals of the Coast', *English Historical Review*, 22 (1907), 468–77, and 23 (1908), 736–57.
[43] W. Stanford Reid, 'Sea-Power in the Anglo-Scottish War, 1296–1328', *Mariner's Mirror*, 46 (1960), 7–23; R. G. Nicholson, *Edward III and the Scots: The Formative Years of a Mili-*

Conflict at sea began with piratical raids on each side of the Channel, mainly directed at merchant vessels or port towns. Raids on port towns were often launched to avenge similar attacks across the Channel. As an element of maritime strategy raids on port towns made sense because the ships were there. The destruction or capture of enemy vessels was the objective rather than to hold territory. The spread of terror was a consequence of sea-borne raids on ports. Among the most terrifying were the Franco-Genoese raids along the south coast in 1338–40. Southampton was burned and raids continued from Plymouth to Harwich. Coastal defence schemes included the use of fire beacons to warn of attacking ships, but they were not very effective.[44] A pre-emptive strike was the best defence. The English attack on the French and Spanish at Sluis in 1340 was a masterful strike that caught the enemy fleet embayed and unable to manoeuvre. The English came sailing in unexpectedly and as Geoffrey le Baker states, Edward III had 'the wind and the sun at his back and the flow of the tide with him, with his ships divided into three columns, . . . an iron shower of quarrels from crossbows and arrows from longbows brought death to thousands of people'. The French lost nearly 200 ships.[45]

There are few parallels to the English naval victory at Sluis, although many naval engagements were fought in harbours, bays or along shore trading routes. Examples include the English victory over the Spaniards off Winchelsea in 1350 and their defeat by Castilian galleys in the battle at La Rochelle in 1372. The most effective vessel for raiding and attack was the galley. It incorporated the principal requirements of speed and manoeuvrability.[46]

The French had a considerable ally in Scotland, a base for naval raids that distracted the English from their designs in France. English naval effort was directed toward the invasion fleets necessary to transport and supply English armies on the Continent. The continued arrest of shipping for this purpose does not suggest that a grand naval strategy for 'sovereignty of the sea' was in play. The English countered at sea, but perhaps most effectively in diplomacy by hiring away Genoese ships and naval commanders. The response to raids on

---

tary Career 1327–1375 (London, 1965). See also C. J. Ford, 'Piracy or Policy: The Crisis in the Channel, 1400–1403', *Transactions of the Royal Historical Society*, 5th ser., 29 (1979), 63–78.

[44] Colin Platt, *Medieval Southampton: The Port and Trading Community, AD 1000–1600* (London, 1973), 109 ff. Michael Hughes, 'The Fourteenth-Century French Raids on Hampshire and the Isle of Wight', in Anne Curry and Michael Hughes, eds, *Arms, Armies and Fortifications in the Hundred Years War* (Woodbridge, 1994), 121–43.

[45] Geoffrey le Baker, *Chronicon*, ed. E. M. Thompson (Oxford, 1899), 68–9.

[46] James Sherborne, 'The Battle of La Rochelle and the War at Sea, 1372–5', *Bulletin of the Institute of Historical Research*, 42 (1969), 17–29, and 'English Barges and Ballingers of the Late Fourteenth Century', *Mariner's Mirror*, 63 (1977), 109–14. Mario Bandioli, Rene Burlet, Andres Zysberg, 'The Naval Architecture and Oar Systems of Medieval and Later Galleys', in Robert Gardiner, ed., *The Age of the Galley: Mediterranean and Oared Vessels since Pre-Classical Times* (London, 1995), 172–205; Ulrich Alertz. 'The Naval Architecture and Oar Systems of Medieval and Later Galleys', ibid., 142–62.

commercial shipping, especially the English wine trade to Gascony, was the use of convoys. Numerous reports attest to the raids on merchant shipping. Convoys afforded some protection for merchants, but they also presented larger targets for enemies. Intelligence was a key factor for all parties in naval warfare. Obviously it would be difficult to disguise the preparations necessary to organise a convoy. Spies were common to all ports. The threat to English shipping was so great that convoys were mandated at various times. The customary escorts for merchant convoys consisted of large armed merchantmen and sometimes the king's ships. This would change with the use of gunpowder weapons aboard ships purpose-built to accommodate them.[47]

The French, their allies and paid *condottieri* used a mixture of strategies to continue the war at sea in an effort to disrupt the English invaders. They were never able to successfully reverse the tide and carry the war to England on more than a limited basis. Vessels did patrol the Channel and North Sea, but on no set schedule and they were unable to stay on station. Blockades were attempted infrequently. But in early-fifteenth-century England ships did cruise in search of the enemy on sea-keeping missions. Henry V understood the value of the navy that he used in his successful invasion of Normandy. The French lost many of their Channel ports and much of their fleet as a consequence. This lesson was lost on his successors who sold off the fleet, opening an era of piracy and losses abroad.[48]

Elements of a maritime strategy can be seen in the literature of the Hundred Years War, perhaps nowhere more pointedly than in the *Libelle of Englyshe Polycye*, written in the 1430s. The anonymous author proposed blockading the passage to Dover while securing Calais and interdicting Flemish trade:

> Cherishe merchandise, keep the Admiralty,
> That we be masters of the Narrow Sea.[49]

These proposals were never implemented, a reminder that maritime strategy remains a subset of a national grand strategy.[50] Another century would pass before all the elements of a standing navy began to come together. Naval historians since Mahan have debated his interpretation of the influence of sea power upon history. Indeed, an attempt was made in 1997 to examine Mahan's

---

[47] *The Calendar of Patent Rolls* includes many references to convoys: see *CPR* (1340–3), 567–70, *CPR* (1350–4), 486; H. J. Hewitt, *The Organization of War under Edward III, 1338–1362* (Manchester, 1966), 23, 67, 77; Timothy J. Runyan, 'Wine and War: The Anglo-Gascon Wine Trade in the Later Middle Ages', in Klaus Friedland, ed., *Maritime Food Transport* (Vienna, 1994), 245–55.
[48] C. F. Richmond, 'The Keeping of the Seas During the Hundred Years War: 1422–1440', *History*, 49 (1964), 283–98; and his 'English Naval Power in the Fifteenth Century', *History*, 52 (1967), 1–15.
[49] *The Libelle of Englyshe Polycye, A Poem on the Use of Seapower*, 1436, ed. G. W. Warner (Oxford, 1926). See G. A. Holmes, 'The Libel of English Policy', *English Historical Review*, 76 (April 1961), 193–216.
[50] John B. Hattendorf, *Naval History and Maritime Strategy: Collected Essays* (Malabar, Florida, 2000), 256.

influence on medieval maritime history at a meeting in New York of the American Historical Association.[51] As more effort has been directed to the study of late medieval history, its link to the subsequent era of the Renaissance/early modern period grows stronger and the distinction blurs. Over the past several decades arguments for a military revolution in late medieval and early modern Europe have faced substantial challenges, as noted above. Perhaps the efforts to ascertain the establishment of state navies with ships, navigational capabilities, armaments and professional crews will experience similar sea changes and challenges. At last reporting, the arguments on the military revolution debate identified several paradigms. There is revolution – a dramatic change, sometimes over a long period of time. There may be multiple revolutions within the framework of the larger revolution, such as an artillery revolution or an infantry revolution. There is also a paradigm derived from the work of scientists labelled 'punctuated equilibria'. The proposal suggests that evolutionary change occurs during rapid bursts of development after long periods of stasis.[52] Each interpretation has its proponents and antagonists. No attempt will be made here to massage, or muscle, the maritime history of Europe into one of these models. But the challenge from this perspective seems to be answered best by the continued investigation of underwater cultural resources, which constitute our best source of new information, coupled with continued careful examination of documentary evidence.

---

[51] Maryanne Kowaleski chaired the session, with papers by Timothy J. Runyan, Richard Unger, Fred Hocker and comment by John Hattendorf.
[52] See C. J. Rogers, 'Military Revolutions of the Hundred Years War', in Rogers, ed., *Military Revolution Debate*, 76–7.

OARS, SAILS AND GUNS:
THE ENGLISH AND WAR AT SEA, *c*.1200–*c*.1500

Ian Friel

THIS is a survey which focuses on technological change and war at sea as seen through the evidence of English sources. England was a regional naval power in northern Europe between the thirteenth and fifteenth centuries. For much of this period, the main enemies were France, and, to a lesser extent, Scotland and the Welsh princes. The French, Scottish and Welsh wars meant that the operations of English ships at war were restricted mostly to the waters around the British Isles and to the coasts between northern Spain and the Low Countries. The demands on English naval forces were limited compared to what would come after the mid-seventeenth century.

The shipping resources available to English governments in this period varied considerably. Although royally owned ships were generally at the core of major naval operations, at no time before the seventeenth century was the government able to undertake major naval expeditions without using substantial numbers of ships owned by commoners. Medieval English governments for the most part also lacked naval dockyards and had to rely on the 'civilian' shipbuilding industry to supply some of its vessels. This means that the financial accounts and other records of medieval English naval activity are also important sources for the history of English merchant shipping and for the general history of maritime technology. The technology of naval warfare changed for England in the later Middle Ages. How much the development of ships and guns changed practice at sea is difficult to assess but certainly the effects contributed to the evolution of standing naval forces.

Until the fourteenth century, oared vessels provided a major part of the striking power in English war fleets. The English called them 'galleys'. As far as we can make out, these were clinker-built vessels with a double-ended hull form, carrying a single square sail. Until the late thirteenth century, or perhaps slightly before, they were steered by a side- or quarter-rudder alone, although it is apparent that by the 1290s stern rudders were also fitted to some big English galleys. It is also clear that by the 1290s, if not earlier, some had fighting castles at the bow, stern and masthead.[1] All this said, there is still much that is not

---

[1] Ian Friel, *The Good Ship: Ships, Shipbuilding and Technology in England, 1200–1520* (London, 1995), 39–115, *passim*.

known about them. Were they Anglicised descendants of Viking *drakkar*, or did they derive ultimately from the big oared warships built for King Alfred of Wessex in the late 890s?[2] Only archaeology can help to answer that question now.

The term 'galley' declined in English usage in the fourteenth and fifteenth centuries. Even by the early fifteenth century, the English were tending to use 'galley' to designate Mediterranean-style vessels. From the second half of the fourteenth century to the late fifteenth century most English oared fighting ships were called balingers or barges, or, latterly, 'barks'.[3] These were also clinker-built oared fighting ships, indistinguishable in their recorded written details from the earlier galleys (apart, in the fifteenth century, from changes in rig), whatever they actually looked like. Some of these oared fighting vessels could be very big. In the early thirteenth century, King John had galleys with at least seventy rowers, and out of eight galleys built for Edward I in the 1290s, five had one hundred oars or more. As late as 1401, a hundred-oar balinger was built for Henry IV.[4] Oared fighting ships remained part of the English naval inventory right into the sixteenth century, although their status and numbers changed. The first English-based navy of any significance to be created after the Norman Conquest was built up by kings Richard I and John in the late twelfth and early thirteenth centuries, to fight the French king. The loss of the Duchy of Normandy to France in 1204 placed an important seafaring region in the hands of an enemy, accentuating the need for naval forces. In 1206, John had forty-seven galleys on station at ports from King's Lynn to Gloucester, plus another five in Ireland, a massive royal fleet for the Middle Ages. He also had sailing ships of various sizes but the galleys were clearly the principal combat arms.[5] Oared fighting ships needed large crews and this probably limited their ability to stay at sea. Their great military advantage was a tactical one: they could move independently of the wind in combat. Long-distance travel under oars was probably never much of an option, but one should not exclude the possibility that such feats did take place. There is little doubt that the English Crown made much use of oared craft between the thirteenth and fifteenth centuries. Contemporary financial accounts record the purchase of large numbers of oars, and the crews of galleys, barges and balingers were generally much larger than those of sailing vessels of equivalent tonnage, because of the need to have enough men to work the oars. Analysis of surviving tonnage and crew data for English royal ships between 1399 and 1422 suggests a sharp disparity between

---

[2] *The Anglo-Saxon Chronicle*, trans. Michael Swanton (London, 1996), 90.
[3] Dorothy Burwash, *English Merchant Shipping 1460–1540* (Newton Abbot, 1969), 103 ff.
[4] L. G. Carr Laughton, 'Naval Accounts for 1209–1211', *Mariner's Mirror*, 28 (1942), 74–7; Friel, *The Good Ship*, 113.
[5] N. A. M. Rodger, *The Safeguard of the Sea: A Naval History of Britain, Volume I: 660–1649* (London, 1997), 45–54.

the crew sizes of oared and sailing vessels of the same tonnage, with oared vessels on average having nearly twice as many men for a given tonnage.[6]

That said, it is evident that by the early fifteenth century, sailing ships had supplanted oared craft as the main striking force in English war fleets. The growing size of sailing vessels, and the adoption of fighting castles, may well have been one reason for the downgrading of the oared vessel in English service. The Danish archaeologist Ole Crumlin Pedersen has put forward the hypothesis that the introduction of fighting castles from the late twelfth century onwards (they are first depicted on a seal of 1199) was perhaps originally developed to give oared craft an edge in combat against higher-sided sail-driven ships like the cog. Cogs and their like of course acquired castles, re-establishing their height advantage. Although other scholars, such as Jan Bill, have challenged this hypothesis, it remains a possibility.[7] Height and crew size were crucial advantages in medieval sea warfare, and it is likely that large, castle-equipped sailing ships could only have been defeated, in most cases, by ships of similar type. This helped to undermine the value of the galley and similar oared vessels as a primary type of warship in late medieval northern Europe, at least in English service. Certainly by the time of king Henry V (1413–22), there had been a decisive shift in the composition of English royal naval forces. Oared balingers and barges were still important, but more as reconnaissance and patrol craft. For example, Henry V's personal fleet was probably at its peak strength, if not peak numbers, in about March 1417. It then had twenty-seven operational vessels with an estimated total tonnage of 6400 tons with 600 tons of this being estimated since the tonnages of one carrack and four balingers are unknown. Eleven of the twenty-seven vessels were oared balingers, but they only made up about 10 per cent of the total tonnage. The other approximately 90 per cent consisted of sailing ships. The English naval victories at Harfleur in 1416 and off the Chef de Caux in 1417 involved the capture of seven very large Genoese carracks, something that would have been very difficult if not impossible for oared ships alone as the carracks enjoyed a substantial height advantage over oared warships. There can be little doubt that these two victories were chiefly gained by sailing ships.[8] In fifteenth-century English war fleets the oared vessel seems to have been an important auxiliary craft, but never much more than that.[9]

Until the early fifteenth century, English ships, like those elsewhere in northern Europe, used the common north European one-masted rig with a single square sail. This rig was exported to the Mediterranean in the late thirteenth and

---

[6] Ian Friel, 'Documentary Sources and the Medieval Ship: Some Aspects of the Evidence', *International Journal of Nautical Archaeology*, 12 (1983), 55.
[7] Ole Crumlin Pedersen, 'The Vikings and Hanseatic Merchants', in G. Bass, ed., *A History of Seafaring Based on Underwater Archaeology* (London, 1972), 181–204.
[8] Public Records Office E364/59, *passim*; Friel, *The Good Ship*, 151–2; Rodger, *Safeguard of the Sea*, 143–4.
[9] N. A. M. Rodger, 'The Development of Broadside Gunnery 1450–1650', *Mariner's Mirror*, 82 (1996), 301–24.

early fourteenth centuries along with the hull form of the cog. In the fourteenth century Mediterranean sailors added a smaller lateen mizzen to this rig to help make the new, large ship-type, the *cocha*, called a carrack by the English and other northerners, more manoeuvrable.

The earliest-known English record of a two-master dates from 1410, when a two-masted Genoese carrack captured by pirates was acquired by King Henry IV. The English Crown began using and building two-masted vessels in the years 1416 and 1417, probably learning about the technology from captured ships and seamen. The purpose-built two-masters were either large sailing ships or long, low balingers, which were perhaps perceived to benefit from the improved manoeuvrability. It seems that the 1400-ton great ship *Grace Dieu*, completed in 1418, had three masts, although the precise arrangement is unknown. However, it is clear that in the 1430s an English royal balinger was rebuilt as a three-master, with a small square-rigged foresail to help improve its handling. It is possible that the square-rigged foremast was an English invention, but such developments could hardly be kept secret. By the 1450s and 1460s the three-masted square-rig was spreading across both northern and southern Europe and undergoing development. The result was a handier ship, undoubtedly much better suited to the rigours of transoceanic travel than the old one-masters would have been. As such, the three-master became one of the major instruments of oceanic colonisation and conquest, along with other types like the Portuguese caravel.[10]

The Portuguese, whether willingly or not, were also significant in the transmission of southern skeleton-building technology to northern Europe between the 1430s and 1450s. The new type was generally called a carvel by northerners, after the 'caravel'. The first known English-built carvel, Sir John Howard's *Edward*, was constructed in the 1460s. By the early decades of the sixteenth century the technique was being used for the construction of major English war carracks.[11] These two epoch-making technological developments in sail plan and hull construction transformed the nature of European shipping and made European transoceanic enterprise feasible, but their precise effect on naval warfare is less easy to chart. The new rig made ships more manoeuvrable, but it became a general standard, not something that conferred a special tactical advantage on any one power. Skeleton construction later made possible the creation of lidded gun ports and gunrooms, but that did not come until the sixteenth century.[12]

The first recorded shipboard gun was a small weapon, used for firing lead pellets and quarrels or crossbow bolts, bought for the English royal ship *All Hallows Cog* in 1337 or 1338. Guns seem to have remained relatively unimportant in English sea warfare until the fifteenth century. Of the thirty or so ships

---

[10] Friel, *The Good Ship*, 84–109 and 157–70.
[11] Ibid., 170–80.
[12] Cf. Rodger, 'Broadside Gunnery'.

possessed by Henry V between 1413 and 1422, only about half had guns and the total of actual weapons did not exceed forty-two. The most heavily armed ship was the 760-ton 'great ship' *Holigost*, with seven guns. Where their material is stated, the guns were almost invariably made of iron, although in 1411 a barge of Henry IV's had both an iron gun and a bronze one. The weapons were called both 'cannons' and 'guns' although the terms were seldom used interchangeably for the weaponry of the same ship, perhaps hinting at technical differences. The guns were breach-loaders, often with two or even three separate powder-chambers apiece, to speed reloading. We do not know if these were wheeled cannon or swivel guns.

Surviving English ship inventories are rare between the early 1420s and the late 1470s and there are no royal ship inventories between the mid-1430s and the mid-1480s. This is unfortunate as major developments in rig and ship-borne gunnery took place in this period. For one thing it is clear that between the 1420s and the 1480s a revolution had occurred in the provision and use of shipboard guns. Although overshadowed by the introduction of lidded gun ports in the sixteenth century, it was clearly one of the major stages in the development of the warship, and comparatively little is known about it.[13]

Records of the 1470s and 1480s reveal that significant increases had taken place in the numbers of ship-borne guns since the 1420s. In the late 1470s Sir John Howard owned two private warships, the *George Howard* and *Edward Howard*. They carried, respectively, 16 and 15 wrought-iron breech-loading 'bombards'. A few years later, in 1485, a royal ship, the *Mary of the Tower*, had 48 guns and 11 chambers, plus 12 hakbushes, a crude form of musket. Another royal vessel, the *Martin Garsia*, had 30 guns, 86 chambers, 100 gunstones, that is, round shot made of stone, and 300 tampions or shot wads. The two largest of Henry VII's ships, the 1000-ton *Regent* and the 600-ton *Sovereign*, built in the 1480s, carried prodigious numbers of guns. The 1495 inventory of the *Sovereign* lists 130 guns of three types, serpentines of iron and bronze and stone guns, all breech-loaders, and all mounted on swivels, called 'miches', rather than carriages. These technological changes were complemented by changes in personnel. Gunners began to appear as separate specialists aboard English warships in the 1470s, and were common on large warships by the 1490s.[14]

Despite the increasing numbers of guns, there is no sign that they had much effect on English naval tactics before the sixteenth century. All late-fifteenth-century English warships carried large numbers of bills, bows and other hand weapons, arms that were used to fight the boarding actions that still decided the outcome of any naval battle. There is no reason to believe that the English had much notion of the effective use of stand-off gunnery until well into the

---

[13] Friel, *The Good Ship*, 150–6.
[14] PRO C76/163, m.6; Michael Oppenheim, ed., *Naval Account and Inventories in the Reign of Henry VII 1495–7*, Navy Records Society 8 (London, 1896), 38, 50, 69, 194–5, 261 and 339–44; Rodger, *Safeguard of the Sea*, 160–1.

sixteenth century. Famously, both the *Regent* and the French warship *La Cordeliere* were destroyed when both caught fire during a boarding action in 1512. Swivel guns of the type which bristled from ships in the 1490s would have been only useful as anti-personnel weapons. It is possible that one reason for their use in large numbers was that it was anticipated that a significant number would be unreliable. Twenty-nine of the *Regent*'s guns were lost in unspecified ways in the 1497 English campaign against Scotland.[15] Heavy ship-borne guns that could sink other vessels only began to make their appearance in north European waters in the early sixteenth century. For most contemporary seafarers the aim in battle was to capture an enemy ship, not sink it, if at all possible. A captured ship could be a valuable prize, and surviving officers could be ransomed. A sunken ship might mean one less enemy vessel, but it was otherwise no use to anyone.

Unlike medieval France, with its impressive galley dockyards at Rouen and elsewhere, medieval England lacked anything like a standing navy. One or more officials of the royal household, assisted by others appointed on an *ad hoc* basis when the pressure of work required it, essentially undertook the management of the king's ships. From the 1330s the clerk, later keeper, of the king's ships, an administrator and finance officer rather than an operational commander, normally ran the ships.[16] The king's ships were far from being a navy in the modern sense of the word, although it was recognised by Crown and commoners alike that they did have some function in the defence of the kingdom and of English shipping, as well as in the prosecution of war. Although fleets of royal ships were sometimes quite large – particularly those of John and Henry V – few medieval English monarchs had the financial resources to keep a large fleet in being for very long. Royal fleets tended to be built up rapidly in times of need, and then demobilised or sold off after the crisis had passed. For instance, after Henry V died in 1422 most of his ships were quickly sold off to help settle his debts. The king's sea and land campaigns had removed the threat of French sea-borne attack and there was no longer seen to be any need for a large royal fleet.[17]

The uses to which the medieval king's ships were put were also not always 'naval' ones, even in time of war. Henry V, for example, revived the royal fleet in order to help pursue his ambition to take the throne of France. The fleet rose in number from seven usable vessels in July 1413, to twenty-seven by March 1417, and at its height in 1420, the king owned something like thirty-six ships. The accounts of the clerk of the king's ships for 1413–22 show that twenty-nine of

---

[15] Rodger, *Safeguard of the Sea*, 170; Oppenheim, *Naval Accounts*, vol. 8, 279.
[16] Rodger, *Safeguard of the Sea*, 128–30 and 158–9.
[17] Susan Rose, ed., *The Navy of the Lancastrian Kings and the Accounts and Inventories of William Soper, Keeper of the King's Ships, 1422–1427*. Navy Records Society 123 (London, 1982), 52.

the king's ships were used at one time or another in naval operations, such as invasion fleets or sea-keeping patrols, but that seventeen also went on merchant voyages, most of them carrying wine from Bordeaux, although a few went further afield to Prussia and Portugal.[18] It is possible that the ships on the Bordeaux run went as convoy escorts, but the crew sizes on these enterprises were generally smaller than those for war operations. The main reason for sending the ships seems to have been monetary. Henry's one-masted sailing ships were used on these voyages and on the face of it they were profitable. Between September 1413 and June 1416, twelve ships completed twenty-six trading voyages, which netted the very large sum of £2055 in freight payments from merchants. The proceeds were ploughed into the financing of the royal ships. However, if one subtracts the costs of crew wages and victuals from this figure, the profit reduces to £400 and the whole enterprise may well have been run at a loss, as £968 was spent on the upkeep of the twelve ships over this period, much of which must have been necessitated by the rigours of the voyages. The deficit was even greater than this as one 220-ton ship, the *Cog John*, was wrecked off Brittany during a Bordeaux voyage. Nevertheless, the fact that these voyages continued suggests that contemporaries saw them as successful.[19]

The king's ships had a multiplicity of uses, but they were seldom intended to be much of a combat force by themselves. Medieval English naval expeditions, large and small, relied on using conscripted merchant ships and other vessels belonging to English owners. As far as one can make out, impressment commands were generally obeyed, although at times they caused serious interruptions to sea-borne trade. Merchant vessels were essential for moving troops, horses and stores, and with the addition of fighting castles, if they did not already have them, could be converted into warships. Although we do not know the full size of the English merchant fleet at any point in the Middle Ages, musters for royal fleets do give us some notion of the numbers of vessels used by English merchants. Edward III used the largest recorded fleets in the 1340s, with 440 ships mobilised for carrying an army to Brittany in 1342 and at least 750 vessels used in the king's voyage to Normandy in 1346. The Black Death of 1348–50, which killed a large portion of the population of Europe, inevitably reduced the shipping resources of every kingdom, leaving fewer mariners to man ships and less demand for shipping. Despite chronicle accounts of Henry V using a fleet of 1500 ships for his 1415 invasion of France, there is little evidence to back this up, and financial records suggest that English fleets were smaller than they had been in the 1340s. Given the fact that the Black Death and later epidemics had substantially reduced the English population by the early

---

[18] PRO E364/54, E364/59 and E364/61, *passim*.
[19] PRO E364/54 D, m.2r – F, m.2v, *passim*, and E364/59 F, m.2r.

fifteenth century, this is not very surprising.[20] English rulers also intermittently hired vessels from friendly foreign powers for use as both transports and combat vessels. In 1417, for example, twenty foreign ships were hired for use in sea patrols, and over fifty more served as transports.[21]

The records of the customs at Bordeaux, an English possession until 1453, give a good idea of the changing sizes of English merchant ships in the late Middle Ages. The Bordeaux wine ton of 252 gallons was the principal container used in the port and the wine trade inevitably used some of the larger contemporary bulk-carriers. As an employer of shipping, the trade seems to have been at its peak in the early fourteenth century. For example, in the three months between late June and Michaelmas 1303, there were 271 wine shipments from Bordeaux. Fifty-five of these shipments were carried in ships capable of carrying between 150 and 250 tons, and in the following year one shipment even reached 303 tons. The tonnage lading figures, although variable, are a good guide to the actual as opposed to alleged carrying capacities of ships. By the 1350s, after the Black Death, English ships in the 150 ton-plus range were much rarer, a situation that persisted into the early decades of the fifteenth century. However, there was also a sharp increase in the numbers of these ships by the 1440s, and the appearance of vessels in the 200 ton-plus range. One ship calling at Bordeaux in 1444–45 was even able to load 380 tons of wine, perhaps the largest cargo of any English-built merchant ship in the Middle Ages. The ship in question was the *Grace de Dieu*, built on the Yorkshire coast in 1439, which later ended up as a derelict royal warship on the river Hamble in the 1480s. A muster of ships in 1450–1 for an expedition confirms that the English at this time possessed significant numbers of large merchant ships. Out of sixty-three vessels collected, eighteen were between 200 and 400 tons' burden. Between the 1420s and the 1450s the English merchant fleet seems to have had more large vessels than it was to have for another century and a half or so. It is ironic that the English government of the time lacked the finance and other capabilities to make effective use of this shipping in the revived war with the French Crown.[22]

Significant numbers of non-royal ships were also private warships, used by pirates and privateers, and were of great value to the Crown in times of war. This fact served to undermine royal efforts to curb piracy. Some of the biggest pirates, like the notorious John Hawleys of Dartmouth, father and son (1370s to

---

[20] Rodger, *Safeguard of the Sea*, 118–19 and 140–1; Christopher Allmand, *Henry V* (London, 1992), 78.
[21] PRO E364/59, H m.2r.; *Rotuli Normanniae*, ed. T. D. Hardy, *1200–1205* and *1417–1418* (London, 1835), 320–9.
[22] PRO E101/158/10; E101/173/4; E101/185/7; BL Add. MS 15524; PRO E364/92, A m.1v – B m.1r. (I am grateful to Dr Wendy Childs for making her transcripts of these accounts available to me); R. C. Anderson, 'The *Grace de Dieu* of 1446–1486', *English Historical Review*, 34 (1919), 584–6.

1430s) were important men, powerful and honoured in their own localities, and too useful to the Crown to ever suffer much for their piratical activities. Pirates favoured speedy oared balingers and barges, and John Hawley the Younger even presented one of his vessels, the balinger *Craccher*, to Henry V. The masters of royal ships could be pirates. John William, who rose to be the master of the great ship *Jesus*, had committed at least one act of piracy when he had earlier worked for John Hawley as master of the *Craccher*. Some monarchs, such as Henry IV, seem to have used privateering campaigns as a means of exerting pressure on enemies without the risks of open war.[23]

What did technology mean in all of this? Actual shipbuilding for the English Crown in the Middle Ages concentrated on the construction of oared fighting ships, rather than sailing vessels. The former were probably much less easy to come by than the latter, and certainly few people but the king would have been able to crew and operate the sorts of big galleys constructed for Kings John and Edward I. Even in Henry V's time, the actual construction of ships for the Crown was restricted to four 'great ships' (super-large, clinker-built carracks) and eight balingers or barges.[24] Purchase played very little part in Henry V's ship procurement 'process': at least seventeen of the twenty-eight other sailing ships acquired by the Crown in this period were prizes. Later in the century, in the time of Henry VII in the 1480s and 1490s, the four new ships built for the king were two carracks and two oared barks. Any other vessels were acquired by alternative means.

The shipbuilding industry that built these vessels was 'civilian' in nature. Despite some naval base or dockyard construction in the time of John and Henry V, there were no specialised warship building yards in the sense of those that existed in the eighteenth century. The Crown had to rely on the dispersed and somewhat disorganised English shipbuilding industry for what construction and maintenance work it required. The industry worked entirely in clinker construction until the mid-fifteenth century, and its gradual conversion to carvel construction from about the 1450s still lacks a complete explanation, although factors such as lower costs (less iron, more wood, fewer specialist workers required) and improved hull serviceability may well have played a part. This, however, was a general change for shipping of all types, and it is clear that not all English warships were being built carvel-fashion until the early decades of the sixteenth century.[25]

Changes in English ship rig may have been fostered by the royal fleet.

---

[23] J. C. Appleby, 'Devon Privateering from Early Times to 1688', in M. Duffy *et al*., eds, *The New Maritime History of Devon*, vol. I: *From Early Times to the Late Eighteenth Century* (London, 1992), 91; Rose, *The Navy of the Lancastrian Kings*, 42, 245 and 250; C. J. Ford, 'Piracy or Policy: The Crisis in the Channel, 1400–1403', *Transactions of the Royal Historical Society*, 5th series 29 (1979), 63–78.
[24] Rose, *The Navy of the Lancastrian Kings*, 245–52.
[25] Friel, *The Good Ship*, 39–67 and 170–80.

Certainly Henry V's fleet changed rapidly from having no two-masters in 1415 to a situation in 1420 where it had one apparent three-master and eleven two-masters, of which four were English-built. Five of the two-masters were former Genoese carracks. Two other ships were possibly from Spain and one from Bayonne. Certainly the 'new' two-masted technology was available in other parts of northern Europe at about the same time, but there is clear evidence of its rapid adoption for ships of the English royal fleet, apparently to improve large sailing ships and long, low balingers.[26]

The four 'great ships' built for Henry V between 1413 and 1420 represented another major innovation. It was not unusual for an English monarch to have a single large sailing ship as a prestige piece. King John had had a 'great ship' called *Dieulabeneie*, and Richard II and Henry IV had had the 300-ton *Trinity*, for example. The first of Henry V's great ships was a rebuild, at about 400 tons, of the old *Trinity*, renamed the *Trinity Royal*. The second, the *Holigost*, was a rebuild of a large Spanish ship, but the biggest ones, the 1000-ton *Jesus* and the 1400-ton *Grace Dieu* were constructed from scratch. As a group, the great ships appear to have been clinker-built versions of Mediterranean carracks. Certainly the Genoese carracks hired by the French at this time represented a major threat to English naval forces. The great ships were different in size and scale from earlier large royal ships, and represented a trend in English and other north European warship building that can be traced into the sixteenth century and beyond. The large war carracks were potent symbols of royal power. They carried as many people as a large village. The *Jesus* had a crew of 201. The tall, heavily manned ships were perceived to be of great use in the form of sea warfare that was resolved by boarding actions. It is difficult to point to the use of such carracks as being particularly decisive, but it should be noted that both the *Holigost* and the *Trinity Royal* were in the thick of the fighting in the battle of Harfleur in 1416, a battle which not only saw the capture of three large carracks, but also resulted in an English victory.[27]

As discussed above, guns *appear* to have had very little effect on the nature of naval warfare in northern Europe before the sixteenth century. However, if this was entirely the case, one does wonder why there was a sudden sharp increase in the numbers of guns carried on English warships in the latter part of the fifteenth century. There must have been a perception that larger numbers of guns made a warship more effective. Although the bulk of these were small, anti-personnel swivel guns, this does not mean that they were mere popguns. In a boarding action, the 600-ton *Regent* would have been able to fire fifty or more such weapons at an enemy ship alongside, and the relatively quick reloading time for a small breech-loader could have meant that the fire from the ship was able to devastate any open decks or perhaps even penetrate light superstructure.

[26] Rose, *The Navy of the Lancastrian Kings*, 245–52.
[27] PRO E101/42/39; Carr Laughton, 'Naval Accounts', 74.

For people who believed in the reality of hell, the noise and smoke alone could have been very daunting. Although it may not merit the title of an 'armament revolution', the rising use of gunpowder weapons on sailing warships in the second half of the fifteenth century was a real phenomenon, one that served to make the ship a deadlier instrument of war. However, it was a phenomenon that had probably already reached its limits by 1500. Until the invention of the lidded gun port in the early sixteenth century, it was not possible to mount guns in any numbers below the castle or the weather deck. This in turn limited the size of weapons that could be used, as a large battery of heavy guns could pose major stability problems. Once the lidded gun port and the gunroom were developed, it became easier to carry heavy guns, as these could go below the weather deck, lowering the vessel's centre of gravity. The ship-borne heavy gun eventually became a destroyer of ships, but the techniques and tactics required to make this possible were not fully developed until the seventeenth century. The rise of the ship-borne gun in the fifteenth century was in the context of existing tactics. It made 'red war yet redder' rather than revolutionised it.[28]

Changing maritime technology did transform the ways in which the English waged war at sea in the Middle Ages, but the transformations in England seem to have been matched by those in other countries. England kept up with new developments, and perhaps led the way in some, but prevailing medieval economic and technological conditions made it impossible for anyone to maintain a decisive technological margin for very long. Superiority in numbers and the ability to raise fleets when needed seem to have mattered more, giving the English a sufficient edge over their naval opponents in Wales, Scotland and France. Although French forces were able to stage many devastating raids on the English coastline during the Hundred Years War, in the fourteenth and fifteenth centuries French armies were never able to invade England. By contrast, the English were able to invade France on a number of occasions, culminating in Henry V's conquest of northern France and his recognition as heir to the French throne. However, medieval England's wars were ultimately won or lost on land. The only way in which the English could gain even partial control of the English Channel was to conquer Normandy, which was achieved, briefly, between 1419 and 1450. The English naval forces could never have won the long series of conflicts between England and her enemies in the thirteenth, fourteenth and fifteenth centuries but they were effective enough to make it possible for the English Crown to undertake periodic sea-borne offensives against those enemies. Without English medieval sea power, disorganised and ramshackle as it sometimes was, there would have been no Hundred Years War and all the terrors that went with it.

---

[28] Thomas Hardy, 'Channel Firing'.

Part II

SOUTHERN EUROPE

BYZANTIUM AND THE SEA: BYZANTINE FLEETS AND THE HISTORY OF THE EMPIRE IN THE AGE OF THE MACEDONIAN EMPERORS, *C*.900–1025 CE

John H. Pryor*

WHEN Basil I (867–86), the founder of the 'Macedonian' dynasty, seized the throne, the Byzantine Empire was at one of its recurrent nadirs. Crete had fallen to Spanish Muslims around 824. Effective authority over Cyprus and Rhodes had been lost much earlier. Cilicia was in the hands of Muslim corsair emirs. In the North, the Empire was under pressure from the Patzinaks, Magyars, and Bulgars. In the West, Byzantine presence in south Italy was ephemeral.

By the death of Basil II (976–1025) it all looked very different. The maritime approaches to the Empire from the south and west had been secured by the re-establishment of firm rule in south Italy during the reign of Basil I and by the reconquest of Crete in 960–1, Cyprus in 965, Rhodes at some unknown date, and Cilicia and northern Syria in the second half of the tenth century. Basil II destroyed the First Bulgarian Empire in 1018 and pushed the northern frontier back to the Danube, where it remained in spite of occasional Patzinak pressure.

In all of this, Byzantine fleets played operational roles at various times. By the Macedonian era, these consisted of an 'imperial' fleet based on Constantinople commanded by the δρουγγάριος τοῦ πλοίμου (*droungarios tou ploimou*), 'admiral of the fleet', and the thematic fleets of the Kibyrrhaiōtai based at Attaleia, the northern Aegean (theme of *Aigaion Pelagos*, Aegean Sea), and the southern Aegean (theme of Samos, based at Samos), each under their στρατηγοί (*stratēgoi*), generals/admirals. Squadrons were also stationed in the Peloponnēsos and elsewhere at various times.

The Sources

What we actually know about the ships of which Byzantine fleets were composed, and the tactics and strategies they employed, is frustratingly little. One of the major problems lies in the sources. One text which has been used by

---

* Much of this paper is founded on research conducted for a forthcoming book by John Pryor and Elizabeth Jeffreys: *The Byzantine Navy: Evolution of the Ships and Their Capabilities*. The authors acknowledge the publisher's permission to reuse in the forthcoming book material presented here.

maritime historians in the past without adequate attention to its character is now known not to have been a description of the construction of tenth-century Byzantine war galleys, δρόμωνες (*dromōnes*) and χελάνδια (*chelandia*) at all, but rather a juvenile exercise in the philology of nautical terminology. This is the anonymous treatise, *Naval Warfare*, commissioned by Basil the Patrician and Parakoimōmenos (the work hereafter referred to as the *Anonymous*), which survives only at folios 339–42 of the manuscript Milan, Biblioteca Ambrosiana, MS B 119-sup. [gr. 139]. Hitherto edited only by Alphonse Dain, his edition was produced under the worst circumstances imaginable during the Second World War and is totally unreliable.[1] The author is now deduced to have been a young retainer of Basil the Parakoimōmenos (fl. 944–85), who ransacked sources such as the *Onomasticon* of Julius Pollux (second century CE), the *Lexicon* of Hesychios of Alexandria (fifth century CE), and a manuscript of Thoukydidēs' *Peloponnesian War* with scholia, to produce a purported description of tenth-century Byzantine war galleys that had much more in common with τριήρεις (*triēreis*) of Themistoklean Athens. His audience would have recognised his treatise for what it was, as he intended.

The other major text to which maritime historians have traditionally turned in order to understand the Byzantine navy is Constitution XIX of the *Taktika* of Emperor Leo VI (886–912). In the Ambrosiana manuscript, this constitution was excerpted from the complete text of the *Taktika* by the compiler of the manuscript and included together with the *Anonymous* in a separate section of the manuscript devoted to naval warfare. Dain's edition of Leo is just as faulty as that of the *Anonymous*.[2] Moreover, in spite of the fact that Leo explicitly said that, in compiling Constitution XIX, he used old or ancient tactical manuals, historians have not appreciated the extent to which the emperor's treatise was an exercise in book learning. He used Thoukydidēs and early manuals of strategy, especially the sixth-century *Stratēgikon* attributed to one Maurice and some chapters on naval warfare attributed to a certain Syrianos Magistros, also dated to the sixth century.[3] Additionally, in spite of the fact that Leo said that he had also consulted with his *stratēgoi*, it can be shown that Constitution XIX fairly reeks of 'arm-chair sailing', of cute stratagems devised by the emperor in front of a fireplace in the imperial palace in Constantinople. Leo VI had no practical experience of warfare, neither at sea nor on land.

Later in the tenth century, Leo's Constitution XIX, as also his whole *Taktika*, was closely paraphrased by Nikephōros Ouranos, a practised general and

---

[1] *Naumachica Partim Adhuc Inedita*, ed. A. Dain (Paris, 1943), 57–68. New editions and translations of this and the other texts used here will appear as appendices to *The Byzantine Navy*. However, for the sake of convenience, references here are still given to Dain's edition.
[2] Ναυμαχικά Λέοντος Βασιλέως, ed. Dain in *Naumachica*, 15–33.
[3] G. T. Dennis and E. Gamillscheg, eds, *Das Strategikon des Maurikios* (Vienna, 1981). The chapters of Syrianos Magistros also survive only at folios 333r–338v of the same Ambrosiana manuscript. It was edited as Syrianos Magistros, Ναυμαχίαι Συριανοῦ Μαγίστρου, in Dain, *Naumachica*, 43–55.

magistros in land warfare, as chapter 54 of his own *Taktika*. Dain's edition of this, from the sixteenth-century manuscript Florence, Biblioteca Medicea Laurenziana, MS Laurentianus LVII–31,[4] is equally as unreliable by comparison to the manuscript Munich, Bayerische Staatsbibliothek, Cod. Monac. 452, from which the Florence manuscript was copied in 1564 and which Dain had wished to use had his transcripts not been lost in the war. Nikephōros Ouranos reiterated many of the impractical stratagems of Leo VI, either because he had no naval experience himself or else perhaps because he was constrained by deference to the revered great-grandfather of the current emperor, Basil II, in order to have his own work accepted for 'publication' in the highest circles of Byzantine court society.

A third major text on which maritime historians have relied heavily is the supposed inventories for the expeditions to recover Crete in 911 and 949, which for some unknown reason were excerpted and included at books 44–5 in the problematic compilation attributed to the auspices of Constantine VII Porphyrogennētos and known as the *De Cerimoniis*. These inventories are incomplete, fraught with orthographical transmission problems, and were the product of non-nautical bureaucratic clerks rather than of seamen. However, at least we have a fundamentally reliable edition of this text from the unique manuscript, Leipzig, Univ./Urb., MS 28 [Rep. i.17],[5] emendations made by scholars in recent years, and a new and definitive edition.

Matters of textuality may seem removed from the concerns here. However, when major texts upon which previous maritime historians have relied can be shown to have been anything but what they have been understood to be, then we must start again. In the case of the Byzantine Empire, virtually every text that survives has to be 'deconstructed'. For us, the reality is the texts, not the ships and the men. In seeking to understand a historical reality, the projection of Byzantine sea power in the interests of the Empire, we are forced at every turn back to texts whose purposes were not those for which we seek to use them.

The Ships

That being said, as long as we comprehend correctly the nature of the texts and the purposes for which they were originally intended, all is not lost. We can know with confidence that the standard *dromon* of the tenth century was a fully decked bireme with two superimposed banks of oars, one rowed from below deck and the other from above it. Both banks of oarsmen rowed fully seated. There were approximately twenty-five oars per side on each bank, for a total

---

[4] Περί Θαλασσομαχίας ed. Dain in *Naumachica*, 69–88.
[5] Constantine VII Porphyrogennētos, *Constantini Porphyrogeniti Imperatoris de Cerimoniis Aulae Byzantinae Libri Duo*, ed. I. Reiske, 2 vols (Bonn, 1829), here vol. I, 650–79; J. F. Haldon, 'Theory and Practice in Tenth-Century Military Administration: Chapters II, 44 and 45 of the *Book of Ceremonies*', *Travaux et mémoires*, 13 (2000), 201–352.

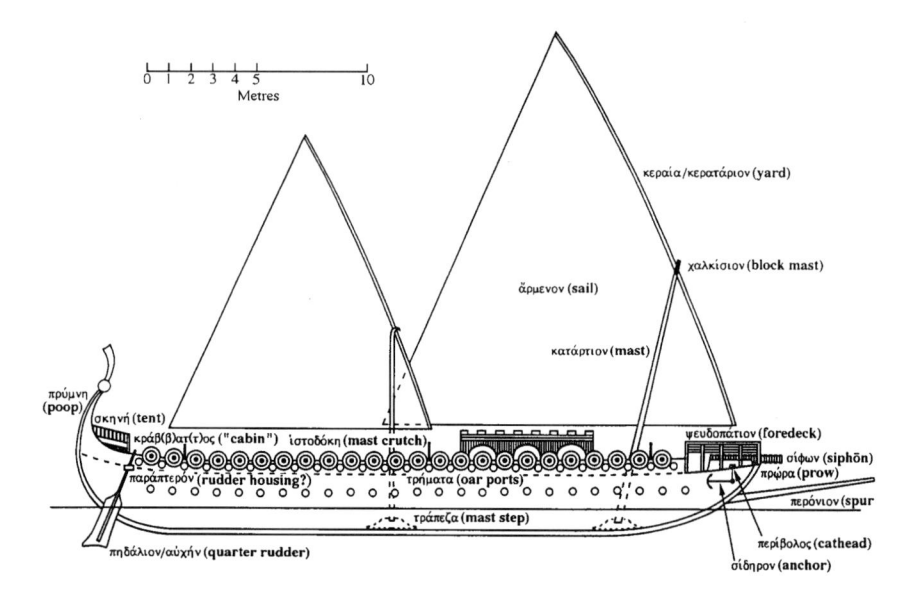

1. Longitudinal section of a tenth-century bireme dromon. © John H. Pryor

crew of around a hundred oarsmen, plus marines and officers up to around a hundred and fifty men. An οὐσία (*ousia*), which was the standard complement of a war galley, its crew excluding officers and marines, and which was definitely not an actual ship as has frequently been supposed,[6] was 108 men. *Dromons* and *chelandia* had two sails, a larger one at the bow and a smaller one amidships. But there is no evidence that will stand up to scrutiny for any Byzantine galleys having either three masts or three banks of oars. There were also smaller *dromons*, which were particularly fast and used especially for scouting and message carrying, and which were known as γαλέαι (*galeai*), 'galleys'. They probably also had two sails, but they had only one bank of oars.

Extrapolating from the length of the 'room' of a seated oarsman, the *interscalmium*, the distance between any two thole pins, σκαλμοί (*skalmoi*), of around one metre, the overall length of a standard *dromon* or *chelandion* was around 31.25 metres and its beam amidships by comparison to later western

---

[6] See, for example, H. Ahrweiler, *Byzance et la mer: la marine de guerre, la politique, et les institutions maritimes de Byzance aux VIIe–XVe siècles* (Paris, 1966), 416–17; K. A. Alexandres, Ἡ Θαλασσία δύναμις εἰς τὴν ἱστορίαν τῆς βυζαντινῆς αὐτοκρατορίας (Athens, 1956), 73–4; E. Eickhoff, *Seekrieg und Seepolitik zwischen Islam und Abendland: das Mittelmeer unter byzantinischer und arabischer Hegemonie (650–1040)* (Berlin, 1966), 137; F. Hocker, 'Late Roman, Byzantine, and Islamic galleys and fleets', in J. Morrison, ed., *The Age of the Galley: Mediterranean Oared Vessels since Pre-Classical Times* (London, 1995), 86–100, here 94; C. Makrypoulias, 'The Navy in the Works of Constantine Porphyrogenitus', *Graeco-Arabica*, 6 (1995), 152–71, here 154–5; W. Treadgold, 'The Army in the Works of Constantine Porphyrogenitus', *Rivista di studi bizantini e neoellenici*, n.s. 29 (1992), 77–162, here 134.

galeae was around 4.46 metres. Its length-to-beam ratio was around 7:1; however, that is misleading, because the upper hull was flared outboard above the lower oar ports. The ratio at the waterline was approximately 8:1 (28:3.5 metres). Its deadweight tonnage was around 25 metric tonnes. The foremast was around 11.85 metres long with a masthead height of around 10.65 metres above sea level and the peak of the sail around 21 metres above the same. The smaller midships mast was only around 8.3 metres long.

Bireme dromons almost certainly had upper hulls flared outboard so that the blades of the two banks of oars would be clear of each other when submerged. The upper oars would also have been longer than the lower ones, so that the strokes of the upper and lower oarsmen would be the same in horizontal plane, which was the important thing. These were small galleys by later medieval standards. Their crews were similar in size to those of western *galeae* of the thirteenth century, but they were packed into hulls of only around 75 per cent of the capacity of the latter. They also had a less efficient oarage system. A fully seated oarsman could not deliver as much power as one using the stand-and-sit stroke of western *galeae*. Moreover, the addition of an outrigger to western *galeae* permitted the development of oars with better gearing, mechanical advantage, and power efficiency. The *galea* replaced the *dromon* and the *chelandion* in the late eleventh century in the West, almost certainly because it was discovered that a bireme galley could be rowed from two oarage positions on the same bench above deck rather than from two superimposed benches.

Among other problems thus overcome would have been the very great one of ventilation of the hold. Fifty oarsmen working below deck would have emitted large amounts of body heat, carbon dioxide, and sweat. Removal of this and replacement of oxygen must have required some system of forced ventilation and even then the mechanical efficiency of the lower oarsmen must have been seriously compromised.

Water Supplies and Logistical Capabilities

When the final expedition of 960–1 against Crete was being contemplated, opposition in the Senate to the plans was only overcome by the arguments of the *parakoimōmenos* Joseph Bringas, who urged that the length of the voyage should not be feared.[7] In the tenth century, even a voyage from Constantinople to Crete was a long-range expedition and a major undertaking for a large fleet. Naval warfare was a matter of coasting for very limited distances and developing strategies that combined possession of the coasts and islands with what naval forces could achieve with regards to control of coastal sea lanes. The

---

[7] Theophanēs Continuatus, *Theophanes Continuatus, Ioannes Cameniata, Symeon Magister, Georgius Monachus*, ed. I. Bekker, 3 vols (Bonn, 1838); VI. Βασιλεία Ρωμανοῦ υἱοῦ Κωνσταντίνου τοῦ πορφυρογεννήτου. 9 (475), '. . . καὶ μὴ δεδιέναι τῆς ὁδοῦ τὸ μῆκος καὶ . . .'.

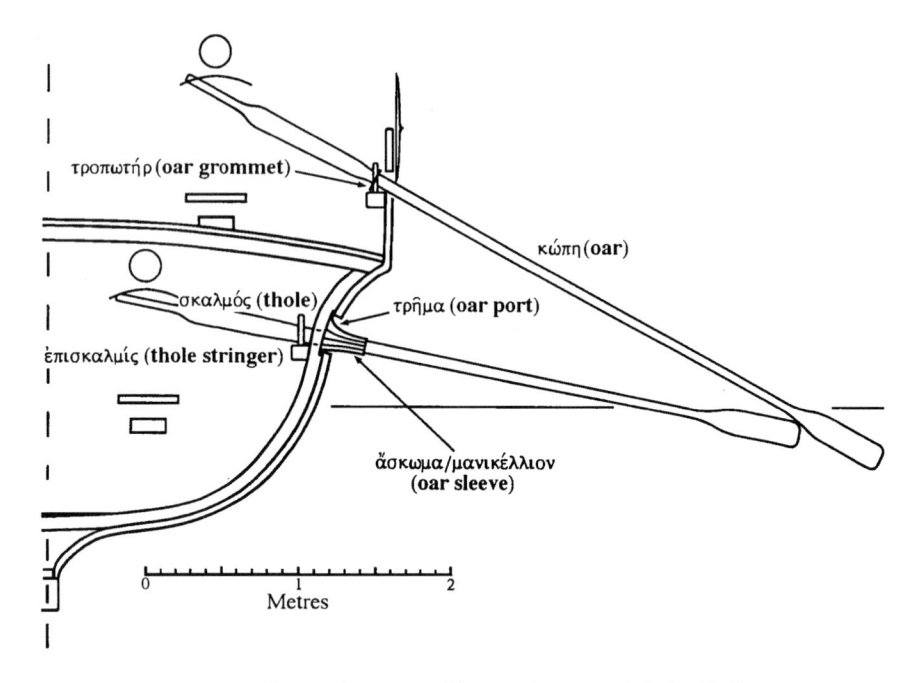

2. Oarage system of a tenth-century bireme dromon. © John H. Pryor

stages of the voyage for the expedition of 949, as revealed by the portulan (*stadiodromikon*) inserted in the *De Cerimoniis*, were each no longer than around 145 kilometres.[8]

Supplies of fresh water were vitally important because they were the 'fuel' that drove any galley. Unless a galley could use its sails, it would come to a stop within hours if water supplies ran out because dehydration would quickly enfeeble the oarsmen. Naval forces had to provide for fresh water and provisions in advance or ensure that they could obtain them en route. Moving into waters off enemy shores deprived fleets of water, unless they could take it by force, which was usually not easy to do since most significant coastal water sources were incorporated into fortified habitations for obvious reasons. 'Foraging' for water from small streams in deserted coves or wells in isolated villages taken over by force might be possible for small flotillas, but such sources would be inadequate for large fleets. Moreover, few ports in the eastern Mediterranean were on large rivers and many had no river at all and were dependent upon wells.

Estimates of the amount of water crews required have been revised upwards dramatically over the past decade or so. During sea trials of the reconstructed Greek trireme *Olympias*, it has been found that oarsmen need a litre per hour,

---

[8] Constantine VII, *De Cerimoniis*, vol. I, 678; Haldon, 'Theory and Practice', 234–5. Note that it is highly improbable that the fleet actually followed this route.

just for drinking, to prevent dehydration.[9] More would have been needed for the soupy stew of salt meat and legumes that was the staple diet of medieval crews.

A range of evidence from antiquity to the seventeenth century increasingly supports around eight litres per day for galley crews.[10] If we consider the standard *ousia* of 108 men of a Byzantine *dromon* or *chelandion*, the water requirement can confidently be expected to have been a minimum of 108 x 8 = 864 litres per day. Increasing that to at least 1000 litres or one tonne of water per ship per day when officers and marines are also taken into account would surely be reasonable. And this would be to discount supernumeraries, *dromons* with two *ousiai* as crews, and the various higher figures for crews reported for the ships of the Cretan expeditions.[11] One tonne of water per day would have been an absolute bare minimum.

By the tenth century, it is probable that Byzantine fleets were using both barrels and amphorae as water containers. One inventory for the Cretan expedition of 949 specified five κάδοι (*kadoi*) per *dromon* and *kados* was a word used commonly since antiquity for a shipboard water amphora.[12] The *kadoi* depicted on the *Cista Ficoronica* of c.300 BC, in a representation of Jason and the Argonauts watering at the spring of the Bebrycians, are estimated to have weighed around 18 kg with a capacity of 27 litres.[13] Five *kadoi* such as those of the *Cista*

---

[9] B. Rankov, 'Reconstructing the Past: The Operation of the Trireme Reconstruction *Olympias* in the Light of Historical Sources', *Mariner's Mirror*, 80 (1994), 131–46, here 138; S. Platis, 'The Greek Crew Trials with *Olympias* in 1988', in Τρόπις *III/Tropis III: 3rd International Symposium on Ship Construction in Antiquity, Athens 1989. Proceedings* (Athens, 1995), 335–45, here 340; J. Morrison, J. F. Coates, and N. B. Rankov, *The Athenian Trireme: The History and Reconstruction of an Ancient Greek Warship*, 2nd edn (Cambridge, 2000), 238.

[10] Earlier estimates of water requirements, as low as 2.25 litres per day, are now regarded as hopelessly inadequate. See A. W. Sleeswyk and F. Meijer, 'The Water Supply of the *Argo* and Other Oared Ships', *Mariner's Mirror*, 84 (1998), 131–8, here 133–5; J. Dotson, 'Economics and Logistics of Galley Warfare', in Morrison, *The Age of the Galley*, 217–23; J. H. Pryor, *Geography, Technology, and War: Studies in the Maritime History of the Mediterranean, 649–1571* (Cambridge, 1988), 75–85; J. H. Pryor, 'From Dromōn to Galea: Mediterranean Bireme Galleys AD 500–1300', in Morrison, *The Age of the Galley*, 101–16, here 114; J. H. Pryor, 'The Geographical Conditions of Galley Navigation in the Mediterranean', in Morrison, *The Age of the Galley*, 206–16, here 210.

[11] The figures for the two expeditions of 911 and 949 and for various types of ships vary considerably: *chelandia pamphyla* of 120 or 150 men, *chelandia ousiaka* of 108 and 110 men, *chelandia* and dromons of 220 men, dromons of 200 or 220 men. Crews were tailored to suit circumstances and expedition objectives and in many cases the ships obviously carried supernumeraries either as landing assault troops or to provide two 'watches' to keep the galleys moving around the clock if necessary.

[12] Constantine VII, *De Cerimoniis*, vol. I, 671; Haldon, 'Theory and Practice', 226–7.

[13] Sleeswyk and Meijer, 'The Water Supply of the *Argo*', 133. The 'Cista Ficoronica' is a bronze water urn from Palestrina (Praeneste) south-east of Rome, dated to the second half of the fourth century BC and of Greco-Etruscan workmanship. It was acquired by the antiquarian Francesco Ficoroni in 1738. It is now in the Villa Giulia museum of Etruscan antiquities in Rome, inv. no. 24787. See T. Dohrn, *Die Ficoronische Ciste in der Villa Giulia in Rom* (Berlin, 1972).

Ficoronica would contain only around 135–50 litres of water and, therefore, they cannot have been the main storage receptacles of *dromons* for water. The inventories did not specify barrels or any other items that might have been. However, a letter from the Cairo Geniza dated to the mid-eleventh century mentioned buckets that contained a 'half a Byzantine barrel'. This is one of the earliest known reference to barrels in Byzantium, but, from it, it is clear that by that period Byzantines were well known to use barrels.[14] How much earlier than this they had been doing so is unclear.

Amphorae were less efficient as water containers and also much heavier as containers in relation to their contents. Their dry weight to capacity ratio was around 1:1.5. Barrels are much more efficient than this. Traditional oak wine barrels weigh between 50 and 65 kg for 225 litres capacity. Their dry weight to capacity ratio is around 1:3.5–4.5.

On bireme *dromons*, both the storage of water and also its weight must have been a problem. Thirteenth-century Sicilian galleys, the earliest for which we have construction details, had only around 50 centimetres freeboard amidships and a tonne of water would sink them by a centimetre or so.[15] No more than a quarter or so of their 40 tonnes of deadweight tonnage could have been used for water because of the weight of the food, armaments, equipment, spare gear and myriad other essentials required. It is extremely improbable that the smaller 25-tonne Byzantine *dromons* could have carried much more than around 5 tonnes of water. Later evidence from Genoa suggests that the larger war galleys of the fourteenth and fifteenth centuries could carry between 4 and 8 tonnes of water,[16] but they had no oarsmen rowing in the hold.

With two files of oarsmen rowing below deck, where could water have been stored? A 245 litre (54 gallon) capacity oak cask has a maximum diameter at its pitch of 28 inches (71 centimetres), a head diameter of 23 inches (58.5 centimetres), a height of 36.5 inches (92.5 centimetres), and would occupy a cylindrical space of around 370 litres.[17] The only place in the hold of a bireme *dromon* that casks such as that could have been stowed would have been on the floor down the centre-line of the ship, and that space would surely have had to have been reserved for the long spare gear that had to be carried: rudders, oars,

---

[14] S. D. Goitein, *A Mediterranean Society: The Jewish Communities of the Arab World as Portrayed in the Documents of the Cairo Geniza*, vol. I: *Economic Foundations* (Berkeley and Los Angeles, 1967), 321. The letter is in the Taylor-Schechter collection of Cambridge University Library, MS TS 12.241. It is written in Judaeo-Arabic, medieval Arabic written in Hebrew script. The relevant lines are recto 6–7, transliterated as follows: '. . . n'ml fy 'l'nbb' b'lnwb' kmsyin dlw w'ldlw 'ldy ystq' bh nṣf bty' rwmy' . . .', translated as '. . . we laboured at bailing by turns of fifty buckets and each bucket that was used for scooping [water] was half a Byzantine barrel [in size] . . .'. Here the Arabic *dlw* meant a 'bucket', *bty'* a barrel', and *rwmy'* 'Roman' or 'Byzantine'.
[15] Pryor, 'From Dromōn to Galea', 112–13.
[16] Pryor, *Geography, Technology, and War*, 77–9.
[17] K. Kilby, *The Cooper and His Trade* (Fresno, 1971), 61.

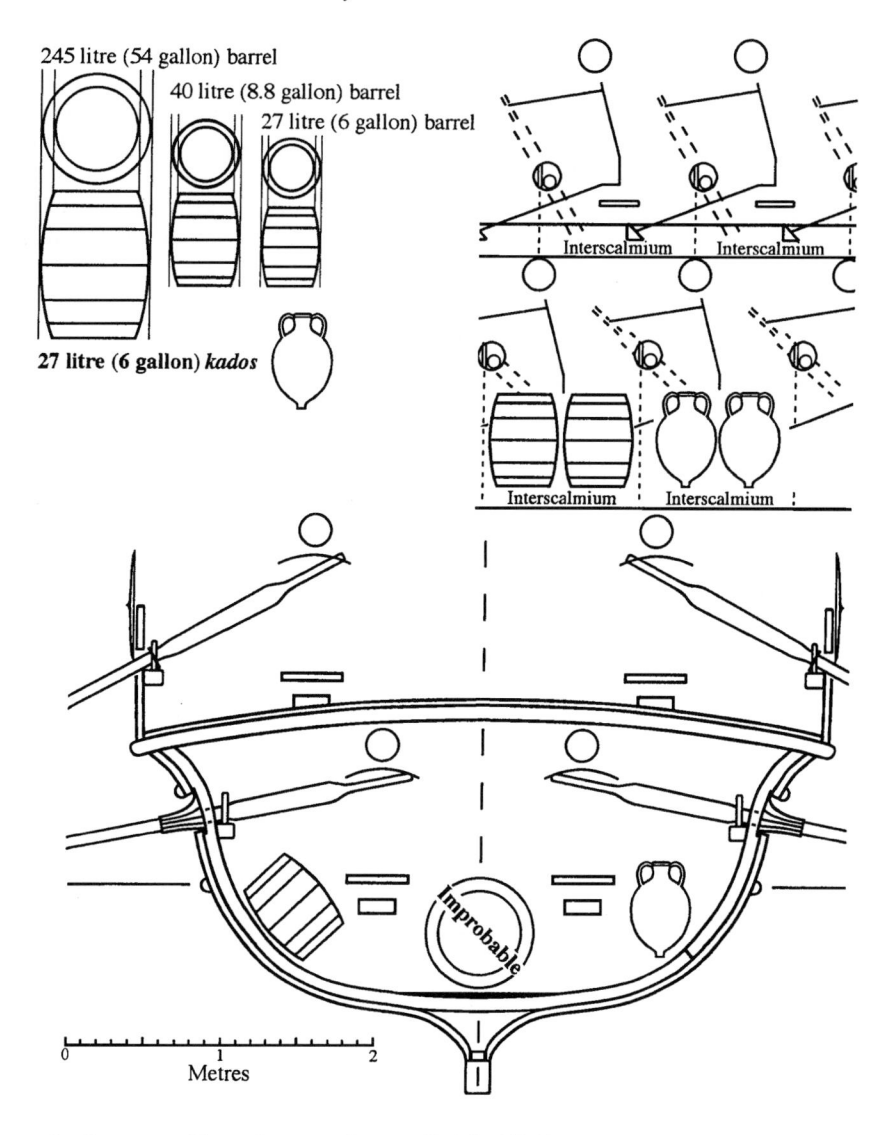

3. Stowage of barrels or amphorae. © John H. Pryor

yards, even masts.[18] Such gear could obviously not have been carried above deck on a warship.

In the case of galleys, such as classical *triēreis* and Byzantine *dromons*, we are forced to conclude that each oarsman carried his own water supply in a *kados* or a small barrel. It is tempting to associate an optimum size for a small

---

[18] Leo VI, Ναυμαχικὰ Λέοντος Βασιλέως, §5 in Dain, *Naumachica*, 19–20.

portable barrel with that of the size of the Genoese *quartarolo* (39.75 litres) or the Neapolitan *barile* (43.625 litres). Barrels much bigger than 40 litres (8.8 gallons) would be too heavy and large to be handled by a single man. Forty litres is also about double the size of a normal bucket and buckets containing more than that and weighing over 20 kg become extremely difficult to manoeuvre. 40 litres would weigh 40 kg (88 lbs), plus around 10 kg (22 lbs) for the weight of the barrel, making a total of 50 kg (110 lbs), and the barrel would measure approximately 35.5 centimetres across the head, 44.5 centimetres at the pitch (circumference of 140 centimetres), and 54.5 centimetres high.[19] A man could not get his arms around anything much bigger than that to lift it in any case.

It would be just possible to stow two 27-litre *kadoi* or two 40-litre barrels alongside the thwarts of the oarsmen of the lower bank between them and the hull, two for each oarsman. Half of the barrels or *kadoi* may well have been stowed similarly above deck for the oarsmen of the upper bank, but obviously they could not have stayed there during battle and there must have been room to stow them below if necessary. Either that, or they were jettisoned before battle.

After reflection, the only logical conclusion to the problem of the water supply of *dromons*, a supply which then governed their cruising range, is that they could stow away around one hundred 40-litre barrels, weighing around 5 tonnes when full, or around one hundred 27-litre amphorae weighing around 4.5 tonnes. This would give a *dromon* a minimum range under oars in summer, using one tonne of water per day, of three days.

The speed that oared ships of all kinds could maintain under oars is a matter of considerable debate. Different scholars have directed their attention to different periods and various types of oared ships and have produced results that are very difficult to reconcile. What one would like, of course, is reliable historical data for voyages made by Byzantine fleets of *dromons* in pressing circumstances in conditions which would suggest that the voyages were made under oars in calm conditions or at worst against light breezes. However, the Byzantine sources contain precious little data and, for the most part, we are compelled to have recourse to that from the sources for classical antiquity and the western Middle Ages and, then, to proceed by analogy. Nevertheless, there is sufficient consistency in the data to suggest that in favourable conditions fleets could maintain around 3–4 knots while at sea. According to his *Life of St Theoktistē of Lesbos*, the narrator, Nikētas Magistros, was told on Paros, by a hermit called Symeon, that from Paros he would sail to Naxos, lie there in harbour for one day, sail for Crete on the second day and reach it on the third.[20] Since, at the time, Nikētas was accompanying the expedition of Himerios to Crete in 910, he was probably on a war galley, a *dromon*, and the voyage predictions read like a reflection of what could normally be accomplished by a *dromon* sailing before the prevailing northerlies of summer south to Crete. Naxos to Chandax

---

[19] Kilby, *The Cooper and His Trade*, 61.
[20] *Acta Sanctorum Novembris*, 4 (Brussels, 1925), 224–33; §13, trans. A. C. Hero in A.-M. Talbot, ed., *Holy Women of Byzantium* (Washington, 1966), 95–116, here 107–8.

(Iráklion) in Crete, via Ios and Thēra is only around 120 nautical miles; easy sailing before the prevailing northerlies of summer in, say, thirty hours at an average speed of around 3.5 knots.

With a figure of that order and an average of around fourteen hours of daylight during summer campaigning seasons, three days' water supply would give Byzantine fleets a range of no more than 170 miles under oars. All things were variable of course. Conditions made all the difference, as also would have using the sails when possible, cool weather, and human endurance, strength, and skill. Fleets could also proceed by night, if out to sea away from coasts and islands, or if the skies were clear and the moon was full, or even if the need was great. But, in normal circumstances, Byzantine fleets would not have ranged much more than around 170 miles without watering. When packed to the gunwales with supernumeraries, as they were for the assaults on Crete, that figure would have to be lowered dramatically.

No wonder that Syrianos Magistros, followed by Nikēphoros Ouranos, recommended that not only a *stratēgos*, but also each and every ship in a fleet should have aboard seamen familiar with the coasts and where fresh water could be obtained. As Nikēphoros wrote:

> It is appropriate for a *stratēgos* to have with him men who have accurate knowledge and experience of the sea in which he is sailing, which winds cause it to swell and which blow from the land. They should know both the hidden rocks in the sea, and the places which have no depth, and the land along which one sails and the islands adjacent to it, the harbours and the distance such harbours are the one from the other. They should know both the countries and the water supplies;[21] for many have perished from lack of experience of the sea and the regions, since winds frequently blow and scatter the ships to one region and another. And it is appropriate that not only the *stratēgos* should have men with this knowledge we have discussed, but also each and every ship should have someone knowing these things to advise well when appropriate.[22]

---

[21] By ὕδατα (*hydata*), Nikēphoros Ouranos and Syrianos Magistros almost certainly meant 'fresh water'. The knowledge required was of where to obtain precious fresh water, rather than knowledge of the 'waters'; i.e. the seas.

[22] Nikēphoros Ouranos, Ἐκ τῶν τακτικῶν Νικηφόρδοῦ Οὐρανοῦ κεφάλαια ριθ´-ρκγ´, §§119.1.1–3, in Dain, *Naumachica*, 93: "Ἁρμόζει τὸν στρατηγὸν ἔχειν μεθ᾽ ἑαυτοῦ τοὺς γινώσκοντας ἀκριβῶς τὴν πεῖραν τῆς θαλάσσης εἰς ἣν πλέει, τὸ ποῖοι ἄνεμοι κυμαίνουσιν αὐτὴν καὶ τὸ ποῖοι φυσῶσιν ἀπὸ τῆς γῆς· ἵνα δὲ γινώσκωσι καὶ τὰς κρυπτομένας πέτρας εἰς τὴν θάλασσαν καὶ τοὺς τόπους τοὺς μὴ ἔχοντας βάθος καὶ τὴν παραπλεομένην γῆν καὶ τὰς παρακειμένας αὐτῇ νήσους, τοὺς λιμένας καὶ τὸ πόσον ἀπέχουσι οἱ τοιοῦτοι λιμένες εἷς ἀπὸ τοῦ ἄλλου ἵνα δὲ γινώσκωσι καὶ τὰ χωρία καὶ τὰ ὕδατα πολλοὶ γὰρ ἐκ τοῦ ἔχειν ἀπειρίαν τῆς θαλάσσης καὶ τῶν τόπων ἀπώλοντο, ἐπειδὴ φυσῶσι πολλάκις ἄνεμοι καὶ σκορπίζουσι τὰ πλοῖα εἰς ἄλλον καὶ ἄλλον τόπον. Καὶ ἁρμόζει ἵνα μὴ μόνον ὁ στρατηὸς ἔχῃ τοὺς γινώσκοντας ὅπερ εἴπαμεν, ἀλλὰ καὶ ἓν ἕκαστον πλοῖον ἵνα ἔχῃ τὸν ταῦτα γινώσκοντα, πρὸς τὸ βουλεύεσθαι καλῶς τὸ συμφέρον.' Cf. Syrianos Magistros, Ναυμαχίαι Συριανοῦ Μαγίστρου, §§5.1–3 in Dain, *Naumachica*, 45–6.

Consider what the problems of water supplies must have really involved. According to the inventories for the expedition of 949 to Crete, the imperial navy was composed of 150 *ousiai*. Not all of these took part in the expedition, since some were deputed for other duties. However, there were definitely 20 *dromons* in the fleet, each carrying 2 *ousiai*. There were also at least 40 *chelandia* of one *ousia* each. For the rest, the figures are arguable, but being exact does not matter here. For the sake of argument, let us postulate 20 *dromons* and 40 *chelandia*, with 80 *ousiai* between them, and halve the water ration for the second *ousia* of the *dromons* on the grounds that both *ousiai* cannot have rowed at once. If they moved under oars, they would require a minimum of 70 tonnes of water per day, 210 tonnes for a three-day supply for the fleet or 280 tonnes for four days.

No rivers anywhere en route were large enough for fleets to sail up them beyond the salt water zone, so that they could water by lowering buckets overboard. Fleets were dependent on ports for water, but, in the tenth century, most of these would have been merely sheltered roadsteads. Developed port facilities were few and far between. Fleets as large as this would have had to anchor offshore or, at best, come in by turns in small numbers to whatever docks existed. Moreover, it is doubtful whether any ports, even Constantinople, had reticulated water supplies fed to any docks that did exist. The earliest known attempt to do this was Genoa's building of an aqueduct along her docks during the thirteenth century. Galleys could be beached; however, to then load tonnes of water onto them would not be such a bright idea in the largely tideless Mediterranean. Water would have to be loaded manually by bucket into *kadoi* or barrels from wells, springs, or streams, and then transported by men, by carts, or by boats to the ships afloat. Admittedly, there were many men in the crews, but that would be useful only if they could pull into a large fresh-water river, and there were very few of those. Only one barrel at a time can be filled from a well. Watering a large fleet in this way must have been a laborious and time-consuming exercise.

In 911 and 960, the final staging port for the last voyage to Crete was Phygela, now Kuşadasi in Turkey. But in 949 the fleet apparently travelled from Mitylēnē to Chios, Samos, Fournoi, Naxos, Ios, Thēra, and Christiana, to Dia opposite Chandax (Iráklion) in Crete. These were small islands, where watering would have to be done from wells or small streams. With portable barrels of 40 litres, watering the 80 *ousiai* of 949 would have needed around 1750 barrel-manlifts per day. A full supply of 210 or 280 tonnes would have needed 5280 or 7000 barrel-manlifts.

Then, there is the problem of wells. How big were well buckets? Again, there would have been an ergonomic optimum. The bigger and heavier the full bucket, the more men needed, or the longer the time taken, to raise it by rope and windlass and empty it. An optimum size for a bucket may have been around 20 litres. A bucket with an internal diameter of 28 centimetres and a height of 32.5 would have a capacity of 19.7 litres and its size seems to be about right. If so, the number of well-lifts required would be double that of the barrel-lifts. How long would 14,000 well-lifts in Samos harbour have taken?

These figures could be varied considerably without affecting the obvious conclusion. Watering large fleets must have been extremely laborious and time-consuming and this helps explain why extended expeditions were regarded as such monumental undertakings. In fact, I believe that we barely begin to comprehend the enormousness of galley warfare in the Middle Ages. During the First Crusade, only the small Genoese fleet attempted the voyage to the East in a single sailing season, and it just barely made it in four months before the onset of winter. The larger Pisan and Venetian fleets left in the autumn, intending to winter en route, despite the considerable expense that would have involved. So also did the large Venetian Crusader fleet of 1122. They apparently did not consider it possible for their fleets to make the voyage in one sailing season. Only that can explain why they were prepared to assume the enormous expense of wintering en route.[23] When horses were also transported, as they were for the Cretan expeditions of 911, 949, and 960–1, the problems must have been exacerbated enormously. Horses consume large amounts of water but cannot load it themselves.[24]

Crews

In spite of the fact that some crews in Byzantine fleets at various times were well regarded, for example the Mardaites of the theme of the Kibyrrhaiōtai, there is little evidence to suggest that, in general, Byzantine seamen were so skilled that this gave Byzantine fleets any edge over their opponents. It is true that Byzantine squadrons managed to defeat the Russians on all occasions when they attacked Constantinople: in 860, probably in 907 under Oleg of Kiev, in 941 under Igor, and in 1043 under Jaroslav. A fleet also defeated the Russians on the Danube in 972. However, rather than being attributable to any qualities of Byzantine seamen, these victories were due to the triple advantages of Greek Fire, *dromons* and *chelandia* being much larger than the Norse river boats of the Russians, and (except in 972) being able to fight in home waters against an enemy far from home. The last is true also of the defeat of the Muslim assaults on Constantinople in 674–80 and in 717–18. In both cases, it was the advantage of home waters against the disadvantage of campaigning hundreds of miles from sources of supplies, the problems faced by the Muslims of surviving on campaign through the winter, and Greek Fire that proved decisive. The same is probably true of the victories over the fleets of Thomas the Slav in 822–3.

---

[23] See J. H. Pryor, ' "Water, water everywhere, Nor any drop to drink": Water Supplies for the Fleets of the First Crusade', in *Dei Gesta per Francos: études sur les croisades dédiés à Jean Richard* (Aldershot, 2001), 21–8. This does leave unexplained, of course, how the Byzantines managed to send a massive fleet to Vandal Africa under Belisarios in 533, including horse transports, and then to do it again in 697 with a fleet of unknown size under John the Patrician, sent to recover the province from the Muslims.

[24] Limitations of space preclude further consideration of the transport of horses here. The issue is addressed at length in *The Byzantine Navy*.

In general, the record of Byzantine fleets from the seventh to the tenth centuries was hardly impressive.[25] To be sure, they did achieve some notable victories: the defeat of the Tunisians off Syracuse in 827–8, the defeat of a Muslim fleet under Abū Dīnār off Cape Chelidonia in 842, the victory of Nikētas Ooryphas over the Cretans in the Gulf of Corinth in 879 and of Nasar over the Tunisians off Punta Stilo in 880, the victory of Himerios on the day of St Thomas (6 October), probably in 905, the defeat of Leo of Tripoli off Lemnos in 921–2, the victory of Basil Hexamilitēs over the fleet of Tarsos in 956, and the defeat of an Egyptian squadron off Cyprus in 963. Against that record, however, have to be balanced many disastrous defeats: of Constans II at the battle of the masts off Phoenix in 655, of Theophilos, the *stratēgos* of the Kibyrrhaiōtai, off Attaleia in 790, a defeat off Thasos in 839, the defeat of Constantine Condomytēs off Syracuse in 859, the annihilation of a fleet off Milazzo in 888, a defeat off Messina in 901, the disastrous defeat of Himerios north of Chios in 911, the defeat of a Byzantine expedition in the Straits of Messina in 965, and of fleets off Tripoli in 975 and 998.

Although the tide of Byzantine naval success ebbed and flowed over the centuries, as other circumstances dictated, nothing suggests that the quality of the Empire's seamen was in any way decisive. Indeed, there are occasional pieces of evidence that suggest that all was not always happy in the fleets. Some time between 823 and 825, John Echimos, the 'deputy governor', ἐκ προσώπου (*ek prosōpou*), the acting *stratēgos*, of the theme of the Kibyrrhaiōtai, confiscated the properties of seamen of the fleet. After he had become a monk and taken the name Antony, later to become St Antony the Younger, he was interrogated as to his reasons for doing so on the orders of the new emperor, Theophilos (829–42). According to the author of his *Life*, his explanation was that they had been partisans of Thomas the Slav in his rebellion of 821–3 and were 'hostile to Christians', thus implying that they were iconoclasts, and that he had confiscated their property and given it to supporters of Theophilos' father, Michael II (820–9). In spite of this explanation, the emperor initially imprisoned him and had him interrogated, suggesting that there was more to the story and that he rejected the explanation.[26] The fleet of the Kibyrrhaiōtai had, indeed, joined Thomas the Slav, as it was also later to join the rebellions of Bardas Sklēros in 976–9 and Bardas Phōkas in 987–9, and it is clear that, at times, there must have been serious disaffection in what was the front-line fleet of the Empire in the ninth and tenth centuries.

In 880, the expedition sent under the command of Nasar, the *droungarios tou*

---

[25] It is obviously not possible to be exhaustive here. What follows is intended to be a limited, but balanced, representative example of the more important Byzantine victories and defeats in fleet engagements.
[26] Anonymous, Βίος καὶ πολιτεία τῦ ὁσίου Ἀντωνίου τοῦ Νέου ('Life and Conduct of the Holy Antony the Younger'), ed. A. Papadopoulos-Kerameus, in Συλλογὴ Παλαιστίνης καὶ Συριακῆς ἁγιολογίας, Православный Палестинскій сборникъ, 19.3 (St Petersburg, 1907), 186–216, here 209.

ploimou, to counter an attack in the Ionian sea by a Muslim fleet from Tunisia was forced to a temporary halt at Methōnē by the desertion of a large part of the crews.[27] Why they deserted is unknown, but we can be fairly sure that it was not a simple question of their having 'lost their nerve', as the *Vita Basilii* suggested.

Tactics and Strategies

Since the chronicles and other sources are devoid of all but the most spare and sketchy descriptions of battles, we are primarily dependent on the *Naumachika* of Leo VI and its paraphrase by Nikēphoros Ouranos for our knowledge of tactics and strategies.

It is clear that, by the heyday of the *dromon*, naval tactics and strategies were very different from what they had been during the age of the *triērēs*. Reduced to a fundamental, these differences can be attributed to the disappearance of the only 'ship-killing' weapon ever known before the invention of explosive projectiles: the waterline ram. For all its potency in some circumstances, Greek Fire was never the ship-killer that the ram had been and no system of battle tactics was ever built around it.[28] The weapon was obviously effective in certain circumstances, but there are many uncertainties about what those circumstances were. Byzantine chroniclers frequently attributed fleet victories to the use of Greek Fire; however, they rarely mentioned its use when fleets were defeated, even though it is obvious that it must have been used unsuccessfully on many such occasions. The spur, which had replaced the waterline ram by the sixth century, was not designed to puncture a hull and sink a ship, but rather to destroy its motive power by smashing its oars. No other weapons, neither projectiles nor any other, now had ship-killing capabilities. Battle tactics, therefore, had to change. Objectives changed from attempts to deliver a 'knock-out' blow to degrading attrition. Rather than manoeuvring to obtain a position to ram and sink, tactics became to degrade an enemy ship's ability to resist, so that it could be boarded and captured. The preliminary phases of battle, therefore, became extensive exchanges of missiles of various types.

Naval warfare became more unpredictable than ever. No longer could any power hope to have such an advantage in weaponry or in the skill of crews that success could be expected. Weaponry and skill could still make a difference, of course, but rarely a decisive one. More often than not, victory or defeat became a matter of circumstances, admiralship, and numbers. To commit to battle was to risk the unpredictable fortunes of war and really decisive victories were hard to achieve in any case. A victor could rarely prevent large sections of defeated

---

[27] Theophanēs Continuatus, V.62 (302–3).
[28] To characterise Greek Fire as comparable to 'the atomic bomb in our own day', as did Ellis Davidson, is grossly misleading. See H. R. Ellis Davidson, 'The Secret Weapon of Byzantium', *Byzantinische Zeitschrift*, 66 (1973), 61–74, here 61.

fleets escaping the 'field' of battle and the Mediterranean powers could replace ships and crews remarkably quickly in any case.

Expeditionary objectives could frequently be achieved best by preserving one's forces intact and actually avoiding battle, since naval warfare was essentially amphibious warfare whose purpose was to secure control of terrestrial objectives rather than to attempt to control maritime space. The latter was an unrealistic and vain hope given the limitations of medieval naval technology with respect to the vast expanses of the sea.

With foremast masthead height 10.65 metres above sea level, the theoretical horizon of a lookout at the masthead of a *dromon* would be only around 11.8 kilometres. Theoretically, the head of a sail 21 metres above sea level could be seen a further 51.7 kilometres away, but, of course, no man could see 63.5 kilometres away with unaided sight. In all probability, around 15–20 kilometres would have been the limit of visibility from the masthead of a *dromon*.[29] Scout ships could not, therefore, patrol a space more than 30–40 kilometres in advance of a fleet and probably no more than 30, since they were smaller than battle *dromon*s and would have had lower mastheads. In fact, in order to be able to actually read signals with unaided eyesight and communicate them back to the fleet, the distances must have been much less than this. Syrianos Magistros advised that a fleet should always proceed with scout ships out ahead, up to 6 *milia* or so. Two scout ships should be 6 *milia* ahead and another two should be between them and the fleet to relay any messages.[30] 6 *milia* was only around 8 kilometres. If the forward scouts then had a range of visibility of another 8–16 kilometres, then the real maritime space that could be 'controlled' had a radius of only around 25 kilometres at best.

Moreover, even if scouts descried an enemy fleet 25 kilometres away from a fleet, it would take hours for the fleets to come to engagement, even if they both cooperated and sailed at full speed to engage. If the weather conditions were favourable for one fleet, they would almost invariably be unfavourable for the other. If either fleet sought to avoid engagement, they could never be forced to do so unless trapped somehow.

Even narrows, such as the Straits of Otranto, are approximately 110 kilometres wide and the entrance to the Aegean between Crete and Rhodes is approximately 180 kilometres wide, although Karpathos does straddle the gap. No medieval power could ever hope to control ingress and egress through such maritime spaces, contrary to the nonsense often written about such matters. Galleys which were incapable of staying at sea in heavy weather and which had limited water supplies and cruising ranges, which lacked any weapon capable of

---

[29] From the masthead of *Olympias*, which is approximately 11.5 metres above sea level, the horizon is 11.25 kilometres distant. A man can just see the deck of a similar low-hulled ship at a range of 16.1 kilometres. See J. Coates, in J. S. Morrison, *Greek and Roman Oared Warships, 399–31 BC* (Oxford, 1996), 258. No data are given for the visibility of sails over the horizon.

[30] Syrianos Magistros, Ναυμαχίαι, §§6.1–3 in Dain, *Naumachica*, 46.

quickly destroying enemy ships, and whose performance capabilities were inadequate to force an enemy to engage if he did not wish to do so, could never control maritime space. In such circumstances, naval forces could rarely be more than an adjunct to land forces, sea power to land power.

Byzantine naval forces were always very secondary to the land armies and the use of sea power was merely an adjunct to that of the land. By themselves, they rarely achieved very much. The reconquest of Crete in 960–1 was an exception to the rule, but that followed at least four failed previous attempts. The history of the Empire reveals that most naval expeditions accompanied terrestrial expeditions. Naval forces ferried land forces and protected their maritime flanks and supply lines. Most naval engagements occurred in these circumstances, rather than in those of opposing fleets seeking each other out. Control of the land meant control of the sea, because control of the land carried with it both control of the refuges to which all galley fleets had to have recourse in inclement weather and also control of the water supplies, without which no naval forces could operate for more than a few days. It also helps to explain the extensive record of fleets lost when caught at sea in inclement weather off coasts that were either geographically or humanly hostile. Reading the record of Byzantine and also Muslim fleets destroyed at sea by storms, and contemplating the horrific loss of human life involved, gives a sobering perspective on the essential futility of naval warfare in the Byzantine-Muslim period. Rarely did naval victories lead to long-term or extensive political gains.

Caution became the first priority. Syrianos Magistros advised that a *stratēgos*, an admiral, should always have good intelligence of the enemy, that he should engage the enemy only if he had superior numbers and not even if the forces were equal, unless the enemy forced the engagement, and that one should not engage at all unless the enemy posed a danger. Nikēphoros Ouranos later repeated some of these recommendations.[31] Leo VI advised planning attacks with forethought, being wary of committing to general engagements, only doing so when confident of superiority over the enemy. He cautioned against becoming overconfident.[32] The first priority of a *stratēgos* was to preserve his own forces intact and then to search for any opportunity or strategy that would enable him to attack the enemy with the least risk to his own forces. Thus, Leo VI recommended giving battle in waters of one's choice off enemy coasts and laying ambushes.[33] The recommendation to engage off enemy coasts so that

---

[31] See Syrianos Magistros, Ναυμαχίαι, §§6.1–3, 9.8, 9.10–11, 9.14 in Dain, *Naumachica*, 46, 49, 50; Nikēphoros Ouranos, Περὶ Θαλασσομαχίας, §§38, 51, ibid., 79–80, 82.

[32] See Leo VI, Ναυμαχικὰ Λέοντος Βασιλέως, §§17, 36–7, 40, 75–6 in Dain, *Naumachica*, 22, 25–6, 32; Cf. Nikēphoros Ouranos, Περὶ Θαλασσομαχίας, §§15, 34–6, 67–8, ibid., 75, 79, 96; Anonymous, §3.1, ibid., 66.

[33] See Leo VI, Ναυμαχικὰ, §§40, 53 in Dain, *Naumachica*, 26, 28; Cf. Nikēphoros Ouranos, Περὶ Θαλασσομαχίας, §§38, 51, ibid., 79–80, 82. Note that in §40, even though he was following Syrianos Magistros quite closely at this point, Leo VI actually reversed the advice of Syrianos, who had advised setting up a battle close to shore if off one's own territory so that there would be a refuge if defeated, and out to sea if off enemy territory. See Syrianos

enemy crews would not fight to the death but would seek safety in flight confirms the fact that almost all medieval galley warfare was coastal. Both Syrianos Magistros and Nikēphoros Ouranos also made that perfectly clear.

Appreciation of the fact that all medieval naval warfare was essentially coastal and amphibious warfare is important, since many of the recommended strategies and tactics were devised in that context. 'Ambushes', for example, are easily comprehensible in coastal warfare. Reserve squadrons might be hidden behind islands or promontories. They are more difficult to envisage on the high seas. How could one hide reserve squadrons on the high seas, except behind fog banks which are unusual in the Mediterranean, or if one came out of the sun catching the enemy with the sun in his eyes? It should be added, however, that to do so was indeed a favourite tactic.[34]

In the approach to battle it was essential to draw up a fleet in formation. Syrianos Magistros emphasised the importance of this and discussed how the commander should maintain the formation.[35] A disorganised fleet dared not engage, because its ships would be unable to lend support to each other and would be overwhelmed. This was the cardinal sin that Constans II committed in 655, when he went into battle off Phoenix without bringing his fleet into formation and was annihilated, barely escaping with his life.[36] In 904, the *droungarios tou ploimou*, Eustathios Argyros, had to break off his attack on the fleet of Leo of Tripoli, because he had not been able 'to draw up in a counter-formation', ἀντιτάξασθαι (*antitaxasthai*), his own fleet.[37] Leo then went on to sack Thessalonikē. The reverse occurred in 956 or 957, when Basil Hexamilitēs, the *stratēgos* of the Kibyrrhaiōtai, successfully beat back a fleet from Tarsos larger than his own because he managed to form his own fleet into a counter-formation, ἀντιπαράταξις (*antiparataxis*), before engagement.[38] One of the classic battle tactics was to disorganise an enemy's formation by feigning flight until the enemy ships in pursuit became strung out and then either to send in fresh

---

Magistros, Ναυμαχίαι, §§9.42–4 in Dain, *Naumachica*, 55. The emperor seems to have been influenced by another sentence of Syrianos which said that off foreign territory ships positioned at the sea end of a line would be most likely to desert while off one's own territory it would be those at the landward end. Ibid., §9.23 in Dain, *Naumachica*, 52.

[34] Roger of Lauria did so at the Battle of the Gulf of Naples on 5 June 1284. See J. H. Pryor, 'The Naval Battles of Roger of Lauria', *Journal of Medieval History*, 9 (1983), 179–216, 192.

[35] Syrianos Magistros, Ναυμαχίαι, §§9.4–7 in Dain, *Naumachica*, 48–9.

[36] Theophanēs the Confessor, *Theophanis Chronographia, Annus Mundi 6146*, vol. I, 346: 'τοῦ δὲ βασιλέως μηδὲν ποιησαμένου πρὸς παράταξιν ναυμαχίας'. On the battle see V. Christides, 'The Naval Engagement of Dhāt aṣ-Sawārī AH 34 / AD 655–6: A Classical Example of Naval Warfare Incompetence', *Byzantina*, 13 (1985), 1329–45.

[37] Theophanes Continuatus, V.20 (366–7): 'ἀποστέλλει οὖν ὁ βασιλεὺς τὸν Εὐστάθιον τὸν τηνικαῦτα δρουγγάριον μετὰ στόλου κατὰ τοῦ Τριπολίτου ὃς μὴ δυνηθεὶς ἀντιτάξασθαι τούτῳ ἀντεστράφη κενός'.

[38] Theophanes Continuatus, VI. Αὐτοκρατορία Κωνσταντίνου. 29 (453).

reinforcements against the disorganised enemy or to turn around in formation and overwhelm the disorganised enemy ships one by one.[39]

According to Leo VI, the standard formation was the line abreast in a shallow, crescent-moon semi-circle, with the flagship at the centre of the line in its 'deep', and the stronger and larger *dromons* at the ends of the line. This was also supposedly the best formation for making a fighting retreat by backing water.[40] The objective was to overwhelm the end of an enemy line, so that the galleys at the end of one's own line could turn in on the exposed flanks of the enemy galleys and attack them where they were most vulnerable, at their sides. Other formations may also have been used in various circumstances: a straight line, or several lines or squadrons, some of which could attack from the flanks or the rear once the enemy was engaged by the main formation.[41] This latter would seem to have been dependent upon having an overwhelming superiority in numbers. As Leo VI himself said, in what must be something of a classic understatement, the same was true of the tactic to disengage a formation that had fought the enemy to a standstill and then to send in reinforcements.[42]

For lack of any ship-killing weapon, it is highly improbable in fact that any tactical manoeuvres whatsoever could prove decisive. By the tenth century, naval battles became a matter of approach in formation, attempts to hold formation above all costs in order to protect the vulnerable sides and sterns of the ships, and then an initial phase of engagement characterised by extensive exchanges of missiles at a distance designed to degrade the enemy's manpower. This continued to be the case into the High Middle Ages throughout the Mediterranean.[43] That was why *dromons* had a forecastle, a 'false floor', ψευδοπάτιον (*pseudopation*), above the Greek Fire tube, σίφων (*siphōn*), at the prow, from which marines could hurl missiles against an enemy ship.[44]

Such missiles included the same 'processed' fire material for Greek Fire as used in the *siphōnes* but hurled by catapult, either in pottery jars or in the form of caltrops wrapped round with tow and soaked in it.[45] There can be no doubt that the former at least were used because examples survive.[46] Quite probably

---

[39] See Leo VI, Ναυμαχικά, §§54, 56 in Dain, *Naumachica*, 29; Nikēphoros Ouranos, Περὶ Θαλασσομαχίας, §§52–3, ibid., 82–3.

[40] See Leo VI, Ναυμαχικά, §§2, 28, 42, 49, 50, 79 in Dain, *Naumachica*, 19, 24, 27, 28, 33; Leo VI, 'Ἐκ τοῦ κυροῦ Λέοντος τοῦ Βασιλέως §2, ibid., 38; Nikēphoros Ouranos, Περὶ Θαλασσομαχίας, §§26, 32, 47, 48, 71, ibid., 77, 78–9, 82, 87.

[41] See Leo VI, Ναυμαχικά, §§51, 52 in Dain, Naumachica, 28; Nikēphoros Ouranos, Περὶ Θαλασσομαχίας, §§49, 50, ibid., 82.

[42] See Leo VI, Ναυμαχικά, §55 in Dain, Naumachica, 29; Nikēphoros Ouranos, Περὶ Θαλασσομαχίας, §52, ibid., 82–3.

[43] See, for example, Pryor, 'Naval Battles of Roger of Lauria', 179, 186–7, 207. See also Alexandres, Ἡ θαλασσία δύναμις εἰς τὴν ἱστορίαν τῆς βυζαντινῆς αὐτοκρατορίας, 62.

[44] See Leo VI, Ναυμαχικά, §6 in Dain, *Naumachica*, 20; Nikēphoros Ouranos, Περὶ Θαλασσομαχίας, §5, ibid., 72.

[45] See Leo VI, Ναυμαχικά, §§64, 66 in Dain, *Naumachica*, 30; Nikēphoros Ouranos, Περὶ Θαλασσομαχίας, §60, ibid., 84.

[46] See V. Christides, 'New Light on Navigation and Naval Warfare in the Eastern

the jars of unslaked lime mentioned by Leo VI were also used, but one may have one's doubts about the practicality of the suggestion of jars full of poisonous reptiles.[47] From his tone, even the emperor seems to have had doubts about that one. However, the most effective missiles, and those which formed the bulk of those exchanged, were rocks, ordinary caltrops, arrows from bows, the small arrows or bolts known as 'flies' or 'mice' shot by the bow-ballistae, and then javelins when closed up somewhat more.[48] The large numbers of such missiles mentioned in the inventories for the Cretan expeditions, and the absence from these of the more 'exotic' projectiles, prove that this was so: in particular, 10,000 caltrops, 50 bows and 10,000 arrows, 20 hand-bow-ballistae and 200 'mice', and 100 javelins per *dromon*.[49]

The great importance of proper management of the preliminary missile phase was indicated by the emperor's insistence on using them effectively, not wasting them against an enemy protected by shields, and ensuring both that supplies were not exhausted and that crews did not exhaust themselves in hurling them.[50] He appears to have appreciated that battles were not won in missile phases. These might influence the outcome but hand-to-hand combat decided it.

In the final phase of battle, the opposing ships grappled. The words used by the *Anonymous*, Leo VI, and Nikēphoros Ouranos to describe this phase were δεσμός (*desmos*), a bond, and δεσμεῖν (*desmein*), to bond or fetter, both connected to δεσμεύειν (*desmeyein*), to bind or fetter or tie together. 'Couple' and 'to couple' are perhaps the closest English translation of what was intended. When it was apparent that the crew of an enemy ship was sufficiently degraded to make boarding and capturing a realistic possibility, iron rods, καμάκες σίδηραι (*kamakes sidērai*), no doubt with grappling hooks at both ends, were used to grapple with it and couple it so that it could not escape. The tactic used in defence against enemy ships trying to grapple and couple in the same way was to keep the ships apart by using even longer poles: ἀκόντια (*akontia*) or κοντάρια (*kontaria*).[51] Coupling and preventing coupling were apparently procedures that required considerable practice and exercise, to judge from Leo

---

Mediterranean, the Red Sea and the Indian Ocean (6th–14th centuries AD)', *Nubica*, III/1 (1994), 3–42, here 19–25.

[47] See Leo VI, Ναυμαχικὰ, §§60–2 in Dain, *Naumachica*, 30; Nikēphoros Ouranos, Περὶ Θαλασσομαχίας, §57–8, ibid., 83–4. Or did the emperor have a recollection of the report of John Malalas that the asp that killed Cleopatra was one of those that she carried in her ships for purposes of battle? See John Malalas, *The Chronicle of John Malalas: A Translation*, trans. E. Jeffreys et al. (Melbourne, 1986), 116.

[48] See Leo VI, Ναυμαχικὰ, §§14, 60, 63 in Dain *Naumachica*, 21–2, 30; Nikēphoros Ouranos, Περὶ Θαλασσομαχίας, §§12, 57, 59, ibid., 74, 83–4.

[49] Constantine VII, *De Cerimoniis*, vol. I, 669–70; Haldon, 'Theory and Practice', 224–5.

[50] See Leo VI, Ναυμαχικὰ, §§15–17 in Dain, *Naumachica*, 22; Nikēphoros Ouranos, Περὶ Θαλασσομαχίας, §§13–15, ibid., 75.

[51] See Leo VI, Ναυμαχικὰ, §§68, 69, esp. 28 in Dain, *Naumachica*, 24, 30–1; Nikēphoros Ouranos, Περὶ Θαλασσομαχίας, §§61, 62, esp. 26, ibid., 77, 84–5. Cf. *Anonymous*, §5.2, ibid., 76.

VI's insistence on the point and his words of warning that the procedure was not always advantageous.[52]

From this point, the fully armed marines on the upper oar banks of the *dromons* came into play.[53] During the missile phase, they were almost certainly stationed on those parts of the decks called by the *Anonymous* (by analogy with the half-decks of *triēreis*) καταστρώματα (*katastrōmata*), along the sides behind their shields slung on what he called the 'pavesade', καστέλλωμα (*kastellōma*); although, neither of these were words used by Leo VI and Nikēphoros Ouranos. At this point, fights must have degenerated into hand-to-hand mêlées The only potentially decisive weapons left at this point were the 'cranes', called γερανία (*gerania*), which, if we can believe Leo VI, could pour Greek Fire already alight onto the deck of an enemy ship coupled alongside, and the rocks or iron weights hurled from the castles in attempts to smash the deck and ultimately the hull of the enemy ship.[54] However, there must be reservations about the practicality of both of these suggestions of the emperor. Both sinking and especially setting fire to an enemy ship coupled alongside would pose obvious dangers to one's own ship.

Conclusion: the Navy in the Byzantine Polity

It is no accident that only two Byzantine 'admirals' ever became emperor: Apsimaros (Tiberios II, 698–705), who had been *droungarios* of the Kibyrrhaiōtai, and Rōmanos I Lekapēnos (919–44), who had been *droungarios tou ploimou*. Nor is it an accident that only once did an emperor take command of the navy as a whole and attempt to seek out and destroy an entire enemy fleet: Constans II at the Battle of the Masts in 655.[55] As opposed to this, emperors took command of land armies on many occasions. The secondary character of the fleets in the Byzantine polity is reflected in the rank accorded to their commanders in the various lists of precedence compiled in the ninth and tenth centuries. In the *Taktikon Uspenskij*, composed around 842–3, the *droungarios tou ploimou* of the imperial fleet in Constantinople ranked only in eighty-fourth position among the officers of state and the *stratēgos* of the Kibyrrhaiōtai, although ranked twenty-fifth overall, ranked only eleventh among the eighteen *stratēgoi* of the themes. In the *klētorologion* of Philotheos of 899, he ranked thirty-eighth out of sixty and the *stratēgos* of the Kibyrrhaiōtai, although ranked

---

[52] See Leo VI, Ναυμαχικὰ, §§28, 37, 69 in Dain, *Naumachica*, 24, 25–6, 31; Nikēphoros Ouranos, Περὶ Θαλασσομαχίας, §§26, 35, 62, ibid., 77, 79, 84–5. Cf. *Anonymous*, §5.2, ibid., 76

[53] See Leo VI, Ναυμαχικὰ, §§9, 14, 20, 74 in Dain, *Naumachica*, 21–2, 23, 32; Nikēphoros Ouranos, Περὶ Θαλασσομαχίας, §§8, 12, 18, 66, ibid., 73, 76, 86. Cf. *Anonymous*, §§2.7, 5. pr., 5.1, ibid., 65, 67.

[54] See Leo VI, Ναυμαχικὰ, §§7, 68 in Dain, *Naumachica*, 20, 30–1; Nikēphoros Ouranos, Περὶ Θαλασσομαχίας, §§6, 61, ibid., 72, 84.

[55] See Christides, 'The Naval Engagement of Dhāt aṣ-Sawārī'.

twenty-first overall, was only the fifteenth of twenty-five *stratēgoi* of the themes. The other two *stratēgoi* of naval themes, those of Samos and of the Aegean Sea, were third and fourth-last among the *stratēgoi*, ranking only above those of far-off Dalmatia and Chersōn. In the *Taktikon Beneševič* of 934–44, the *stratēgos* of the Kibyrrhaiōtai was only the twenty-first of thirty-two *stratēgoi* and those of the Aegean Sea and Samos were fourth and fifth-last respectively. The *droungarios tou ploimou* ranked a further seventeen places below the *stratēgos* of the Aegean Sea. By the time of the *Taktikon* of the Escorial (971–5), the *stratēgoi* of the Kibyrrhaiōtai, Samos, and the Aegean Sea ranked fifty-fifth, sixty-seventh, and sixty-eighth respectively, with the *droungarios tou ploimou* in a miserable hundred and thirtieth position, below even such essential dignitaries as the palace doorkeepers, ὀστιάριοι (*ostiarioi*).[56]

That Mahanian theory of naval warfare is not applicable to the centuries of galley warfare in the Mediterranean has now become a commonplace of maritime history.[57] Nevertheless, the parameters of just how inapplicable it is have still to be mapped out fully. In the case of the Byzantine Empire, it is perfectly clear that the limitations of the technology of shipping and armaments from the sixth to eleventh centuries meant that the defence of the Empire could never rest on wooden walls. The authorities realised this perfectly clearly and that is why the fleets always remained greatly inferior to the armies in the polity of the Empire. It had nothing to do with such cultural factors as Byzantine conservatism or dislike of the sea, as has sometimes been asserted. The fleets were never able to control maritime space or to maintain maritime frontiers. They could never prevent large scale incursions by Muslim and even Russian fleets into Byzantine home waters. They could never even control corsairs operating in the Aegean. The fleets were important in so far as they were an adjunct to land armies that they ferried or operated in conjunction with, but it was the latter on which the defence and advance of the Empire rested.

---

[56] See N. Oikonomides, *Les Listes de préséance byzantines des IXe et Xe siècles* (Paris, 1972), 57, 102–4, 246, 264–8.
[57] See in particular J. F. Guilmartin, *Gunpowder and Galleys: Changing Technology and Mediterranean Warfare at Sea in the Sixteenth Century* (Cambridge, 1975); Pryor, *Geography, Technology, and War*.

IBERIAN NAVAL POWER, 1000–1650

Lawrence V. Mott

AT the beginning of the eleventh century, one would have assumed the future naval power of the Iberian Peninsula would be the Caliphate of Cordoba. The Christian kingdoms of Castile, Aragon and the counties of Catalonia, were small entities restricted to the northern portion of the peninsula, while the kingdom of Portugal did not yet exist. The Caliphate of Cordoba on the other hand had a highly developed naval organisation, due in large part to the Viking raids of 844. In that year a fleet of approximately a hundred longships attacked and sacked Lisbon, Seville, Cadiz, Medina Sidonia, and Algeciras. They were eventually driven off, but the raids had made an impact on the Muslim government. The response was to establish permanent arsenals and squadrons at the coastal cities along with a series of coastal watchtowers. When the Vikings returned in 859 they found the Caliphate to be a much tougher opponent and, though able to sack Algeciras, they suffered a series of defeats that discouraged them from ever returning in force.

By 1000 a sophisticated naval administration had developed in the caliphate headed by the *amir al-bahr*, who was responsible for the administration of the port squadrons and the arsenals. As such the admiral was responsible for the security of the entire coastline. The breakup of the caliphate in 1002 saw the office of the *amir al-bahr* disappear, although it would reappear under the later Muslim administrations of the Almoravids and the following Almohads. This administration would be absorbed when Castile finally captured Seville in 1248 and would form the basis for its naval administration.

Compared to this centralised approach to naval warfare, the Christian kingdoms relied on a rather *ad hoc* system in which the defence of the northern coast was left to local ports. Part of the reason for this was that Castile and Aragon were occupied with expanding their kingdoms southward on the peninsula. However, by the twelfth century both kingdoms were beginning to augment their naval presence primarily in a response to their growing maritime commerce and the problem of endemic piracy. The line between piracy and commerce was often blurred and merchants often preferred to use galleys, which could quickly switch to an offensive posture when a target of opportunity presented itself.

Whereas the use of the galley for commerce and warfare had a long history in the Mediterranean, it was also the preferred warship in the Bay of Biscay at this time. In 1120 the bishop of Santiago de Compostella hired a Genoese shipwright to build two bireme galleys at the local arsenal to combat Muslim pirates.[1] Muslim pirates operating on the north coast were a continuing problem in the tenth and eleventh centuries, but this was somewhat diminished by the establishment of the kingdom of Portugal and the fall of their base at Lisbon in 1147. The galley would remain the preferred warship in the Atlantic well into the fourteenth century. The most common warship in the major battles fought between Castile and Portugal in the thirteenth and fourteenth centuries was the galley, though by the thirteenth century the northern ports of Galicia and the Basque region were beginning to use armed keels, clinker-built ships based on Viking construction techniques. While primarily a merchant vessel, a keel could be quickly transformed into a warship with the addition of light castles fore and aft. In the siege of Seville in 1248 these northern vessels were used to blockade the Guadalquivir River to prevent Muslim vessels from relieving the city.

The twelfth century saw the expansion of the naval power of Castile, Aragon and Portugal, but these nascent naval powers were not dominant in any sense. Aragon was rapidly expanding its maritime presence in the Mediterranean following its merging with Catalonia in 1137. In an attempt to stamp out the endemic piracy emanating from the Balearic Islands, the count of Barcelona enlisted the help of Pisa in an expedition against the islands. Likewise the short-lived conquest of Almería in 1147 by a combined force from Castile and Aragon relied heavily on Genoese ships.[2] The Portuguese, while having some success at sea against Muslim forces, still did not have a fleet sufficient to threaten them effectively. In 1182 the Portuguese attacked Ceuta with twenty-one galleys, but were overwhelmed by a defending Muslim fleet of fifty-four vessels.[3] All of these states were relying heavily on private vessels for naval operations. While for specific undertakings the monarchies might build some vessels, none of them maintained a royal fleet. In large part this was due to the fact that the states had not consolidated their territories or authority, nor had they the fiscal mechanisms to maintain a permanent fleet.

The thirteenth century would see a number of profound changes in how naval warfare was conducted and organised. Much of the change was brought about by the consolidation of the territorial boundaries of Portugal, Castile and Aragon by the mid-thirteenth century. By 1251 Alfonso III of Portugal had expelled the Muslims from the Algarve, while Castile had captured Seville in 1248 and the mouth of the Guadalquivir River. The result of this expansion was that Castile found itself in possession of two significant coastlines separated by the sometimes hostile kingdom of Portugal. Aragon had expanded rapidly also, first by capturing Mallorca in 1229 and then by the complete conquest of Valencia in 1245. By 1250 the Crown of Aragon controlled the eastern seaboard

---

[1] Cesáreo Fernández Duro, *La marina de Castilla* (Madrid, 1995), 20.
[2] Antonio de Capmany y de Monpalau, *Memorias históricas sobre la marina, comercio y artes de la antigua ciudad de Barcelona* (Barcelona, 1961), vol. I, 30–1.
[3] Armando Da Silva Saturnino Montiero, *Batalhas e combates da marinha portuguesa, 1139–1521* (Lisbon, 1989), 16.

of the Iberian Peninsula as well as the strategic island of Mallorca. The rapid expansion of all the kingdoms and decreasing open territory also meant that they would soon be involved in naval operations against each other as well as against the Muslims. By the second half of the thirteenth century these monarchies began to solidify their power and authority with attempts to regulate maritime trade and to control and monopolise maritime violence along their coasts. It is no coincidence then that the first state naval organisations began to appear at this time and while they had much in common, they also differed substantially. In a sense, the problems with financing and political authority encountered by these nascent organisations were precursors of the difficulties that would bedevil the Spanish monarchy in the sixteenth and seventeenth centuries.

Aragon by the second half of the thirteenth century had expanded its interests to North Africa, and in doing so had come into direct conflict with Angevin pretensions for control of the Mediterranean. When the Aragonese invaded and captured Sicily in 1282 they obtained a strategic location and, more importantly, absorbed a naval administration dating back to the Norman period. For a period of thirteen years Aragon was able to operate a permanent royal fleet on a year-round basis. The reason this was sustainable was that the Crown of Aragon was able to establish a centralised naval organisation under the control of the office of the admiral. The old Norman and Hohenstaufen administrations provided an organisation and network of arsenals capable of maintaining a fleet. More importantly, Sicily had an established system of taxes for supporting the fleet so that the crown did not have rely on Iberian sources for funding, which would have been problematic at best.[4] The result was that, until the Aragonese left Sicily by treaty in 1295, the Catalan-Aragonese fleet was one of the most effective naval units in the Mediterranean.

The Crown of Aragon also had the additional asset of an established maritime community in Catalonia that designed and built warships for the fleet. The result was the design of galleys with particularly high forecastles and poops to accommodate and protect the deadly accurate Catalan crossbowmen. This enabled the fleet to engage the much larger Angevin fleet, which used galleys with low bulwarks, and to defeat it on a consistent basis.[5] The Catalan community also provided experienced commanders to the fleet. The combination of the Sicilian and Catalan maritime communities, organised under the control of a central naval authority, proved highly effective and was one factor contributing to the collapse of French ambitions in the Mediterranean during the thirteenth and fourteenth centuries. However, when the Catalan-Aragonese fleet left in 1295, the system essentially collapsed. The Sicilians lost most of the officer corps and the amphibious units. For the Crown of Aragon it was an issue of

---

[4] Lawrence V. Mott, 'The Best Manned Fleet Ever Beheld: The Catalan-Aragonese Fleet in Sicily 1282–1295' (Ph.D. dissertation, Univ. of Minnesota, 1999), 172–95.
[5] Lawrence V. Mott, 'The Battle of Malta: Prelude to Disaster', in Donald Kagay and L. J. Andrew Villalon, eds, *The Circle of War in the Middle Ages* (New York, 1999), 164–6.

finances. From 1285 until 1348 the Crown was constrained by the union of Aragon and Valencia, which restricted the king's ability to impose any new taxes. This political fragmentation ensured that the Crown would not be able to introduce fleet taxes in any form. Without consistent funding for the fleet, the centralised organisation developed in Sicily could not be maintained in Aragon. The office of the admiral would remain, but it only controlled the Arsenal and ships at Barcelona and did not have the overarching control of the other ports of the kingdom as it had in Sicily. The Catalan fleet was still a force to be reckoned with as the Genoese discovered in the loss of their fleet while fighting for the control of Sardinia in 1353. In 1382 the Catalans would defeat a Milanese fleet, ensuring that Sicily stayed in the Aragonese sphere of influence. However, the inability to impose a fleet tax and a small population base would constrict Catalan-Aragonese naval power.

Castile during the thirteenth and fourteenth centuries was confronted with a somewhat different set of problems. Whereas Fernando III had appointed an admiral to command the fleet assembled on the north coast for attacking Seville in 1248, there is no mention of any office of the admiral.[6] However, by 1254 under Alfonso X there appeared the office of the *almirantazgo*. What evidence does exist suggests that the Crown had simply absorbed the existing Muslim naval administration and modified it for its particular needs. Unlike the office of the admiral in Aragon, the *almirantazgo* had direct control over the arsenals and ports in Castile as well as responsibility for regulating maritime commerce in the kingdom. Moreover, the king of Castile had substantially more authority to raise taxes to fund the fleet.

However, Castile had its own set of problems. Because of the location of Portugal, Castile found itself in control of two separate coastlines with substantially different environments and maritime traditions. The Mediterranean and the Strait of Gibraltar required a different set of naval forces from those required for operations in the Atlantic and the Bay of Biscay. The initial solution was to divide the *almirantazgo* into two districts. One was centred at Seville and responsible for the Strait of Gibraltar and the Mediterranean, while the other was at Burgos and was responsible for the Atlantic. The geographical reality necessitated this division, but it did not change the fact that Castile would have to marshal and operate naval units with distinctly different characteristics.

Castile also had a rather surprising problem with regard to ship design and construction. Whereas the northern ports had expertise in constructing the keels and cogs that were playing an important role in northern trade and naval warfare, this knowledge did not transfer to the realities of galley warfare as conducted around southern Castile and the Strait of Gibraltar. Castile still had to rely on Genoa to provide shipwrights, naval commanders and vessels for major operations, such as those conducted in 1284 and 1292 against Muslim forces. For the attack against Tarifa in 1292 the Castilian fleet under the command of

[6] Florentino Pérez-Embid, 'El almirantazgo de Castilla, hasta las capitulaciones de Santa Fe', *Anuario de estudios americanos*, 1 (1944), 10, 86.

the Genoese admiral Zacarias required eleven galleys from Aragon. In a letter to Zacarias, King Sancho IV recognised the necessity of obtaining Genoese experience in naval matters.[7] In a sense, the taking of Seville put Castile in a position from which it would never be able to escape completely. During the thirteenth and fourteenth centuries Castile would fight a series of naval battles with both the North African states and with Portugal for the control of the waters near the Strait of Gibraltar. All of these conflicts would require galley warfare, including the blockade of Seville by Portugal (1369–70) and the Castilian naval assaults against Lisbon (1384). Yet while Castile was conducting galley warfare in the south, throughout the fourteenth century it also had to confront growing hostilities with England in the Bay of Biscay and the English Channel. In 1350 hostilities broke out when twenty English warships raided a Castilian convoy of forty armed merchantmen and captured twenty in a battle known as Les Espagnols sur Mer. Though a peace treaty would end this conflict, Castile was soon dragged into the Hundred Years War. In 1372, a Franco-Castilian fleet crushed the English at the Battle of La Rochelle and in 1376 a Castilian fleet raided the English coast and sacked Walsingham. The Castilians would return in 1405 when hostilities broke out again, raiding Jersey and sacking Poole. What is of importance is that the vast majority of combatants were cogs and nefs common to northern waters, not the galleys employed by Castile in the South.

For this same period very little is known about the naval organisation of Portugal. While documents indicate there were royal galleys being operated by the Portuguese monarchy, there was no formal naval organisation as had developed in Castile and Aragon.[8] Unfortunately, there is a dearth of information concerning developments in Portugal from the late thirteenth to the fourteenth century. Initially, Portugal had shown itself to be the naval equal of Castile, but because it could not match Castile's resources, and possibly due to the lack of development of a strong naval organisation, Portugal's naval strength actually weakened while that of the other Iberian powers was strengthening.

As all of these states discovered, naval warfare was an expensive proposition and one of the most cost-effective ways to conduct warfare against an opponent was indirectly through the use or tacit support of pirates. However, as these Iberian kingdoms began to rely on maritime commerce for revenue the regulation of this form of violence became increasingly important. The unregulated piratical activities of a subject could quickly drag the kingdom into a conflict or commercial reprisals with the kingdom or city of the offended party and that might not be in anyone's interest. Governments usually responded to acts of piracy by another city or country against one of its merchants by seizing the goods of the offending party in its port, or by authorising reprisals. The Castilian-Aragonese War of 1357 was started when Catalan pirates attacked

---

[7] Fernández Duro, *La marina de Castilla*, 52.
[8] Da Silva Saturnino Montiero, *Batalhas e combates da marinha portuguesa*, 28.

Genoese ships in Castilian waters.[9] The result was a nasty war in which Aragon came out the worse for wear.

The Mediterranean had a long history of piracy and had developed mechanisms for regulating it. In both Castile and Aragon those wishing to embark as corsairs were required to place a deposit with the authorities that would be forfeit if the corsair attacked friendly shipping. In Castile, the *almirantazgo* was responsible for regulating piracy. In Aragon during the War of the Sicilian Vespers (1282–1302) the admiral controlled these activities, but following 1295 the bailiff general of each realm was responsible.[10] In both kingdoms there was a stipulation that, if the deposit did not cover the damage to a friendly party, the admiral or the bailiff general would pay for any indemnities incurred by licensed corsairs. In both kingdoms, the Crown received one fifth of the booty collected by a licensed corsair. As pointed out by N. A. M. Rodger in this volume, this system for regulating piracy was essentially lacking in Atlantic waters.

Because the expense of maintaining even the local port squadrons was considerable, besides licensing private individuals both Castile and Aragon would often supply galleys to private individuals for corsairing. The thirteenth-century law code called the *Siete Partidas* outlined the different levels of governmental involvement that might occur. The three different types of royal involvement were:

1. Where the crown provided the ships and their equipment, the provisions and arms, and the pay for the crews.
2. Where the crown provided the ships, their equipment and arms, but others organised the squadron and provided the provisions and pay.
3. Where the crown provided only the ships and their equipment, and others supplied the arms, provisions and pay.

The percentage of loot claimed by the crown varied depending on the level of royal participation. The advantage of the last example of royal participation was that it allowed the Crown to keep a number of vessels in service at a minimal cost. This point was crucial for Aragon, because there the ability of the king to tax was severely limited, and maintaining a fleet was an expensive proposition. By the late thirteenth century 75–80 per cent of the cost of operating a galley went to pay the crews. It is little wonder then that when the fleet was not in service, the galleys were hauled out and stored at the main arsenals at Barcelona and Valencia, while the crews were mustered out of service. Following the plague of 1348, the problem of finding crews and paying for them would become progressively more intractable. Pedro IV tried futilely to impose controls on the pay of rowers. Up to the sixteenth century the oarsmen were still

---

[9] Thomas N. Bisson, *The Medieval Crown of Aragon* (London, 1986), 112.
[10] Andrés Diaz Borras, 'La lucha anticorsaria en Valencia durante la edad media. El episodio protagonizado por Pere Cabanyelles (1417–1418)', *Revista de Historia Naval*, 7 (1989), 115–16. Mott, 'The Best Manned Fleet', 90, 181–3.

freemen, but by the mid-sixteenth century the bulk of the rowers in the galleys would be convicts and slaves, if for no other reason than to hold down the cost of operating the galleys.[11] For Castile the problem lay not only in finding funds to operate a fleet but also in the case of the north coast there was the problem of ship maintenance when the vessels were laid up. Whereas galleys could be hauled out and stored, this option was not available in the North where cogs and nefs were the predominant warship types. This problem would only become worse as the full-rigged ship developed in the fifteenth century. As the kingdom lacked the resources to maintain a permanent fleet, the only recourse was to charter armed merchantmen as needed. Neither Castile nor Aragon could simply requisition ships without paying for them, but even paying for the use of armed merchantmen during times of war proved useful in relieving the government of the cost of a permanent fleet. It is a system that worked well until the late sixteenth century. In part the decision to use armed merchantmen was driven by the changing nature of warfare in the Atlantic. During the fourteenth century, in all of the naval battles fought between Castile and Portugal the primary combat vessel had been the galley. However, by the fifteenth century both combatants were beginning to use full-rigged vessels. Nothing exemplifies this change better than the Battle of Gibraltar between Castile and Portugal in 1476. Castile had assembled a squadron of three full-rigged *naos* from Vizcaya, five *carabelas*, and four Catalan galleys to blockade the Strait of Gibraltar. In the spring of 1476 this squadron intercepted a group of four Portuguese and Genoese ships, capturing two and burning the others.[12] What is of importance is that the main combatants were full-rigged ships armed with wrought-iron cannons propped up over the caprails in the waist of the ships.[13] While the galleys would remain the predominant combat vessel in the Mediterranean, the full-rigged sailing ship had come to dominate combat in the Atlantic and North Sea.

Gunpowder itself was not a new development in the Iberian Peninsula. Small cannons began appearing on both Castilian and Aragonese vessels in the fourteenth century. Ambiguous comments in the early fourteenth century concerning Castilian ships firing *barras de hierro* (iron bars) appear in several chronicles. An inventory of the fleet sent to Naples in 1419 by Alfonso V of Aragon shows that at least three galleys carried *bombardas* and that two of them had two cannons each.[14] The wrought-iron cannons used in both the Atlantic and the Mediterranean from the fourteenth well into the sixteenth century were

---

[11] David Goodman, *Spanish Naval Power: Reconstruction and Defeat, 1589–1665* (Cambridge, 1997), 215. John F. Guilmartin, Jr, *Gunpowder and Galleys* (Cambridge, 1980), 111.
[12] Fernández Duro, *La marina de Castilla*, 202.
[13] A famous votive painting of the battle done by a father to honour his son who died in the battle clearly shows the full-rigged ships and cannons. The painting is located in the Parochial Church of Zumaya.
[14] Antonio de Capmany y de Monpalau, *Ordenanzas de las armadas navales de la Corona de Aragon* (Madrid, 1787), appendix, 4–7.

anti-personnel weapons, if for no other reason than that they lacked both the power and accuracy to make them effective ship-killing instruments. In both the Atlantic and the Mediterranean combat at sea was still being decided at close quarters and ship losses were still due either to fire or grounding.

The end of the fifteenth century brought a number of profound changes to the Iberian Peninsula. In 1479 Aragon and Castile were technically joined under Ferdinand and Isabella. However, while the two kingdoms were joined politically, there were institutional, fiscal and economic differences that would haunt this united Spain in the sixteenth and seventeenth centuries. Moreover, Castile would find itself heavily involved in the Mediterranean while at the same time it tried to establish an Atlantic empire. Aragon would provide much of the expertise for Mediterranean naval operations, but political, demographic and economic turmoil from the late fourteenth into the fifteenth century had sapped the kingdom of much of its resources. Portugal, while being shut out of the Mediterranean by Castile, had begun to establish an overseas empire first in West Africa and then in the Indian Ocean. In 1502 following the voyage of Vasco da Gama to India, the Portuguese rapidly expanded their influence throughout the Far East through the use of armed caravels and carracks. In 1510, the Portuguese took Goa in India and then Malacca in 1511. The primary vessels used for Portuguese expansion were called carracks. The distinctive feature of these vessels was their sheer size and built-up forecastles and poops. Though they carried few large cannons, the high superstructure bristled with small wrought-iron weapons. Whether by design or sheer fortune this combination of size and numerous anti-personnel weapons proved the perfect combination for naval warfare in the Indian Ocean and South-east Asia. Although the Portuguese were faced with local opposing forces that were often more numerous, there was no organised naval force with ships large enough or sufficiently armed to challenge them. The Turks would contest the Portuguese control of the Indian Ocean throughout the sixteenth century, but they would use Mediterranean galleys that lacked the range and sea-keeping ability to gain control of the ocean.[15] Even after Portugal came under Habsburg rule in 1580 the Portuguese operated their overseas empire virtually independently of the Spanish government. The entire enterprise was operated by the state, and the initial success of the Portuguese at sea suggests that a highly efficient naval organisation operated from Lisbon, though there have been few studies of it. However, as has been suggested by Jan Glete, because Portugal faced no European threat in South-east Asia during the sixteenth century there was no impulse to develop faster and more powerful ships.[16] While the Portuguese continued to use the large carracks into the seventeenth century, the carrack fell out of use in Europe because of the inability of this type of vessel to contend with the faster, heavily armed and more manoeuvrable galleons appearing in northern waters. When confronted with the swifter

---

[15] Jan Glete, *Warfare at Sea, 1500–1650: Maritime Conflicts and the Transformation of Europe* (London, 2000), 76–84.
[16] Glete, *Warfare at Sea, 1500–1650*, 89.

merchantmen of the Dutch and English armed with cast-iron cannon in the mid-seventeenth century the Portuguese found it impossible to prevent them from taking over their trade in South-east Asia. Spain was also establishing an overseas empire during the sixteenth century, first in the Americas and later in Asia. Charles, grandson of Ferdinand and Isabella, became heir to the growing empire shortly before the Aztecs and Incas were conquered in his name. The inclusion of Spain into the Habsburg Empire would eventually draw it into a series of conflicts that would literally span the globe. From 1494 until 1559 Spain was engaged in a series of wars with France for the control of Italy. It was also in a conflict with the Ottoman Empire for control of the western Mediterranean that would last until 1580. Spain also became the champion of Roman Catholicism in the era of the Protestant Reformation. Besides these conflicts, Spain was attempting to establish itself in the New World and protect the developing trade with its colonies. In confronting these multiple challenges, the problem was that Spain was neither politically nor fiscally unified.

To provide money for the fleet required not only the approval of the parliament of Castile but also separate approval from the Crown of Aragon. Initially Spain relied on the *avería*, a tax on goods transported to the New World, to pay for naval forces to protect the New World trade, but this was changed to a direct tax called the *milliones* in 1590 in order to build a permanent fleet. However, this tax could only be applied to Castile as the *cortes* of Aragon refused to approve it. Separate funds from the papacy, known as the Three Graces, were used to support the galleys operating in the Mediterranean. Besides having disparate sources of funding for its far-flung naval commitments, the Habsburg government was plagued by a series of bankruptcies in 1560, 1575, 1607, 1627, 1642 and 1652. The periodic shortage of funds directly affected the fleets' ability to function.[17]

From 1479 until the truce with the Ottoman Empire in 1580, the bulk of the funds went to support the large galley fleets required to counter Turkish incursions into the western Mediterranean. During this time the Spanish fleet would fight major battles at Tunis in 1535, Prevesa in 1538, Djerba in 1560 and Lepanto in 1571. The Spanish fleet also had to combat the plague of pirates that was devastating the eastern seaboard of the Iberian Peninsula. Operating galleys was increasingly expensive and the cost of operating a galley from 1523 to 1587 more than tripled.[18] Equally important, while warship design was rapidly evolving in the Atlantic, the galley was still the dominant warship in the Mediterranean in the sixteenth century. Warfare there was still as much amphibious as naval in nature, and this, combined with the shoal waters and fickle winds of the Mediterranean, meant that galleys were still the best warships for the region. However, by their very design galleys were essentially useless for warfare in the Atlantic. Whereas they were employed sporadically by Spain in

---

[17] Goodman, *Spanish Naval Power*, 39–60.
[18] Guilmartin, *Gunpowder and Galleys*, 270.

the Netherlands, the Bay of Biscay and even the Caribbean, the narrow hulls and low freeboard of the galley made it at best marginally useful in the Atlantic. The result was that Spain had to maintain a large fleet that essentially could not be deployed outside the Mediterranean to support Spain's growing overseas empire.

The enormous cost of maintaining a year-round fleet of galleys in the Mediterranean is undoubtedly one of the reasons the Spanish government continued to lease armed merchantmen for protection of the New World trade and for naval operations against the French and then English well into the 1570s. While the ability to draft private ships into government service relieved the government of having to maintain a permanent fleet, it also brought its own set of problems. Since the government was attempting to use merchant vessels for military purposes, it was in its interest to see that ships being constructed had features suited for naval warfare, the main consideration being size. To this end the government tried to influence the merchant community to build larger ships by issuing a regulation in 1511 giving loading preferences at ports to larger ships, and in the 1560s Philip II began supplying subsidies for the construction of larger merchantmen.[19] The problem was that the merchant community preferred smaller vessels because they were easier to unload and they handled better in the shoal waters of the Netherlands and the North Sea. Spain was in a difficult position. It could not afford two separate fleets and yet it had to protect shipping in the New World as well as confront the Ottoman Empire in the Mediterranean. First the French in the 1530s and then English in the 1560s took advantage of the situation by sending privateers into the Caribbean to raid towns and capture shipping. In 1526 the king responded to the increasing piracy by ordering all merchant vessels in the Atlantic to travel in convoy. Between 1536 and 1543 the Crown issued a series of additional ordinances concerning the outfitting and manning of ships for the New World trade. By 1564, a system of two yearly convoys to America had been established, but this proved to be only a partial solution.[20] In 1567 the Crown was forced to build twelve small galleons for defence of the convoys, which in turn were replaced by larger versions in 1583. These vessels constituted the first permanent royal Spanish fleet outside the Mediterranean.[21]

One of the major criticisms levelled at the Spanish government concerning the organisation of the Armada of 1588 has been the fact that there were so many Mediterranean ships in the fleet, which admittedly fared poorly in the fighting and particularly the storms the fleet encountered in the North Sea and

[19] William D. Phillips, 'Spain's Northern Shipping Industry in the Sixteenth Century', *Journal of European Economic History*, 17.2 (1988), 77.
[20] Carla Rahn Phillips, *Six Galleons for the King of Spain* (Baltimore, 1986), 9–13.
[21] These vessels are often considered the first permanent Spanish royal fleet. However, during the sixteenth century the Crown already maintained permanent galley fleets in the Mediterranean. Glete, *Warfare at Sea*, 150–1.

off Ireland. Yet when one looks at the strategic position Spain was in, it is no wonder that the fleet consisted of so many Mediterranean vessels. A truce with the Ottoman Empire had only been signed in 1580 and whereas the crown had begun by building more galleons suited for Atlantic duty, there were few available in the 1580s. It took time to create a new fleet suited for the Atlantic rather than Mediterranean combat. Of the thirty-four ships lost from the 1588 fleet of a hundred and thirty, either in conflict or on the voyage home, none was a Spanish-built galleon.[22] The Armada disaster brought a series of reforms in the Spanish fleet. Under Philip III new naval ordinances appeared in 1607, 1613 and 1618 designed to standardise the construction of galleons and ensure they had characteristics that could serve the fleet. Moreover, the government formed the Junta de Armada to oversee the fleet. Up to the sixteenth century, the *almirantazgo* had controlled naval matters, but it had been dissolved and naval matters had been handled in the *Consejo de Guerra*.[23] The reforms created a revitalised Spanish fleet in the first quarter of the seventeenth century. Until the 1630s, the Spanish fleet was a formidable force and had success against the English and the Dutch. For example in May 1624, the Dutch invaded Brazil but within six months the Spanish had marshalled a fleet and ousted the Dutch after defeating their fleet. In 1625 the Spanish fleet successfully repelled an attack on Cadiz by a combined Anglo-Dutch fleet. However, these successes were soon undermined by series of major setbacks. In 1635 the French declared war on Spain and in 1638 French forces crossed the Pyrenees and burned or captured several galleons under construction at Pasajes. The French fleet went on to destroy a fleet of twelve Spanish galleons and blockade the north coast. In 1639 Spain responded by assembling a fleet of one hundred ships with the intention of sailing into the Channel and destroying the French and Dutch squadrons there. However, in September the Dutch fleet caught the Spanish one at the Downs and utterly destroyed it. This disaster was followed in 1640 by a revolt in Catalonia, and then one in Portugal. In 1648 treaties ended most of the conflicts of the Thirty Years War, but Spain and France would fight on until 1659. Exhausted and overextended in the 1650s and 1660s, Spain could not adequately protect its colonies or even its home waters. France had usurped Spain's position as the dominant power on the Continent, while England and the Netherlands became the dominant naval powers. In 1668 Spain was forced to recognise Portugal's independence and the inroads made by the French and English into the Caribbean and North America.

A number of criticisms have been levelled at both the Spanish and Portuguese for their inability to thwart the incursions of the English, Dutch and French into

---

[22] Carla Rahn Phillips, 'The Caravel and the Galleon', in Richard W. Unger, ed., *Cogs, Caravels and Galleons: The Sailing Ship 1000–1650* (London, 1994), 105–6.
[23] Francisco-Felipe Olesa Muñido, *La organización naval de los estados mediterraneos y en especial de España durante los siglos XVI y XVII*, 2 vols (Madrid, 1968), 384–8, 450.

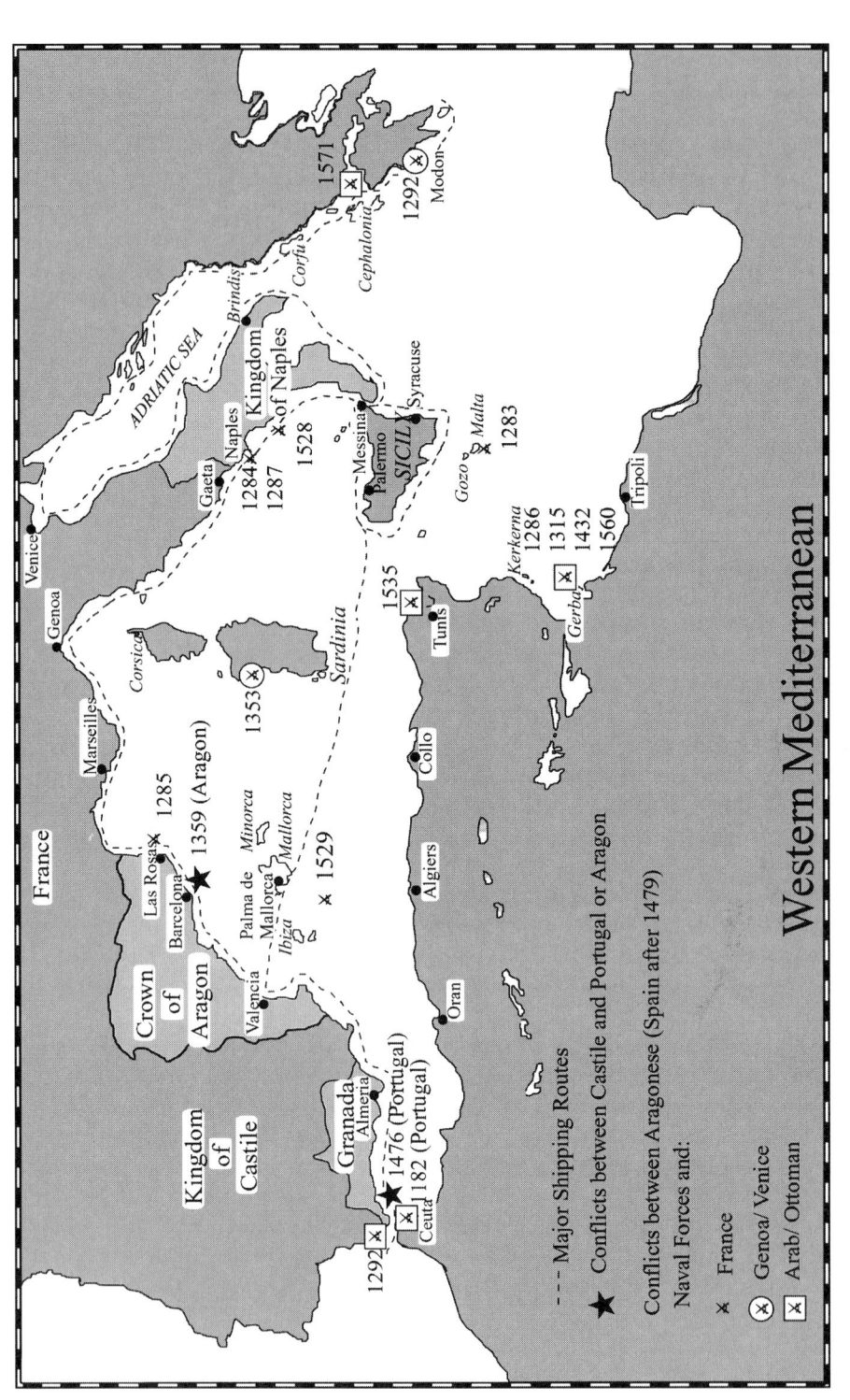

Map 1. The Western Mediterranean

their overseas empires. The most persistent charge has been that neither country modified its ship designs to counter the fast race-built galleons and armed merchantmen being produced by their opponents. Moreover, there has been criticism of Spain's inability to adopt the cheaper cast-iron artillery and its continued use of land carriages for many of its naval guns instead of using the four-wheeled gun trucks developed at the end of the sixteenth century.[24] There is no doubt that Portugal persisted in the use of the carrack in the Indian Ocean and Far East long after that ship-type had disappeared in Europe. However, it had served extremely well against both the Ottomans and Indian Ocean opponents. It is easy to criticise the Portuguese for clinging to a design in the face of change, but most institutions are loath to abandon a proven design until it has been patently shown to be defective or outmoded. A series of hot debates had revolved around changing the design, and the Portuguese were well aware of the shortcomings. However, it was not clear that a change in design was necessary or prudent.[25] Moreover, between 1640 and 1668 Portugal was engaged in a revolt against Spain that undoubtedly put a damper on any movement to change ship designs or adopt newer, larger ordinance.

In the case of Spain, the problem was quite different. It has been noted that each country designed galleons to fit particular national needs.[26] By the seventeenth century Spain controlled an empire that literally stretched around the world. The design of Spanish galleons had to take into account a variety of needs of a navy seriously overstretched. The Spanish galleon not only had to operate as a warship but also had to have the capacity to act as a troop carrier or to transport needed supplies to distant colonies. When seen in this light it is clear that the Spaniards were not behind in ship design compared to the Dutch and English, but simply making design decisions based on need. The English could afford to build race-built galleons because they had no need to transport men or supplies to a global empire. The Spanish had to design galleons that could do all of the tasks reasonably well. Spain's opponents did not have to stretch resources to cover a scattered empire and so were not saddled with having to make such compromises. The Spanish did have trouble in manufacturing cast-iron guns and the Dutch and English generally had cannon firing heavier shot.[27] However, the major problem was numbers. Spain had to produce guns not only for the Atlantic fleet, but also for the Mediterranean galleys and more importantly for numerous forts scattered around the globe. For this reason the artillery was removed from a ship once it docked at a port and often was used on land for defence or a land campaign.[28] To this end the carriages of the

---

[24] For a discussion of these perceived short comings see Glete, *Warfare at Sea*, chapter 10. Goodman, *Spanish Naval Power*, 114–24, 145–9.
[25] Carla Rahn Phillips, 'Manuel Fernandes and His 1616 *Livro de traças de carpintaria*', *American Neptune*, 60.1 (2000), 7–29.
[26] Phillips, 'The Caravel and the Galleon', 102–4.
[27] Goodman, *Spanish Naval Power*, 148.
[28] Phillips, *Six Galleons for the King of Spain*, 91.

guns had to be adaptable. While the four-wheeled gun truck introduced by the English was more efficient at sea, it was nearly useless on land. The continued use of two-wheeled carriages by Spain was dictated by the necessity of having artillery flexible enough to serve on land or sea as needed.

In the seventeenth century Spain was confronted with a series of obstacles that any nation would have found nearly impossible to surmount. All of Spain's opponents were afflicted with some financial or political problems, but never to the degree nor in the same totality as Spain. Whereas the Iberian Peninsula was technically united from 1580 to 1640, the fact was that the government was split into three separate administrations that precluded the fiscal unity necessary to finance a large fleet. Moreover, whereas the Portuguese operated their maritime empire relatively independently, Spain found itself dragged into protecting it along with its own colonies. Spain was also forced into fighting a true two-ocean war in both the geographical and technical sense. Spain had to operate separate naval forces in the Mediterranean and Atlantic that could not operate well in the other's environment.

Strategically, all of the advantages lay with the Dutch, English and French. Given the primitive state of communications in the seventeenth century, Spanish colonies and convoys were easy targets, since by the time any defence could be mustered the raiders would have simply moved on. Spain's opponents, with few colonies to protect, had the luxury of designing and operating ships for raiding and privateering, while Spain on the other hand had lengthy lines of communication to guard. Its far-flung global commitments forced Spain into making a series of naval decisions and compromises that her opponents never had to confront.

When seen in this light, Spanish and Portuguese naval power achieved a great deal. They thwarted attempts by the Ottoman Empire to control the western Mediterranean while at the same time helped establish a global network of colonies and outposts. Although the other European powers would make inroads into Spanish holdings and effectively replace Portugal in Asia, Spain and Portugal held on to the vast majority of their holdings in the Americas. By the second half of the seventeenth century, although the Spanish navy was in decline, it had effectively secured Spain's overseas empire for at least another century. Both Spain and Portugal had evolved effective naval forces and administrations in the fifteenth and sixteenth centuries, laying the foundation for the navies which competed more or less globally in the era described by Mahan.

VENICE, GENOA AND CONTROL OF THE SEAS IN THE THIRTEENTH AND FOURTEENTH CENTURIES

John Dotson

WHEN trying to find the underlying and developing ideas of naval operations and strategy in the events of the naval conflicts between the Italian maritime states of the thirteenth and fourteenth centuries, the fundamental questions are: (1) What do the actions of the hostile parties reveal about the war aims of the participants? (2) How did these change over time if, indeed, they did? (3) What strategies were developed to achieve those aims? In practical affairs, it is common for theory to lag well behind practice.[1] Alfred Thayer Mahan's influential analysis of naval strategy was based on a study of sailing navies that were obsolete in the time that he was writing. This is not to suggest that the commanders of the sailing navies of the sixteenth to the eighteenth centuries did not grasp the concept of global strategy nor that naval commanders in the fourteenth century did not have clear goals. Rather, it suggests that the theoretical articulation of complex concepts often follows a thorough testing of ideas in the practical sphere. That, in turn, suggests that to understand the development of certain ideas in their contemporary context, one must look to the actions of the participants as indications of the thought processes that guided them.

The north Italian maritime communes, Pisa, Venice, and Genoa, found themselves increasingly in competition and conflict during the eleventh century. In the Tyrrhenian Sea, Pisa and Genoa at first cooperated in operations against Muslim states. Pisa was apparently the senior partner in these early efforts. As Genoa grew rapidly in the first decades of the eleventh century, alliance gave way to competition and growing enmity. Control over the islands of Corsica and Sardinia became the focal point of the developing conflict.

The First Crusade brought a greater presence of Genoese and Pisan shipping into the eastern basin of the Mediterranean than ever before. Since 1082 Venetians had enjoyed the commercial advantage of special status in the Byzantine Empire and were sensitive to any perceived encroachment into their economic

---

[1] Richard Unger, in a paper presented to the August, 1999 meeting of the Association of the History of the Northern Seas, suggested that the wars between the two great Italian maritime republics of Venice and Genoa led in the fourteenth century to 'what could be called a struggle for command of the sea'. He later observes that 'It is also hard to find among Venetians or Genoese or any other players in the naval battles of the high Middle Ages ideas about naval dominance'.

sphere.[2] In 1099 Venetian and Pisan forces clashed in the harbour at Rhodes en route to support the efforts of the First Crusade. It is significant that Pisan prisoners were released only when they promised not to engage in commercial activities within the Byzantine Empire.[3] Nonetheless, naval and logistical support that could only be provided by the Italian maritime cities was necessary to the long-term success of the crusading movement. As the Crusader States were established, the Italians were given commercial privileges and designated quarters in the cities of Oltremare.[4] Frequent quarrels erupted as they manoeuvred for mercantile advantage in the eastern Mediterranean ports and commercial centres.

The first war fought between Genoa and Venice, the War of San Saba, broke out after years of tension in the ports of the Crusader States, especially in Acre, the largest. Economic competition and civic pride led to disputes that sometimes escalated into violence. An anonymous Genoese chronicler stressed that the conflict in the East was not just between Venetians and Genoese, but included Pisa as well.[5] The local conflict between rival colonial populations in the Levant became a war in 1257. In that year the Venetians – in response to Genoese attacks on their compatriots in Acre and amidst charges and counter-charges about various grievances – sent a fleet of fourteen galleys with their annual caravan to Oltremare. The goal was immediate: to punish the Genoese and to expel them from Acre. Under the command of Lorenzo Tiepolo they drove Genoese shipping out of the harbour of Acre and forced those who remained to withdraw to a strongly fortified tower.[6]

The wars between Venice and Genoa were never between those two cities alone, but involved different constellations of alliance. For much of this period Pisa and Genoa were locked in a struggle over Sardinia so that according to the principle that 'the enemy of my enemy is my friend' the citizens of the Arno city were natural allies of the Venetians in spite of their animosity in earlier times. In addition, the Genoese chronicler reports, virtually the whole of Oltremare united against Genoa. Only the Anconitans, the Catalans, and Philip of Montfort, Lord of Tyre and King of Armenia, sided with the Ligurians. The Anconitans and Catalans, he says, were of little help because of their fear of the

---

2   In 1082 the Byzantine emperor Alexius I in a 'Golden Bull' rewarded Venice for its help in fighting off an invasion by Robert Guiscard, the Norman ruler of south Italy, by granting trading privileges and exemption from customs duties within the Empire.
3   Frederic C. Lane, *Venice: A Maritime Republic* (Baltimore, 1973), 32.
4   'Oltremare' or 'Overseas' or 'Beyond the Sea' was the western term for the area in which the Crusader States were being established.
5   *Annali Genovesi di Caffaro e dei suoi continuatori*, trans. Ceccardo Roccatagliata Ceccardi and Giovanni Monleone, vol. VI (Genoa, 1929), 56.
6   Son of Doge Giacomo Tiepolo (r. 1229–49) and operating in conjunction with Venetians in Acre under the leadership of the *bailo*, Marco Giustiniani. F. C. Hodgson, *Venice in the Thirteenth and Fourteenth Centuries* (London, 1910), 122 ff.

numbers arrayed against the Genoese.[7] But the Lord of Tyre proved to be a crucial ally and his territory a decisive refuge.

The following year, an attempt by a Genoese fleet to relieve their besieged compatriots in Acre failed in a disastrous defeat just outside the harbor.[8] The remaining Genoese in Acre fled when they saw that their only hope of relief had been destroyed. Their quarter in the city was destroyed and columns from their fortified tower were taken back to Venice where they still stand near San Marco. The conflict in Acre had ended disastrously for the Genoese. They had been expelled from the most important commercial centre of Oltremare. They maintained a presence only in Tyre, a distinctly secondary port. The growing conflict among the Italian maritime cities in Oltremare caused a good deal of concern in the West. The papacy intervened to negotiate a peace and exchange of prisoners among the warring parties.[9] This War of San Saba, so called after the disputed monastery that was its putative cause, was primarily a conflict among the overseas residents of the maritime cities that grew to include the home cities. It centred on Oltremare, and peace came quickly when it became evident that the Genoese would not be able to evict the Venetians and Pisans from Acre, nor they the Genoese from Tyre. Naval strategy was bluntly aimed at the point of conflict.

Certainly there were economic goals behind the clashes in Oltremare. Any city that could control one of the three great entrepôts for Oriental goods – Constantinople and the Black Sea, Oltremare, or Alexandria – would reap great riches. Alexandria, under powerful Egyptian control, was out of reach. But the Venetian conquest of Constantinople in 1204 had demonstrated that it was possible for an ambitious and aggressive power to gain control of that strategic point. It also must have seemed credible that competitors could be expelled from at least the major ports of Oltremare. The expulsion of Genoese merchants from Acre was a severe blow, but not a fatal one because they remained ensconced at Tyre. Unable to react effectively to the Venetians and Pisans in Syria, the Genoese turned to diplomacy and to another strategic area. In effect, frontal assaults in Oltremare were proving costly and ineffective. The Genoese shifted their attack to a different point where they could find an ally in their struggle against the Venetians.

Around 1260 the Genoese sent ambassadors to negotiate with Michael Palaeologus, the most plausible claimant to the Byzantine throne at Constantinople. In 1261 the parties reached an agreement in the Treaty of Nymphaeum in which the Genoese promised armed support to Michael's claims and he, in turn, promised to put them in the Venetians' place at Constantinople when he had occupied it. As things developed, Greek forces entered the city in the night of 24 July 1261 without encountering any significant resistance.[10] The Venetians im-

---

[7] *Annali Genovesi*, VI, 65. See also Steven A. Epstein, *Genoa and the Genoese* (Chapel Hill, NC, 1996), 146.
[8] Georg Caro, *Genova e la supremazia sul Mediterraneo* (Genoa, 1974), I, 74–75. *Annali Genovesi*, 3, 86.
[9] Epstein, *Genoa and the Genoese*, 146; *Annali Genovesi*, VI, 66–7.
[10] Caro, *Genova*, I, 110–11; *Annali Genovesi*, VI, 79.

mediately dispatched a fleet of eighteen galleys to Constantinople to protect their citizens and property there, but the Genoese arrived first and burned much of the Venetian quarter of the city. Though Greeks had regained Constantinople without the promised aid of the Genoese, their intervention parried the Venetian riposte. The emperor kept his bargain, realizing that Genoese naval power might yet be necessary to protect his gains. But, he sought to limit their influence in the city itself by confining them to a suburb across the Golden Horn. The Genoese would turn Pera into a thriving city and powerful naval base in its own right.

Pope Urban IV promptly threatened Genoa with excommunication because of its alliance with the schismatic Greeks. Papal pressure did not deter the Ligurian city from its very profitable alliance, but did threaten to create difficulties for its inhabitants. War between the maritime cities resumed and during 1262 diplomatic and military manoeuvring continued. The Latin Emperor, Baldwin II, appealed to the Venetians to aid him to regain Constantinople while Urban IV urged the monarchies of the West to deny the excommunicated Genoese access to their lands and markets.[11] Constantinople, and later Pera controlled entrance and egress to and from the Black Sea more completely than any other naval base could control a major route. The Genoese seemed to have found ample compensation for their expulsion from Acre. The Genoese continued to cooperate with Michael in his reconquest of the Empire. At his command they dispatched thirty-eight galleys to transport munitions and supplies to Malvasia (Monemvasia) in the Morea. When they arrived at Settepozzi (Spetsai) they learned that a Venetian fleet *en route* to Negroponte was in the vicinity. Outnumbering the Venetians thirty-eight to thirty-two, they decided to attack, but the Venetians claimed immunity as crusaders. This was apparently enough to cause most of the Genoese fleet to hesitate. Only fourteen of them pressed forward and of those, four – including the galleys of the two admirals – were captured.[12] Throughout the war Genoese fleets performed uniformly badly, often because of divided or ineffective command. Their commerce-raiding efforts were often more successful.

In 1264 Simone Grillo sailed from Genoa toward Oltremare with a fleet of twenty galleys and two large *navi*. In violation of orders to proceed directly to Tyre that he had sworn to obey, he instead led his forces in a brilliant raid, evading the Venetian war fleet and intercepting their annual Levant caravan near Durazzo, capturing all of it but the great *Roccafortis*. Despite this success, Genoese competence in battle between war fleets did not improve. During the campaign of 1266 the Genoese fleet of Lanfranco Borborino, in spite of superior numbers, was utterly destroyed by Jacopo Dandolo's Venetian galleys near Trapani in Sicily. In this battle the Genoese admiral, like Rosso della Turca

---

[11] Caro, *Genova*, I, 126; *Annali Genovesi*, VI, 81 ff.
[12] Caro, *Genova*, I, 132 ff.; *Annali Genovesi*, VI, 90–3.

at Acre, clung to defensive tactics even though his war council advised him to attack.[13]

In 1269 Genoa began negotiations to provide naval support and transport for Louis IX's crusading expedition against Tunis. Under pressure from the French king, and because the war seemed to have reached an impasse, the three maritime cities concluded a truce. In Genoa Oberto Spinola and Oberto Doria seized power in a coup that saw the two of them confirmed as Captains of the People. Events in the central Mediterranean were beginning to overshadow the stalemated situation in the eastern basin. While Venice was able to control the Adriatic and could concentrate on defending its position in the East, Genoa had to face complex situations across the entire Mediterranean basin. Pisa was the first and nearest enemy of the Genoese, but Provençals and Catalans soon emerged as economic competitors and naval rivals. Genoa had been drawn into a conflict in Sicily that had begun with Charles of Anjou's descent into Italy in 1264. In the years following the truce of 1270 they were absorbed by factional strife within the city and war with the Angevin prince who ruled Provence to the west of the city as well as Sicily which dominated their routes to the East. Thus, the truce in the East was continued.

It was in confrontation with Pisa, not Venice, that the armistice first broke down. When a Corsican noble rebelled against the Genoese and then found refuge in Pisa in 1282, that was enough to rekindle the war in the Tyrrhenian Sea. Most important the Ghibelline Captaincy of Spinola and Doria organised the resources of the Genoese state for war. They established a new magistracy, the Credenza, that was charged with financing and procurement of *matériel* for war.[14] They also seem to have established a more effective command structure. In the last two decades of the thirteenth century Genoese prosperity reached its medieval zenith, enabling the newly established Credenza to build fleets of unprecedented size and effectiveness. While Venetian fleets were built by the state in the famous Arsenal, Genoese fleets were always made up of a combination of communal and private vessels in varying proportions. Often, communal vessels made up the lesser proportion of the fleet. While the Genoese system was certainly more administratively awkward, it may also have been more open to technological innovation.[15] Late in 1282 the Credenza made plans for a fleet of one hundred and twenty galleys, including fifty newly built by the commune. Such a large fleet – almost three times the size of the largest used up to this point – put severe demands upon the ability of the Genoese to provide manpower for it.[16] A Genoese raid on Elba in February 1283 indicates a change in the conditions of naval warfare in the Mediterranean. The seas were no longer closed in winter, due in part to new navigational techniques developed with the

---

[13] See John E. Dotson, 'Fleet Operations in the First Genoese–Venetian War, 1264–1266', *Viator*, 30 (1999), 165–80, for a detailed discussion of both these actions.
[14] Epstein, *Genoa and the Genoese*, 158.
[15] See p. 124 below at note 18.
[16] Epstein, *Genoa and the Genoese*, 158–9.

introduction of the compass at about this time.[17] It would be increasingly difficult to predict when ships could be found in the strategic narrows of the Mediterranean shipping lanes as Simone Grillo had done with the Venetian caravan of 1264. There were also evolutionary developments in the ships used in war. The last decade of the thirteenth century saw the introduction of the trireme galley, a heavier vessel with a crew half as large again as the bireme galleys heretofore used and a capacity three times that of the bireme.[18] Larger crews and increased capacity for marines and mechanical artillery at little or no cost in speed and manoeuvrability would make this new galley type the most effective warship of its day. There is some evidence to indicate that Genoese prosperity and efficient fiscal organisation led to earlier, or at least more extensive, adoption of trireme galleys in their fleets than was the case with their opponents. During 1283 the war for Corsica and Sardinia developed with several indecisive sea battles and much commerce raiding. In July 1284 a Pisan fleet commanded by the Venetian, Albertino Morosini, attempted to bring Benedetto Zaccaria's Genoese squadron to battle near Portofino. Finding themselves almost trapped between Zaccaria and another large force that sortied from the port of Genoa, the Pisans retired to Porto Pisano where they found refuge behind its fortifications and the great chain across the mouth of the harbour. Oberto Doria's Genoese fleet of ninety-three galleys followed them there and with a clever ruse tricked the Pisan fleet of seventy-two galleys into a battle near the Meloria reefs. The Pisan fleet was entirely destroyed and the mariners who were not killed were taken captive to Genoa. An alliance with Pisa's rivals in Tuscany, Florence and Lucca, further weakened Pisa, which never recovered from these events. Though not totally eliminated, Pisa was reduced to a condition where it was never again a serious maritime threat. In fact, there were almost certainly many factors at work other than the defeat at Meloria that explain the decline of Pisa.

The fall of Acre to the Saracens in 1291 set the stage for a second Genoese–Venetian war, the War of Curzola. Since 1258 the Venetians and Pisans had dominated in Acre. But after its capture new ports, Famagusta in Cyprus and Lajazzo in Armenia, became more important. In these areas the Genoese were competitive.[19] Venice and Genoa each wanted to expel the other from the Black Sea. The armistice of 1270 had been renewed repeatedly, but that war had ended without any clear result.[20] Any incident would do to reignite hostilities. There were many points of friction between the rivals. Genoese

---

[17] Frederic C. Lane, 'The Economic Meaning of the Invention of the Compass', *American Historical Review*, 68 (1963), 605–17; reprinted in *Venice and History: The Collected Papers of Frederic C. Lane* (Baltimore, 1966), 331–44.

[18] John E. Dotson, 'Merchant and Naval Influences on Galley Design at Venice and Genoa in the Fourteenth Century', in Craig L. Symonds *et al.*, eds, *New Aspects of Naval History* (Annapolis, 1981), 25.

[19] Caro, *Genova*, II, 172–3.

[20] Ibid., II, 174.

corsairs captured Venetian ships, chartered by Pisans. Some Venetians were robbed and roughed up by Genoese in Palermo. Genoa, wanting to prevent Pisa from receiving any aid from Venice, established a blockade of Pisa. Venetians were accused of carrying horses and mercenaries to the Pisans in Sardinia. Both sides were inclined to resume hostilities to seize an advantage in the rapidly changing economic environment of the late thirteenth century. All of these factors rekindled the old enmity between Venice and Genoa. The Genoese showed a new feeling of confidence, no doubt engendered by the experience gained in the war with Pisa. The Venetians began the war with the old certainty that they could easily defeat twice their number of Genoese.[21] In July 1293 there were no formal hostilities, but tensions were running high. When seven Genoese merchant galleys from Romania encountered four Venetian galleys near Corone they expected the smaller squadron to yield the right of way as was customary. Instead, the Venetians formed a battle line and rowed to the attack. The Genoese captured and sacked the entire Venetian flotilla.[22]

At the end of the thirteenth century, Genoese tactical superiority was as overwhelming as the Venetians' had been at mid-century. The extension of the sailing season year round, however, made the task of choking off an enemy's commerce by interception of a single convoy impossible. The galley's limitations as a blockading craft were considerably more evident in these new conditions of navigation. As already noted, there were no spectacular convoy victories in this second Genoese–Venetian war like Grillo's victory over the *Roccafortis* convoy.

The value of the colony at Pera to the Genoese was demonstrated in the opening phases of the Second Genoese–Venetian War. When Venice sent fourteen war galleys to Cyprus and Armenia with their merchant fleet in 1294 intending to drive the Genoese from Famagusta and Lajazzo, the Genoese of Pera raised a scratch fleet of hastily armed merchant galleys. Though outnumbered, this makeshift flotilla inflicted a severe defeat on the overconfident Venetians, capturing most of their vessels. Their rapid and successful response saved the Genoese merchant communities in Cyprus and Armenia.[23]

The average size of fleets in the second Genoese–Venetian war and, despite the Black Death, even in the third war, was much greater than in the first war. The average fleet size in the major engagements of the first war was around thirty galleys. In the second and third wars the average was around sixty (see Table I). Early in the Corsican War both Pisa and Genoa made use of very large fleets. This was almost certainly made easier by the very restricted theatre of operations in that war, confined as it was to the Tyrrhenian Sea and the Gulf of Genoa. Even when this general increase in the size of forces is taken into consideration, the fleet, which the Genoese sent out in 1295, was truly remarkable. That summer they strained to arm two hundred galleys and, in the event,

[21] Ibid., I, 185 ff.
[22] Ibid., II, 177.
[23] Caro, *Genova*, II, 183 ff.; Lane, *Venice*, 83.

Table I

Size of Selected Fleets: 1258–1379

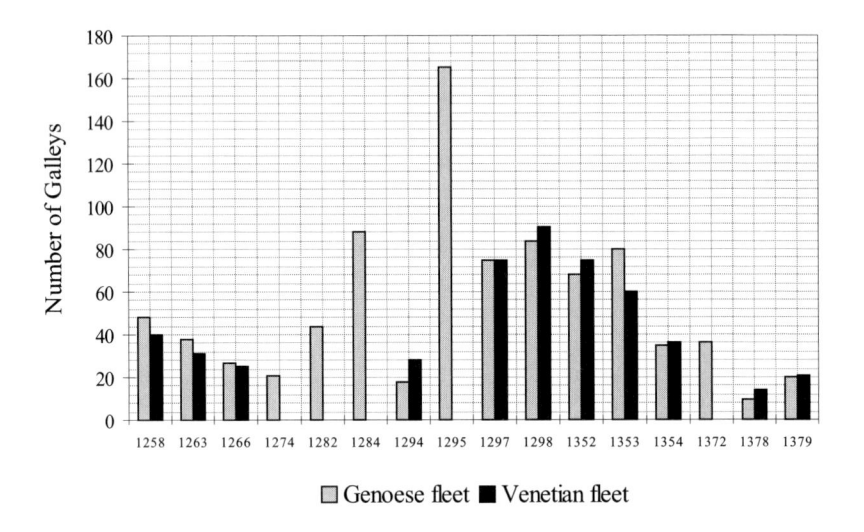

☐ Genoese fleet ■ Venetian fleet

put to sea with around one hundred and sixty-five. The majority of these were new trireme galleys, larger and heavier than the earlier bireme types.[24] A formal challenge was sent inviting the Venetians to meet this formidable fleet in battle, even offering to meet them near Messina so that they would not have to endure the fatigue of a long voyage to Genoa. This huge fleet did, in fact, travel to Messina, where it waited in vain for almost three weeks for the Venetians.[25] Even if the Venetians had had a comparable fleet, they would have been foolish to attempt the passage of the Strait of Messina in the face of so powerful a force. In fact, it appears that the Genoese were operating at the limits of their capacities just to get this assemblage to Sicily and back. If not, why did they not go on to the Adriatic when the Venetians did not come to them?

The great fleet of 1295 represented a maximum effort for the Genoese, requiring the mobilisation of virtually all the private galleys, manpower, and money of the Riviera.[26] Following this unparalleled and fruitless effort, and to

---

[24] Ibid., II, 196 and n. 52. Cf. also Dotson, 'Merchant and Naval Influences'. The Genoese chronicler Jacopo da Varagine gives the figure of 165 galleys and says that only vessels with at least 220 men on board 'as is commonly reckoned' were allowed to sail with the fleet, but that many had 250 and some as many as 300 men. He places the total number of men in the fleet at 45,000 which would make an average of 272 men per galley. *Annali Genovesi dopo Caffaro e suoi continuatori*, G. Monleone, trans. and ed., vol. I (X in the series of *Annali Genovesi*), 22 ff. The problems of victualing, watering, and sanitation for these numbers in the limited space of even the larger triremes must have been monumental.

[25] *Annali Genovesi*, X (I), 24 ff.

[26] Ibid., 26 ff. What Jacopo da Varagine actually wrote was that there remained in Genoa and the Rivera enough men to equip a further forty galleys left behind as a home guard.

some extent as a result of the strain of financing and manning it, bitter internecine fighting broke out among the opposing parties at Genoa. No fleet at all was sent out the next year while a Venetian fleet of some seventy galleys attacked Genoese possessions in Romania, including even Pera and Caffa.[27] In 1297 the Genoese sent a large fleet of about seventy-five galleys to sea, but divided the command between two admirals. This fleet entered the Adriatic to challenge the Venetians. Predictably, the commanders, Gando de Mari and Tomaso Spinola, soon fell out and parcelled the fleet out between them, de Mari taking the larger part to Sardinia while Spinola returned to Sicily. The Venetians had sent out a number of small squadrons raiding Genoese possessions in Sicily, Armenia, Cyprus and Byzantium. These were united off Sicily under the command of Andrea Dandolo. He chased the smaller part of the Genoese fleet there all the way to North Africa without bringing it to battle.[28] Internal dissensions would eventually prove fatal to the Genoese efforts. Toward the end of August 1298, a Genoese fleet commanded by Lamba Doria, originally of eighty-four galleys but due to losses to a storm in the Adriatic finally of seventy-seven, harried Venetian possessions on the Dalmatian coast, forcing the Venetian fleet to accept battle near Curzola Island early in September.[29] Andrea Dandolo's Venetian fleet was considerably larger, with ninety-six galleys, but was out-manoeuvred and outfought by the Genoese. Fewer than a dozen of the Venetian galleys escaped and thousands of Venetian mariners were taken prisoner. A contemporary Venetian analyst, Marin Sanudo, observed that the Genoese galleys were larger and better equipped than the Venetians'. This appears to be yet another indication that the Genoese had a greater number of the new triremes in their fleet.[30] In spite of the overwhelming victory, no attack on the Venetian lagoon followed. The Genoese had also suffered heavily and Doria feared internal dissension at home where Genoese Guelfs, based at Monaco and allied with Venice, threatened the city.[31] By this time, both sides had reasons to seek a peace. The Genoese, with the civil war between the Guelfs and the Ghibelline government of the metropolis growing increasingly dangerous and with the expense of maintaining hostilities growing increasingly burdensome, needed to end this war on two fronts. Venice and Pisa, with so many of their citizens imprisoned at Genoa, also had reason to seek an armistice. The Venetian failure to achieve decisive results by their attempt to destroy all of Genoa's eastern commerce in the strenuous campaign of 1297 and the inability of Genoa to follow a naval victory with an attack on the enemy home city led to the peace.

---

[27] Ibid.; Caro, *Genova*, II, 220 ff.
[28] Caro, *Genova*, II, 227 ff.
[29] Ibid., II, 233 ff.
[30] The exact composition of the fleets is unknown, but it is possible that the manpower of the Genoese fleet might have equalled or even exceeded that of the Venetians. Considering an extreme case in which all seventy-seven of the Genoese galleys were triremes carrying crews one and a half times as large as a bireme, and all ninety-six of the Venetian galleys were biremes, the disparity might have been as great as the proportion of 115.5 to 96.
[31] Caro, *Genova*, II, 236 ff.

Matteo Visconti, ruler of Milan, acted as broker for the accord. The treaty between Venice and Genoa established peace on terms of relative equality. Venice promised to stay out of any conflict between Genoa and Pisa and abandoned its support of the Genoese Guelfs. Likewise, the Genoese promised not to enter the Adriatic in the event of war between Venice and any of its neighbours. Genoa's peace with Pisa was considerably more harsh, signalling the imbalance of power that had existed between the two since the Battle of Meloria.[32]

Nonetheless, at the end of the War of Curzola, Genoa was arguably the most formidable maritime power in the Mediterranean. It was rich and populous. It could put to sea larger and more effective fleets than any other state. Not only were the fleets large, but the skill and bravery of their crews and commanders were acknowledged by all. Pisa was no longer a threat and Venice was checked.

During the first half of the fourteenth century the Genoese tightened their hold on the Black Sea trade. The third Genoese–Venetian war arose from this fact. The war began in 1350, only two years after the Black Death had devastated Italy. Both cities were hard pressed for manpower. The distinguished historian of Venice Frederic Lane estimated that the usual draft in Venice would have manned only twenty-five galleys. Additional manpower had to be sought in Dalmatia and Greece. The Venetians faced further difficulties when many of those drafted hired substitutes and discipline proved to be a problem. This was obvious in the first battle of the war when thirty-five Venetian galleys attacked fourteen Genoese merchant galleys at Castro, near Negroponte. The Venetian authorities were scandalised to learn that four of the Genoese galleys had escaped as the Venetian crews scrambled to plunder those vessels already taken.[33] Worse, the escaped galleys joined with several others out from Genoa and sacked the harbour at Negroponte.[34] Large fleets had, however, become the standard in naval war between the two cities. If local drafts and mercenaries were not sufficient, allies might be found. The Venetians found them in the Aragonese, who were contesting with Genoa for domination of Corsica and Sardinia,[35] and the Greek Emperor, John Cantacuzene. Venice offered subsidies to the king of Aragon and the Byzantine emperor in an effort to raise a fleet comparable to those that had operated during the second war.[36] In 1351 it was evident that the Genoese would move as quickly as they could to reinforce their colony at Pera. From there they might intimidate the Byzantine emperor into withdrawing from the coalition and shore up their strategic position there. King Pedro IV of Aragon's instructions to his admiral made it clear that destruction of the Genoese fleet was his primary objective. He would have preferred a strategy based on intercepting the Genoese before they could reach the East and only

---

[32] Ibid., II, 246.
[33] Lane, *Venice*, 175–6.
[34] *Annali Genovesi dopo Caffaro e i suoi continuatori*, ed. and trans. Giovanni Monleone, II (XI in the series), *Giorgio Stella* (second part) (Genoa, 1972), 76. Cf. Mario Brunetti, 'La battaglia di Castro (1350)', *Rivista marittima*, 43 (Jan.–Mar. 1910), 269–82.
[35] Caro, *Genova*, II, 224 ff.; Lane, *Venice*, 84.
[36] Lane, *Venice*, 175 ff.

reluctantly permitted his admiral the discretionary power to proceed to Romania if he failed to intercept the enemy. The allied plan was a good one. The Catalan and Venetian fleets would rendezvous near the Strait of Messina to intercept the Genoese if they moved toward the East.[37] However, they underestimated the size of the Genoese fleet and the alacrity with which their admiral, Paginino Doria, could move. He was on his way to Pera before the allies could get their fleets in position. The Venetians and Catalans were forced to pursue him to Constantinople.

The Genoese fleet of sixty galleys proceeded to Romania in the winter of 1351. The only Venetian force in its path, a fleet of twenty galleys, fled to Negroponte where the commander, Niccolo Pisani, scuttled it and undertook the defence of the port with the crews. When the Venetian and Catalan main force arrived to help the defenders, the Genoese lifted the siege and proceeded to their base at Pera. The Venetians and their allies strengthened their fleet by refloating Pisani's galleys. They then moved to join with the Greeks in order to dislodge the Genoese from the Bosporus.[38] There the fleets met in February 1352. Doria drew up his sixty galleys in a narrow part of the Bosporus so that their flanks could not be turned by the more numerous allied fleet. The allied fleet amounted to some eighty-nine galleys, forty-five Venetian, thirty Aragonese and fourteen Greek.[39] By all accounts the Greeks were never engaged and fled at the first opportunity, so the effective strength of the allies was only slightly greater than that of the Genoese. The battle was considered an especially bitter one, the more horrifying because it continued into the night as a storm broke over the sea. Losses were high on both sides. The Genoese chronicler, Giorgio Stella, said that there were reports of four thousand Venetian and Catalan dead and seven hundred or so Genoese.[40] Despite claims of victory by both sides the Genoese were clearly the victors. The Venetians and Aragonese had to withdraw their fleets and the Byzantine emperor was forced to accept a peace that recognised a strengthened Genoese position at Pera. Still, the Venetian–Aragonese combination was a potent one, even if the Greeks had been knocked out of the war. The focus of interest of the allies was different: Venice hoped to expel the Genoese from their strategic position on the Bosporus and in the Black Sea while Aragon wanted to wrest control of Sardinia from Genoa. Having failed to dislodge the Genoese from Constantinople in the bloody Battle of the Bosporus, the scene of battle shifted closer to the Aragonese area of interest. In August 1353, the allied fleet of eighty galleys, again under the command of Nicolo Pisani, inflicted a crushing defeat on Antonio Grimaldi off the harbour of Alghero in Sardinia. Forty-one of the sixty Genoese galleys were captured along with their crews.[41] The Genoese Guelfs and Ghibellines blamed one another for

---

[37] C. Manfroni, 'Il piano della campagna navale veneto-aragonese del 1351 contro Genova', in *Rivista marittima*, 35 (July–Sept. 1902), 323–32.
[38] Lane, *Venice*, 178.
[39] Giorgio Stella, II, 77.
[40] Ibid.
[41] Ibid., 78.

the disaster and civil war again threatened. This was averted by placing the government in the hands of the ruler of Milan, its archbishop Giovanni Visconti.[42]

The following year, 1354, the Genoese were still able to assemble a fleet of twenty-five galleys. Command was given to Paganino Doria who cruised first along the coast of Catalonia, then into the Adriatic where he burned the Istrian town of Parenzo (Porec). Another ten galleys were sent to reinforce this fleet. Venice armed thirty-six galleys and five great ships as well as smaller vessels to oppose him.[43] The fleets met near Porto Longo on the island of Sapienza (Sapiéntza) just south of Modon on 4 November. In the battle Doria's forces captured the entire Venetian force with very little loss to their own.[44] Both sides seem to have reached the end of their resources. Archbishop Giovanni Visconti had died and his nephews, Maffeo, Bernabó, and Galeazzo, did not want to continue to be entangled in Genoa's quarrel. A peace was negotiated that gave no great advantage to either side.

An incident in 1372 revealed the extent of hostility that still existed between the Genoese and the Venetians and led to the fourth war between Venice and Genoa, the War of Chioggia. At the coronation of King Peter II of Cyprus in Famagusta a quarrel broke out between them over a question of precedence. The Genoese seem to have got the worst of it. Genoa reacted by organising an expedition under Pietro Campofregoso, the doge's brother, to Cyprus. While this main force was being readied, a squadron of seven galleys commanded by Damiano Cattaneo went ahead to harry the island kingdom. The financial situation of the commune was so straitened that it had to turn to a private company, a *maona*, to raise the necessary money to pay for the main fleet. In early August thirty-six galleys and various other ships carrying fourteen thousand men set sail for Cyprus.[45] By 10 October Famagusta had been captured. Peter II was forced into a peace that eventually made Cyprus a virtual Genoese colony.[46] When the Genoese were granted control of the small island of Tenedos at the mouth of the Dardanelles by the Byzantine usurper, Andronicus IV, Venice became very concerned by this growing presence in two sensitive strategic areas. Besides, Venice had claims of her own to Tenedos. War threatened and the Genoese began with a diplomatic offensive that made clear that their strategy was to deliver a knockout blow to Venice itself. They tried to assemble a combination of allies on land to complement their naval forces to crush Venice, as Pisa had been crushed in a similar vise almost a century earlier. First, Aragon was neutralised at great sacrifice to Genoese interests by an agreement not to interfere in Sardinia. Alliances were forged with the king of Hungary and Francesco Carrara, the despot of Padua. Other local enemies of Venice entered the alliance, but provided little help.

---

[42] Epstein, *Genoa and the Genoese*, 220.
[43] Giorgio Stella, II, 80.
[44] Ibid.
[45] Ibid., 114; Epstein, *Genoa and the Genoese*, 236.
[46] Epstein, *Genoa and the Genoese*, 237.

Venice also found allies in, not surprisingly, Peter II, the king of Jerusalem and Cyprus, but also Bernabó Visconti of Milan. The latter would prove very valuable to them. Venice and Milan encouraged revolt in Liguria while Milan prepared to invade, hoping to re-establish Milanese lordship over Genoa. Fourteen Venetian galleys under the command of Vettor Pisani were sent to support these efforts. On 30 May, near Cape Anzio, south of Rome, they intercepted ten Genoese galleys under Luigi Fieschi on their way to join forces with the king of Hungary.[47] The considerably smaller size of these fleets is an indication of the reduced circumstances of both cities in the last quarter of the fourteenth century. Five of the Genoese galleys were lost, one ran aground, and the remaining four fled back to Genoa. These unfortunate events provoked another turnover in the government of Genoa. Doge Domenico Campofregoso was deposed and imprisoned by his successor, Nicolo Guarco. The new regime continued the war with Venice along the previously established lines. At the end of the summer, Luciano Doria was sent with seventeen galleys to Zara, now controlled by the king of Hungary. There he linked up with three of the survivors of the Battle of Cape Anzio who had returned to sea to harry Venetian shipping.[48] The following spring Doria cruised north-west along the Dalmatian coast. He found the Venetian fleet of twenty-one galleys refitting at Pula (Pola) in Istria on 5 May 1379. Only six of the Venetian galleys escaped the battle with their captain general, Vittore Pisano. Luciano Doria was killed in the fighting.[49] The victory was celebrated as a major triumph in Genoa and a kinsman, Pietro Doria, was appointed to replace the fallen Luciano. Within two weeks of the battle he sailed from Genoa with another fifteen galleys to take command.

Vettor Pisani's reception at Venice was quite different. He was arrested, charged with incompetence and cowardice, and imprisoned despite much popular support, especially from the sailors.[50] Carlo Zeno had earlier taken five galleys to harass Genoese shipping. After the Battle of Pula (Pola), six more were sent to reinforce him, apparently with the intent that an attack along the Riviera would force the Genoese fleet to withdraw as they had after Curzola. The Genoese were determined to end the conflict with Venice as it had the one with Pisa and conditions seemed right to make that possible. Hungarian forces threatened from the north, the Carrarese occupied Terra Ferma to the west and the Genoese fleet, far from returning home, dominated the Gulf. With supplies cut off Venice was threatened with starvation. Then in August 1379, combined Genoese and Paduan forces captured Chioggia at the southern entrance to the

---

[47] Giorgio Stella, II, 122; Epstein, *Genoa and the Genoese*, 238.
[48] Giorgio Stella, II, 127. Stella says that the total Genoese fleet was twenty-two galleys, but seventeen plus three is only twenty.
[49] Ibid., 128–9. Stella repeats that the Genoese fleet had twenty-two galleys. He also reports that the Venetian fleet had 425 mercenaries aboard 'the usual complement of the galleys' as well as many men from Pula (Pola). The Venetian galleys and 2407 prisoners were sent back to Zara. Fifteen captured galleys with 2407 prisoners would be about 160 men per galley, a perfectly believable figure.
[50] Lane, *Venice*, 192–3.

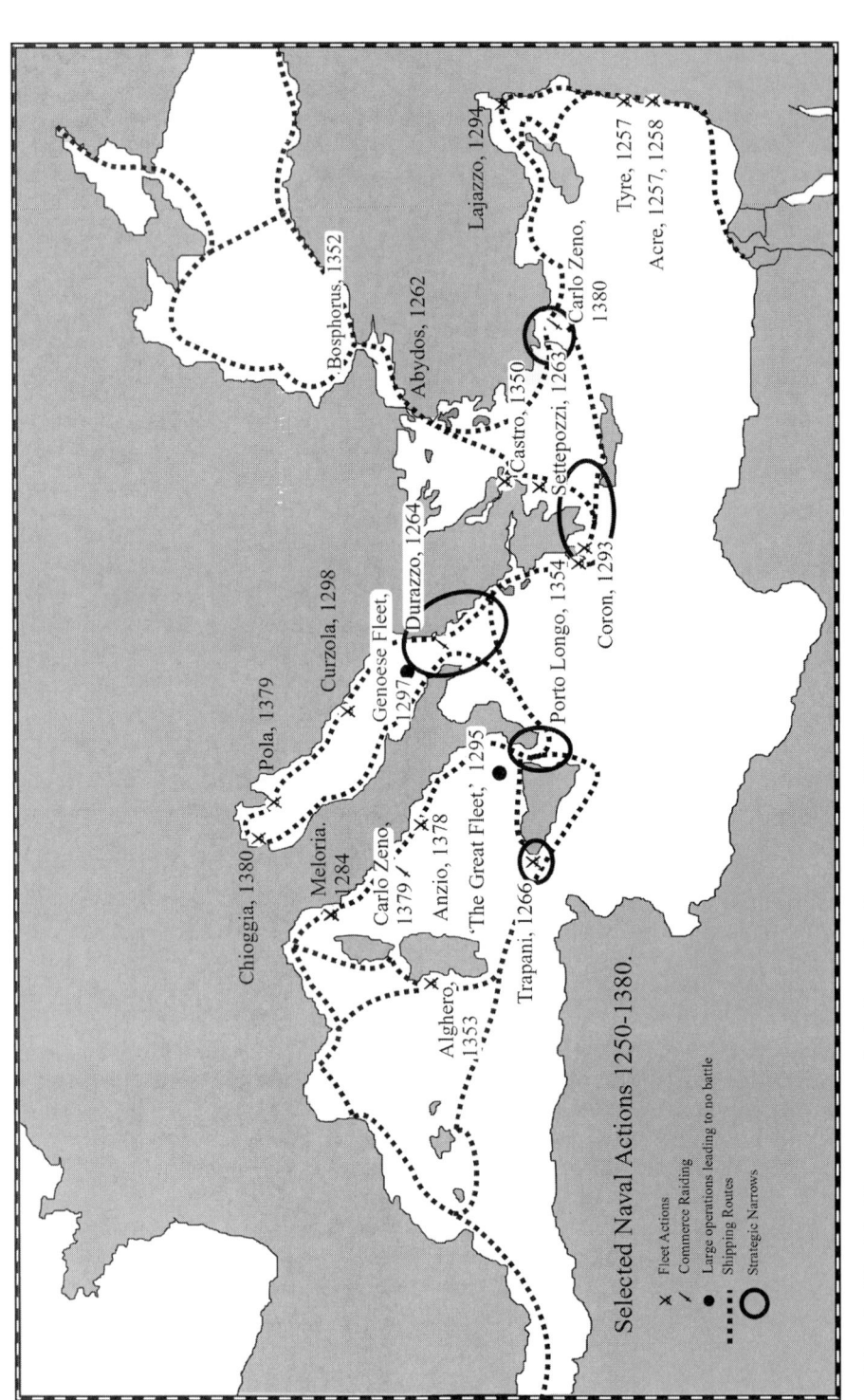

Map 1. The Mediterranean: selected naval actions, 1250–1380

lagoon. Venice sued for peace. In an often-quoted reply the Genoese refused to negotiate 'until they bridled the horses of San Marco'.[51] Clearly, they intended to occupy Venice itself. However, instead of pressing an assault on the unfortified city, they settled down at their base in Chioggia to starve the Serenissima into submission. Given the difficulties of navigating through the tortuous and unknown channels of the lagoon, this was, on the surface, a prudent strategy though it proved fatal in the end. In extreme danger, and needing the complete support of the population, the Venetian government turned to Vettor Pisani. With extreme difficulty another thirty-four galleys were armed. Finding crews for them was more difficult and a draft brought many landsmen to the benches where they learned to row between the Giudecca and the Lido. Pisani planned to sink stone-laden hulks in the major channels of the lagoon to make them impassable to large ships that might carry an army to the Rialto. Under cover of a dark winter night in December and a diversionary attack on Chioggia, the obstacles were placed. The siege of the besiegers had begun.[52]

Meanwhile, with virtually the entire Genoese fleet involved in the attack on Venice, Carlo Zeno had a free hand to sweep the Mediterranean attacking Genoese ships wherever he found them, from Portovenere to Beirut. Even after he received an urgent recall from Venice, he attacked and captured a large and richly laden Genoese cog in the harbour at Rhodes. Even after his return the Venetians did not give battle to the Genoese fleet in the Adriatic, but doggedly kept to their siege of Chioggia. The War of Chioggia is notable in another respect. It appears to be the first time that gunpowder artillery was used on a large scale and from on board ships. Pietro Doria was killed by a shot from a bombard.[53] The Genoese sent reinforcements, thirteen galleys in March, and another five in May, to relieve their besieged forces in Chioggia. The efforts were in vain. Even an attempt to subvert mercenaries in the Venetian forces with a large bribe failed.[54] Finally, in June, running out of food and ammunition, the Genoese forces in Chioggia surrendered. The Venetians captured four thousand Genoese citizens and nineteen galleys. The war continued for several more months. Milanese forces captured Novi in September. Vettor Pisani died in battle against the remaining Genoese forces in the Adriatic.[55] But, for all practical purposes the War of Chioggia ended with the failure of the Genoese and their allies to capture Venice itself.

The Peace of Turin, concluded in August 1381, ended the war. Possession of Tenedos, the immediate cause of the war, was ceded to Genoa. But the Genoese agreed not to fortify it. The Venetians promised not to interfere in the conflict

---

[51] Ibid., 192; Epstein, *Genoa and the Genoese*, 239.
[52] Lane, *Venice*, 193.
[53] Giorgio Stella, II, 140; Lane, *Venice*, 195. Whether he was killed directly by a stone projectile, or by a stone from a collapsing tower, is unclear. The Genoese seemed to have been surprised by the extensive Venetian use of these new weapons (Giorgio Stella, II, 141, n. 436).
[54] Lane, *Venice*, 195.
[55] Epstein, *Genoa and the Genoese*, 241; Lane, *Venice*, 195.

on Cyprus. Thus ended the last major episode in the conflict between Venice and Genoa that had lasted for a century-and-a-quarter. It can be argued that the terms of the peace were favorable to Genoa; after all they had possession of Tenedos. The cost of the war and, one suspects, the failure to finish off the old enemy after coming so near, was more than Genoese society could bear. Venice recovered, ultimately coming to dominate the Terra Ferma. Genoa slipped into a period of foreign domination, first by the Milanese and then by the French. Very soon the naval power of both cities would be overshadowed by national monarchies and great empires.

Over a series of wars spanning nearly a century-and-a-half, much changed. Technology evolved, but did not yet change the fundamental nature of naval warfare in the Mediterranean Sea. That would occur only when northern powers introduced full-rigged ships with broadside batteries. The ships used in combat became larger as the trireme galley replaced the bireme. By the 1370s gunpowder artillery had made an appearance, though not a decisive one. The deadliest weapon in naval warfare was still, at the end of the fourteenth century, almost certainly the crossbow. The Genoese seemed to have gained a slight technological edge for a time late in the thirteenth century if, indeed, they did lead in the introduction of the trireme, but it was not decisive.

Strategic goals evolved from the rather limited attempts to expel the enemy from the immediate point of conflict to the aim of eliminating his ability to conduct war at all. Complex naval operations over large stretches of the Mediterranean involving a sophisticated understanding of time and geography, utilizing intelligence gathering, subterfuge, and a variety of stratagems to bring enemy fleets to battle on favorable terms could be, and were, mounted. Still, the limitations of galley warfare are clear. While the interception of major merchant fleets might be the effective equivalent of a blockade, this became more difficult from the late thirteenth century as navigational and other technical advances opened the seas to year round navigation. Even under the earlier conditions of limited sailing seasons the interception and capture of a merchant convoy was a difficult and chancy affair. Only Simone Grillo's operation in 1264 actually succeeded in such an endeavor on a major scale. On the whole, merchant activity could be harassed, but not interdicted. Nonetheless, the Eastern luxury trade was a high-stakes commerce that moved goods of enormous value and huge profit margins in a very few vessels. The loss of even individual ships could inflict painful, if not fatal, economic damage.

The elimination of a war fleet, while serious, did not spell ruin for the maritime cities. Great naval victories seem to have brought only minimal results. The capture of the entire Genoese fleet at Trapani in 1266 did not end the war, nor did other seemingly stunning victories by one side or another. The loss of trained manpower that such a defeat entailed was apparently more damaging than the loss of galleys. Successive defeats could wear down an opponent as indispensable skilled mariners were killed, disabled, or taken away into captivity. The huge numbers of Venetian and Pisan prisoners held by Genoa at the end of the War of Curzola seems to have been a major factor in persuading them to seek a peace. In the end, though, manpower losses could lead to a suspension of hostilities, but not to long-term control of the seas.

The amphibious nature of galley warfare is evident in the wars between the Italian maritime republics. Decisive actions focused on the control of ports and bases. Venice gained the upper hand in Oltremare when the Genoese were forced out of Acre. The very effective Genoese reply was an alliance that forced the Venetians out of Constantinople. Even when the Venetians returned to the city on the Bosphorus they found themselves trumped by the independent Genoese base at Pera. The most decisive naval battle of the era occurred when Benedetto Zaccaria crushed the Pisans at Meloria in 1284. Pisa, however, was a relatively small city caught between Genoa at sea and its Tuscan neighbors, Lucca and Florence, on land. This combination, in which a victory over an enemy fleet was followed by an attack on its home city, supported by land-based allies, seems to have provided the Genoese with a paradigm for victory which they would attempt to repeat in subsequent wars with the Venetians.

Relatively quickly after the Latin conquest of Constantinople in 1204, Venice built a chain of bases from the lagoons of the northern Adriatic, along the Dalmatian coast, across the Aegean to the Bosphorus. This enabled the Venetians to rely on an essentially defensive strategy to protect their position in the eastern basins of the Mediterranean. Genoa was able to establish powerful bases in the East, but they did not form a nearly continuous chain as did the Venetian bases. Even Pera was, at times, less effective than one might expect because its population could be at odds with the metropolis during Genoa's frequent internecine struggles. Venices's Aegean bases were strongly held. In the end, it took the Ottoman Turks over a century of combined military and naval assaults to uproot them. Genoa did not have comparable resources at its disposal. On the other hand, Venice was never able to mount a major fleet operation within the Tyrrhenian Sea and the Gulf of Genoa to compare with those of the Genoese in the Adriatic.

In the final analysis, the strategic situation put the burden of offensive on the Genoese. The Venetian bases gave them not outright domination of the Eastern Seas but a dominant position. Lacking the resources to grind away at the Venetians as the Ottomans would later do, the Genoese struck at the two anchor points: first, at Constantinople and then at Venice itself. In the War of Chioggia, they came very near to succeeding.

The Venetians with their Arsenal and state-owned ships perhaps more nearly approached the modern idea of a navy than did the Genoese combination of state and privately financed fleets. Still, the conduct of the wars, with their economically-driven enmities, the search for a decisive battle between fleets combined with intensive commerce raiding, certainly seems to foreshadow the undeniably modern wars of the eighteenth century.

GENOESE NAVAL FORCES IN THE MEDITERRANEAN DURING THE FIFTEENTH AND SIXTEENTH CENTURIES

Michel Balard

A REPUBLIC that does not possess the art of war is deprived of that which makes it a republic.[1] Thus spoke Doge Matteo Senarega, at the end of the sixteenth century, in a debate that involved all the ruling groups of Genoa at the time. Was it necessary to create a real state fleet, capable of making the power of the Republic respected and of preserving its liberty, or was it better to leave matters in the hands of private ship-owners from whom the state could charter services in case of a foreign threat, imperial naval obligations, or corsairs who dared to attack the vessels of *la Superba*?

The imbalance between public naval forces and private ones was a constant feature of Genoese history. The galleys of the state counted for little compared to the fleets that the great familial clans could assemble, especially at the beginning of the sixteenth century. Was this a consequence of the Genoese individualism so dear to Roberto Lopez,[2] or was it due to a delayed development toward a modern state, leaving Genoa slow to put into place the means of defence necessary for its survival? To explain the reason for these disproportions it is necessary to determine the importance of Genoese naval forces raised during the fifteenth and sixteenth centuries. It is also necessary to evaluate the frequent, often debated, efforts to construct a real state fleet and, finally, to demonstrate the conditions which were required for such efforts to establish a fleet to be realised.

The studies of Jacques Heers, followed by those of other modern Genoese scholars,[3] allow a characterisation of the Genoese fleet over the course of the two centuries examined here. Indeed, its major features hardly changed from one century to the next. Merchant ships were distinguished by their ample displacement, designed for transporting heavy goods such as alum or salt, and

---

[1] C. Costantini, 'Aspetti della politica navale genovese nel Seicento', in *Guerra e commercio nell'evoluzione della marina genovese tra XV e XVII secolo*, 2 vols (Genoa, 1970–3), I, 209.
[2] R. S. Lopez, 'Le Marchand génois, un profil collectif', in *Annales. Economies. Sociétés. Civilisations*. 13e année, no. 3 (1958), 501–15, reprinted in his *Su e giù per la storia di Genova* (Genoa, 1975), 17–33.
[3] J. Heers, *Gênes au XVe siècle. Activité économique et problèmes sociaux* (Paris, 1961), 642; *Guerra e commercio*.

the grain necessary to feed the city. They are, on the whole, much better known than the galley, whose commercial use seemed to decline over time, the type principally shifting to its military tasks. According to Heers, in 1458 the Genoese fleet included twenty-six ships with a total capacity of 340,000 cantars, i.e. about 16,200 tons for an average of about 620 tons per ship.[4] A decade later, in 1465–6, the composition of the Genoese fleet had scarcely changed: twenty-four ships represented a total of about 321,000 cantars, about 15,300 tons or close to 640 tons capacity per vessel.[5] As for galleys, their number changed according to the demands of war. Rarely did more than ten or so take to sea at one time, and there were never more than a few under construction in the shipyard each year. In 1459, the Council of Elders, noting that the Commune had only three galleys and two *fuste*, decided to arm seven to ten galleys, under unquestionably exceptional circumstances.[6]

At the end of the fifteenth century, the forces provided for the naval expedition of King Charles VIII of France are known in detail. In 1494, the Genoese fleet was composed of nineteen *navi*, six *barche*, thirty-six *galioni* and *saette*, twenty-nine galleys, three *fuste*, and five *brigantine*, with a total of approximately 19,000 tons, excluding the galleys.[7] Between 1474 and 1509, the number of *navi* larger than 8000 cantars capacity ranged from a minimum of eleven vessels in 1502 to a maximum of twenty-one in 1494. The total tonnage of the Genoese fleet oscillated between 250,000 and 300,000 cantars, i.e. between 12,000 and 14,200 tons. That would be slightly smaller than the Venetian fleet, which is estimated at 355,000 cantars (17,000 tons) at the end of the fifteenth century. Genoa constructed, on average, two *navi* per year with an aggregate tonnage of 30,000 to 40,000 cantars (1430 to 1900 tons). In 1548 the Genoese fleet grew to around 20,000 tons, a figure that is slightly greater than that of the Venetian fleet, estimated at 16,000 tons in 1560.[8]

That 1560 figure was the maximum, however, because beginning in the 1520s, in Genoa as in Venice, there was a crisis in naval construction arising from the difficulty of recruiting crews and the rising price of materials, especially of timber needed by the arsenals. Further, the increasing threat of piracy made commercial navigation ever more precarious. The scarcity of timber was the major factor in making naval construction more expensive after 1550. To maintain its fleet Genoa found it necessary to grant loans to ship-owners at a rate of interest sufficiently attractive to encourage naval investment. This is one indication of greater state intervention in maritime affairs. The government of

---

[4] Heers, *Gênes au XVe siècle*, 639–42.
[5] Ibid., 642–4.
[6] Ibid., 270 n. 3.
[7] M. Calegari, 'Navi e barche a Genova tra il XV e il XVI secolo', in *Guerra e commercio*, I, 15.
[8] M. Calegari, 'Legname e costruzioni navali nel Cinquecento', in *Guerra e commercio*, II, 107–8.

Genoa was becoming aware that maintaining a fleet was an important element in the power and prosperity of its citizens and even of the state itself.

Over several centuries, in fact, Genoa had entrusted the defence of its territory and the undertaking of large naval operations to private ship-owners. As early as 1263, the Commune sent twenty-five galleys, one *saetta*, and five *barche* under the command of Pietrino Grimaldi and Pescetto Mallone, who had loaned their government 36,000 *lire genovesi*, to fight against Venice. The government, in turn, imposed a forced loan of 30,000 *lire genovesi*, granting to the creditors revenues arising from an increase in the tax on imports of grain. For the first time the terms *luoghi* and *colonna* were used to designate the shares held by the creditors of the state and the blocs of shares that they held.[9]

Table I shows the size of fleets armed by the Commune from 1298 to 1400, a period that is well known for three great colonial wars between Genoa and Venice. The chronicler Giorgio Stella recorded the mobilising of a fleet approximately every two years. At the beginning of the century these fleets put to sea as the result of confrontations between Genoese Guelfs and Ghibellines. In the years around 1330, the struggle against the Catalans took priority. From 1350 to 1354, the conflict with Venice and Catalonia required prodigious naval endeavours. In 1373, the expedition to Cyprus was organised and, from 1378 to 1381, the War of Chioggia necessitated the mobilisation of all available units. However, during the whole century, there was never a question of a permanent state navy. The great Genoese *alberghi*, the towns of the Riviera, and the feudatories of the Commune participated in financing efforts that were always considered exceptional: forced loans and increases in previously instituted taxes led to the formation of the *compere*, associations of the creditors of the state who joined together when they were not repaid, so that their collective strength could ensure that public resources would be dedicated to the payment of the interest on the debt. In this way the arming of fleets was the principal cause of the rise in the public debt that led to the creation of the Banco di San Giorgio in 1408.

The process can be made more clear by looking at some examples. Under the leadership of Simone Vignoso, the conquest of Chios was achieved in 1346. Twenty-nine ship-owners put their galleys at the disposal of the Commune, which could define a policy of overseas expansion but was not capable of providing the means to carry it out.[10] The *Annali* of Giorgio Stella are explicit in the reporting of this event: 'Considering that in Genoa the public treasury was deprived of money, the Council decided to arm twenty-five galleys or more [there were actually twenty-nine] with money taken from the citizens, in such a way, however, that the Commune of Genoa . . . was obliged, after the expedition was over, to pay the ship-owners a return of 20,000 *lire genovesi* that the Republic receives every year from the *compere* of the *luoghi del Capitolo* and

---

[9] C. Imperiale di Sant'Angelo, *Annali genovesi di Caffaro e de' suoi continuatori*, vol. IV (Rome, 1926), 49–50.
[10] P. P. Argenti, *The Occupation of Chios by the Genoese and Their Administration of the Island 1346–1566*, 3 vols (Cambridge, 1958), vol. I, 86–105.

other revenues.'[11] Once the conquest of Chios was successfully achieved, the ship-owners then returned to Genoa and advanced the sum of 250,000 *lire* to cover the expenses of the campaign. After long deliberations, an agreement was concluded on 26 February 1347 between the Commune and the group of its creditors represented by Simone Vignoso. This association took the name of the *Maona* of Chios. The debt owed to the ship-owners was repaid in shares, or *luoghi*, to an amount of 203,000 *lire genovesi*. This was less than the commanders of the ships demanded, but nonetheless they got property and the administration of Chios and the two Phocaeas, in addition to the revenues provided by the *luoghi*.[12] The more-or-less forced benevolence of the ship-owners made up for the deficiencies of the state, which was then obliged to hand over public revenues to them to meet its obligations.

Four years later, during the War of the Bosporus (1350–5), the Commune was again taken by surprise. On 25 November 1350, Doge Giovanni Valente imposed a forced loan of 300,000 *lire genovesi*. The lenders were grouped into a new *compera*, the *Compera Magna Venetorum*. The revenue from twenty-two indirect taxes was assigned to them to guarantee the payment of the interest on the loan. The *Officium Guerre Venetorum*, established to coordinate the war effort, chartered merchant galleys that were easily converted into warships. Of the sixty galleys that comprised the fleet commanded by Paganino Doria, only eighteen were new: five constructed in Sampierdarena, five by the *darsena* of Genoa, two at Sarzano, two at the Molo, one at the mouth of the Bisagno, while three communes of the Riviera: Savona, Recco, and Sestri Levante each built a new galley.[13]

The same system was used in two later expeditions to the east. In 1373, the Commune set out to avenge the humiliations visited upon its citizens during the riots that accompanied the coronation of Peter II of Lusignan as king of Cyprus. It decided to levy a tax of 104,000 *lire genovesi* in the city and in the towns of the Riviera, and still the Commune could equip only a few small craft. A group of individuals had to help the government to finance the projected naval expedition: seven galleys arrived in Cyprus under the command of Damiano Cattaneo, ahead of the main fleet of thirty-six vessels led by Pietro di Campofregoso, the brother of the doge. Thus was the *Maona Vecchia di Cipro* born, made up of the *patroni* of the ships that participated in the expedition and the individuals who had provided the necessary funds. The sums advanced were divided into *luoghi*, which were backed by money paid in by the king of Cyprus. A list compiled in August 1374 contained two hundred and twenty-two names of participants,

---

[11] Georgius and Johannes Stella, *Annales Genuenses*, ed. G. Petti-Balbi, Rerum Italicarum Scriptores 2, XVII/2 (Bologna, 1975), 145.
[12] M. Balard, *La Romanie génoise (XIIe–début du XVe siècle)*, 2 vols, Bibliothèque des Ecoles Françaises d'Athènes et de Rome no. 235 (Rome, 1978), vol. I, 123–5.
[13] M. Balard, 'A propos de la bataille du Bosphore. L'expédition de Paganino Doria à Constantinople (1351–1352)', in *Travaux et mémoires du centre de recherche d'histoire et civilisation byzantines*, vol. IV (1970), 435, reprinted in his *La Mer noire et la Romanie génoise (XIIIe–XVe siècles)*, Variorum Reprints (London, 1989), II.

among them some of the greatest *alberghi* of Genoa, owners of the expedition galleys. The *maona* which was thus created oversaw the accounts of the Genoese colony of Famagusta, received the remittances of the king of Cyprus and distributed them among its members. This gave them the right to intervene in decisions taken by the Commune regarding the affairs of Famagusta.[14]

In January 1403, a loan of 32,000 florins was floated to arm the expedition planned by Marshall Boucicault, governor of Genoa for the king of France, who intended to reply to the failed attempt by King Janus of Cyprus to take Famagusta. Nine galleys, seven *navi*, a galeass, and a *huissier* were all fitted out with money from individuals who formed a new *maona* of Cyprus.[15] These profited from the payments imposed upon King Janus by the treaty of 1403, i.e. 15,000 ducats per year realised from taxes collected in the kingdom of the Lusignans. Boucicault, trained in the French royal school of administration, conceived the idea of providing Genoa with a permanent fleet for defence and for the high seas. However, the royal governor was expelled from Genoa in September 1409 and was never able to bring this idea to fruition.

During the war against Alfonso V of Aragon the Commune had to negotiate endlessly with private ship-owners to obtain vessels, with the protectors of the Banco di San Giorgio for funding, and with the towns of the Riviera to institute new taxes or to determine their individual contributions. Although an *Officium Balie Marittime* had been established and was charged with organising the arming of the fleet, its departure under the command of Tommasino di Campofregoso for the expedition against Naples was delayed for financial reasons. The government had to get loans from the richest citizens.[16]

Though entirely without suitable financing, the Commune did not turn away from its maritime life. It immediately set about elaborating its maritime laws that touched upon the commercial aspects of navigation as well as naval policy. From the beginning of the fourteenth century the *Officium Gazarie* assumed such tasks as the fixing of crew strengths, establishment of safety measures in the stowage of goods, organisation of reserve shipping, and the inspection of ships on arrival or departure. The *Officium*'s regulatory activities continued until 1528 even though its role began to diminish from the last years of the fourteenth century.[17] In 1498 its duties were absorbed by the *Officium Maris*, which, from the time of its creation at the end of the fourteenth century, was primarily occu-

[14] C. Otten, 'Les Institutions génoises et les affaires de Chypre', in M. Balard, ed., *Etat et colonisation au Moyen Age* (Lyon, 1989), 169–70; C. Otten, 'Les Relations politico-financières de Gênes avec le royaume des Lusignans (1374–1460)', in M. Balard and A. Ducellier, *Coloniser au Moyen Age* (Paris, 1995), 62–3.
[15] *Annales Genuenses*, 263; cf. F. Surdich, 'Genova e Venezia fra Tre e Quattrocento', in *Atti della Società ligure di storia patria*, n.s. 7 (81), fasc. 2 (Genoa, 1967), 248 n. 34.
[16] On all of these, see G. Olgiati, *Classis contra Regem Aragonum (Genova 1453–1454). Organizzazione militare ed economica della spedizione navale contro Napoli* (Cagliari, 1990), 115–215; E. Basso, *Genova: un impero sul mare* (Cagliari, 1994), 243–61.
[17] V. Vitale, *Le fonti del diritto marittimo ligure* (Genoa, 1951). Cf. M. Calegari, 'Patroni di nave e magistrature marittime', in *Guerra e commercio*, I, 62.

pied with the supervision of crews and the recognition of guarantors presented by sailors when they were recruited.[18] This office also disappeared in 1528, much to the profit of the *conservatori del mare*, private ship-owners who thus got from the state prerogatives of supervision and intervention over the craftsmen who built and repaired ships and ship fittings as well as over harbour discipline. Finally, in 1559, a new commission was formed, *Il magistrato delle galee*, whose mission was to organise a state fleet for the defence of Genoese coasts and ships.[19]

The first initiatives in this direction, however, began in the second half of the fourteenth century. When Domenico Campofregoso was doge (1370–8), the first attempt was made to finance a naval force with state funds.[20] One of his successors, Leonardo Montaldo, achieved this goal in 1383 by arming ten galleys to free Pope Urban VI, besieged at Nocera by Louis III of Duras.[21] With Boucicault having free rein for his projects of Mediterranean expansion, two fleets began to be prepared, one of Africa against the Barbary Coast, the other of Cyprus and Syria against the Mamlukes. In the end, only one expedition, that of Cyprus and Beirut, was actually carried out by the marshal in 1403.[22]

These were only ephemeral projects, yet by comparison to them, the lone enduring operation of the sentry galley appears totally derisory. Beginning in 1369, one can follow in the ordinary budget of the Commune, but only very irregularly, sums dedicated to this galley that patrolled along the Ligurian coast with the mission of signalling the presence of hostile fleets or corsairs. One can, nevertheless, extrapolate that practice to other zones, since a document of 1402 mentions the surveillance of Provence, Corsica, and Sardinia among the tasks assigned to the sentry galley.[23] The cost to the Commune ranged from 1500 to 12,000 *lire* depending on the year and, especially, on the duration of service.[24] Indeed, it seems that only the officers were paid by the year while the pay of sailors and ship's boys was calculated according to the time that they were at sea.[25] A coastguard vessel, whose expenses did not exceed 300 *lire* per year, was attached to the sentry galley beginning in 1398. The modest sums recorded in the regular budget of the Commune for its naval defence confirms that this duty was still essentially entrusted to private initiative. The expenses incurred were covered by loans, by the organisation of *maone*, and by the assignment of indi-

[18] Ibid., I, 62.
[19] V. Borgese, 'Il magistrato delle galee', in *Guerra e commercio*, II, 189.
[20] G.-G. Musso, 'Armamento e navigazione a Genova tra il Tre e il Quattrocento (appunti e documenti)', in *Guerra e commercio*, II, 21.
[21] R. di Tucci, 'Costruzione di galee genovesi durante il dogato di Leonardo Montaldo', in *Ad Alessandro Luzio – Miscellanea di studi* (Florence, 1933), 331–8.
[22] Surdich, 'Genova e Venezia', 238–65.
[23] Musso, 'Armamento, e navigazione', 32.
[24] M. Buongiorno, *Il bilancio di uno Stato medievale. Genova 1340–1529* (Genoa, 1973), 374–438.
[25] Calegari, 'Navi e barche', 41.

rect taxes to those who really wanted to participate in the extraordinary financing of these galleys.

Overseas, the situation was just as difficult. Caffa maintained only one galley on duty and some *brigantine* to oversee commerce in the Black Sea and to protect communications with other Genoese commercial centres.[26] In 1402, the bourgeois of Pera were required by Boucicault to commit some support to his expedition against Cyprus. They advanced 34,838 hyperpers, 22 carats, which the French marshal promised to repay from a portion of the excise taxes collected at Pera after the return of peace.[27] The expenses of equipping the sentry galley, as well as the pay of its crew, were raised from the budget of each community. These costs became intolerable when a local conflict exploded and required the simultaneous equipping of several vessels, and especially when the metropolis called on its overseas colonies for naval support, as happened, for example, at the time of the various conflicts with Venice. Between April 1379 and January 1382, Caffa was required to arm five galleys, at a cost to its treasury of close to 7500 *sommi*, while, at the same time, the *podesteria* of Pera and the *maona* of Chios each put two galleys at the disposal of the Commune.[28] Here again, public mobilisation was financed, in part or in whole, by forced loans or by the imposition of new indirect taxes whose yield was assigned to the creditors of the Commune.

In spite of this constant recourse to the private ship-owners of Genoa itself and of its overseas colonies the need for state galleys became increasingly clear during the fifteenth century. In 1402, under the government of Boucicault, the *Officium super gubernatione Darssine Communis Janue et armamentorum gallearum* was created. It was composed of four officers who maintained the inventory of supplies and equipment necessary for arming the galleys of the Commune.[29] Between 1400 and 1450, an average of four galleys were constructed each year. At least some of them must have been built in the state arsenal.[30] In 1494, at the time of Charles VIII's expedition to Italy, Genoa prepared twenty-two galleys, of which four were owned by the Commune.[31] On the other hand, Andrea Doria had a permanent fleet of twenty to thirty galleys, a superiority that explains why, when he chose to side with Spain, he had no difficulty in imposing this choice on his city and instituting a centuries-long aristocratic republic of biennial doges. Against his fleet in 1527 the city could only deploy its two sentry galleys and two others belonging to Fabrizio Giustiniani.[32]

It was not until the second half of the sixteenth century that a Genoese war fleet was established. Its creation caused much debate at Genoa. After 1528, little by little, the idea of establishing a permanent fleet alongside that of the

[26] Balard, *La Romanie génoise*, I, 397.
[27] Ibid., I, 396–7 and 448–52.
[28] Ibid., I, 451.
[29] Musso, 'Armamento e navigazione', 32.
[30] Calegari, 'Legname e construzioni navali', 140.
[31] Ibid., 114.
[32] Borghesi, 'Il magistrato delle galee', 199.

1. The Genoese Fleet and the Arsenal of Genoa, by Christoforo Grassi.
By courtesy of the Museo Navale di Genoa

Dorias took hold. The poet Paolo Foglietta saw the surest guarantee of the autonomy of the republic in that development.[33] Though the creation of a fleet might have been seen as a competitor threatening to Genoa's Spanish ally, it seems highly doubtful. Again, in 1535, at the time of the expedition against La Goulette, the Republic could only muster three galleys, while the Doria family had thirty afloat and one under construction.[34] Until 1559 the two sentry galleys secured coastal defence, while galleys chartered by the Republic or private galleys undertook the expeditions launched against corsairs.

The institution of the *magistrato delle galee* in 1559 was a decisive turning point that marks the final outcome of the debate on the naval rearmament of Genoa. The four nobles who were elected to make up this new magistracy were charged to look after the management of funds dedicated to the establishment and maintenance of a fleet of state-owned galleys, to construct and to sell new galleys, and to manage the Arsenal. The communities of the Riviera were obliged to pay two-thirds of the expenses associated with each of the public galleys. Most of the expenses were covered by income from chartering of those galleys and by the yield from several excise taxes, in particular the *Ripa grossa*, a tax on the sale of personal property.[35] Results were slow in coming: four public galleys in 1559, then only three in 1564, four again in 1583, then six in 1586.[36] Up to that date, the incomes from the various excise taxes were far from covering expenses: 80,000 *lire* in receipts against 130,000 *lire* of expendi-

---

[33] Ibid., 191.
[34] Ibid., 199.
[35] D. Gioffre, *Liber Institutionum Cabellarum Veterum (Comunis Janue)* (Milan, 1967), index.
[36] V. Borghesi, 'Il magistrato delle galee', 192.

tures.[37] Yet, the movement toward the foundation of a state navy had begun. It was far from equalling the naval strength that Venice (twenty galleys in 1580), the Papal States (fifteen in 1550), or even Sicily (ten galleys) could muster. Nevertheless, Genoa had become aware of the need to preserve the integrity of its Ligurian territory just at the moment when the Barbary corsairs were at their most aggressive. The victory of Lepanto as well demonstrated the importance of state fleets in the struggle against the Ottomans.

It remains to explain this surprising Genoese contrast: on one hand it had one of the most powerful merchant marines of the Mediterranean world while on the other its war fleet was weak, indeed laughable, in comparison with the forces of its naval competitors. The first explanation for this situation arises from the weakness of the Genoese state, a conglomeration of diverse economic interests incapable of establishing a stable government and obliged to call on foreign protectors: Valois France, Milan, then Spain. The great familial clans, recognising only their own economic and financial interests, were scarcely supporters of investing in naval forces whose under-utilisation would be obvious except in times of great conflicts. Only then would they accept forced loans or put their own vessels at the disposal of the state with the intent of defending its threatened interests or to profit by skimming from the public purse.

The second explanation comes then from the emphasis placed upon large-capacity merchant ships able to transport raw materials and foodstuffs over long distances economically. Genoa was concerned with the protection of these maritime transports so that it required them to operate in convoys furnished with accompanying fighting personnel who were considered indispensable.

The third explanation derives from the astonishing agility with which the Genoese were able to transform their naval resources. A merchant ship such as the great galley could become, in an emergency, a warship, just as a merchant could become a corsair preying on his government's enemies. The Arsenal of Genoa, as illustrated in the famous picture by Christoforo Grassi,[38] held a sufficient reserve of galleys and war *matériel* to allow a naval campaign to be launched with very little delay because of the exceptionally high degree of competence of its workforce.

In short, the domination of the sea by the Genoese essentially meant freedom of the trade routes to the orient and then toward the west, routes that intersected with those of the Venetians and which might be blocked by Catalan imperialism in the central Mediterranean. The desperate battles that Genoa fought in the fourteenth and fifteenth centuries, interrupted by long periods of truce and of peace, gave rise to freedom of commerce. Curiously, it was at the time when the Genoese passed under the protection of Spain and became the bankers of Europe that they finally asserted the need for a public war fleet as guarantor of the prosperity and of the autonomy of their city.

---

[37] Ibid., 195.
[38] Naval Museum of Genoa.

Table I. Genoese fleets in the thirteenth and fourteenth centuries

Years	Ships	Commanders	Destination	Source
1205	2 galleys	Henry, count of Malta	Romania	*Annali Genovesi*, II,98
1206	3 galleys		Constantinople	*Annali Genovesi*, II,104
1207	7 galleys		Ultramare	*Annali Genovesi*, II,106
1208	galleys and *naves*		Crete	*Annali Genovesi*, II,109
1209	*naves*		Ultramare	*Annali Genovesi*, II,112
1210	8 galleys, 1 *tarida*, 3 *naves*		Crete	*Annali Genovesi*, II,114
1213	*naves*		Alexandria	*Annali Genovesi*, II,126
1217	galleys, *naves, taridae*		Ultramare	*Annali Genovesi*, II,144
1219	10 galleys	Iohanes Rubeus de Volta, Petrus Auriae	Damietta	*Annali Genovesi*, II,153
1222	*naves*		Beirut	*Annali Genovesi*, II,184
1226	4 galleys, 2 *sagitteae*, 1 *bucius*	Belmustus Vicecomes	Savona, Albenga	*Annali Genovesi*, III,15
1229	1 *caravana* of *naves*		Ultramare	*Annali Genovesi*, III,42–43
1229	4 galleys	Octobonus Malonus	Nizza Marittima	*Annali Genovesi*, III,48
1231	*naves*		Ultramare	*Annali Genovesi*, III,55
1231	10 galleys	Carbonus Malocellus, Nicolaus Spinula		*Annali Genovesi*, III,56
1232	5 galleys	Guglielmus son of N. Malonus		*Annali Genovesi*, III,63
1232	10 galleys	Ansaldus Boletus, Bonifacius Panzanus		*Annali Genovesi*, III,64
1234	14 galleys, 18 *naves*	Lanfrancus Spinula, Octobonus de Camilla	Ceuta	*Annali Genovesi*, III,72–74
1235	4 galleys, 70 *naves*	Ugo Lercarius	Ceuta	*Annali Genovesi*, III,75–76
1238	14 galleys	Fulco Guercius, Rubeus de Turcha	Ventimiglia, Galinara	*Annali Genovesi*, III,85
1239	13 galleys	Fulco Guercius	Riviera	*Annali Genovesi*, III,93
1241	1 *caravana* of *naves*		Ultramare	*Annali Genovesi*, III,115
1241	30 galleys	Iacobus Malocellus	Roma	*Annali Genovesi*, III,116
1241	53 galleys and *taridae*	Ansaldus Soldanus, Iacopus de Levanto	Against the imperial fleet	*Annali Genovesi*, III,116
1242	40 galleys		Pisa	*Annali Genovesi*, III,127
1243	10 galleys		Pisa	*Annali Genovesi*, III,146
1244	25 galleys	Podestat of Genoa	Ultramare	*Annali Genovesi*, III,150
1245	galleys		Trapani	*Annali Genovesi*, III,161
1245	galleys	Nicola Lercarius, Iacopus de Levanto	Louis IX's Crusade	*Annali Genovesi*, III,168

Year	Ships	Commander(s)	Destination	Source
1247	25 galleys	Podestat of Genoa	Pisa	*Annali Genovesi*, III,173–174
1248	32 galleys		Louis IX's Crusade	*Annali Genovesi*, III, 178
1251	4 galleys		Pope's escort	*Annali Genovesi*, IV,5
1256	12 galleys	Paschetus Mallonus, Petrus Advocatus	Massa	*Annali Genovesi*, IV,22
1256	24 galleys	Simon Guercius, Nicola Cigala	Sardinia	*Annali Genovesi*, IV,23
1256	16 galleys	Ugo Ventus, Iacopus Niger	Sardinia	*Annali Genovesi*, IV,28
1257	1 caravana of *naves*		Ultramare	*Annali Genovesi*, IV,29
1258	25 galleys, 4 *naves*	Rubeus de Turcha	Venice	*Annali Genovesi*, IV,34
1258	8 galleys		Tyre	*Annali Genovesi*, IV,34
1261	10 galleys, 6 *naves*	Marinus Buccanigra	Constantinople	*Annali Genovesi*, IV,42–43
1262	10 galleys	Otto Ventus	Constantinople	*Annali Genovesi*, IV,49
1263	25 galleys, 1 *sagittea*, 5 *barchae*	Petrinus de Grimaldo, Peschetus Mallonus	Constantinople	*Annali Genovesi*, IV,49
1264	3 galleys, 2 *naves*		Acre	*Annali Genovesi*, IV,54–55
1264	20 galleys	Symon Grillus	Eastern Mediterranean	*Annali Genovesi*, IV,54
1265	10 galleys	Symon Guercius	Against Venice	*Annali Genovesi*, IV,68
1266	18 galleys, 1 *navis*	Lanfrancus Borboninus	Against Venice	*Annali Genovesi*, IV,89
1266	25 galleys	Obertinus Auriae	Crete	*Annali Genovesi*, IV,91
1267	25 galleys	Luchetus de Grimaldis	Acre, Tyre	*Annali Genovesi*, IV,103
1270	55 galleys, *naves* and *ligna*		Tunis, Louis IX's Crusade	*Annali Genovesi*, IV,131
1272	2 *naves*		Ultramare	*Annali Genovesi*, IV,149
1280	3 galleys		Ancona	*Annali Genovesi*, V,9
1280	4 galleys		Romania	*Annali Genovesi*, V,9
1282	4 galleys		Bonifacio	*Annali Genovesi*, V,21
1282	galleys		Romania	*Annali Genovesi*, V,27
1285	3 galleys		Constantinople	*Annali Genovesi*, V,61
1286	5 galleys		Romania	*Annali Genovesi*, V,73
1287	5 galleys		Ultramare	*Annali Genovesi*, V,76
1288	4 galleys	Leonellus Advocatus		*Annali Genovesi*, V,82
1288	4 galleys, 1 *galionum*	Petrus Embronus	Pisa	*Annali Genovesi*, V,84
1288	7 galleys	Benedictus Iacharia	Tripoli	*Annali Genovesi*, V,89–90
1289	3 galleys	Polinus Aurie	Cyprus	*Annali Genovesi*, V,95
1289	12 galleys			*Annali Genovesi*, V,113
1290	6 galleys	Enricus de Mari	Pisa	*Annali Genovesi*, V,115

Years	Ships	Commanders	Destination	Source
1290	14 galleys	Conradus Aurie	Romania	*Annali Genovesi*, V,117
1290	20 galleys	Conradus Aurie	Pisa	*Annali Genovesi*, V,119
1291	2 galleys	Thedisius Aurie, Ugolinus de Vivaldo	Atlantic Ocean	*Annali Genovesi*, V,124
1291	6 galleys	Franceschinus Porcellus	Pisa	*Annali Genovesi*, V,124
1291	7 galleys	Nicolinus de Petracio		*Annali Genovesi*, V,124
1291	2 galleys	Benedictus Iacharia	Riviera	*Annali Genovesi*, V,127
1292	7 galleys		Romania	*Annali Genovesi*, V,145
1293	7 galleys		Romania	*Annali Genovesi*, V,167
1294	18 galleys, 2 *ligna*		Romania	*Annali Genovesi*, II,97
1298	165 galleys	Lamba de Auria	Against Venice	G. Stella, *Annales*, 35
1299	78 galleys	Tedisus de Auria	Against Venice	G. Stella, *Annales*, 35
1300	galleys	Accelinus Grillus		G. Stella, *Annales*, 70
1310	10 galleys	Lamba de Auria	Rhodes	G. Stella, *Annales*, 77
1312	galleys	Conradus de Auria	Pisa	G. Stella, *Annales*, 78
1319	28 galleys	Gaspar de Grimaldi		G. Stella, *Annales*, 89
1319	32 galleys			G. Stella, *Annales*, 90
1320	66 and 13 galleys	Petrus de Goano	Guelfs against Ghibellins	G. Stella, *Annales*, 93–95
1321	16 and 18 galleys		Guelfs against Ghibellins	G. Stella, *Annales*, 98
1322	17 and 20 galleys		Guelfs against Ghibellins	G. Stella, *Annales*, 102
1323	10 and 16 galleys		Guelfs against Ghibellins	G. Stella, *Annales*, 105–106
1325	24 and 20 galleys	Gaspar de Auria	Guelfs against Ghibellins	G. Stella, *Annales*, 108
1328	40 and 33 galleys	Luchinus de Nigro	Guelfs against Ghibellins	G. Stella, *Annales*, 113–14
1330	15 galleys	Aitonus de Auria		G. Stella, *Annales*, 113–14
1332	45 galleys	Antonius de Grimaldi	Against Catalans	G. Stella, *Annales*, 121
1333	10 galleys	Octobonus de Marinis	Against Catalans	G. Stella, *Annales*, 122
1333	10 galleys	Ianotus Cigala	Against Catalans	G. Stella, *Annales*, 122
1334	10 galleys	Sologrus de Nigro	Against Catalans	G. Stella, *Annales*, 122
1335	7 galleys	Odoardus de Auria	Against Catalans	G. Stella, *Annales*, 126
1335	28 galleys	Odoardus de Auria		G. Stella, *Annales*, 126
1336	14 galleys	Neapolionus Spinula		G. Stella, *Annales*, 127
1337	9 galleys	Franciscus de Marinis		G. Stella, *Annales*, 127
1338	40 galleys	Aitonus de Auria	For the King of France	G. Stella, *Annales*, 128

Year	Galleys	Commander	Destination	Source
1340	9 galleys	Simon de Quarto		G. Stella, *Annales*, 134
1341	20 galleys	Egidius Buccanigra	For the King of Castille	G. Stella, *Annales*, 134
1344	15 galleys	Martinus Zacharias	Smyrna	G. Stella, *Annales*, 140
1345	19 galleys			G. Stella, *Annales*, 143
1346	29 galleys	Symon Vignosus	Chios	G. Stella, *Annales*, 145
1350	14 galleys	Nicolaus de Magnerri	Constantinople	G. Stella, *Annales*, 150
1352	60 galleys	Paganinus de Auria	Constantinople	G. Stella, *Annales*, 151
1353	60 galleys	Antonius de Grimaldis		G. Stella, *Annales*, 152
1354	25 galleys	Paganinus de Auria		G. Stella, *Annales*, 153
1355	15 galleys	Philipus de Auria	Tripoli	G. Stella, *Annales*, 154
1367	8 galleys			G. Stella, *Annales*, 161
1371	10 galleys	Thomas Muritius		G. Stella, *Annales*, 164
1373	43 galleys	Damianus Cattaneus	Cyprus	G. Stella, *Annales*, 166–67
1377	10 galleys	Aron de Struppa		G. Stella, *Annales*, 169
1378	32 galleys	Ludovicus de Flisco, Lucianus de Auria		G. Stella, *Annales*, 170–73
1379	69 galleys	Petrus de Auria	Against Venice	G. Stella, *Annales*, 175
1380	13 galleys	Matheus Maruffus		G. Stella, *Annales*, 179
1380	5 galleys	Ivanesius de Mari		G. Stella, *Annales*, 181
1380	13 galleys			G. Stella, *Annales*, 181
1381	13 galleys	Isnardus de Guarco		G. Stella, *Annales*, 183
1383	10 galleys	Nicolaus Maruffus	Cyprus	G. Stella, *Annales*, 189
1385	10 galleys	Clemens de Facio		G. Stella, *Annales*, 191
1386	10 galleys			G. Stella, *Annales*, 192
1388	15 galleys	Raphael Adurnus		G. Stella, *Annales*, 193
1389	40 galleys	Iohanes Centurionus	Tunis	G. Stella, *Annales*, 194
1396	11 galleys			G. Stella, *Annales*, 215
1397	4 galleys		Romania	G. Stella, *Annales*, 222
1398	4 galleys	Georgius Granellus	Romania	G. Stella, *Annales*, 225

AN EXEMPLARY MARITIME REPUBLIC: VENICE AT THE END OF THE MIDDLE AGES

Bernard Doumerc

IN VENICE, 'the sea was all that mattered'. Truly, this was the founding principle that marked the history of this celebrated city.[1] For a very long time historians made the Serenissima a model of success, wealth, and opulence, sometimes asserting that the Venetians 'had a monopoly of the transit trade in spices from the Orient' and 'that they were the masters of the Mediterranean'.[2] Such accounts, flattering to the pride of the inhabitants of the lagoons, emphasised the prestige of Venetian navies and the patriotism of its noble lovers of liberty, united to defend the city against the adversities of nature and of men. All this is entirely misleading.

The Venetians were not the only ones who used the maritime routes of the Mediterranean Sea, an area that they were forced to share with great rivals.[3] Beginning in the eleventh century, the Venetian government, determined to take a place in international affairs, intervened vigorously against the Normans who had recently installed themselves in southern Italy and Sicily. At that time all of the Christian West, not only the Venetians, was excited by the success of the crusaders, and tried to find advantage in these unsettled commercial conditions. So it was that the drive to establish a trading presence on the southern shores of the Mediterranean, from Ceuta in Morocco to Lajazzo in Cilicia, began with violence. The Middle Ages were a time of war in which periods of peace were extremely brief. Governments knew how to manage unpredictable economies that were continually buffeted by the repeated conflicts of the age. The Venetians were not the masters in the western basin of the Mediterranean. There the Genoese and the Catalans reigned. In the East they were forced to share the wealth of the Byzantine Empire, the Armenian kingdom and caliphates with their competitors, the Pisans, the Amalfitans, and the Genoese. Though faced

---

[1] F. C. Lane, *Venise, une république maritime* (Paris, 1985), 96, and in 'Venetian Shipping during the Commercial Revolution', in *The Collected Papers of F. C. Lane* (Baltimore, 1966), 3–24.
[2] F. Braudel, *La Méditerranée et le monde méditerranéen à l'époque de Philippe II*, 2 vols (Paris, 1982), I, 493.
[3] J. H. Pryor, 'The Naval Battles of Roger of Lauria', *Journal of Medieval History*, 9 (1983), 179–216, and also in his *Geography, Technology, and War. Studies in the Maritime History of the Mediterranean (649–1571)* (Cambridge, 1988).

with fierce opposition from the other Italian cities, little by little, the tenacity and the communal spirit of the Venetians succeeded in lifting the Serenissima to dominance. They knew how to build the foundations of their maritime power.

From the eleventh century onward, the successive governments of the city wanted above all to take control of navigation in the narrow Adriatic Sea, from the Po Valley with its populous and prosperous cities, and reaching out toward distant lands. It is the Adriatic problem that gave the first impetus to Venetian imperialism. Later, the peace that Venice concluded in 1177 with the emperor Frederick I established the Republic's 'Lordship of the Gulf', which it alone would dominate until the middle of the sixteenth century.[4] For some Italian maritime cities the first Crusades in the Near East provided an opportunity for conquest, but the Venetians would wait until the Fourth Crusade when, in 1204, they finally dismembered the Byzantine Empire for their own gain. Their naval power rested upon constantly growing trade, closely following a considerable growth in the demand for maritime transport between the two shores of the Mediterranean. These conditions allowed the creation of an overseas colonial empire, the *stato da mar*. Radiating outward from major islands such as Euboea and Crete, and from bases at strategic points along the coast, such as Coron and Modon in the Peloponnese or, in the Aegean Sea, from the many islets of the Duchy of Naxos, the enterprise of Venetian colonists and tradesmen grew unceasingly. Great successes, as much in battle as in the marketplace, are the mark of a powerful state. Without a doubt these successes rested on three critical and all-important determining elements. First was the creation of that unique institution, the Arsenal, by the communal authorities. Second was the implementation of vigorous oversight of the Republic's naval potential as is clearly demonstrated in the establishment of convoys of merchant galleys. Finally, there was the continuing concern for associating the defence of economic interests with preoccupations of territorial expansion aimed at the founding of a colonial empire. These, it seems, were the reasons why Venice became a great maritime power.

There was a technological solution to the new equation that determined the relation between time and distance. This 'world economy', as defined by Fernand Braudel, saw new kinds of sailing craft brought into use. In Venice, even as the traditional role of sailors was called into question, the galley remained the preferred vessel. Venetians saw no reason to force cargo ships to evolve in a different way from warships when the galley could fill both these functions that were intimately bound together in medieval deep-sea navigation.[5] If the numerous crew of a galley was expensive, it was much less so than the loss of the vessel and its cargo. The galley was the favourite weapon of the Venetians and all means were employed to optimise its capabilities within the parameters

---

[4] G. Cracco, *Un altro mondo, Venezia nel medioevo dal secolo XI al secolo XIV* (Turin, 1986), 52.
[5] F. Melis, *I trasporti e le comunicazioni nel medioevo*, ed. L. Frangioni (Florence, 1984), 111.

dictated by necessity. From a very early time Venice had several shipyards, the well-known *squeri*, within the city itself. Perhaps from the beginning of the twelfth century – some have suggested that it was as early as 1104 – the ruling elite decided to provide the city with a shipbuilding establishment controlled by the government.[6] Archival documentation from 1206 confirms the existence of such a state-controlled naval shipyard and also attests that the construction of ships for the Commune was to be confined to this facility. In 1223, the first evidence appears for the existence of the *patroni arsenatus*, directors of the Arsenal, elected from among the nobles of the Great Council and salaried by the Commune. Their task was clearly defined: to provide necessary raw materials to the craftsmen, especially wood for ships' frames, hemp for sails, and cordage, and to see to the timely delivery of sound and robust ships. The details of Doge Enrico Dandolo's direct intervention in the preparation for the attack on the capital of the Byzantine Empire during the Fourth Crusade of 1204 are well known. This intrusion of the public authority into the management of naval construction would continue until the end of the Republic. In 1258, the *capitulares illorum de arsena* defined the role of the directors. From 1277, after some hesitation, the state attempted to retain its skilled labour force by forbidding craftsmen from emigrating. Within two years, between 1269 and 1271, the government decided to codify the regulations that governed the craft guilds in the Arsenal. The statutes of the caulkers', shipwrights', and rope-makers' guilds also date from this period. By 1265, the districts that produced wood and hemp for the Arsenal were managed by public administrators. Then, in 1276, the government required that at least one squadron should always be prepared to put to sea at a moment's notice, which required the continual presence of craftsmen at the Arsenal. Finally, in 1278, an arms manufactory completed the complement of activities sheltered within the protecting walls of the shipyard.[7]

In 1302, the Venetian government implemented a revision of 'the corrections and additions' to the Arsenal regulations.[8] This action was necessary to encourage the full development of the technological revolution that would maximise the Republic's naval potential. A short time later, between 1304 and 1307, the Arsenale Novo was created.[9] By 1325 every sector of maritime activity had been reformed. The speed with which the authorities decided, the promotion of *utilitas* favourable to the public good, and a real will to innovate gave expression to a powerful movement toward a goal of dominating the sea. In 1301, the Senate declared that it was necessary to arm a permanent squadron for the protection of 'the Gulf' (the Adriatic Sea). The cramped port facilities in the

---

[6] E. Concina, *La casa dell'Arsenale*, in *Storia di Venezia*, Temi, Il Mare (Rome, 1991), 147–210.
[7] G. Luzzato, *Studi di storia economica veneziana* (Padua, 1954), 6.
[8] F. Melis, *I mercanti italiani nell'Europa medievale e rinascimentale*, ed. L. Frangioni (Florence, 1990), 9.
[9] E. Concina, *L'Arsenale della Repubblica di Venezia* (Venice, 1984), 26 ff.

lagoon led to a natural expansion with new basins in the Arsenale Novo.[10] This expansion of facilities was completed by the creation of naval bases at Pola and Pore? in Istria. Until the final phase of renovation at the end of the fifteenth century, this naval establishment was the pride of Venice's oligarchy. In 1435, the Senate declared, 'our Arsenal is the best in the world' and encouraged visits by the famous and powerful as they journeyed toward Jerusalem. This evocation of the labour, ingenuity, and efficiency of the seamen of Venice resounded all across Europe and flattered the pride of the subjects of the Serenissima. The myth of Venice, forged by the political powers around the Arsenal, helped to elicit respect, fear, and effective administration.[11]

It is necessary to pause for a moment to consider this assertion of a clever political will that quickly adapted to circumstances. In looking at the overall situation in the Mediterranean basin it is clear that by the late thirteenth century the Venetian position had weakened. In 1261, a Byzantine–Genoese coalition took control of Constantinople and a part of Romania that, up until that time, had been controlled by the Franks and Venetians. Meanwhile, the Republic relentlessly defended Crete, the coastal bases of the Peloponnese, and the important islands of the Aegean Sea.[12] In 1291 the fall of Acre marked the final defeat of the Crusaders in the Latin States of the Levant. It appears that the Venetians had already begun a withdrawal toward the west when, in 1274, Doge Lorenzo Tiepolo prohibited investment in agricultural estates on Terra Ferma 'to oblige the Venetians to take an interest in naval affairs'. A little later, in 1298, their perpetual rivals, the Genoese, entered the Adriatic to support the Hungarians with an attack on Venetian possessions in Dalmatia.[13] Naval war within the confined spaces of the Adriatic forced the government to undertake a major reform effort to confront this threat from the enemies of the Republic. This was more than a territorial conflict. It was also an economic war that engulfed the entire Mediterranean basin. The desire to capture commerce and to dominate distribution networks for goods placed great importance on the ability to keep fleets at sea. The last phase in the creation of Venice's magnificent Arsenal took place between about 1473 and 1475. After the fall of Constantinople in 1453, fear seized the Venetians who dreaded a naval assault on their colonial possessions. The defence of the *stato da mar* was undertaken by reinforcing the defences of the system of naval bases. First, Negroponte and

---

[10] Ibid., 28, and E. Concina, 'Dal tempio del mercante al piazzale dell'Impero: l'Arsenale di Venezia', in *Progetto Venezia* (Venice, n.d.), 57–106. Originally the 'gulf' or 'Gulf of Venice' referred to that part of the Adriatic north of a line between Pola and Ravenna. As Venetian control of the Adriatic expanded, so did their definition of 'the Gulf'. See F. C. Lane, *Venice: A Maritime Republic* (Baltimore, 1973), 24.
[11] E. Crouzet-Pavan, *Venise triomphante, les horizons d'un mythe* (Paris, 1999), 122.
[12] B. Doumerc, *La difesa dell'impero*, in *Storia di Venezia, dalle origini alla caduta della Serenissima*, vol. II, *La formazione dello stato patrizio*, ed. G. Arnaldi, G. Cracco and A. Tenenti (Rome, 1997), 237–50.
[13] B. Krekic, *Venezia e l'Adriatico*, in *Storia di Venezia*, III, 51–81 and P. Cabanes, *Histoire de l'Adriatique* (Paris, 2000), 191.

Nauplia, and then, the Arsenal of Candia, an important strong point on Crete, were completely renovated between 1467 and 1470. At home, in Venice, momentous changes in circumstances created a need to augment the Republic's naval forces. Henceforth, fierce naval war against admirals in the pay of the Ottomans brought unaccustomed reverses. In this context, the senate asked Giacomo Morosini (called *el zio*, 'Uncle') to prepare plans for an extension of the Arsenal in 1473. With an additional eight hectares added to its area, it became the greatest shipyard in Europe and 'the essential foundation of the state'.[14]

By demonstrating its undeniable concern for optimising the financial and technical resources devoted to naval construction, the government showed the way for the whole people. The authorities obtained indispensable support from all those social groups whose destiny was tied to the vigour of the city's maritime activity. At the same time, the desires of those groups corresponded to the announced public policy of giving priority to the naval forces. It is not true that a permanent and effective naval force did not appear until the sixteenth century.[15] A navy existed in Venice from the fourteenth century. As described above, the patrol squadron charged with policing the Adriatic was at the heart of that force, but there were other available units. First among them were the galleys armed by the port cities that had gradually come to be included in the *stato da mar*. In the event of conflict these Dalmatian, Albanian, Greek, and Cretan cities were required, by the terms of their submission to Venice, to provide one or more galleys for the naval draft due to the metropolis. There are many instances of these drafts. One example is sufficient to indicate their nature.[16] During the conflict against the Turks during the 1470s, the Arsenal could not quickly provide the thirty galleys demanded by the Senate. All the subject cities of the Empire were required to contribute to the fleet. Crete provided eleven galleys, four came from the occupied ports of Puglia, two from Corfu, eleven from Dalmatia (three from Zara, two from Sebenico, one each from Cattaro, Lesina, Split, Pago, Arba, and Trau). Cadres of loyal 'patriots' known to Venetian administrators leavened the crews gathered from these various ports. Neither the ardour of these fighters from 'overseas' nor their fidelity to St Mark was taken for granted. The Senate did reward loyal commanders such as Alessandro de Gotti of Corfu, Francesco Chachuni of Brindisi, and Jacopo Barsi of Lesina.

The second Venetian trump card was the initiation of an unprecedented system for the administration of sea-borne trade. This system provided a formidable tool, designed to respond to the needs of *la ventura*, of commerce, laying a

---

[14] Archivio di Stato, Venice, senato, mar, reg. 15, fol. 14 for example, and S. Karpov, *La navigazione veneziana nel mar Nero (XIII–XV sec.)* (Ravenna, 2000), 12.
[15] J. Meyer, 'Des liens de causalité en histoire: politiques maritimes et société', *Revue historique*, 614 (2000), 12.
[16] A. Ducellier and B. Doumerc, 'Les Chemins de l'exil, bouleversements de l'Est européen et migrations vers l'Ouest à la fin du Moyen Âge' (Paris, 1992), 163; Archivio di Stato, Venice, senato, mar, reg. 15, fol. 161.

foundation for a dominating and expansionist people. These innovative procedures put in place by the ruling oligarchy were developed to take advantage of an exceptional organisation that would raise Venice into the first rank of Mediterranean naval powers. During the first twenty years of the Trecento, there was a period of maturation punctuated by different attempts to develop a system of navigation that eventually evolved into the galley convoys known as *mude*. Having achieved this objective with the consensus of all the participants in the financial and business world, it was then necessary to create an efficient system of management. Even if maritime trade was prosperous, it remained fragile and subject to unforeseeable risks. It was always possible that a major conflict with the Genoese or the Catalans, or even a brief outbreak of extreme violence due to piracy, might place the whole economic structure of the Republic at risk.[17] Meanwhile, in the city of Venice as well as in the small island market towns of the lagoon, in the warehouses and in the tradesmen's shops or the craftsmen's booths, men pursued gain, but they did so without an overall plan and without looking for any really consistent method in their approach. Around the middle of the fourteenth century Venetian patricians came to realise the necessity of undertaking ambitious measures to surmount the major obstacles to a rational exploitation of the merchant fleets by making major changes in their organisation. Perhaps the terrifying War of Chioggia (1379–81) accelerated the rapid development of this concept. The patriciate instituted regulations providing for general communal equipping of merchant fleets to offset the disadvantages of the privately outfitted trading expeditions that had been paralysed during this long conflict. It is clear that the implementation of this new system affected all of the Republic's economic and social structures. Progress toward fully implementing this model for the unique and exemplary management of Venetian maritime potential took place only slowly, but it was to dominate the Republic's actions at sea up to the middle of the sixteenth century.[18]

The founding act of this state-controlled regulation was the *Ordo galearum armatarum*, decreed on 8 December 1321. It concerned both the galleys and sailing cargo ships. The experimental phase lasted until the end of the Venetian–Genoese war of 1379. The cooperation of several outfitters was needed for a merchant convoy so the galleys received collective financing. This innovative policy originated after the fall of Acre in 1291. The entrepreneurial merchants, far from pulling back from risky undertakings, soon became involved in the conquest of the Atlantic routes to Flanders and England. This rapid expansion encouraged new initiatives, sometimes hesitant and disorganised during the first half of the Trecento, then coordinated by the public authorities under the careful supervision of the city's aristocratic patriciate. Opening navigation routes

---

[17] B. Doumerc, *Il dominio del mare*, in *Storia di Venezia*, IV, 11; A. Tenenti and U. Tucci, eds, *Rinascimento* (Rome, 1996), 113–80.
[18] D. Stöckly, *Le Système des galées du marché à Venise (fin XIIIe–milieu XVe)* (Leiden and New York, 1995), 158; F. C. Lane, *Navires et constructeurs à Venise pendant la Renaissance* (Paris, 1965).

toward the west, along with intensification of maritime relations with the Levant, placed the keys to international trade in Venetian hands after 1350. They also profited from a remarkably favourable position in relation to the Alpine passes leading to northern Europe. By this time the system of auctioning the charters of galleys belonging to the Commune had been definitively established. To avoid a destructive confrontation between the authorities and the merchants (even though at Venice it is sometimes difficult to discern a difference between the two groups) the state asked that the Black Sea convoy be managed according to this new principle. After some years it was adopted for all navigation routes, to the general satisfaction of both groups. Besides the galley convoys, there was also a whole sector of maritime endeavour involving sailing round ships with high freeboard (*naves*). Sometimes their operation is described as free outfitting, because it was subject to fewer regulatory constraints. These *naves* transported necessary bulk products such as grain, all kinds of raw materials of high volume, construction materials, salt, ashes, and so forth. The primary purpose of the more strongly defended galleys was to transport costly cargoes of spices, silks and precious cloths, metals, and weapons. In the middle of the fourteenth century, when the Church lifted its prohibition of trade with the Muslims, the Venetians had a fleet ready to open trade once again with the Syrian and Egyptian ports of the Levant. In 1366, a sailing route involving both galleys and *naves* established connections from the lagoons to Alexandria and Beirut, beginning a promising trade. In the 1440s, nearly ninety *naves* and fifty-five galleys sailed for the Near East, and about thirty for Constantinople. The volume of the goods continued to increase, as did the pattern of massive investment and fiscal returns for the treasury. The reform of maritime statutes that had become obsolete, the creation of new work contracts that imposed a minimum wage, improvements in living conditions on board ships and a mariners' residence in the city attracted a skilled labour force, mostly from Dalmatia, Albania, and Greece. These immigrants, originating from its overseas colonies, allowed the Republic to raise the banner of St Mark throughout the Mediterranean.[19] The Senate, the real architect of this system, far from putting the system of private management in opposition to the one controlled by the Commune, took the best of each of the two systems and combined them. For that reason, some historians speak disparagingly about bureaucracy or state control to describe the Venetian system of trade.

Henceforth, the state owned the merchant fleet, chartering galleys to merchants who operated them. The operator was the highest bidder in the auction for charters. Only nobles were allowed to participate in this auction, an exclusive privilege that gave them control of the financial and commercial operations of the fleet, in return for which they were expected to respect rigorously the specific terms and conditions of the charters. After 1420 all merchant

---

[19] E. Ashtor, *Levant Trade in the Later Middle Ages* (Princeton, 1981), 381; J. C. Hocquet, *Voiliers et commerce en Méditerranée, 1200–1650* (Lille, 1976), 442; B. Doumerc, *Venise et l'émirat hafside de Tunis* (Paris, 1999), 172.

galleys were constructed on the same model according to the plan of the 'galley of Flanders'. This was a vessel of 250 tons burden, delivered as a bare hull (a 'barebones charter') for which the operator furnished all the necessary equipment – sails, cordage, oars, and maintenance materials. The Commune thus freed itself completely of the need to invest in those lesser items. On the other hand, the merchant, knowing that the necessary capital for naval construction was provided by the state, could keep most of his financial resources free for the commercial transactions that were the goal of the expedition. In addition, the winning bidder who took charge of the galley (called the *patrono*) got priority in loading the most precious goods and a monopoly in the transportation of these goods at fixed prices. These incentives earned the merchants' approval because they no longer dreaded aggravated competition amongst themselves, the law was the same for everyone, the costs of transport were fixed and conditions on board were identical for all galleys.

There is often a feeling of modernity about a state when its economic functions predominate. This would make Venice of the Quattrocento a real laboratory of modernity.[20] The economic stakes involved in these operations were very high. In 1409 a *muda* to Flanders carried in its holds merchandise worth 460,000 ducats, equivalent to a tonne and half of gold! In the 1430s, cargoes of spices and drugs loaded on galleys voyaging to Alexandria were often valued at more than 150,000 ducats. Figures like these justify the care taken by the authorities to supervise such transactions, which, after all, provided the bulk of the state's tax revenues.[21] This was remarkable for the time since surely a patrician merchant, following his own bankruptcy, would not have turned to the communal authorities expecting financial assistance. On the contrary, it was to improve competitiveness and to establish its supremacy that the government accepted a transfer of power to merchants even while introducing a measure of coercion into the process. The organisation of the maritime economy took on the characteristics of a mixed economy, promoting private interests while safeguarding the public interest. This was the strength of the Venetian system.

Consider two examples of constraints freely accepted by the operators of merchant galleys. The first concerns the financing of the expeditions. As was mentioned above, it was necessary to invest a considerable amount of capital. At the end of the fifteenth century, the cost to charter a merchant galley for one voyage was 9200 ducats (33 kg of fine gold). Not only was it necessary to pay for the charter of the galley but also the cost of operating the vessel during a voyage of five to eleven months – depending on the destination – including victualling and salaries for a crew of a hundred and fifty rowers and some twenty specialists and officers. The Commune required that a company be established to manage the operation of the galley so that a complete bankruptcy caused by insolvency of any of the partners might be avoided. A magistracy, the *avogaria*

---

[20] B. Doumerc, *Il dominio del mare*, 123.
[21] J. Day, 'Les Instruments de gestion du monde', in *Venise 1500, la puissance, la novation et la concorde: le triomphe du mythe* (Paris, 1993), 142–56.

di Comun, supervised all financial commitments proposed by the *patrono*. The total amount of the estimated cost for the operation of the galley was divided into twenty-four equal shares (*carati*) as was the case for the purchase of a ship. The value of a share varied according to the actual length of the voyage, any unforeseen expenses, and risks at sea. An adjustment was made when the convoy returned to Venice allowing the distributed operating expenses to be deducted from the profits of the voyage. Merchant literature is full of descriptions of these temporary companies aimed at limiting each partner's financial risk, because the cost of operating a galley exceeded the investment potential of a single entrepreneur. Such associations were indispensable, and since the objective was to verify financial investments and the quality of commercial transactions, the *patrono*'s family played an essential role. In these cases, the family enterprise was preferred above all other options, especially the *fraterna*, which created a core of investors around the brothers of the *patrono*.[22] Little by little during the fifteenth century, the circle of the financial partners was limited to the members of a single family. This cut down considerably on the number of shareholders from an average of twelve in the 1450s to, in many cases, as few as two by the beginning of the sixteenth century. Under these conditions the prevailing commercial regulations benefited certain participants who were henceforth free to set sale prices as they wished because they had the advantage of a transportation monopoly. This perversion of the *incanto* system eventually caused its demise and its being denounced by Marino Sanudo in his *Diarii*.

The second constraint imposed on merchants engaged in the state-controlled sector concerns the presence of a *capitanio*, an agent of the government elected by the members of the Great Council and paid by the Commune. The *capitanio* of the galley convoy supervised the activities of the *patroni* of the individual galleys, enforcing adherence to the terms of the charter to maintain regularity, speed, and security during these long voyages.[23] It was also the responsibility of this state representative to decide, in accordance with the merchants, to change course or to shorten a stay in port when circumstances warranted. As guarantor of the common interest, he had to limit the ambitions of entrepreneurs who would not hesitate to compromise the interests of their rivals if, by so doing, they could increase their personal gain. Disagreements were numerous and litigation frequent, but in the event of a serious breach of the rules of the *incanto*, a *patrono* could be banned from participation for a period of several years.[24] The role of the *capitanio* was essential to the regulation of this complex mixed management system and crucial to the smooth operation of the voyages. The reports read in the Senate upon return of the *muda* were complicated because of

---

[22] B. Doumerc, C. Judde de Larivière, 'Le Rôle du patriciat dans la gestion des galères marchandes à Venise au début du seizième siècle', *Studi veneziani*, 36 (1998), 57–84.
[23] B. Doumerc, D. Stöckly, 'L'Evolution du capitalisme marchand à Venise au XVe siècle, le financement des mude', *Annales H. S. C.*, 1 (1995), 133–57.
[24] B. Doumerc, 'La Crise structurelle de la marine vénitienne au XVe siècle: le problème du retard des mude', *Annales E.S.C.*, 40 (1985), 605–25.

the difficulties encountered by these agents of the government as they confronted the representatives of capitalist enterprise. Despite it all, and this was part of the miracle, the collusion of interests maximised profits for both individuals and for the enterprise as whole.

This system of managing the merchant galleys hid a little-known aspect, which was in fact the keystone of the success of the Venetian thalassocracy in the Mediterranean during the closing centuries of the Middle Ages. Until now, historians have placed the Venetian system of navigation only in a context of maritime transport and trade. In fact, the political decision by the Senate to manage maritime commercial expeditions of the merchant galleys directly by organising them in convoys was exemplary and innovative in more ways than one. First, the government avoided maintaining a naval patrol squadron outside of the Gulf. It would have been a vain hope to eradicate the plague of piracy in the waters extending from the Channel to the Aegean Sea. Instead, the captains of the *mude* were ordered to intercept and to neutralise any pirates that they met and sometimes to engage in hot pursuit, even if it meant diverting from their planned course. However, the Republic did not supply letters of marque or of reprisal to ships' captains hoping to participate in the *guerre de course*. To maintain control of these high-risk activities that might put the vital interests of the state at risk, the Senate almost always preferred to entrust them to meticulously organised expeditions, avoiding any improvisation with the attendant possibility of dangerous and harmful consequences[25] Often, the communal galleys of the cities of the *stato da mar* participated in these operations to police the seas but, on the whole, this tactic did not produce satisfactory results. Second, another lesser-known aspect of Venetian policy must also be taken into consideration: the requisition of merchant galleys. After having encouraged the development of regular convoy routes, which may have seen as many as fifty great galleys in service, the Venetian government in 1465, forced to react to an unfavorable military situation, found that its fleet, as a whole, did not contain enough warships.[26] Social concerns regarding the employment of a large number of seamen on board the 'man-eating' galleys, and fiscal considerations resulting from the fixed pricing of the *noli* (charters) and the control of cargos which this facilitated, concerns which were as important as worries about the defence of merchant ships, led to the galley becoming a privileged instrument of Venetian maritime expansion. The choice of the Venetian authorities in favour of convoys of merchant galleys (*mude*), however, must have been somewhat detri-

---

[25] A. Tenenti, 'Venezia e la pirateria en Levante: 1300–1460', in A. Pertusi, ed., *Venezia e il Levante fino al secolo XV. Atti del i convegno internazionale di storia della civiltà veneziana*, 2 vols. (Florence, 1973–4), I, 705–71.
[26] B. Doumerc, 'Le Rôle ambigu de la muda vénitienne: convoi marchand ou unité de combat', in *Histoire maritime: thalassocratie et période révolutionnaire, Actes des 114e et 115e Congrès Nationaux des Sociétés Savantes* (Paris, 1989; Avignon, 1990; Paris, 1991), 139–54 and R. Cessi, *Storia della Repubblica di Venezia* (1968), 191.

mental to the profitability of the unarmed *naves* that remained in private operation.

The security of trade relations was the source of all profits, so an argument was put forward that the companies of the wealthiest aristocrats should be favoured by making them the only ones authorised to organise the profitable *mude*. Over the years this point of view became a determining factor in the evolution of the place of the *galere da mercato* in the complex whole of the Venetian maritime economy, reviving the basic debate, which set in opposition the objectives of the private managers of the voyages and the objectives of the government. The great network of navigation routes favoured the noble entrepreneurs who collaborated with the authorities within the system of the *incanto*. Whenever an accident of circumstances threatened the regularity of the voyages, the state encouraged the *mude*, sometimes forcing independently equipped and operated ships to remain inactive in port. This transfer of activities worked to the profit of the galleys as demonstrated by the creation of the route to Aigues Mortes in 1415 and then to the Barbary Coast in 1436 in response to the problem of maritime insecurity. Indeed, the senate announced that it was preferable 'in any case to fit out two galleys on the Aigues-Mortes route for one alone does not seem safe'.[27] Here is the heart of the debate: the Venetian *muda* was a merchant unit but also a combat unit and it is necessary to consider that it made a permanent contribution to the naval forces placed at the disposal of the government's military commanders. These galleys were armed 'for war and for trade' and the terms of their charter agreed to after the auction provided that the government could exercise its right of requisition at any time. During the fifteenth century this procedure was often used. This was the third element of Venetian maritime supremacy.

It is necessary to see the activities of the *mude* in another context as well. The galleys provided the state with a very efficient naval potential for general tasks aimed at preserving the supremacy of the Empire. From the beginning, the Senate specified that the *patroni* of galleys had to accept some missions 'in the service of the Signoria' in return for the numerous advantages from which they benefited.[28] What did this mean? A few examples make the Senate's intention clear. The least coercive of these requirements concerned the transportation of officials designated by the government, *baili* and ambassadors, as well as colonial administrators. These voyages were always made aboard communal galleys protected by the flag of St Mark. Sometimes the captain of the merchant convoy played the role of government representative in dealings with local authorities in Tunis, Alexandria, or London. In 1438, the Senate asked the captain of the Aigues Mortes convoy to agree to the request of the Grand Master of the Order of St John of Jerusalem who wished to travel from the great Provençal port of

---

[27] Archivio di Stato, Venice, senato, misti, reg. 53, fol. 29, and Antonio Morosini, *Annali, extraits de la chronique de Morosini relatifs à l'histoire de France* (Paris, 1898), I, 374.
[28] B. Doumerc, 'Les Flottes d'état, moyen de domination coloniale à Venise (XVe siècle)', in M. Balard and A. Ducellier, eds., *Coloniser au Moyen Âge* (Paris, 1995), 115–29.

Marseilles to Rhodes. The clamour of protest from the expedition's investors had no effect on the Senate's decision and for several weeks the galleys remained far off their planned course. Another kind of requisition for peaceful missions concerned the transportation of funds or strategic materials destined for the administrators of the cities of the overseas empire. At the beginning of the fifteenth century, the *mude* of the Levant carried a considerable quantity of oars, yards, and cordage, as well as timber and cut stone in order to renovate the arsenals of the Peloponnese and Crete. In the middle of the fifteenth century, these requisitioned services were frequent because it was then necessary to add the transportation of troops and the repatriation of refugees resulting from an expansion of the area of hostilities.[29] In addition, the *capitanio* was often assigned to inspect the strongholds of the colonial domain to provide an objective report on the needs, genuine or not, put forward by the rectors 'of our overseas possessions'. During the Venetian–Genoese war in the 1430s, and then again during the one against the Turks in the 1460s, the *mude* participated in naval actions under the orders of the Captain General of the Sea. The dramatic break in ranks at the defeat of Zonchio in 1499 revealed the reluctance of the crews and merchants to assume the task of national defence. Strikes broke out among crews 'who refused to fight so often' and demanded a salary increase of 30 per cent. The investor's mistrust was often in evidence, putting the effectiveness of the government in peril.[30]

The only mission willingly accepted by the *patroni* of the galleys was to hunt for corsairs. This service of policing the seas was profitable to their private activities since they were all owners of cargo vessels operating in the unregulated shipping sector. Be that as it may, the government had succeeded in reducing unproductive investment in a permanent naval squadron. The evolution of international political conditions among the countries along the coasts of the Mediterranean requiring increasing participation by the merchant galleys 'in the service of the state' had grave consequences for the peace of mind of the entrepreneurs. Indeed, the threat of a requisition always hung over every departure and the meagre and consistently tardy indemnities from the government discouraged the sailors as much as the ship-owners.

By the beginning of the sixteenth century, the reconciliation of economic policy with the constitution as well as with the defence of a colonial empire was no longer appropriate. Then, it was said, 'the whole navy is devoured by the army' and numerous voyages of merchant galleys cancelled at the last moment or diverted from their course put an end to the trust of the Venetian merchant partners.[31] Henceforth, the fleet of the state, giving priority to the defence of empire, could no longer play a leading role in trade. Venice remained the maritime power that it had always been, but was no longer a first-rank naval power.

---

[29] Doumerc, 'Le Rôle ambigu', 152.
[30] Marino Sanudo, *I diarii* (Bologna, 1969), vol. I, chapter 30.
[31] Girolamo Priuli, *Diarii (diario veneto)*, ed. A. Segre, in *Rerum Italicarum Scriptores* 24, 2nd edn (Citta di Castello, 1912–1941), 39.

An Exemplary Maritime Republic 163

One after another the sailing routes closed at the turn of the sixteenth century: the Barbary Coast, then Aigues Mortes, and finally Flanders.[32] Only the Levant routes continued to be active but even those suffered long interruptions in their traffic. The disaster of 1484 was fresh in everyone's mind; in that year, French pirates had attacked the *muda* of Flanders. The consequences were dreadful. The galleys had been captured after a hard fight. A hundred and thirty sailors were killed, three hundred wounded, and, of course, their cargos had been confiscated by King Charles VIII's representative. A few months later, a major incident provoked a panic around the Rialto, the financial centre of the city. To save the last bit of the Languedoc spice import market, the Senate demanded that the Aigues Mortes convoy depart, knowing that another interruption in shipping would sound the death knell of any claim to trading in that region. It took six auctions before one was successful, and the *patroni* were able to extract important fiscal advantages from the government for the voyage including the payment of a 3500-ducat subsidy for each *patrono* and a 30 per cent increase in the charter rate. The voyage was an exceptionally long one because it included stops along the Barbary Coast. This course full of pitfalls made martyrs of the sailors and merchants. When they had returned, the accounts told the story. The cost of stopping for forty-five days to defend Zara, which was besieged by the Turks, was estimated at 10,000 ducats per galley, due to expenditures for the supplementary purchase of victuals for the crews and the payment of higher wages than had been foreseen. The *patroni* also asked for 8000 ducats for the lack of profit on lost charters and unsold merchandise. All this added up to an indemnity of 25,000 ducats for each *patrono* who had been forced to make this voyage against his better judgement.[33] The government faltered because, in a backhanded way, the difference of opinion at the heart of the system of managing the galley fleet was expressed virulently in debates at the meetings about the accounts.

A census of the naval forces undertaken in 1496 by the Ministers of the Marine (*Savii ai Ordini*) demonstrated the naval inferiority of the Republic 'because there are too few armed ships at sea'. This explanation given by the chronicler, Marino Sanudo, is astonishing because, he adds, 'there are few ships because, until now, we had no fear of the Turks'.[34] The result was that the obligations imposed upon the captains of the *mude* increased continually. In 1496, for example, the galleys of the Barbary Coast convoy participated in a massive counter-attack, launched to limit the audacious actions of the Barbary pirates.

Two dramatic episodes permit an evaluation of the interventionist role of the Venetian government in the management of the fleet. The first concerns the conflict involving the kingdom of Naples during the Italian Wars. In 1495, a league including Venice, the Duke of Milan, the Pope, and the king of Aragon, wanted to oppose the plan of the French king, Charles VIII, to annex a part of

---

[32] Sanudo, *Diarii.*, I, column 302.
[33] Priuli, *Diarii*, 273.
[34] Sanudo, *Diarii*, I, column 30.

southern Italy. The Senate issued a general requisition order 'to retain all ships and large merchant galleys'. The Captain General of the Sea, Marco Trevisan, could, with great effort, assemble a war fleet of only about twenty galleys. That is why the contribution of eleven merchant galleys was absolutely necessary, so he waited for the arrival of galleys from the Dalmatian cities. The second episode, with more tragic consequences, was that of the Battle of Zonchio in 1499. The animosity between Antonio Grimani, the Captain General and the *patroni* of the merchant galleys led to a catastrophe in which the disheartened crews' weariness and the merchants' rebellion caused a military disaster. Some months later, outside the port of Modon, which was besieged by the Turks, the *patroni* of the *galere da mercato*, by their unforgivable refusal to fight, caused the loss of the city. Despite sensational court proceedings and some sentences based on principle, the *patroni* were absolved since the state was willing to acknowledge its share of the blame because of the incompetence of its representatives in the battle.[35] Naval battles in the following years offered further proof of the problem. During the spring of 1500 off the island of Cephalonia Captain General Marco Trevisan, warned by Grimani's unhappy experience, considered sending back the merchant galleys that he had received as reinforcements because they seemed poorly equipped to fight, and the *patroni* were outspokenly critical of their mission.[36] The weariness of the demoralised crews and the condemnation of the *patroni* of the merchant galleys, little involved as they were in safeguarding the *stato da mar*, heralded the end of an exemplary system. The redefinition of the specific role of the *muda del mercato* had not taken place because of the lack of a clearly expressed political will. Contrary to what had happened in the middle of the Trecento, this crisis of confidence in the Cinquecento quickly turned into open opposition.

In this way it is possible to discern the main lines of power that lead the Republic of Venice to dominate a large portion of the Mediterranean. The senatorial nobility, uniting the most important investors and committed merchants in the maritime economy, patiently forged a tool without equal among the rival nations and competitors: the system of regular navigation routes plied by convoys of merchant galleys. The modest ship-owners, nobles or not, were discouraged by the regulatory and fiscal obstacles that favoured the *mude* and by the permanent insecurity of sea-borne commerce, but were powerless to compete efficiently against the mixed private and public management of the naval potential. This was all the more true when *raison d'État* generated an indisputable argument for the use of these convoys, at times in the form of five galleys with 1200 men in each crew ready to intervene quickly in any zone on missions in the public interest. At the end of the fifteenth century and especially

---

[35] Ibid., IV, columns 337, 360.
[36] B. Doumerc, 'De l'incompétence à la trahison: les commandants de galères vénitiens face aux Turcs (1499–1500)', in *Félonie, trahison, reniements au Moyen Âge, Les Cahiers du Crisima*, 3 (Montpellier, 1997), 613–34, and F. C. Lane, 'Naval Actions and Fleet Organization (1499–1502)', in J. R. Hale, ed., *Renaissance Venice* (London, 1973), 146–73.

at the beginning of the following century, this senatorial nobility, united into the 'Party of the Sea', even after having gained considerable advantages, often in violation of the law, was no longer able, considering the circumstances, to protect their essential prerogatives. The nation, threatened by sea and by land, no longer gave priority to this system which for two hundred years had given glory and fortune to those who lived around the lagoon. This was the beginning of the downfall of the Venetian colonial empire in the Mediterranean and, at the same time, of this unique and long-effective system of operating the merchant marine.

Part III

SIXTEENTH AND EARLY-SEVENTEENTH-CENTURY EUROPE

THE NAVIES OF THE MEDICI:
THE FLORENTINE NAVY AND NAVY OF THE SACRED MILITARY ORDER OF ST STEPHEN, 1547–1648

Marco Gemignani

AT the beginning of the fifteenth century, the Republic of Florence obtained its long-awaited connection with the Tyrrhenian Sea, when it conquered Pisa in 1406. In 1421, it expanded further when it acquired the coastal towns of Leghorn and Porto Pisano from the Genoese.[1] Before long, Florentine galleys began to ply the Mediterranean and to push through the Strait of Gibraltar, trading as far away as Flanders and England. In the last quarter of the century, Florence, whose government was by now largely run by the Medici family, was engaged in a war against the kingdom of Naples and the Papal States. The huge expenses sustained during this conflict, the danger of piracy, and the competition from Basque, Catalan, English and French merchant ships, which could import and export goods from the Florentine State at costs notably lower than those of the Florentine galleys, forced the Florentines to disarm their fleet.

In 1537, Cosimo I de' Medici became Duke of Florence and began a foreign policy aimed at increasing his own dominions and reducing the influence of Emperor Charles V over Florence.[2] Cosimo I achieved his first success in 1543, when the Emperor relinquished the fortresses of Leghorn and Florence.[3] The duke was aware that he could not withdraw completely from the protection of the Habsburgs, so instead he tried to alter the alliance between Florence and the Empire to create a relationship whereby he became the key supporter of the Habsburgs' presence in the Italian peninsula. Cosimo I was convinced that Charles V would agree to this, preferring to tolerate Cosimo's plans for territorial acquisitions, along with the aim of greater autonomy for the Florentine state, rather than cause friction.

---

[1] Michael E. Mallett, 'Pisa and Florence in the Fifteenth Century: Aspects of the Period of the first Florentine Domination', in *Florentine Studies. Politics and Society in Renaissance Florence*, ed. by N. Rubinstein (Evanston: Northwestern University Press, 1968), 413.
[2] Rudolf von Albertini, *Firenze dalla Repubblica al Principato. Storia e coscienza politica*, translated into Italian by C. Cristofolini (Turin: Einaudi, 1970), 281.
[3] Furio Diaz, *Il Granducato di Toscana – I Medici*, vol. XIII of G. Galasso, ed., *Storia d'Italia* (Turin: UTET, 1976), 83; Giorgio Spini, *Cosimo I e l'indipendenza del principato mediceo* (Florence: Vallecchi, 1980), 195 ff.

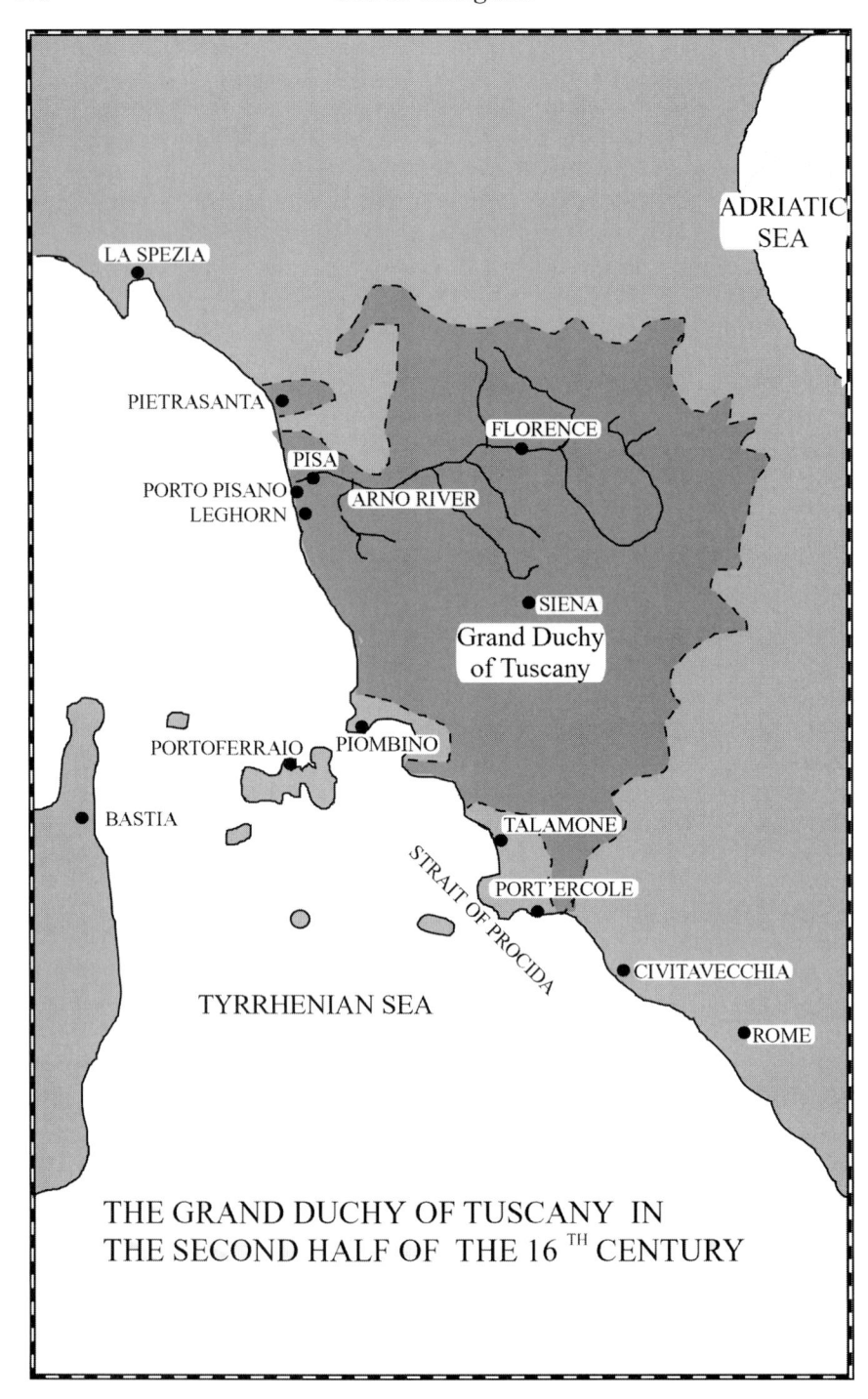

Map 1. The Grand Duchy of Tuscany and the Tyrrhenian Sea

The opportunity for Cosimo I to show the emperor how useful the contribution of a small state such as the Duchy of Florence could be arose with the increasing Muslim presence in the Mediterranean. Control of this sea, which had been maintained by Christians for centuries, was brought into question by the Islamic fleet's resounding victory in 1538 in the waters off Preveza and by Charles V's failure in 1541 to conquer Algiers, the principal base of Muslim privateers.[4] The defeat at Preveza gave new vigour to the Barbary privateers, intensifying their voyages to seize Christian merchant ships and to raid the coastal towns and villages of Spain and the Italian peninsula.

Cosimo I realised that navies were acquiring increasing importance, given the evolution of the international political situation, and thus felt it necessary to devote his time to creating his own naval force to gain greater recognition at an international level and to protect the coasts of the state from Muslim raids. Moreover, he needed to safeguard the maritime communication lines leading to Leghorn, the main port of the duchy. In particular, Cosimo I realised the need to protect trade, especially at sea. To encourage the merchants to import and to export their commodities from Leghorn, it was necessary to reassure them with the presence of warships to keep the waters of the northern Tyrrhenian safe from privateers. The Duke of Florence, always aiming to support commerce, allowed his own galleys at least partial self-financing, through freight charges. He would, on occasion, permit merchants to load goods onto his own ships, especially those destined for Naples and Messina.

As he consolidated power in his dominions, Cosimo I began to implement the outline of a naval policy, partly resuming the one begun in the fifteenth century. He started work on the construction of an arsenal in Pisa, along the north shore of the Arno River, using the structures of the pre-existing port. In 1547, he launched the *Pisana*, the first galley built entirely within the territory of the Florentine state, and he soon added a further three galleys. His choice of building galleys, as opposed to other types of ships, was dictated both by the technical knowledge of the men working in the Arsenal, most of whom originated from the territories of the Republic of Genoa, and by the lack of sailors trained to utilise the complex equipment of sailing ships. In addition, the galley was considered, at that time, to be an excellent warship, which, thanks to its oars, did not need to rely on the wind and was thus more manoeuvrable than a sailing ship. Obviously, the low freeboard limited the use of galleys to the months between spring and autumn, when there were few storms in the Mediterranean. In winter, the galleys remained disarmed and in port.[5] Within

---

[4] Alberto Santoni, *Da Lepanto ad Hampton Roads* (Milan: Mursia, 1990), 18; Antonio Perria, *Andrea Doria il corsaro* (Milan: Sugarco, 1982), 158–64, 177–87; Roger C. Anderson, *Naval Wars in the Levant 1559–1853* (Liverpool: University Press, 1952), 4–5.
[5] For just two brief periods, at the beginning of the 1570s and at the beginning of 1630s, the Medici would also have had at their disposal some galleasses, which however would soon be revealed as unsuitable for the privateering war both for their low speed and because of the excessive expenses of maintenance. In addition, haphazardly, the Medici's fleet would have

the scope of the naval policy that Cosimo I intended to follow, the duke attempted to appropriate bases in the northern Tyrrhenian Sea, to be used both by his own growing fleet and as support bases for Spanish ships, since these vessels preferred to sail along the coast rather than follow the direct route between the Iberian and Italian peninsulas.

From 1540, Cosimo I tried to convince Charles V to hand over control of the island of Elba and the state of Piombino, where he had sustained substantial expenses for fortifications. In 1548, Cosimo obtained both of these, although the possession of Piombino lasted little more than a month. The Duke of Florence, however, did not give up and continued trying to retrieve Piombino, whilst also intensifying work at Portoferraio, which had remained in his possession. His efforts resulted in an ephemeral success when in August 1552 he signed a treaty with his cousin Iacopo VI Aragona Appiano for the state of Piombino to be redelivered to him.[6]

The increase in the Medici ships, the work undertaken in Pisa, Portoferraio and Leghorn to furnish these ships with effective land-based infrastructures and the promulgation of a set of rules for the fleet, its operation and organisation, aroused the apprehensions of both the republics of Venice and Genoa. The two states saw that Florence had built a navy from scratch and, if it continued to develop at the same rate, would soon be able to threaten their positions in the hierarchy of Christian fleets in the Mediterranean.[7] In fact, the Medici court's policy also aroused anxiety in Spain. King Philip II, who succeeded his father Charles V in 1556, hesitated for some time after the victorious war of 1555 (fought alongside Florentine troops against Siena) before investing Cosimo I with the conquered town and its territory, including the Maremma coast.[8]

---

included some small galleys (called in Italian *galeotte*) and some galleons, especially at the beginning of the seventeenth century. About the galleys built in the Arsenal of Pisa it is necessary to note that a characteristic that distinguished them from other ships of the type in service in the remainder of Mediterranean navies was that they had the smallest holds. Although it reduced their range, it did give them the possibility of going faster in the water.

[6] Archivio di Stato di Firenze (hereafter ASF), *Manoscritti*, 128, fol. 92r; Licurgo Cappelletti, *Storia della città e stato di Piombino dalle origini fino all'anno 1814* (Leghorn: Giusti, 1897), 159 ff. Besides the desire to hold Elba and Piombino, Cosimo I also showed an interest in Corsica, Civitavecchia and finally succeeded in acquiring, in the name of his consort Eleonora of Toledo, only the island of Giglio and the Castiglione of Pescaia. See Rodolfo Bernardini, 'Due insuccessi della politica estera di Cosimo I de' Medici: i tentativi di annessione della Corsica e dell'Ordine di S. Lazzaro all'Ordine di S. Stefano P.M.', *Quaderni Stefaniani*, 7 (1988), 27–42.

[7] The Venetians particularly feared repercussions for their relations with Turkey because of the privateering activity in the eastern Mediterranean by the Medici's galleys, so much so that they seized one of them that stopped in Cyprus in July 1559; see Marco Gemignani, 'Rappresaglia veneziana per atti di pirateria in Levante (1559–1561)', *Rivista storica*, 9 (1996), 2, 38–44.

[8] One must remember that in 1556 Charles V in abdicating had divided the dominions of the House of Habsburg between his brother Ferdinand I, who got, besides the title of emperor, Austria, Bohemia and Hungary, and his son Philip II, who got Spain, Flanders, the possessions in the Italian peninsula and the colonies in the New World.

The treaty, signed on 3 July 1557, on the one hand granted Siena to Cosimo I making him Duke of Florence and Siena, and on the other allowed Spain to keep Mount Argentario and the towns of Orbetello, Port'Ercole and Talamone, which belonged to the defeated Siena, to make up the state of Presidios. The treaty also forced Cosimo I to hand over Piombino and Elba to Iacopo VI Aragona Appiano, allowing him to retain only Portoferraio.[9] Repudiation of the debts due from Charles V, Philip II and Iacopo VI was a serious blow for Florentine finances. Furthermore, Cosimo I was laden with the burden of supplying the Spanish with troops, ammunition, provisions and galleys.[10]

The requirement to provide Philip II with men, supplies and ships at the same time reflected the Duke of Florence and Siena's correct intuition about the maritime needs of Spain in the Mediterranean. At the same time, he also apprehended the Catholic King's desire to keep the Medici navy under control. Despite this, Cosimo I decided to continue his policy of naval expansion. To carry this out, Cosimo named Piero Machiavelli, son of the famous Niccolò, Commissioner of the Galleys in March, 1557.[11] Machiavelli also saw the importance of the fleet and suggested to Cosimo I that by increasing the number of ships he could become 'the needle in the balance' for possible future disputes which were likely to arise between France and Spain. He also made the duke aware of the need to maintain a good relationship with the Papacy, given the importance that religion posed in society at the time, marked by contrasts between Protestants and Catholics. This last point also coincided with Cosimo I's firm belief that religious stability would support the status quo in the states and would serve to maintain the power of the dominant classes. This policy toward the Papacy did not, however, succeed straight away and it was only with the election of Pius IV as Pope on 25 December 1559 that relationships between the Roman and Florentine courts improved, thanks to the financial and diplomatic support of Cosimo I.[12]

Secure in the new Pope's favour, Cosimo I presented a series of applications to Pius IV in January 1560 through his loyal secretary, Bartolomeo Concini. Among them was an application for the creation of a chivalric Order.[13]

The Duke of Florence and Siena, during this period, had written a memo pointing out the three targets that he and his eventual successor would have to

---

[9] Arnaldo d'Addario, *Il problema senese nella storia italiana della prima metà del Cinquecento* (Florence: Le Monnier, 1958), 399–424.
[10] The document of investiture of Cosimo I as Duke of Siena and the terms of the treaty on 3 July 1557 are in ASF, *Manoscritti*, 128, fols 80r–92r.
[11] Ibid., *Mediceo del Principato*, 468, fol. 48r.
[12] Josefs Gelmi, *I papi*, translated into Italian by C. Milesi (Milan: Rizzoli, 1986), 167.
[13] 'Memoria di quanto ho passato in Roma con Sua Santità per ordine di S[ua] Eccellenza dalli 15 sin alli 22 di gennaro 1559 [ab inc.]', see ASF, *Mediceo del Principato*, 616, file 27, fols not numbered (hereafter n. nn). The other appeals concerned the nomination to cardinal of Giovanni, seventeen- year-old son of Cosimo I, the establishment of bishoprics in the Medici's territories, the dispatch of an apostolic messenger to the Florentine court and finally the preparation of a visit of Cosimo I to the Pope.

follow to further strengthen the regional-level state that he governed.[14] These three targets were the creation of an Order, the formation of a cavalry unit and the continued expansion of the ducal navy. In the creation, organisation and operation of this new military Order the duke was inspired by the already existing Orders of the Knights of Alcantara, Calatrava, Christ, St Iacopo of the Sword and St John. Those admitted into the new Order would undertake the defence of both the Catholic faith and the Medici state. To develop its military activities, Cosimo I thought that the Order would initially have just two galleys, using other resources to increase their strength ashore as funds allowed. The duke provided most of the initial funding. In his memorandum, Cosimo I chose Pisa as principal base for the Order, where a convent would be built. Barracks were also to be built at Portoferraio.

In constituting this military Order the Duke of Florence and Siena successfully combined his three aims in a way that was advantageous for both his foreign and internal policies. The first objective was to improve Florentine relations with the papacy, which, as mentioned previously, would also have beneficial effects on relations with other Catholic powers and help to guarantee the loyalty of his subjects. The Order satisfied the second aim and provided the duchy with a noble institution of elevated rank on the basis of the extremely selective criteria for recruiting its members. This aspect of the Order would also raise Cosimo I's personal prestige, as well as the stature of both his family and of the state he governed. The chivalric Order would serve to tie the duke to members of the noblest and most important families not only of the duchy but also of other Catholics states. The third objective that Cosimo I attained with the establishment of the Order, of which he became Grand Master, was to carry out the duty of fighting against Islam, and for that warships were needed. Thus, the Medici family would have had at its disposal a fleet which was independent of that controlled under his title as the Duke of Florence and Siena. Thanks to the good relationship between Florence and Rome, Pius IV signed the *breve Dilecte Fili*, on 1 October 1561, authorising Cosimo I to create the Order. Four months later on 1 February 1562, the Pope signed the *breve His Quae* approving the statutes of the Chivalric Militia which was dedicated to St Stephen, Pope and Martyr, and had as its insignia a red cross with eight points on a white background.[15]

On 15 March following, during a grand ceremony in Pisa's cathedral, Giorgio Cornaro, bishop of Treviso and apostolic messenger at the Florentine court, invested Cosimo I as Grand Master of the Order. Before long, Cosimo I, as detailed in his memorandum, ordered the construction of the convent of St Stephen's Militia in Pisa, but did not proceed with the original plan to have a

---

[14] Ibid., 327, fols 7r–8v.
[15] The new Order owes its name to the fact that St Stephen's day was 2 August, the day the Medici's troops defeated the escaped Florentine rebels at Montemurlo in 1537 and the soldiers of Pietro Strozzi at Scannagallo in 1554 during the War of Siena.

barracks for its members in Portoferraio.[16] Cosimo I and his successors maintained the Order's navy, providing for any and all of their operating expenses. As to expenses for the ducal navy, including the acquisition of *matériel*, weapons, provisions and the payment of salaries for personnel not members of the Order both at sea and in service at installations on land, the full burden fell on ducal finances. The treasury of the Order of St Stephen, for the whole of the sixteenth and for most of the seventeenth century, was limited to paying only the salaries and other living expenses of the Order's knights, that is of the admiral, the knights commanding the ships and of the infantry units of the Duchy (and later the Grand Duchy) who were often on board ships, and of the other members of the Chivalric Militia who, voluntarily or by obligation, sailed both on the St Stephen's galleys and on those of the ducal navy.[17]

In March 1563 the first General Assembly of the Order was held in Pisa, presided over by Cosimo I, during which the highest-ranking knights were elected for the following three years and Giulio de' Medici, a distant relative of Cosimo I, was chosen as admiral.[18] Following what he had written in his memorandum, Cosimo I decided to give two galleys to the Order of St Stephen from the ducal navy which had suffered some losses recently that partly jeopardised its operational ability.[19] The ship assigned to carry out the duty of *Capitana* (flagship) of St Stephen's fleet was the *Lupa*, while the *Padrona* (vice-flagship) was the *Fiorenza*. Both were delivered to Admiral Giulio de' Medici on 30 May 1563 in the port of Leghorn.[20]

The Order's first naval mission took place in cooperation with the ducal

---

[16] In the convent all the knights lived for three years of apprenticeship during which they would have learned the basics of mathematics, geometry, cosmography, history, geography, and land and naval tactics, besides which they would have been trained in gymnastics, wrestling, swimming, fencing, and use of crossbow, arc and portable fire weapons. In the three years also included were six months for the *Professione al Convento* during which the knights had to participate in all religious ceremonies in the Church of the Order. Another semester was devoted to further practical training in both naval and military activity. See Mario Salmi, *Il palazzo dei cavalieri e la scuola normale superiore di Pisa* (Bologna: Zanichelli, 1932), 1–20; Ewa Karwacka Codini, 'Edifici dell'Ordine di Santo Stefano a Pisa: aspetti architettonici e artistici', *Quaderni Stefaniani*, 11 (1992), 133–95; Rodolfo Bernardini, 'Istruzione e obblighi militari dei cavalieri carovanisti da Cosimo I a Pietro Leopoldo I', in *L'istituto della Carovana nell'Ordine di Santo Stefano. Atti del Convegno, Pisa 10 maggio 1996* (Pisa: ETS, 1996), 230–1.
[17] Only during the years from 1625 to 1649 did the Order, on precise application of the then Grand Duke Ferdinando II, partially contribute to the maintenance of the galley; see Archivio di Stato di Pisa (hereafter ASP), *Ordine dei Cavalieri di S. Stefano*, 7118, fols n. nn.; 7119, fols. n. nn.; 7120, fols. n. nn.; 7121, fols n. nn.; 7122, fols n. nn.; 7123, fols n. nn.
[18] Ibid., 4391, fols 3v–4r.
[19] From May 1560 to February 1563 five galleys and a small galley were sunk or captured by the Muslims, cf. ASF, *Mediceo del Principato*, 212, fol. 83v; 214, fol. 30r; 219, fols 279v–280r; 504, fols 287r–288v, 321r–323v; Archivio di Stato di Genova (hereafter ASG), *Archivio Segreto* 2795, file 1541–65. 'Lettere di Cosimo I° de Medici, detto il Grande, primo Gran Duca di Toscana alla Repubblica di Genova', fol. 111r.
[20] ASF, *Manoscritti*, 128, fols 257v–258r.

galleys *Capitana* and *Regina*, when the four galleys went to Spain to be at the disposal of King Philip II for taking supplies to Oran in North Africa, a town besieged by the Muslims. While sailing alone towards the Spanish port of Tortosa to have repairs done arising from earlier damage, the St Stephen's *Capitana* was attacked and captured by two Algerian ships.[21] Cosimo I was greatly disappointed by this debut of the Order's navy and, although he did not start proceedings against the admiral of the militia, he soon ordered his dismissal. From 6 March 1564 Cosimo employed the *Fiorenza*, together with the ducal galleys, under the command of Iacopo VI Aragona Appiano, who had previously commanded the Medici navy from 1552 to 1555.[22] In the meantime Cosimo I knew that Philip II was hiring galleys to transport an expeditionary force to conquer Peñon de Velez, a place along the northern Africa coast opposite Malaga. The Duke of Florence and Siena, taking advantage of the Spanish sovereign's great need for ships, succeeded in having set aside the accord made with Philip II in 1557, by which he had been forced to lend his ships without payment. In fact, in the contract (called *asiento*) signed by the king of Spain on 17 May 1564, Spain agreed to take ten galleys on lease for five years, each of which was to have a full complement of the necessary rowers and a crew of at least sixty-five sailors. These ships were placed under the command of Don Garcia de Toledo, Philip II's General Captain of the Sea. In return, Cosimo I's father-in-law, the Spanish sovereign, would pay a substantial amount of money to the Duke of Florence and Siena for the leasing of the ships.[23] The ten galleys rented to the Spanish included the Order's *Fiorenza*. Although the expedition to conquer Peñon de Velez ended in success, there were many deaths among Cosimo I's crews, due to a contagious disease. Among the dead was the Commissioner of the Galleys, Piero Machiavelli.

In March, 1569, Cosimo I again put his galleys and the Order's *Fiorenza* at the disposal of the Spanish, as he had done in previous years. That year, when the squadron was going west to the Iberian peninsula, it encountered bad weather. As meteorological conditions worsened, the galleys sought shelter on the island of Pomegues, not far from Marseilles. Despite Aragona Appiano's

---

[21] Ibid., *Mediceo del Principato*, 500, fols 85r, 163r–164r, 343r and v. Loss of *Capitana*, like losses of other ships during the sixteenth century afflicted the Order of St Stephen. No trace is found of the loss in the first works published that have dealt with the navy, such as Fulvio Fontana, *I pregi della Toscana nell'imprese più segnalate de' Cavalieri di Santo Stefano* (Florence: Pier Mattia Miccioni e Michele Nestenus, 1701); Aldigherio Fontana, *Le glorie immortali della Sacra, ed Illustrissima Religione di S. Stefano tanto nelle Armi, quanto nelle Lettere* (Milan: Sirtori, 1706) (after Fano: Bernardino Vigolini, 1708); Giorgio Viviano Marchesi, *La Galeria dell'Onore Ove sono descritte le Segnalate Memorie del Sagr'Ordine Militare di S. Stefano P. e M. e de' suoi Cavalieri* (Forlì: Marozzi, 1735).
[22] ASP, *Ordine dei Cavalieri di S. Stefano*, 45, fol. 62v; ASF, *Mediceo del Principato*, 2077, fol. 63r; ASF, *Miscellanea Medicea*, 23, file 28, fols 3r–8r. In 1565 Iacopo VI would have been placed side by side in command with his half-brother Alfonso Aragona Appiano, natural son of Iacopo V, of the Order of St Stephen on 25 May 1563: see ASP, *Ordine dei Cavalieri di S. Stefano*, 600, file 3, fols n. nn.; 145, file 90, fol. n. n.; 1186, fol. 10r.
[23] ASF, *Miscellanea Medicea*, 23, file 29, fol. 1r and v.

recommendation to wait in the shelter of the island for the weather to improve, the Spanish ordered the ships to depart as soon as the mountainous seas and strong wind appeared to be calming. On 19 April, while they were sailing across the Gulf of Lions, they were caught in a storm and five galleys were lost.[24] Dismayed at the loss of these ships due to the stubborness of the Spanish who wanted to continue the trip at all costs, Cosimo I complained to both Philip II and to Don Garcia de Toledo.[25] Despite his position, Cosimo I was obliged to accept the losses without compensation. During the following months, the Arsenal in Pisa began work on building new galleys. If 1569 had been an unlucky year for the Medici's navy, the same cannot be said for Cosimo I, who, thanks to the good relationship established with the new Pope Pius V, succeeded in acquiring the title of Grand Duke of Tuscany. At the beginning of 1570, Cosimo I continued construction of more ships and annulled the *asiento* with Philip II when the Madrid court failed to pay the remuneration due. At that point, Spanish finances were heavily overcommitted to maintaining the troops containing the revolt in Granada and in fighting in Flanders.[26]

The following July, the Turks landed on the island of Cyprus, then under Venetian control. In response, an accord was reached in August between Venice, Philip II and Pius V, to send a fleet of galleys, commanded by Marc' Antonio Colonna, against the Ottoman fleet.[27] Cosimo I intensified diplomatic relations with the Papal States in order to sign an *asiento* with Pius V. The negotiations continued over the following months, when the Pope needed additional ships after his twelve galleys had gone to the Levant in an unsuccessful attempt to aid Cyprus and to defeat the Turks. Only three of them returned in November, all in a sorry state. The remaining nine had been lost in bad weather.[28]

In order to place twelve galleys at the Pope's disposal, Cosimo I had to recruit new workmen for the Arsenal of Pisa. Numerous experienced woodcutters were brought from Lombardy to cut the necessary trees in Tuscany for the construc-

[24] The *Padrona* and *Colonna* were sunk at sea with their entire crews. *Toscana* and *Lupa* were wrecked on the cliffs in Sardinia and the *Pace* had the same fate on the island of St Peter, all three losing many men. ASF, *Mediceo del Principato*, 541, fol. 82r; 294r and v; 541a, fols 668 bis r–669 bis r.
[25] Ibid., 233, fols 16r, 18v–19r.
[26] Fernand Braudel, *Civiltà e imperi del Mediterraneo nell'età di Filippo II*, translated into Italian by C. Pischedda (Turin: Einaudi, 1986), vol. I, 1099–1148; ASF, *Mediceo del Principato*, 551, fols 318r and v, 329r; 553, fol. 9r and v; 554, fols 210r and v, 245r; ASP, *Pia Casa di Misericordia*, 110, fol. n. n.
[27] ASG, *Magistrato delle galee* 2, fols n. nn.; ASF, *Mediceo del Principato*, 235, fol. 113v; 562, fols 5r and v, 21r, 27r and v.
[28] The ships of Venice, Spain and the Papal States took some weeks to reach the waters off Crete. By then their commanders knew that on 9 September Nicosia and a large part of Cyprus had fallen to the Turks. Only Famagosta remained. Since the Winter season was approaching and it would have been impossible to provide for the crews in Crete because of the lack of supplies, Marc'Antonio Colonna ordered the squadrons to move to ports of the Italian peninsula. During the passage, storms sank numerous ships. ASF, *Mediceo del Principato*, 235, fol. 116v; 554, fol. 159r and v.

tion of these ships.[29] Thanks to this productive effort, when the Holy League was founded on 20 May 1571, Cosimo I was able to lend Pius V the St Stephen's *Fiorenza* and another eleven Grand Duchy galleys.[30] These twelve ships, carrying the Pope's insignia, participated in the famous battle of Lepanto on 7 October 1571. The only loss among them was the *Fiorenza*, which, having been seriously damaged in the fight, was scuttled by knights of the Order at the end of the battle.[31]

In order to replace the Order's unit lost at Lepanto, Cosimo I ordered, in early 1572, that the next galley to be launched from the Arsenal of Pisa be assigned to the Order, christening it *Fortuna*.[32] That same year, the Grand Duke of Tuscany decided again to lend his twelve galleys to the Papacy. Although Pius V had died on 1 May 1572, his successor, Gregory XIII, continued his policy against the Ottoman Turks. At the same time, Cosimo I granted in an *asiento* to Philip II, two galleasses, a small galley (recently built in Pisa) and a galleon, which would also serve in the Christian fleet. During the summer, the Christian fleet, commanded by Don Juan of Austria, sought to fight the Turks, who preferred instead to flee. After an attempt by the Christians to take possession of Navarino failed, Don Juan authorised all ships furnished by Cosimo I to return to Leghorn that November.[33]

In the meantime, Cosimo I was apparently struck down by a type of progressive paralysis, which eventually caused him to lose the use of his right hand and his speech. As it progressed, he gradually entrusted the direction of the state and the Order of St Stephen to his son, Francesco, who, after his father's death on 21 April 1574, became Grand Duke of Tuscany and Grand Master of the St Stephen Militia with the name of Francesco I.[34] Even before his father's death, Francesco found himself administering a naval complex of considerable size. Besides the small ships, it included two galleasses, a galleon, a small galley and twelve galleys, one of which was the *Fortuna* belonging to the Order of St Stephen. The burden of maintaining a similar fleet had proved to be hard on the Grand Duchy's finances. Earlier his father, Cosimo I, had removed Iacopo VI Aragona Appiano from the position of commander of the Grand Duchy's navy, perhaps to save money, and nominally replaced him with his son, nineteen-year-old Pietro de' Medici, with the agreement of his older brother, Prince Francesco.[35]

---

[29] Ibid., 562, fols 150r and v, 221r and v.
[30] Ibid., *Manoscritti*, 128, fol. 529v; Archivio di Stato di Lucca, *Anziani al tempo della libertà*, 552, fol. 17v; ibid., *Biblioteca Manoscritti*, 13, 668–70.
[31] ASF, *Mediceo del Principato*, 566, fol. 102r.
[32] ASP, *Ordine dei Cavalieri di S. Stefano*, 1366, fol. 484r.
[33] ASF, *Mediceo del Principato*, 240, fol. 47v; 241, fol. 71r; 583, fols 269r and v, 293r and v, 323r and v.
[34] Ibid., *Manoscritti*, 128, fols 578v, 619r.
[35] Ibid., *Mediceo del Principato*, 241, fol. 86v. Since Pietro de' Medici did not have any experience in the naval field, Cosimo I thought about placing beside him as lieutenant the Flor-

Another important change concerning the St Stephen's navy came on 22 January 1573, when the admiral of the Order, Tommaso de' Medici, was made captain of *Fortuna*.[36] This appointment was not intended to be a demotion from admiral of the militia. An admiral was responsible, theoretically, for a fleet, but at that time it consisted of only one galley. This appointment was to show the wish of the Florentine court that the head of St Stephen's navy should be an experienced sailor, something which was not true of the man who had held that title since the spring of 1564.[37]

Cosimo I and Francesco both hoped that in 1573 Gregory XIII would have again hired their galleys, but following the peace between Venice and Constantinople on 12 March, the Holy League of Venice, Spain and the Papal States ceased to exist and the Pope did not renew the contract of *asiento* with Florence. Similarly, Philip II was not willing to contract for either the Grand Duchy's ships nor those of St Stephen for his service, since he would hardly have been able to pay to lease them. These circumstances forced the Medici to decommission a large part of the fleet on which Cosimo I had, over the years, lavished so much money and for which he had held such high hopes. Agreeing with his father, Prince Francesco was forced in April 1573 to dismantle two galleasses and a small galley, maintaining in service only one galleon and six galleys, of which five were Tuscan and one of the Order of St Stephen. The prince did this to prevent Philip II from borrowing numerous units from the Grand Duchy of Tuscany without honouring his financial agreement, as he had done in the past. The prince decided to increase the number of galleys of the Order to four and, at the same time, to reduce the Tuscan number to two. In this way, the Florentine court hoped to be able to justify refusal of the Spanish application for the loan of its galleys, showing that most of the ships at the base in Leghorn belonged to the Order of St Stephen, an autonomous corporate body separate from the Grand Duchy of Tuscany.

With regard to the employment of the fleet, both Cosimo I and Francesco, despite their intentions not to lend their own units to Spain, knew that Philip II was assembling a fleet under the command of Don Juan of Austria to attempt an attack on North Africa. In order for the Medici to maintain good relations with the Spanish court, they thought it a good idea to send both the Grand Duchy's two galleys and the Order's four galleys to serve in the Christian fleet, without any remuneration.[38]

After Francesco became Grand Duke and Grand Master, it became apparent

---

entine Simeone Rossermini, an expert soldier who had already sailed for some time on board the Medici's ships, see ibid., 240, fol. 59r and v.

[36] Ibid., fol. 60r.

[37] Nevertheless Tommaso de' Medici did not have the opportunity to do much during that voyage. A short while after he was named captain of *Fortuna*, he fell ill and was forced to ask the court to be exempted from going to sea, ASP, *Ordine dei Cavalieri di S. Stefano*, 1322, fol. 41r.

[38] ASF, *Mediceo del Principato*, 4904, fol. 28r and v.

that, once again, neither Phillip II nor Gregory XIII wanted to use his ships. At this point, Francesco I decommissioned the Grand Duchy's two galleys and sent the Order's four ships on an offensive operation in the central Mediterranean along the Barbary coast and to the Levant. Ships based at Leghorn had not carried out such a mission for many years, so, on 13 May, Francesco I issued a set of instructions to be followed on board the galleys of St Stephen under the command of the admiral of the Order, Tommaso de' Medici.[39] During this five-month cruise, the Order's ships sank or captured eleven Muslim ships and imprisoned around three hundred enemy sailors.[40]

In 1575, Francesco I put his galleys at the disposal of Philip II, who ordered them to assemble at Naples under the command of Don Juan of Austria. To prevent idleness among the Tuscan crews in port, the ships of the Order made two voyages along the North African coast, during which they tried to attack the town of Susa. At first, the galleys were unable to approach the coast, because of rough seas. A second attempt also failed, due to an error in navigation. The troops disembarked about ten miles from the Tunisian town, but, making do, the Knights of St Stephen had to be satisfied with ransacking the small fortress of Reclia.[41]

This small success at Reclia represented the first amphibious operation completed by the Order. Actions of the same kind would be carried out with increasing frequency in the following years, especially when, following Francesco I's death on 20 October 1587, his brother, Ferdinando I, became Grand Duke of Tuscany and Grand Master of the Order of St Stephen.[42] Ferdinando I instituted a foreign policy aimed at further loosening the ties between Tuscany and Spain, while at the same wanting closer relations with France. To achieve this, Ferdinando I arranged the marriage of his own niece, Maria de' Medici, daughter of Francesco I, to King Henry IV in October 1600.[43] However, neither the new blood ties nor the conspicuous dowry provided by Ferdinando I served to improve relationships between Florence and Paris, instead the Grand Duke was forced to look toward reconciliation with Spain. The decision of the new Spanish king, Philip III, to conquer Algiers furnished Ferdinando I with an occasion. In order to transport the Spanish expeditionary force to Africa in 1598, Phillip III was forced to ask the Italian states to furnish

---

[39] Ibid., *Carte Strozziane*, I serie 146, fols 19r–20r; a similar copy is ibid., *Mediceo del Principato*, 1203, file 1, fols 192r–193v.
[40] Biblioteca Comunale di Siena, *Manoscritti*, K.III.56, fol. 2r. Many of the Muslims taken imprisoned in this case, as in the preceding and succeeding ones, were employed as rowers on board the Medici's galleys.
[41] ASF, *Mediceo del Principato*, 678, fol. 204v. For further details about this operation see Marco Gemignani, 'Il concetto di operazione anfibia del Sacro Militare Ordine di Santo Stefano sotto i gran magisteri di Francesco I e di Ferdinando I de' Medici', in *Aspetti ed attualità del potere marittimo in Mediterraneo nei secoli XII–XVI. Atti del Convegno, Napoli 27–9 ottobre 1997* (Rome: Ufficio Storico della Marina Militare, 1999), 173–5.
[42] ASF, *Manoscritti*, 129, fol. 260r.
[43] Diaz, *Il Granducato di Toscana – I Medici*, 288–9.

him with ships.[44] Seizing the opportunity for improving relations, Ferdinando I put the Order of St Stephen's four galleys at the disposal of the Spanish sovereign. The ships eventually joined the Christian fleet that was being assembled in Sicily under command of Gian Andrea Doria in the summer of 1601.

This large fleet set sail from Messina on 5 August 1601, and called at Majorca. En route they stood offshore near Algiers for a time while people who were in contact with Doria tried to disrupt the town as a prelude for an assault by the troops of Philip III.[45] These plots in which the commander in chief of the Christian fleet put so much faith did not produce the desired results and Doria withdrew, losing the opportunity to bring an end to Barbary privateering.[46] Subsequently, Ferdinando I allowed Spain to use the Order's navy only occasionally. Instead, he increasingly used cruises to protect the shores of Tuscany from Muslim raids and to undertake raids along the coasts of Greece, Turkey and North Africa.[47]

The attacks against the Ottomans' coastal towns and fortresses usually had the advantage of supplying prisoners which could be used as rowers on board the galleys, allowing the St Stephen's ships to boast to other Christian states of their navy's strength, demonstrated by such clear successes against the Muslims.[48] In August 1607, the Order's navy, now increased to eight galleys and strengthened by sailing ships, was used for executing a more ambitious enterprise than the usual amphibious operations of the 'hit and run' type.[49] Ferdinando I made plans to conquer Famagusta, as the first stage in occupying

---

[44] Godfrey Fisher, *Barbary Legend. War, Trade and Piracy in North Africa 1415–1830* (Westport: Greenwood Press, 1974), 129–30.

[45] ASF, *Mediceo del Principato*, 295, fol. 138v; 2081, fol. 762r.

[46] Ibid., 904, fol. 263r.

[47] When the Squadron of St Stephen operated with the ships of Spain, of the Order of St John and other states of the Italian peninsula, friction often occurred over precedence. Sometimes incidents even went as far as shoot-outs with casualties of Christian sailors and soldiers, as happened in the port of Messina in September 1614; see Marco Gemignani, 'Esempi di collaborazione in seno all'Armata Navale cattolica', *Quaderni Stefaniani*, 14 (1995), 94–103.

[48] To spread the news of these victories and to perpetuate their memory, the Grand Duke, besides ordering the painting of pictures and frescos, also occasionally printed brochures reporting on the amphibious operations and the results achieved; see for example *Relatione dell'impresa della Prevesa fatta per ordine del Serenissimo Gran Duca di Toscana. Dalle Galere della Religione di Santo Stefano, seguita a 3. di Maggio 1605* (Florence: Sermartelli, 1605); *Relazione di tre imprese fatte dalle galere di Santo Stefano, quest'anno MDCVI, cioè di Laiazzo in Soria, di Namur in Caramania, e della Finica in Satalia* (Florence: Sermartelli, 1606); *Relazione della presa della Fortezza, e porto di Seleucia, detta Agliman, in Caramania; e di Due Galere Capitane, & altri Vasselli Turcheschj. Fatta da sei Galere della Religione di Santo Stefano il giorno dell'Ascensione 16. di Maggio 1613* (Florence: Cosimo Giunti, 1613). The victories of that period by the Order's navy can almost all be attributed, from a tactical point of view, to the ability of St Stephen's Admiral Iacopo Inghirami who, in addition to deep knowledge of maritime problems, also had solid experience of land operations developed during his service in the Wars of Religion in France at the end of the sixteenth century. For further details on his life, see Marco Gemignani, *Il cavaliere Iacopo Inghirami al servizio dei granduchi di Toscana* (Pisa: ETS, 1996).

[49] ASF, *Carte Strozziane*, I serie 147, fol. 249r and v.

the whole of Cyprus. With Cyprus under his command, he could create an advanced base to begin expansion in the eastern Mediterranean, using the support of the populations of that area, which at that time were in revolt against the Turkish Empire. Through this plan, Ferdinando I would have increased, by almost half, the territory of his dominions and, moreover he would have been able to add the title of king to that of Grand Duke. With possession of Cyprus, Ferdinando I would clearly have garnered respect from rulers of the other states of the Italian peninsula with whom he often disagreed in matters of precedence. However, because of the lack of coordination among the forces employed, the operation ended in failure. Not wanting to appear discouraged by this debacle, Ferdinando I resumed the usual amphibious operations of the 'hit and run' type, and undertook a raid against the Algerian town of Bône (Al Anabas). During this operation, the Knights of St Stephen and Tuscan troops, at the cost of forty-seven casualties, captured 1464 prisoners and killed 470 Muslims.[50]

When Ferdinando I died on 7 February 1609, his son, Cosimo II, became the new Grand Duke of Tuscany and Grand Master of the Order. Under his direction, the Order kept on effecting only small raids against coastal objectives, continuing defensive cruises in the northern Tyrrhenian Sea and offensive cruises in both the Aegean Sea and in the central and eastern Mediterranean. During these years, the fleet occasionally participated in actions with larger Christian fleets.

Cosimo II died on 28 February 1621, and his son Ferdinando II succeeded him to rule the Grand Duchy and head the Order up to 1670.[51] During his long reign, he increasingly employed the navy of the Order of St Stephen, using it to defend the Tuscan coast and to escort diplomats and important people by sea. Meanwhile, he reduced the number of cruises along the Muslim coast and amphibious raids hardly ever occurred. At the beginning of the 1640s, Ferdinando II was busy in the First War of Castro, also known as the War of the Barberini, in which Tuscany was allied with the Republic of Venice, the Duchy of Modena, and the Duchy of Parma against Pope Urban VIII.[52] During this war,

---

[50] Archivio Inghirami, Volterra, 58, file 'Protocollo degli ordini e rescritti sovrani per il servizio delle galere comandate dal Generale Iacopo Inghirami e documenti relativi a detto servizio', fol. n. nn.; also on the occasion of the victory of Bône the brochure *Relazione del viaggio e della presa della città di Bona in Barberia. Fatta per commessione del Sereniss. Granduca di Toscana in nome del Serenissimo Prencipe suo primogenito dalle Galere della Religione di Santo Stefano il di 16. di Settembre 1607* (Roma: Lepido Facii, 1607) (after Florence: Sermartelli, 1607; after Bologna: Benacci, 1607) was published. For further details related to this enterprise, which was surely the greatest amphibious operation completed by the Order of St Stephen, see Marco Gemignani, 'La conquista di Bona', *Società di Storia Militare*, 2 (1994), 7–36.

[51] Ferdinando II initially, since he was still a minor, was assisted by his paternal grandmother, Cristina of Lorena, and his mother, Maria Maddalena of Habsburg Diaz, *Il Granducato di Toscana – I Medici*, 375–7.

[52] The conflict began following the occupation by the Papal States' troops of lands of the Duke of Parma, Odoardo Farnese, that is Castro and Ronciglione. They were encumbered by previously contracted large debts to the Pope and did not have the resources to pay those debts. After this easy success, the Papal States' soldiers tried also to conquer the whole of the

in order to avoid clashes with other Christian navies, the ships of the Order of St Stephen were limited to operations that loosely patrolled the shores of the Grand Duchy and the Papal States.[53]

In 1645, the War of Crete, also called the War of Candia, began between Venice and Turkey. The new Pope, Innocent X, asked and got from Ferdinando II the dispatch of the galleys of St Stephen along with those of other Christian navies to aid the Serenissima Republic. Despite the long wait in the waters around Crete, the ships of the Order were never involved in serious fighting against the Ottomans. In 1646, while the ships of the Order were in Leghorn, news spread that a large French fleet was operating in the Tyrrhenian Sea, very probably intended to attack Spanish possessions in the Italian peninsula and the states allied with Madrid, including the Grand Duchy of Tuscany. The king of Spain, Philip IV, who had succeeded his father Philip III in 1621, was engaged alongside the Holy Roman Empire in the Thirty Years War. Informed of the intentions of the French fleet, he decided that, in order to avoid strengthening his harbours in Italy, to sell those bases to Ferdinando II.

At that point, however, Tuscany, was in a serious financial predicament, because of expenses sustained during the First War of Castro. It was not able to take advantage of the opportunity of acquiring these bases that would have allowed it to control the Channel of Piombino. At the same time that Tuscany refused the Spanish proposal, Ferdinando II also rejected an offer from Cardinal Mazarin for Tuscany to ally itself with France. To avoid being involved in the war, the Grand Duke proclaimed his neutrality and declared himself ready to receive the French ships in his own ports.[54]

The French, after having repeatedly defeated the Spanish both in land battles and in a naval clash, demanded and got from Ferdinando II a supply of provisions. Otherwise, they would have carried out raids against Tuscany. This made the financial situation of the Grand Duchy even more precarious, forcing Ferdinando II to decrease expenses. When the treasury of the Order was not able to assure their maintenance, he took the serious decision of reducing the number of galleys of the Order of St Stephen. The negotiations to sell three galleys with rowers started in the second half of 1646 and, initially, they were offered to Naples and to the Republic of Genoa, two states strongly linked with Spain.[55] Subsequently, Venice was also contacted. It needed to reinforce its own navy for use against the Turks, who were occupying Crete, but, in the event, it proved

---

Duchy of Parma. The nearby states allied themselves against the Pope, saying that he was obliged at the end of the war to return the contested lands to the Duke of Parma; see Ciro Paoletti, 'La prima guerra di Castro (1640–1644)', *Rivista marittima*, 131 (1998), 4, 89–91.
53 Ibid., 92–100.
54 Letter from Pandolfo Ottavanti to Domenico Pandolfini from Leghorn on 2 September 1647, see ASF, *Mediceo del Principato*, 2425, fol. n. n.; Jean Meyer and Martine Acerra, *Histoire de la marine française des origines à nos jours* (Rennes: Ouest-France, 1994), 34.
55 ASF, *Mediceo del Principato*, 2163, fols 434r, 626r.

impossible to agree on a price with the Venetians.[56] Ferdinando II decided to sell the three vessels to the French, who also agreed in order to prevent their ending up in the hands of their Spanish adversaries. To avoid creating diplomatic embarrassment for the Grand Duke with Philip IV, the Medici officially sold the ships to the principality of Monaco in the spring of 1647. Monaco then delivered them to the French.[57] Ferdinando II, with this sale, reduced the operational fleet of the Order to only two galleys. They would primarily be used for protecting the northern Tyrrhenian Sea from raids of Barbary privateers, to escort important people and especially to transport commodities to and from Sicily.[58]

Those were in general terms the circumstances which characterised the rebirth of the Florentine navy in the second half of the sixteenth century, its expansion, the creation by the Medici of the Order of St Stephen endowed with its own fleet, which in the 1570s gradually merged with the Grand Duchy's navy. In examining the nature and evolution of these two navies belonging to the Medici, it becomes clear that they were built to give the Medici greater importance in the international context. Cosimo I was the first to understand how necessary it was to have a fleet in the Mediterranean, which during the sixteenth century became a basin where tensions between Christians and Muslims were increasing. Cosimo I can justly be considered the father of the Medici navy of the period.

The duties of the Florentine ships were manifold. They were to control the northern Tyrrhenian Sea, to protect the Tuscan coasts and the merchant ships headed for Leghorn because Cosimo I and his successors understood that to allow the development of the state that they governed it was absolutely necessary to favour commercial exchange. The ships were to attack Muslim warships and merchantmen to show other Christian states the desire of the Florentine court to oppose Islam. The Medici also considered their ships as 'objects of exchange', to rent to Spain or to the Papal States to get, in addition to money to cover part of the expenses of maintaining the fleet, their support in matters of foreign policy.

Another purpose of the creation of the Order of St Stephen was to create a link between the Medici and the most important families of the Tuscan nobility and also of other Christian states, subsequently to improve relations with the papacy and to have an autonomous fleet separate and different from that of the government.

The huge expenses of maintaining these two navies were initially almost entirely paid through government financing. After some years, when the Florentine court realised that the Papal States and Spain did not wish to rent the Grand

---

[56] The Venetians, rather than buying the galleys, decided to acquire just the rowers, ibid., cc. 512r, 518r, 522r; Archivio di Stato di Venezia, *Senato, Dispacci degli ambasciatori e residenti, Firenze*, 57, fols 39r–41r, 83r–86v, 91r–93v.
[57] ASF, *Mediceo del Principato*, 2167, fol. 343.
[58] ASP, *Ordine dei Cavalieri di S. Stefano*, 3041, *passim*; 3042, *passim*; 3043, *passim*; 3044, *passim*.

Duchy's or the Order's ships, and what is more that the Spanish often did not pay the amount due, it was forced to suppress the government navy and to combine its ships with those of the Order of St Stephen. In this way the Medici could justify their refusal to rent ships to the Spanish, saying that these galleys did not belong to the state that they governed but to an autonomous chivalric Order that had no dependent relationship with Spain. Ships of the Order of St Stephen, especially under the leadership of Ferdinando I and Cosimo II, were then employed in amphibious operations and used initially only to provide prisoners to employ on board the galleys of the Order. Subsequently, the ships were also used to increase the prestige of the Medici family because the grand dukes sometimes entrusted the direction of their operation to relatives. Only in one case, the attack against Famagusta in 1607, was the fleet of St Stephen – on that occasion supported by some rented sailing ships – employed for conquering a territory. The plan was to use that town as a base in the eastern Mediterranean to promote the Medici dynasty from the rank of grand dukes to that of kings, but the enterprise failed. Later, in the 1630s and 1640s, the fleet of the Order of St Stephen was transformed from a primarily offensive posture to a defensive one and given the task of representation. To reduce the costs of the maintenance of the fleet, Ferdinando II was even forced to sell three of its galleys.

Strategic factors and naval technology also evolved in the Mediterranean in the roughly one hundred years from the launching in 1547 of the first Medici galley of the period to the mid-seventeenth century. A squadron of five or six galleys could and did have some importance at the time of Cosimo I and his immediate successors. By around 1650 a small fleet of this kind was not enough either to carry out amphibious operations against the Islamic coasts, now better protected by fortresses and patrols of cavalry, or to effect attacks against the maritime commercial trade routes, now often served by large sailing ships equipped with large amounts of artillery. Spain no longer required the ships since by the mid-seventeenth century it had a large permanent fleet of its own. Only in the 1680s did the navy of the Order of St Stephen, engaged alongside other Christian fleets in the War of Morea, increase its forces to four galleys and other small ships. Its weight, both from a military point of view and from a diplomatic one, would have been small in comparison to the Medici navy at the time of Cosimo I,[59] but he had appreciated, as much as or more than most of his contemporaries, the changing character of naval warfare in the sixteenth century.

[59] ASF, *Miscellanea Medicea*, 672, file 'Per le Galere'.

THE STATE OF PORTUGUESE NAVAL FORCES IN THE SIXTEENTH CENTURY

Francisco Contente Domingues

> Portuguese sea-power was, in its day and for its time, immensely impressive[1]

ALMOST every attempt made so far to provide a theoretical basis for naval power has failed to consider Portugal among the elite club of powers that, at some historical moment, could be considered global maritime powers. This exclusionary analysis dated back to Alfred Mahan[2] and almost every subsequent essayist and historian has followed him.[3] Nevertheless, in 1988, George Modelski and William Thompson proposed a new vision of how naval power has evolved since the end of the fifteenth century to today. They came to the conclusion that four major naval forces have appeared on a worldwide scale: Portugal, Holland, England and the United States of America. Like Mahan, Modelski and Thompson did not consider Spain to be a part of this group, because it should only be considered a regional power.[4] Comparison between these two works immediately highlights the obviously different methodologies and criteria adopted which inevitably and, as expected, conditioned any final conclusions drawn. However, the different perspectives are also a result of factors other than just methodological criteria. The reason that led Modelski and Thompson to propose Portugal as the first major naval power in the modern period was clearly, above all, the chronological period covered by their study. In fact, specialists usually take the middle of the seventeenth century as the first moment to consider, following Mahan. Bringing this date back by over a century obviously turned the spotlight on the power which first navigated the high seas. There are varied different grounds to justify this change.

---

[1] George Modelski and William R. Thompson, *Sea Power in Global Politics, 1494–1993* (Houndsmills and London: The Macmillan Press, 1988), 174.
[2] *The Influence of Sea Power upon History, 1660–1783* (Boston: Little, Brown & Co., 1890).
[3] The last one was Richard Harding, *Seapower and Naval Warfare 1650–1830* (London: UCL Press, 1999).
[4] Mahan ignored Spain for a very different reason, as shown by Jesus Salgado Alba, *El poder naval ante la realidad politica española* (Madrid: Instituto de Historia y Politica Naval, 1982), 3.

The first reason has to do with the simple fact that Portugal has not, in general, been historiographically considered as a maritime power. This is easily explained by the existing supply of information about European navies, with historians focusing on the period when England and Holland appeared as the major naval powers, that is, from the mid-seventeenth century on. In contrast, studies of the navies of southern European countries, particularly in the case of Portugal, have had no significant international projection. The main exception is everything to do with Columbus' voyages, well known in international scholarship. In fact, published studies are the primary (and frequently only) source of information for attempts to produce global interpretative syntheses such as the ones mentioned.

Examining the most important world naval powers from that time and the number of years they held this position, Modelski and Thompson drew up a framework which was very clear about the sources available to calculate those countries' naval strengths, as can been seen by the following numbers:

Table 1. Sources available to calculate total warship numbers, 1494–1860

Country	Number of years	Number of sources
Portugal	87	1
Spain	113	51
England/Great Britain	367	85
Netherlands	105	50
France	367	92
Russia	75	20
USA	45	1

George Modelski and William R. Thompson, *Sea Power in Global Politics, 1494–1993*, 46. The source for the USA is an official contemporary report.

The second reason is the shifting of focus to the specific instrument of naval power: the ship. Much of the information on this subject, perhaps the essential part, is still in manuscript form, although Portuguese treatises on naval architecture from the early modern period have been systematically published in recent years.[5] This seriously hampers any attempt at a comparative study of European countries' naval resources up to the seventeenth century. Consequently, the necessary details are found by analysing characteristics of the vessels that can reasonably be considered a major element in establishing naval power: warships.

The third major obstacle is the lack of reliable documentation on European

---

[5] Fernando Oliveira, *O Livro da Fábrica das Naus* (Lisbon: Academia de Marinha, 1991 [original MS c.1570]); João Baptista Lavanha, *Livro Primeiro da Architectura Naval* (Lisbon: Academia de Marinha, 1996 [original MS c.1600]); *Livro de Traças de Carpintaria por Manoel Fernandez. Transcrição e Tradução em Inglês* (Lisbon: Academia de Marinha, 1995 [original MS 1616]).

ships until at least the end of the sixteenth century, compared to the mass of detail obtainable for later periods. The description found in *Anthony Anthony's Roll* of English ships from Henry VIII's time is unique. Even if it were not, it is legitimate to wonder whether a warship from *c.*1500 or 1550 (excepting oared ships, which are not totally relevant here), can be accurately defined.

Generally, in terms of ocean-going ships, the further back in time one goes, the harder it is to make a generic distinction between merchant ships and warships from European naval forces. The principal issue is whether this question, which makes perfect sense from the eighteenth century onwards, can be asked for such a distant past as the sixteenth century. This implies that the documentation may never solve a problem that reflects a criterion which, hypothetically, may not be applicable to the century when the Portuguese navy dominated navigation on the high seas.

Modelski and Thompson see the real issue as being the global and political question of when and where naval power has been and is an effective instrument of political domination. Thus, they find a close relationship between hegemonic naval power and a series of more or less identical cycles of around 120 years, each of which evolved in parallel fashion and featured global wars that gauged who held global power:

> The long cycle approach . . . raises basic questions of world organisation: the conditions of world leadership and the causes and consequences of major warfare in a framework that suggests that these basic processes might be subject to regularities that are both repetitive (cyclic), and also revolutionary. Global war, for instance, may be shown to have recurred, in the experience of the modern world, with surprising regularity.[6]

It is through examining these long cycles that the authors can expand Mahan's problem and establish the fundamental link between naval power and these cycles. This in turn focuses attention on two of the cycles' characteristics: global war and innovation. Each global war was above all else a naval war, since the organisation of the world system depends essentially on continental interaction, which since 1500 was essentially maritime.

> Global wars have been naval wars in the most general sense because global wars are contests for world leadership and world leadership requires sea power.[7]

Consequently, coming to the central question of the real possibility of measuring the instruments of naval power, a change in the balance of power existing at any specific time is not merely a change in the naval means held by the powers in real or potential conflict, but also a change which affects the world's established political order. This means that one navy's loss of supremacy over another sparks off a fundamental alteration in the status quo.

---

6 Modelski and Thompson, *Sea Power*, 15.
7 Ibid., 19.

> If the distribution of sea power is indicated by the ratio or relationship of battle fleets or major naval combatants, then adverse changes in that relationship tell a great deal about changes in the word's political structure.[8]

Everything seems to boil down to very simple questions: knowing who had the navy or navies that guaranteed naval power, and knowing the measurement criteria that provide objective indicators capable of going beyond a qualitative analysis of the relative forces present in any political and military circumstances. The increased importance that Modelski and Thompson attribute to navies is a result of the role that they also attribute to those navies in defining naval power:

> 1. A dominant power's navy achieves and exercises naval control by neutralising or destroying the opponents' navies;
> 2. It defends its naval bases from attacks and invasions, and attacks its opponents' bases;
> 3. It controls its trade and communication routes, and tries to intercept those of its enemies;
> 4. It plays a fundamental role in joint defence of and with friendly others, thereby strengthening alliances.

Navies and their enormous importance form the central issue of this theory. They are seen as the fundamental instrument of naval power and this power, in turn, is understood as a *sine qua non* for dominating the cycles that successively defined the world systems. This means that other questions, which are normally taken into consideration, such as economic and social factors, are to some extent excluded. Alternatively, in a potential reading that is justified by a series of comments made throughout the work, they try to give the naval factor its due value, something that has not been done in similar works.

The natural consequence is that Modelski and Thompson focused on the questions raised by their specific view, without considering other visions such as those noted above and not examining them at the same level. Even so, António José Telo's recently expressed reservations are still completely relevant. They can be summarised as follows:[9]

> 1. There is no fundamental justification for the rigid 120-year cycle which repeats itself and follows the same principles. Besides, the very concept of cycles in history 'is very uncertain, precisely because social reality does not repeat itself';
> 2. Naval power is always considered decisive and is hegemonically held by a single state in each cycle. Both these ideas are simplistic and neither matches the facts.

---

[8] Ibid., 17.
[9] António José Telo, *Do tratado de Tordesilhas à guerra fria: reflexões sobre o sistema mundial* (Blumenau, Brazil: Editora da FURB, 1996), 68–70.

And at the end of it, the true role of the warship remains to be accurately defined as does the measurement processes used to quantify naval power within any century. According to Modelski and Thompson, as long as a nation has 50 per cent of the global naval resources or 50 per cent of all war vessels, it qualifies as a world naval power. They consider that, between 1494 and 1654, an ocean-going warship can be defined as any armed ship that belongs to and is maintained by a state. This rather conservative ownership criterion is relevant in that it avoids situations of casual use, which do not in themselves reveal the state's capacity actually to have access to ships that it could call up at specific moments, as happens with freighting. Consequently, they only identify two powers that had Crown navies – Portugal and England – during the sixteenth century. Of these, England was a regional power and Portugal a world power. However, some practical difficulties in assessing the suggested terms must be pointed out.

Henrique Quirino da Fonseca's book,[10] heavily used by these two authors, was the result of extensive research in primary sources and is unique in Portuguese historiography on this subject. It offers the most complete description of Portugal's naval resources until around 1640. While the relevant elements of the vast array of documents on which it was based would nowadays need reassessment, there is no reason to think that any re-elaboration would lead to significantly different results from those presented. Equally, there is nothing to suggest that Portuguese documentation will one day allow us to find something like a systematic and exhaustive identification of all the ships on the India run in the sixteenth century (much less other runs or fleets), similar to the one for Dutch ships sailing to Asia in the seventeenth and eighteenth centuries.[11]

While the available instruments must be seen as insufficient for a full assessment of Portuguese naval resources in the sixteenth century, it is equally evident that the expression 'naval resources' needs precise definition. Simply counting the ships and establishing a percentage that, a priori, defines a relationship of comparative strength does not seem to be a complete answer. The ships themselves were of little or no use without the support of a logistic structure to help in the war effort or simply to equip them for trading voyages. In the first case, naval bases are truly important, no matter how rudimentary the sixteenth-century versions might seem, and ports of call were equally relevant in both cases for the longer routes, as exemplified by the India run.

A precise definition of a sixteenth-century naval base is a question that deserves proper analysis, since the concept is projected back in time from when its use became usual. A well-established port of call could well be considered

---

[10] Henrique Quirino da Fonseca, *Os Portugueses no mar. Memórias históricas e arqueológicas das naus de Portugal*, 2nd edn (Lisbon: Comissão Cultural da Marinha, 1999).
[11] J. R. Bruijn, F. S. Gaastra and I. Schöffer, with assistance from A. C. J. Vermeulen, *Dutch-Asiatic Shipping in the Seventeenth and Eighteenth Centuries*, vol. I – introductory volume (The Hague: Martinus Nijhoff, 1987), 271 ff. for the list of references used by the authors; vols II and III contain all the data on Dutch fleets sent to the Orient.

essential for sixteenth-century ocean navigation, a case in point being the Ilha de Moçambique (Mozambique Island) on the India run – a voyage between Lisbon and India carried out annually from 1500 to 1863.[12] What was needed was a port with dockyards and warehouses, like Goa in the 1500s. However, it is not possible to go much further than these examples.

The main criticism of Modelski and Thompson's theory is undoubtedly their definition of the 50 per cent mark as a criterion to define world naval power. Why 50 per cent? If a navy has 40 per cent of all the warships could it not be a world naval power? And would 30 per cent not be enough? This ignores another essential criterion: the qualitative aspect. How many Indian armed *paraus* were equivalent to one Portuguese galleon from the mid-sixteenth century?

Clearly, the need to consider the qualitative criterion makes it substantially more difficult to assess which countries were or were not naval powers, although the authors' purpose was exactly that of reducing the level of subjectivity in this type of analysis. However, some level of subjectivity is simply inescapable in questions relating to the sixteenth century.

On the other hand, ownership of vessels is a different matter. Study of this question is seriously hampered by the lack of reliable information. It is known that private ships sailed alongside the Crown's ships on the first voyage on the India run, using Portugal's most extensive trade route, the Cape Route. According to Moacyr Soares Pereira, the first *nau* to return to Lisbon, *Nossa Senhora Anunciada*, belonged to D. Álvaro de Bragança and his associates, Italian merchants Bartolomeo Marchioni, Girolamo Sernigi and possibly António Salvago. Equally, one of the caravels that was lost belonged to D. Diogo da Silva e Meneses, the king's tutor and first count of Portalegre, and to his partners.[13] By cross-referencing broader information, A. A. Marques de Almeida identified ships belonging to three private financiers in this same fleet.[14] This reveals the difficulty in establishing what belonged to whom, or of establishing who owned or financed the ships on the India run or to what extent they did so. Up to now, accurate information on this subject is only available for the first half of the sixteenth century.

It is impossible to provide an objective definition of ownership by only considering the construction and fitting out of galleons. Leonor Freire Costa

---

[12] Vasco da Gama's voyage was a one of exploration. The India run really started with the thirteen ships in the fleet of Pedro Álvares Cabral, who left Lisbon in 1500 and discovered Brazil on his way to India. See Francisco Contente Domingues, *A Carreira da Índia. The India Run* (Lisbon, 1998).

[13] Moacyr Soares Pereira, *Capitães, naus e caravelas da armada de Cabral* (Lisbon: Centro de Estudos de História e Cartografia Antiga, offprint no CXV, 1979), the most complete account about Cabral's fleet, although some of the conclusions are open to discussion. On Cabral and his voyage in general see António Dias Farinha, 'A Viagem de Pedro Álvares Cabral ao Brasil e à Índia', *Oceanos*, 39 (Lisbon, 1999), 54–68, and Luís Adão da Fonseca, *Pedro Álvares Cabral. Uma viagem* (Lisbon: Inapa, 1999).

[14] A. A. Marques de Almeida, *Capitais e capitalistas no comércio da especiaria. O eixo Lisboa–Antuérpia (1501–1549). Aproximação a um estudo de geofinança* (Lisbon, 1993), 99.

came to the conclusion that both the crown and private ship-owners used essentially the same strategies. The king sent galleons to war at his expense and the private ship owners sent the *naus* on trading voyages at their expense. However, as was the case with the tables drawn up by A. A. Marques de Almeida, the data supplied do not give specific details about galleons in the contingent of ships going to India.[15]

Therefore, any conclusions about potential convergence in strategy between private ship owners and the king seem immediately open to question. It remains to be seen whether the information will reveal precisely which ships really went to sea, that is, whether there is any architectural or morphological distinction between *naus* on the India run and war galleons, which would consequently suggest functional specialisation.

All the reservations about Modelski and Thompson's theory derive from the fact that they were forced to project concepts like 'warship' or 'naval base' back onto the sixteenth century, while we understand those concepts the way they are generally accepted from the late seventeenth and eighteenth century onward. Their aim was to create a norm that could, in the long term, define a group of stable criteria for what were or were not world naval powers. Despite these shortcomings, their work has one undeniable merit: it pushed the question of naval power back to times where it was not previously applied, sidelining Alfred Mahan's chronologically limited vision.

As the aforementioned evaluation criteria cannot be applied *ipsis verbis*, we must now try to understand to what extent we can assess their theory from a more qualitative point of view. The first and most basic question is, 'Did the Portuguese have real warships in the sixteenth century?' The need to prepare long-haul ships to make the journey from Lisbon to the Orient and back became clear immediately after Vasco da Gama's journey. This led to the appearance of the *nau*, a broad carvel-built ocean-going ship with a bulging cross-section, quarterdecks and forecastles, three masts with square sails on the foremast and mainmast and a lateen sail on the mizzenmast. It is extremely difficult to differentiate between the Portuguese *nau* and its equivalents in other European navies. Leaving aside the obvious difficulties in converting measurements of volume, there were no significant differences in size. Vasco da Gama's *naus* were not of more than 120 Portuguese tons displacement, but these numbers soon rose and quickly. The largest ships of the 1500 fleet under Pedro Álvares Cabral were of 300 tons, and 400 and 500-ton ships soon appeared. What does seem to have distinguished these ships from other European vessels was their robustness, which resulted from the fact that they were designed to undertake the extremely arduous journey from Lisbon to India. The other factor was the sail area, which images clearly show to be far greater than was usual. The first reliable drawings

---

[15] Leonor Freire Costa, *Naus e galeões na ribeira de Lisboa. A construção naval no século XVI para a Rota do Cabo* (Cascais: Patrimónia, 1997); see also 'A construção naval', in *História de Portugal*, ed. José Mattoso, vol. III: *No alvorecer da modernidade (1480–1620)* (Lisbon: Círculo de Leitores, 1993), 296; Marques de Almeida, *Capitais*, 99–125.

are from the two illustrated *Books of Fleets*, from the period around 1565–70, but reflect quite well this distinctive character of Portuguese ocean-going ships.[16]

The *nau* was a transport ship, as was required for the India run. However, two other types of ocean-going ships – the fleet caravel and the galleon – soon appeared, probably mainly developed for naval military purposes. As Henrique Quirino da Fonseca noted, the fleet caravel had already appeared at the end of fifteenth century.[17] Its design was evidently based on a standard one from that time, with lateen sails on all masts except for a square sail on the foremast, that plan to make use of steady winds blowing from the stern. Columbus used this sail plan on his first journey, as stated in his diary, but the technique was evidently known long before that time in the Mediterranean. The fleet caravel evolved very quickly into a specific kind of warship. While the small lateen caravels from the fifteenth-century voyages of discovery were of around fifty tons and of sixty or eighty tons at the most, a standard round caravel was of 150 or 180 tons. It had two covered decks, four masts, three with lateen sails and a square sail on the foremast, and was armed. It also had a narrow hull, making it perfect to escort fleets of larger ships, act as a coastguard and fulfil other, similar functions.

The problem is that hardly anything definite is known about this vessel before technical documentation appeared. We can only assume that the references made to caravels used for those missions or in the India fleets refer to fleet caravels and not lateen caravels, a problem that arises because the documentation rarely refers specifically to either kind. But this is an obvious conclusion, considering the testimony from a number of people that the lateen caravel was considered inappropriate for long-distance voyages, immediately after Vasco da Gama's return in 1499. Portuguese technical documents on naval architecture only exist from *c.*1570 onwards, which means that before that date the available information found in documents is inaccurate, and frequently even mistaken, while reports were generally made by men who knew little of seamanship. This is particularly true with reference to the Portuguese galleon.

The word 'galleon' is used to define a specific type of ship from the begin-

---

[16] Among fifty or sixty full accounts of Portuguese ships sent to India, some covering very short periods, and others two centuries or more, although none of them reflects official data as far as we know, two are extremely valuable because they present illustrations of the fleets, ship by ship. Both are from the third quarter of the sixteenth century. There are good reasons to believe that these are accurate representations of the Portuguese ships at the time, and the most impressive thing to be seen in those drawings is precisely the unique size of the sails: *Memória das armadas*, facsimile edition (Macao: Instituto Cultural de Macau *et al.*, 1995) (1st facsimile edn: Lisbon: Academia das Ciências, 1982), and *Livro de Lisuarte de Abreu*, facsimile edition (Lisbon: Comissão Nacional para as Comemorações dos Descobrimentos Portugueses, 1992).

[17] Henrique Quirino da Fonseca wrote the reference book on the Portuguese caravel, but it must be read in the second edition, organised by Pimentel Barata: *A caravela portuguesa e a prioridade técnica das navegações henriquinas*, comentário preliminar, notas e apêndices de João da Gama Pimentel Barata, 2nd edn, 2 vols (Lisbon: Ministério da Marinha, 1973).

ning of the sixteenth century onwards. In brief, from the shape of the hull, the type of the sails and their identifiable functions Portuguese historiography concluded that the galleon was specifically prepared for war at sea, a view summarised in João da Gama Pimentel Barata's study on the galleon in 1979.[18] Comparison between a 600-ton *nau* and a 500-ton galleon, found in technical documentation from *c.*1590 certainly suggests this. The galleon had a longer keel though its volume was smaller, which indicates a narrow hull. The few surviving images reveal that the galleon's quarterdecks were lower than in the *nau*, and that while the *nau* has three masts with a square sail on the foremast and mainmast and a lateen sail on the mizzenmast, the galleon had a fourth mast, a bonaventure-mizzen or jigger, which also had a lateen sail. As the rigging is quite similar, it was the galleon's superior qualities as a sailing ship that distinguished it. The uses of the two ships were also different. There were few galleons on the India run, but they led the fleets that guarded straits and the coastal guard fleets, where ships' functions were clearly military.

The Portuguese galleon bears little relationship to the Spanish galleon, which could be a warship or part of the merchant navy. The Portuguese galleon was instead essentially a single type of ship, already considered the first ocean-going vessel specifically designed for war at sea. This idea is, however, misleading. The morphological characteristics of the galleon are surely enough to guarantee that this ship was conceived as a warship, but the available sources suggest that the galleon was bi-functional, that is, although a warship it was also heavily used as a cargo ship, of course with less cargo capacity than the *nau*, but with superior military effectiveness. Almost as big as a *nau*, that is based only on the technical evidence, not the literary, which is usually used, the galleon could in fact be used like a cargo vessel.

Things were rather different with the fleet caravel. Developed earlier than the galleon, it was almost completely useless for cargo due to the limitation of the 150–80 average tonnage, which left little if any capacity for anything other than crew needs, and artillery, powder and ammunition. From its appearance in the late fifteenth century, the fleet caravel was used in guard fleets almost everywhere, and more than once in war fleets sent to North Africa or India, fleets that had thirty or forty ships. The fleet caravel must then in fact be considered the first ocean-going sailing ship developed exclusively for war at sea by any European navy.

Sixteenth-century Portuguese naval history records no great moments of conflict with other European navies but there is no room for doubt that the Portuguese navy was highly efficient in Oriental waters, both in terms of military victories and in controlling shipping in the Indian Ocean. The impressive expansion of Portuguese maritime influence can only be explained through its

---

[18] João da Gama Pimentel Barata, 'The Portuguese Galleon (1519–1625)', *Five Hundred Years of Nautical Science* (Greenwich, National Maritime Museum, 1979), 181–92; reprinted *Estudos de arqueologia naval* (Lisbon: Imprensa Nacional-Casa da Moeda, 1989), vol. I, 303–26 and 327–38 (Portuguese and English versions).

naval superiority. Yet the rapid creation and maintenance of this long-lasting naval presence covering half the globe by a country of Portugal's population and financial resources at the beginning of the sixteenth century is still unexplained. In the sixteenth century, *grosso modo*, the Portuguese sailed almost everywhere:

They went to the ports of Flanders, as they had done since the twelfth century;
They traded in the Mediterranean;
They linked Portugal to the Atlantic archipelagos of the Azores, Madeira, São Tomé and Príncipe and Cape Verde through regular runs (especially to the Azores, where a permanent fleet kept a watchful eye on corsairs, waited for the *naus* coming from India and escorted them to Lisbon);
They watched and tried to control the Straits of Gibraltar and patrolled the Portuguese coast;
They went to Brazil, where several journeys of exploration were made from 1501 onwards and where trade grew slowly until the real boom at the end of the sixteenth century, starting an intense maritime traffic up to early nineteenth century;
They did the trade run to Mina (Elmina), the nerve-centre of West African coastal trade, up to the early seventeenth century, and kept naval resources based at Arguim;
They patrolled the Indian Ocean, hoping to control access to the Red Sea, the Persian Gulf, and watching the Malabar and Coromandel coasts;
They guaranteed the maritime link from India to Malacca, and from there to the Far East, China (Macao) and Japan with annual runs, from the mid-sixteenth century onwards.

They also sailed to every coastal area that they passed in the Orient, stimulating extremely rich local trade, even in areas where the Portuguese state of India did not rule, such as the Bay of Bengal. They created a vast network of trade routes stretching from Flanders to Japan. These often crossed paths with the naval fleets that were trying to impose a 'Portuguese Sea' around the world, both through the great ships such as fleet caravels and galleons on the high seas and the oared ships in the coastal areas of the Orient, all used very proficiently. Trading posts and fortresses everywhere, over 300 of them from Brazil to the Far East, along with dockyards that sometimes produced better ships than in Lisbon, as happened in Bahia (Brazil) and Goa (India), guaranteed the essential logistic and trade support, together with controlled ports of call. These were real naval bases to use a terminology which is more modern than that used in that day and age.

How many warships did Portugal have? What was their value in comparison to the warships of other European and of Oriental navies? How many warships existed in the world? There are no definite answers to these questions. However, looking at the geographical distribution of sixteenth-century Portuguese naval actions and abandoning an impossible quantitative analysis for that period, Modelski and Thompson certainly did not exaggerate in their vision of Portugal as the first, and, at the time, the only world naval power.

Mahan's concept of sea power makes sense considering its singular historical perspective, the circumstances in which the author wrote his major work, and the goals he was trying to achieve. This concept must be approached with caution, as John Hattendorf suggested,[19] but there is no good reason to reduce the concept to Mahan's perspective a century after he wrote. Our knowledge of and perspectives on maritime and naval history must be different – or should be. Naval history did not start with the Royal Navy, nor were the first naval wars to dispute maritime supremacy in the mid-seventeenth century between the English and Dutch. We should look to the Portuguese–Castilian naval war in the Atlantic in the 1470s, as Dias Farinha suggested,[20] or the naval wars during the first years of the sixteenth century in the Indian Ocean. In both cases the result was the complete control of offshore navigation for a certain period of time, firstly in the South Atlantic, secondly in the Indian Ocean. Perhaps the concept of maritime supremacy, as suggested by Louis Sicking,[21] could be more effective and historically accurate for the sixteenth century and in general for the period before the mid-seventeenth century. But there is no doubt that what makes sense is to revise the chronology to be considered. The period 1000–1650 proposed for examination by John Hattendorf and Richard Unger should allow us to explain the deep origins of European sea power and maritime supremacy, searching for their origins and first developments instead of considering only their most well-known and commonly discussed manifestations.[22]

---

[19] For the best general introduction to Mahan's life, career and writings see *Mahan on Naval Strategy. Selections from the Writings of Rear Admiral Alfred Thayer Mahan*, with an introduction by John B. Hattendorf (Annapolis, Maryland: Naval Institute Press, 1991). The introduction explains every essential concept in Mahan's thought.
[20] In his remarks at the seminar at Arrabida.
[21] See chapter 12 of the present volume.
[22] I would like to express my gratitude to the Fundação Oriente, for supporting my participation in this seminar, and Dr José Virgílio Pissarra.

NAVAL POWER IN THE NETHERLANDS BEFORE THE DUTCH REVOLT

Louis Sicking

IN historical studies, the term 'sea power' – meaning control over the sea – is usually connected with the work of the American naval officer A. T. Mahan. He established the principle that the sea could only be brought under control through the domination of the enemy's naval forces. According to Mahan this could only be realised in sea battles, and, if necessary, by blockades combined with the threat of an attack.[1] The greatest care should to be exercised with regard to Mahan's concepts of sea power in the period preceding the one on which he based his conclusions. The danger has not discouraged historians from finding inspiration in his ideas on sea power.

The present paper seeks to contribute to the debate about the relevance of Mahan's concept of sea power for the early modern period by studying the case of the Habsburg Netherlands. Although the Netherlands were not engaged in any major sea battle during the first half of the sixteenth century a certain notion of sea power does seem to have played a role in naval strategic thinking. It will be argued that naval superiority alone over enemy forces did not ensure the exercise of sea power. After all, merchant ships played an important role in naval warfare well into the seventeenth century. Therefore the total seagoing merchant fleet of a town, region or country – the maritime potential – had to be taken into account when considering its sea power. The concept 'maritime potential'[2] seems preferable to that of 'naval forces' for the period up to 1650. Before then, seagoing vessels were useful both in an economic and a politico-military sense. The distinction between merchant ships and warships was not clearly defined, at least in north-western Europe. Whereas merchant ships were used for warfare, it was not uncommon for merchandise to be transported by warships.[3] The 'maritime potential' of the Habsburg Netherlands, its standing navy created in 1550, and finally the contemporary notions of sea power in the country will be

---

[1] G. Parker, *The Military Revolution. Military Innovation and the Rise of the West, 1500–1800*, 2nd edn (Cambridge, 1996), 82. A. T. Mahan, *The Influence of Sea Power upon History 1660–1783* (Boston, 1890).
[2] J. Huizinga and other Dutch historians used the word 'scheepsmacht' for which no literal English equivalent is available. It is something like 'shipping power'.
[3] J. R. Bruijn, *The Dutch Navy of the Seventeenth and Eighteenth Centuries* (Columbia, 1993).

Map 1. The Netherlands in 1543

discussed and related to each other. This approach is important for understanding sea power in the early modern period in general and the rise of the Dutch Republic in particular.

Holland and Zealand's maritime potential was one reason why the originally 'continental' Burgundian dynasty had been interested in extending its power to these provinces.[4] Over the course of the fifteenth century, Holland possessed the greatest maritime potential within the Low Countries. Ship-owners from Holland were responsible for an important part of the maritime trade of entrepreneurs based in the metropolis, Antwerp, and in Flanders. In the first half of the sixteenth century, Holland's merchant fleet alone is supposed to have exceeded the combined merchant fleets of England and France.[5] In the 1530s, it is thought to have consisted of approximately 400 large seagoing ships.[6] According to the tables of the tolls of the Sound (the seafaring straits between the North Sea and the Baltic), the number of Holland's ships reached 640 in 1545, 745 in 1546, 917 in 1547, 906 in 1557 and 819 in 1558.[7] Such figures probably represent commercial developments more than an increasing size of the merchant fleet. It can nevertheless be asserted that, over the course of the sixteenth century both the number of Holland's ships as well as the total tonnage of the fleet rose considerably.[8]

The Burgundians and the Habsburgs hardly ever possessed ships of their own. Their maritime presence or policies therefore depended almost completely on the potential of their subjects, and the sea power of the sovereign was thus determined by the extent to which he had access to the ships of private individuals. The question of how the central government in Brussels tried to enhance its influence over maritime affairs was, therefore, crucial. A central official appointee was created in 1485 as the representative of the sovereign ruler at sea with the title 'Admiral of the Sea' or 'Admiral-General of the Netherlands'. In

---

[4] A. G. Jongkees, 'Holland in Erasmus tijd', in D. E. H. de Boer and J. W. Marsilje, eds, *De Nederlanden in de late middeleeuwen* (Utrecht, 1987), 379–92, 383 and Jongkees, 'La Hollande bourguignonne: son intérêt pour les ducs Valois', in E. O. van der Werff *et al.*, eds, *Burgundica et varia. Keuze uit de verspreide opstellen van prof. dr. A. G. Jongkees hem aangeboden ter gelegenheid van zijn tachtigste verjaardag op 14 juli 1989 door de Kring van Groninger Mediaevisten Amici* (Hilversum, 1990), 150–61. For Philip the Good's naval policy see J. Paviot, *La Politique navale de ducs de Bourgogne (1384–1482)* (Lille, 1995).

[5] J. D. Tracy, 'Herring Wars: The Habsburg Netherlands and the Struggle for Control of the North Sea, ca. 1520–1560', *The Sixteenth Century Journal*, 24 (1993), 249–72, 252 n. 6, and Tracy, *Holland under Habsburg Rule, 1506–1566. The Formation of a Body Politic* (Berkeley, Los Angeles and Oxford, 1990), 95 n. 16.

[6] R. W. Unger, *Dutch Shipbuilding before 1800. Ships and Guilds* (Assen and Amsterdam, 1978), 11.

[7] F. Snapper, *Oorlogsinvloeden op de overzeese handel van Holland, 1551–1719* (Amsterdam, 1959), 13.

[8] The average tonnage of the ships participating in the Baltic trade probably decreased slightly during the course of the sixteenth century, but the effect of this on the strong growth of the fleet was small. M. van Tielhof, *De Hollandse graanhandel, 1470–1570. Koren op de Hollandse molen* (The Hague, 1995), 106–8.

1488 the admiral was accorded exclusive powers: he alone took decisions on the equipping of warships and privateers and he was given sole jurisdiction in maritime cases. Between 1491 and 1558 the lords of Veere held the office of Admiral General. As the most powerful nobles of Zealand – 'the province surrounded by Flanders, Brabant and Holland' – the lords of Veere enjoyed a perfect base for the exercise of this high office. They controlled most of Zealand's main island, Walcheren, centrally located between the metropolis of Antwerp and the sea. Walcheren became the focus of Habsburg naval policy in the Netherlands. Contemporaries called the island 'the key of the Netherlands'.[9]

Zealand was the best province in the Netherlands for the selection and the equipping of ships for warfare because of the presence of the natural harbour of the island of Walcheren, Arnemuiden, which served as an outport of Antwerp. The Italian Ludovico Guicciardini in his *Descrittione di tutti i Paesi Bassi* (1567) considered Arnemuiden the central point of Europe since he reported the distances to all of the main European harbours from that place. The presence of the seigniorial power base of the admiral as well as the greatest harbour of north-western Europe made Walcheren the centre *par excellence* for shipping and naval warfare.[10]

Here all kinds of foreign and Netherlandish seagoing ships were available. Whenever the central government, for war or for other reasons, needed ships they were rented or confiscated. In 1542, for example, Mary of Hungary, regent of the Netherlands (1531–55), needed ships for the transport of 4000 men to Spain. She requested the bailiff to make a list of all the ships lying before Arnemuiden with a description of their size and equipment. The bailiff had to have them claimed under pretext of their risk of being taken at sea. Two weeks later ten ships, which were ready to leave for Spain, were held for the transport of the troops.[11] This is just one of many examples of collecting and using privately owned ships for warfare and other naval activities. Most of the necessary ships for the naval expeditions launched from the Netherlands during the French–Habsburg wars between 1521 and 1559 were collected in the same way. Even for his three great expeditions to the Mediterranean – Tunis in 1535, Constantinople in 1538 and Algiers in 1541 – emperor Charles V collected part of the ships and crews in Zealand, most of which were from Holland in origin.[12]

---

[9] L. Sicking, *Zeemacht en onmacht. Maritieme politiek in de Nederlanden, 1488–1558* (Amsterdam, 1998), 42–5, 55–6, 152–3.

[10] W. Brulez and J. Craeybeckx, 'Les Escales au carrefour des Pays-Bas (Bruges et Anvers, 14e–16e siècles)', in *Les Grandes Escales. I Antiquité et moyen-âge. Colloque organisé en collaboration avec la Commission internationale d'histoire maritime (10e colloque d'histoire maritime),* Recueils de la Société Jean Bodin pour l'histoire comparative des institutions 32 (Brussels, 1974), 431–5. J. P. Sigmond, *Nederlandse zeehavens tussen 1500 en 1800* (Amsterdam, 1989), 23.

[11] Mary of Hungary to Hieronimus Zandelin, 15 September 1542; Zandelin to Mary of Hungary, 29 september 1542, Algemeen Rijksarchief Brussels, Archives of the Council of State and 'Audience', 1656/3.

[12] R. Fagel, *De Hispano-Vlaamse wereld. De contacten tussen Spanjaarden en Nederlanders, 1496–1555* (Brussels and Nijmegen, 1996), 408–13.

Thus the maritime potential of the Netherlands available in Zealand and also Holland was of crucial importance for the execution of Charles's naval policy in north-western Europe and of significance for his naval policy in the Mediterranean.

In general all kinds of ships were used for warfare and convoying in the Netherlands. In the sources no indications are found that certain types of ships were especially appropriate for warfare. Philip of Cleves, the first to have occupied the new office of Admiral General, between 1485 and 1488, attributed great importance to the use of heavy artillery on board. Around 1516 he wrote his *Instruction de toutes manières de guerroyer tant par terre que par mer*, which is one of the few treatises from the sixteenth century in which the equipping of warships is treated in a more-or-less systematic way. His work is modern for its time.[13] He mentioned the invention of the gun port, which was introduced only about twenty years earlier. Furthermore he attributed a crucial role to the use of artillery in battle, thanks to which a victory was possible without boarding.[14] Philip's vision, as expressed in the *Instruction*, was implemented for the warships equipped by Netherlandish admirals during the French–Habsburg wars between 1521 and 1559. The placing of artillery on board determined the choice of the ships as well as the way in which they were rebuilt. Besides the creation of gun ports the inner reinforcement of the ships, which had to survive the impact of the firing of the cannon, was of the utmost importance.[15] Philip suggested that warships had better have a double deck so that they could be more heavily armed. They would also better sustain bad weather than ships with just one deck.[16] The Netherlandish warships seem to have fulfilled this demand. According to Cornelis de Schepper, privy councillor and commissioner of the fleet, Netherlandish ships, especially the hulks, were more solid than Spanish ones. Therefore ships from the Low Countries could be used at sea during the whole year and were much better suited to carry heavy artillery.[17]

The transforming of merchant ships into fully fledged warships continued to be a common practice in the Netherlands during the French–Habsburg wars, that is after the introduction of gun ports and heavy artillery on board. It emphasises the continuing reality of the military importance of the Netherlandish maritime potential in the post-medieval era. This means that the general idea that the introduction of heavy artillery on board led to specially built warships needs to

---

[13] P. Contamine, 'L'Art de la guerre selon Philippe de Clèves, seigneur de Ravenstein (1456–1528): innovation ou tradition', *Bijdragen en mededelingen betreffende de geschiedenis der Nederlanden*, 95 (1980), 363–76, 376.
[14] J. K. Oudendijk, *Een Bourgondisch ridder over den oorlog ter zee. Philips van Kleef als leermeester van Karel V* (Amsterdam, 1941), 84–5, 100, 134–5.
[15] J. Glete, *Warfare at Sea, 1500–1650. Maritime Conflicts and the Transformation of Europe* (London, 2000), 35.
[16] Oudendijk, *Ridder*, 69.
[17] R. Häpke ed., *Niederländische Akten und Urkunden zur Geschichte der Hanse und zur deutschen Seegeschichte*, I, 1531–57 (Munich and Leipzig, 1913), 535.

be relativised. Even for the creation of a standing navy in the Netherlands merchant ships were used.

The most important characteristics of standing war fleets or navies are: (1) the ships are owned by the sovereign or the state, and (2) the ships are kept in peacetime. Generally it can be stated that in the sixteenth century permanent war fleets were not yet decisive for the naval forces of a country. War fleets were fitted out for a limited time and consisted mainly of hired ships. The English navy, which under Henry VIII developed as the most important factor of the country's naval force, and probably also the French navy were exceptions. Not only the Tudors and the Valois but also various other royal houses had warships of their own: the Aviz in Portugal, the Oldenburgs in Denmark and the Vasas in Sweden. But these formed no more than a small nucleus of ships, which, themselves, were of limited military importance.[18]

The Habsburgs would only in 1550 join these royal ship owners with the purchase of eight ships in the town of Veere, where the Admiralty had its seat. This is quite remarkable because the Habsburgs were supposed to be not particularly interested in possessing ships. This probably had to do with the enormous potential of ships and seamen in the countries that they ruled. Spain was at the height of its maritime power with flourishing trade and shipping both in the Mediterranean and in the Atlantic. The enormous maritime potential of the Netherlands has already been discussed above. More than the other European rulers, the Habsburgs used privately owned ships for their naval expeditions.[19]

However, the long war with France during the 1550s made it necessary to have naval resources permanently available. The purchase of the first ships by the central government in 1550 was nothing new for the Netherlands as local and regional authorities had done so before.[20] It was rather a new step by the central government, which had become convinced of the advantages as presented by the admiral and the fleet commissioner, Cornelis de Schepper. Purchase was cheaper than renting and owned ships were permanently available and could thus be brought into action immediately. Most ships, fourteen in total, were bought in 1550 and 1551. This first navy of the Netherlands was referred to as 'the warships of the emperor in Zealand'. During the reign of Philip II it was called 'the royal majesty's ships of war'.[21]

The commissioner of the fleet bought the ships in Zealand. Their size varied from a maximum of three hundred tons for a ship called the *Falcon* to less than

---

[18] J. Glete, *Navies and Nations. Warships, navies and state building in Europe and America, 1500–1860* (Stockholm, 1993), I, 3, 13–15, 102, 125–31, 146.
[19] Ibid., 147, 150.
[20] Various towns along the coast of the Zuyderzee and the so-called Four Members of Flanders (Bruges, Ghent, Ypres and the Freedom of Bruges). P. M. Bosscher *et al.*, *Het hart van Nederland. Steden en dorpen rond de Zuiderzee* (Bussum, 1973), 102–4. N. Maddens, 'De Vlaamse Oorlogsvloot tijdens de regering van Karel V', *Belgisch tijdschrift voor militaire geschiedenis*, 22 (1978), 389–99, 389–90, 393.
[21] ARA Brussels, Archives of the Exchequer, Account 26110, fol. 1v, 6r. Inventory general of the royal warships, 1561, ARA Brussels, Archives of the Exchequer, 26117.

forty tons. In the latter case it was a small yacht or a big boat. The small size of the Netherlandish warships was a reason for the English denigratingly to call them mussel shells.[22] Various ship-types seem to have been used for warfare, although the sources – mostly accounts and their annexes – are not often very clear about the type of ships equipped for war.

The economic characteristics generally attributed to warfare in the sixteenth century, that is being very labour-intensive and demanding relatively few permanent investments, were also valid for the standing navy of the Netherlands. The acquisition of the first eight ships and two boats in 1550 cost 19,788 guilders and represented only 19 per cent of the total expenditure for the fleet between January 1550 and April 1551.[23] The purchased ships were merchant vessels, which could be sold again at any time. The artillery used was not specially developed for warfare at sea but could also be used on land. So in the case of the Habsburg Netherlands the formation of a permanent war fleet did not lead to high and permanent investments as has been suggested for the creation of standing navies in general.[24] Only with the development of purpose-built warships in the seventeenth century did the sunk investments rise considerably.

The formation of a standing fleet did have a few closely connected implications for the development of the Zealand town of Veere as a naval base. The successive lords of Veere, who all did their best to favour their own town, occupied the office of Admiral General of the Netherlands. Veere became the seat of the Admiralty. All major war fleets from the beginning of the wars between Valois and Habsburg in 1521 were equipped in Veere. The town was well situated on the north-eastern side of the island of Walcheren and had a very well-equipped harbour within the town walls. For all these reasons the choice of Veere as the naval base of the Netherlands was more or less inevitable. One of the most notable characteristics of Veere as a naval base was the building of an arsenal for which the town had donated land to the emperor in 1554. Because of lack of money the first arsenal in the Netherlands was only built in 1565. Furthermore a small naval administration and an officer corps came into being.[25]

The most important disadvantage of a permanent war fleet was its costs, especially in times of peace. The permanent costs are difficult to estimate since the accounts of the war fleets do not distinguish between incidental and permanent costs. One should also take into consideration that ships, the artillery and other navy-related possessions of the sovereign were not always written off. According to a rough estimate the permanent costs of the navy, artillery and rigging excluded, would have been 7250 guilders a year. This amount represents just a fraction (4.8 per cent) of the average annual expenditures on war fleets in

---

[22] R. Tyler, ed., *Calendar of Letters, Despatches and State Papers Relating to the Negotiations between England and Spain*, XII (London, 1949), 271, 285.
[23] ARA Brussels, Archives of the Exchequer, 23336, fols 21r–25r, 139r.
[24] Glete, *Navies*, 14–15.
[25] Sicking, *Zeemacht*, 207–10.

the Habsburg Netherlands, which during the 1550s amounted to an average of almost 151,000 guilders annually. Fleet commissioner de Schepper had been right when he had stated in his advice to the regent that with small extra cost a permanent war fleet could be kept. De Schepper did, however, underestimate the fact that unused ships rotted away and had to be replaced quite often. The average length of time the ships were in use was about five years, when one excludes the ships that were lost (see Table I). When the peace of Cateau-Cambrésis of 1559 with France seemed to have taken on a permanent character it no longer seemed necessary to keep a standing navy. The advantage of its availability did not counterbalance the disadvantage of the rotting ships. At a public auction held in Veere in 1561, the remaining royal ships of war were sold to the highest bidder.[26]

Despite this permanent navy, which was adequate for the undertaking of modest expeditions, the Habsburgs still depended on private vessels and crews. Fortunately, the natural harbour of Walcheren was the most important market for vessels in the Netherlands and the port of Arnemuiden on the island was a major labour market for seamen. Thanks to these circumstances, the Habsburg navy in Zealand could be strengthened when necessity required. Thus the renting of vessels for the duration of an expedition continued to be the most commonly used method for the equipping of war fleets. By such means the Habsburg government in the Netherlands had a much greater potential for warfare at sea than might be expected given the size of the Veere navy.

The creation of the Habsburg navy was primarily motivated by the wish to deploy warships permanently. The design of the ships was of secondary importance. In spite of the modern equipment of the ships, the professional naval organisation and the local support – motivated by both the admiral as Lord of Veere and by the inhabitants, who benefited economically – the military importance of the navy was limited. Ten warships without other forces were not able to resist the powerful French fleet in the Channel. The Habsburgs' Netherlands navy has to be compared with the navies of Portugal, Denmark and Sweden, rather than with those of England and France. The existence of a war fleet of their own, in the first place, was to confirm the reputation and independence of the Habsburgs at sea. Therefore, the ships were richly decorated, so much so that they even impressed the English.[27] The navy, being based on Walcheren, can be considered as proof of the strategic importance the central government attributed to the island. For the town of Veere, the creation of a permanent war fleet within its walls formed the height of its specialisation in naval warfare. Looking back, the Veere navy has to be considered a temporary experiment. It was a reaction to the continuous menace from France. In spite of its limited military importance, from a historical and institutional point of view the Habsburg navy was a novelty in the Low Countries. In that respect, the origins of the

[26] Ibid., 210–12.
[27] Tyler, *Calendar*, 271, 285.

Table I. The standing navy of the Habsburg Netherlands, 1550–61

Ship's name (size in tons or brouage)	Year acquired	Price of purchase in guilders	Year of sale	Returns from sale in guilders	Depreciation *per annum* in guilders	Depreciation in percentage *per annum*
Dragon (300 tons)	1550	5200	1561	546	423	8
Eagle (150 tons)	1550	2800	1561	540	205	7
Esprivier (60 tons)	1550	893	1551	300	593	66
Flying Griffin (90 tons)	1550	580	1551	420	160	28
Roaring Lion (90 tons)	1550	865	1551	486	379	44
Flying Deer	1551	3000	1557	588	402	13
Salvator (150 b)	1551	3450	1557	654	466	14
Raven (130 tons; 700 b)	1551	1600	1554	360	413	23
Goat (1100 b)	1551	3450	1557	1140	385	11
Mary	1555	3725	1561	1530	366	10
Sea Knight	1555	6300	1561	2230	678	11
Golden Lion	1558	5250	1561	2286	988	19
Total/Average		37,113		11,080	455	21

The average depreciation *per annum* being 21 per cent means that the warships of the Habsburg standing navy in the Netherlands were written off, on average, in about five years. The wrecked ships have not been included. They were *Jonas* (1550–1), *Swallow* (1550–3), *Fox of Dieppe* (1553–4), *Falcon* (1550–9).

Source: L. Sicking, *Zeemacht en onmacht. maritieme politiek in de Nederlanden, 1488–1558* (Amsterdam, 1998) tables 5 and 10, pp. 189 and 211.

present navies of the Netherlands and Belgium, which for a few years now have been under a joint command, are to be found in Veere.

Having narrowed our view to the development of the Habsburg Netherlands navy, we shall now broaden it to consider the wide and often vague concept called sea power. The utility of Mahan's concept of sea power for the period prior to that which he investigated (1660–1783) has been called into question by several historians, such as C. Starr, J. Guilmartin, G. Parker, and more recently, by J. D. Tracy, R. W. Unger and J. Glete. Tracy divided Mahan's concept into two parts by distinguishing between: (1) the use of sea power (warships) for the advancement of the commercial interests of the state and its merchants, and (2) the recognition that effective control of the seas for commercial purposes means attacking the enemy's capacity to make war at sea.[28]

It is important to realise that strategic ideas and notions from Antiquity were sources of inspiration for the development of Renaissance strategies.[29] In north-western Europe the concept of 'control of the sea' was probably introduced as the Hundred Years War came to a close. England and France disputed, in literary narrative at least, the mastery or control of the Channel and the Narrow Seas. In *The Libelle of Englyshe Polycye* (*c*.1440) the expression 'We be maysters of the narowe see' is used.[30] The same notion was used in the sixteenth-century Netherlands. Laurent Vital wrote on the occasion of Charles V's voyage from the Netherlands to Spain in 1517: 'Et ose bien dire, que pour XII jours que le Roy tint la mer, que, après Dieu et ses sainctz, il en fut le sire et maistre, et mettant tout ce qu'il rencontroit et trouvoit en son obeisance'.[31] In 1544, when the Habsburgs and England agreed to undertake joint naval action against France, both Charles V and Henry VIII were expected to become 'lords of the sea'.[32] In 1551, the States of Holland, attempting to ensure the coastal defences against French attacks, proposed to the central government of the Netherlands in Brussels that warships be equipped instead of building fortresses. If the sovereign was 'meester van de zee' ('master of the sea'), such fortresses would not be necessary.[33] A few years later, in 1558, when the Hollanders developed a plan for naval action on behalf of the States General of the Netherlands, they implied that Philip II was to become 'master of the sea'.[34] The examples presented here indicate that the notion 'master of the sea' is

---

[28] C. G. Starr, *The Influence of Sea Power on Ancient History* (New York and Oxford, 1989), 3–6, 83–4; J. F. Guilmartin, *Gunpowder and Galleys: Changing Technology and War at Sea in the Sixteenth Century* (New York, 1974), 16–41; Parker, *Military Revolution*, 82–3; R. W. Unger, 'Alfred Thayer Mahan, ship design, and the evolution of sea power in the late middle ages', *International History Review*, 19 (1997), 505–21; Glete, *Warfare at Sea*, 8; Tracy, 'Herring Wars', 249–51.

[29] G. Modelski and W. R. Thompson, *Seapower and Global Politics, 1494–1993* (London, 1988), 4–8.

[30] M. Mollat du Jourdin, *L'Europe et la mer* (Paris, 1993), 154–5, 158.

[31] L. P. Gachard and C. Piot, eds, *Collection des voyages des souverains des Pays-Bas*, vol. III (Brussels, 1881), 58.

[32] G. Mattingly, ed., *Further Supplement to Letters, Despatches and State Papers, Relating to the Negotiations between England and Spain (1515–1542)* (London, 1940), 125. L. Sicking, 'La Maîtrise de la mer. Coopération navale entre l'Angleterre et l'empire des Habsbourg pendant la première moitié du XVIe siècle', in *Publication du centre européen d'études bourguignonnes*, 35 (1995), 187–97, 192.

[33] Maximilian of Burgundy to Mary of Hungary (1 October 1551), ARA Brussels, Aud. 1659/2, fol. 215r. J. C. M. Warnsinck, 'De memorie van Cornelis de Schepper van den 12-den februari 1552 over de verdediging van Holland, Zeeland en Vlaanderen, in den oorlog tegen Frankrijk', in *Historische opstellen aangeboden aan J. Huizinga op 7 december 1942 door het historisch gezelschap te 's-Gravenhage* (Haarlem, 1948), 247–73, 248.

[34] 'que Sa Majesté se face maître de la meer', P. A. Meilink, 'Notulen en generaal advies van

closely connected, on the one hand to ideas about sovereign honour and reputation, and to sea power and maritime strategy on the other. The importance of honour for Habsburg naval policy is illustrated by the frequent use of the word *reputación* with reference to naval and maritime affairs.

In order to know whether a notion of sea power or a way of strategic thinking is hidden behind the expression 'master of the sea', it is important to examine the debates and decisions concerning the defence of seafaring trade, for which the central government published a specific ordinance in 1550. According to the trading towns of Holland the ordinance was much too defensive in nature and did not offer effective protection to trade on the high seas. The Hollanders stated that it was far more useful for the safety of their trade to have a squadron of about twenty-five ships take offensive action against Scottish pirates.[35] In this context they used the expression 'nettoyer la mer de pirates' ('cleaning out the sea of pirates'), which was inspired by texts from Antiquity.[36] In 1551 the Hollanders seemed to mean the same thing when they emphasised that the sovereign should become master of the sea for the sake of the security of trade at sea. Maximilian of Burgundy, Admiral of the Netherlands (1540–58) and governor of Holland and Zealand (1547–58), wrote to the regent, Mary of Hungary, that if the sovereign was not master of the sea and the Netherlanders and the Spanish did not equip warships, seafaring trade would move to foreign countries.[37] Holland's suggestion of an offensive strategy can be connected with the 1549 decision to introduce the so-called wine-impost, a special tax on wine for all the provinces of the Netherlands. This new tax was to be levied for four successive years in order to raise the capital needed for the standing navy of the Habsburg Netherlands.[38] In 1550 and 1551, the ships cruised the North Sea and the Channel chasing pirates. They were also expected to protect the Netherlandish coast, fishing boats and merchantmen. Early in 1552, after the experiences with the standing navy in the previous two years, Cornelis de Schepper concluded that little could be done with the eight imperial warships alone.[39] They could not pass the Straits of Dover without great risk of being overpowered by the much stronger French navy. There being so few of them, the ships were of no use for coastal defence either. Moreover, heavy weather would force the warships to leave the coast or withdraw to harbour. Patrolling was better left to coastal fishermen, who could signal watchmen in the lighthouses.

---

de Staten Generaal van 1557/1558', *Bijdragen en Mededelingen van het Historisch Genootschap*, 55 (1934), 263–369, 308.

[35] 'pour offenser et debouler hors de la mer les pirates, veu que ledit concept n'estoit que deffensiff et n'estoit soufissant d'asseurer par mer la negociation' and 'seroit besoing user de force'. Cornelis de Schepper to Mary of Hungary (15 October 1549), ARA, Aud. 1665/1, fol. 190r.

[36] Mary of Hungary to De Schepper (14 June 1550), ARA, Aud. 1665/1, fol. 219r.

[37] Maximilian of Burgundy to Mary of Hungary (10 September and 1 October 1551), ARA, Aud. 1659/2, fols 200r, 215r.

[38] Tracy, *Holland*, 139.

[39] Warnsinck, 'Memorie', 265–8.

1. The seal of the Admiralty at the time of Admiral Maximilian of Burgundy (1540–58). The legend reads: 'MAXIMILIANI A BURGONDIA D[OMINI BE]VERIS AC VERIS M[A]RIS PREFECTI' (Maximilian of Burgundy, Lord of Beveren and Veere, prefect of the sea). At the mainsail of the ship represented, the coat of arms of Maximilian is visible. The other sails represent the Burgundian cross. It is possible that sails were adorned in this way. In the ship's hull six gun ports with the barrels of canons are recognisable.

Source: H. Ewe, *Schiffe auf Siegeln* (Rostock 1972) no. 233, p. 218, where it is wrongly described as the seal of Maximilian of Austria.

According to De Schepper, it made no sense to equip warships against pirates and corsairs, 'because they would not leave off anyhow to seek their luck, even if the sea was full of warships'.[40] In the Netherlands sufficient vessels and boats were available for driving off pirates. De Schepper's observations offer a direct and contemporary reference to the military importance of the available maritime potential. Damage that might or might not be caused was out of all proportion to the high cost of equipping and maintaining warships.

Likewise de Schepper did not see much point in equipping a large war fleet to make Emperor Charles V master of the sea. By the time such a fleet was readied, French naval forces would in all likelihood already have withdrawn of their own free will and the expenses incurred to equip a large fleet would have been lost. Furthermore, the harm that might be done to the French coast with a

[40] Ibid., 267.

fleet of forty to fifty warships was out of proportion to the costs of equipping the fleet. How wise the latter words were became clear in 1558 when an Anglo-Netherlandish joint fleet of some 170 ships – 30 of them from the Netherlands – carried out an amphibious attack on the coast of Brittany. It failed miserably.[41]

Rather than equipping large war fleets or occasionally operating the small standing navy, the privy councillor pleaded to keep this naval force prepared. In combination with rented vessels it could be deployed more effectively for a variety of goals.[42] This proposal was indeed realised. The imperial warships that formed the standing navy of the Netherlands during the 1550s were used for convoying the herring fleet and for two enormous commercial convoys to Spain in 1552 and 1553. They also formed the nucleus of several war fleets, one equipped in 1554 to guarantee, jointly with an English fleet, Phillip II's safe passage from Spain to England and another to convoy Charles V and his sisters, Mary of Hungary and Eleonora of France, to Spain in 1556, and, finally, the above mentioned fleet of 1558 which carried out a landing in Brittany. From this it becomes clear that the small imperial war fleet in the Netherlands only carried strategic weight when combined with rented vessels equipped for war. Another conclusion to be drawn is that in reality much of the execution of Habsburg naval policy was focused on securing the sea link between the Netherlands and Spain. Although the convoys between the Netherlands and Spain primarily served a defensive purpose, they were also to impress outsiders. This not only increased the honour and glory of the emperor but also helped to 'clean' the seaway of pirates.[43] In de Schepper's realistic vision the idea of the sovereign as master of the sea could only be realised with the assistance of merchant vessels.

The privy councillor's ideas did not tally with opinions of Hollanders, who expected that the emperor, being their sovereign, would protect them with a large war fleet. In a memorial of 1554, the county of Holland stated that it 'is necessary that the emperor equips a large number of warships at sea in such number and equip them in such fashion that his majesty may remain master and dominator of that sea and may keep with violence all his majesty's enemies from the sea'. Further into the text, it is stated 'that if this is not done all his majesty's Netherlands and especially those of Holland and Zealand will suffer irrecoverable damage and will fall into such poverty as the said countries have never been in for the last two hundred years'.[44] The prosperity of these countries depended heavily on seafaring, as the text goes on to explain. Exaggeration was customary in texts dealing with securing economic interests, but the message is clear: Holland wanted violence used so that the sovereign would become 'master of

---

[41] D. Loades, *The Tudor Navy. An Administrative, Political and Military History* (Aldershot, 1992), 173.
[42] Warnsinck, 'Memorie', 270–2.
[43] Gachard and Piot, *Collection*, III, 58. De Schepper to Mary of Hungary (22 April 1553), ARA, Aud. 1665/2A, fol. 108v.
[44] Memorial (1554), ARA, Aud. 1659/2, fol. 338r.

the sea' or 'the strongest at sea'[45] for the benefit of Holland's commercial interests. This vision corresponds with what Tracy defined as the second part of Mahan's concept of sea power: the recognition that effective control of the sea for commercial ends implies that enemy warfare at sea should be made impossible by attacking him.[46]

Holland's preference for an offensive strategy may at first glance seem surprising. In fact, the county had had a long tradition of using warships for the advancement of commercial interests, a tradition which corresponds with the first part of Mahan's concept of sea power and which stemmed from its Baltic trade. Free passage through the Sound was crucially important in order to guarantee the import of grain from the Baltic. Each time the threat of a closure of the Sound occurred, Holland, with Amsterdam in the lead, was prepared to equip a war fleet and force the passage by violence. Such was the case in 1369, 1438, 1511, 1533, 1565 and 1644.[47] A remarkable continuity is noticeable in the decision-making processes of the expeditions and in the practical development of an offensive strategy over a long term.

However, the offensive strategy based squarely on Holland's commercial interests in 1554 went beyond anything that had been done in the Sound up to that point. Holland's demand was directly related to the approval of the wine tax, introduced in 1550 to finance the standing navy. In 1554 the tax was extended for another four years. In exchange for paying the tax Holland demanded that the central government take measures to guarantee no less than total security at sea. The rapid increase in long-range, direct trade (*voorbijlandvaart*) motivated this desire. Merchandise collected in France and Spain was transported in transit directly to the countries in the Baltic, with no stop in the Netherlands.

Before, the so-called 'west trade' between the Netherlands, France, and Iberia, and the 'east trade' between the Netherlands and the Baltic, were more or less separate cycles.[48] New patterns of trade placed new demands on security at sea. Holland's ambitious strategic vision of the central government's responsibility contrasted sharply with contemporary reality. The yields of the wine tax were too limited to realise anything like the formulated aspirations. A high official in Brussels remarked in 1552 that the income from the wine tax in Holland

---

[45] Ibid., fol. 341r.

[46] Cf. Tracy, 'Herring Wars', 250–1, 270–1.

[47] L. Sicking, 'Die offensive Lösung. Militärische Aspekte des holländischen Ostseehandels im 15. und 16. Jahrhundert', *Hansische Geschichtsblätter*, 117 (1999), 39–51; J. R. Bruijn, *Varend verleden. De Nederlandse oorlogsvloot in de zeventiende en achttiende eeuw* (Amsterdam, 1998), 37–8, 108; F. Snapper, 'Commerce, Ships and War in the Baltic from the Rise of the Hanseatic League till the French Revolution', in G. W. Heeres *et al.*, eds, *From Dunkirk to Danzig. Shipping and Trade in the North Sea and the Baltic, 1350–1850* (Hilversum, 1988), 405–28.

[48] J. Lameere a.o. eds, *Recueil des ordonnances des Pays-Bas*, 2nd series, 1506–1700, vol. VI (Brussels, 1922), 335. Gerrit van Assendelft to Mary of Hungary (20 April 1554), ARA, Aud. 1643/3, fol. 195r. Memorial (1554), ARA, Aud. 1659/2, fol. 338r–v.

was not enough even to equip one single boat, let alone a warship.[49] The implementation of Cornelis de Schepper's ideas, which were cast in a more modest mould, was difficult enough. Whether the protection of commerce or the fishery was at stake, each time de Schepper was confronted with Hollanders unwilling to pay for the necessary expenses, unwilling to arm their merchant vessels, and unwilling to make their ships available for warfare. In other words, the central government had no free access to Holland's enormous maritime potential.

The relationship between the maritime potential of the subjects and the sea power of the sovereign was also recognised after the Dutch Revolt broke out in April 1572. In a letter addressed to the Duke of Alva, then regent of the Netherlands, Anthony of Burgundy, Lord of Wakken, superintendent of the island of Walcheren and temporarily responsible for the then vacant Admiralty, and Philip of Lannoye expressed their great concern about the risk of losing control over Arnemuiden and its natural harbour. The two high officials underlined the importance of Arnemuiden by referring to three hundred vessels loaded with salt which were lying in the harbour 'Once such a country [the islands of Zealand, mainly Walcheren] and such a treasure of vessels loaded with salt were lost, there would be no hope of recovering them and the enemies [the rebels] would be as much reinforced as by having conquered a kingdom, because they will have more means to maintain their position as masters of the sea and of these islands'.[50] In fact, the two officials stressed the importance of Zealand and its great merchant fleet, from which enormous power could be derived: the power to dominate at sea and thus to control a kingdom. Time proved their view was in no way an exaggeration, since the rebels would indeed build their state on its maritime potential.

It seems clear, then, that when studying naval forces in the late medieval and early modern era, the merchant fleet cannot be excluded. Its size and quality determined, to a large extent, the possibilities for naval warfare. The central authorities, as well as the inhabitants of the Netherlands, were very well aware of the military importance of the maritime potential. The harbour of Arnemuiden on Walcheren was the most important market for renting ships for naval expeditions. In nearby Veere, the admiral could easily deploy the necessary ships. Since most war fleets were equipped in Veere, the town developed into a naval harbour culminating in the creation of a standing navy in 1550 with a naval administration, an officer corps, and an arsenal. The navy was, by and large, not important enough to operate independently. The small number of ships, never more then ten, were no match for the much stronger French naval

---

[49] Tracy, *Holland*, 140.

[50] 'laisser perdre un tel pays et tresor de hulckes chargees de sel estant une fois perdues il n'y a plus d'espoir de recouvrer et que les ennemis seront renforcez d'aultant que de la conqueste d'ung royaulme par [ce] qu'ilz auront plus de moyen de se maintenir maistres de la mer et de ces isles.' Antoine de Bourgogne, Lord of Wakken and Philip de Lannoye to Don Fernando Alvarez de Toledo, Duke of Alva, regent of the Netherlands (decoded letter) (Middelburg, 2 September 1572), ARA Brussels, Aud. 1724/2, fol. 12 r–v.

forces. Only in combination with rented ships could any effective naval operations be undertaken. Thanks to the proximity to Arnemuiden, the Habsburg standing navy could always be reinforced with merchant ships and crews. Thus, the renting of ships was and remained the most important method for the equipment of war fleets in the Netherlands. Therefore, Habsburg naval policy had a much wider reach then one would expect on the basis of the standing navy alone, but that policy kept a largely traditional character.

The way of acquiring the ships may well have been traditional. It was, all in all, quite efficient since the authorities could put in place a 'flexible fleet', as owners were prepared to rent ships or were forced to do so. The presence of the admiral nearby was an important element in making it possible for the central government to collect the necessary ships. The fact that the ships had to be transformed seems to have been no disadvantage. All the available evidence indicates that warships in the Netherlands during the French–Habsburg wars were equipped according to the modern standards as formulated by Philip of Cleves in his *Instruction*, i.e., above all, to be fitted for carrying heavy artillery on board.

Since the standing navy founded in 1550 only fulfilled a marginal role compared to that of merchant ships, which were transformed into warships, it is no surprise that the concept which contemporaries defined as being 'master of the sea' was above all linked with merchant shipping. The expression 'master of the sea' was used in various ways. To the sovereign and the central government in Brussels 'master of the sea' referred primarily to the honour and prestige of the sovereign. Honour was to a large extent decisive in Habsburg naval policy. 'Master of the sea' also carried a strategic meaning, which was, however, more ambiguous than the prestige element. The expression was used whenever the sovereign travelled at sea in person. In that event, it meant that during the voyage he was the most powerful man of the sea. The use of the expression in relation to an imperial fleet 'cleaning' the sea of pirates implies a certain control over the sea. The use of the words 'master of the sea' by Holland points most explicitly to a strategic concept: the use of military violence at sea to support commerce. Due to its Baltic trade, Holland had a long-standing tradition in the use of warships for the advancement of its commercial interests. The offensive strategy formulated by Holland in 1554, however, went further. It entailed attacking the enemy and chasing economic competitors from the sea in order to gain control of the sea for Holland's own commercial interest. It was a view which bore testimony of the future as with the violence which the Dutch East India Company (VOC) and other European merchant companies used to penetrate Asian seas for the construction of overseas trade networks.[51] Within the context of the

---

[51] Tracy, 'Herring Wars', 250–1, 271, and introduction in Tracy, ed., *The Political Economy of Merchant Empires* (Cambridge, 1991), 2–5; J. E. Thomson, *Mercenaries, Pirates, and Sovereigns. State-Building and Extraterritorial Violence in Early Modern Europe* (Princeton, 1994), 36–8.

2. Detail from a map of the Netherlands by Hieronimus Cock in 1557
Reprinted by permission of Biblioteca Nazionale in Florence

Habsburg Netherlands 'mastery of the sea' only had a practical meaning for the honour of the sovereign.

The expression 'master of the sea' as a strategic notion gave way to a remarkable paradox: whereas the Habsburg specialist in naval affairs, de Schepper, argued for a modest, but attainable, defensive strategy, the Hollanders formulated an ambitious offensive strategy, which aimed at control of the sea by the sovereign through the use of violence for the sake of their high-seas trade. In exchange for paying the wine tax, Holland considered the sovereign responsible for their security at sea. Because of the disappointing yields of the tax, the designs of the Hollanders remained an illusion. Without the enormous maritime potential of the Hollanders, the Habsburgs could never guarantee security at sea. Only Holland's merchant fleet could have made the Netherlands a sea power. But of all maritime provinces, Holland was least prepared to equip ships for the execution of a defensive strategy. Holland preferred the equipping of warships for offensive action but refused to pay for it unless its own commercial interests were at stake. As long as the commercial interests of the Hollanders did not correspond with the dynastic interests of their sovereign, the Netherlands could not become a sea power. Consequently, the concept 'master of the sea' remained only an idea.

This, however, was no obstacle for the representation of the sovereign as master of the sea, inspired by Antiquity and by the discovery of the New World. On a 1557 map of the Netherlands by Hieronimus Cock, Philip II is represented as sitting in a shell drawn by horses. Neptune, who drives the horses, calls to the king that his kingdom, that is the sea, belongs to him, as far as the world reached at that moment. The god of the sea predicted that when the whole world served the king, the rights of the trident would be his.[52] This prediction certainly refers to Spanish overseas expansion. At a more abstract level, it refers to a notion which to this very day plays a crucial role in strategic thinking: the interdependence between sea power and world power.[53] On Cock's map, Philip II and Neptune form the liaison between the Netherlands, Spain, and its overseas empire.

However, it was not to be. Philip never succeeded in realising world domination as Neptune had imprudently announced. A little over a decade later, the Dutch Revolt marked the beginning of the end of the Spanish dream of world domination. From this moment onward, Neptune was more kindly disposed towards the Dutch than towards Philip II. As is well known, the Republic of the United Provinces based its independence, above all, on its sea power or mastery of the sea. This was possible, because, in the Dutch Republic, political-military goals and economic goals usually corresponded.

[52] 'Neptunus ad Phillippum Regem/ Esto, Philippe, mei pars haec pro tempore regni/ Terrarum ut quantum terminat illa, tuum/ Olim tota tibi tellus ut seruiat uni/ Sic tua totius iura tridentis erunt'. H. A. M. van der Heijden, *The Oldest Maps of the Netherlands. An Illustrated and Annotated Carto-bibliography of the 16th Century Maps of the XVII Provinces* (Utrecht, 1987), 58.

[53] The conceptualisation of sea power in relation to world power began in Western Europe with the treaty of Tordesillas of 1494. Modelski and Thompson, *Seapower*, 7. For the Spanish and Portuguese claims on the mastery of the seas and legal grounds for these claims and the resisting of them by France, England and the Dutch Republic see W. G. Grewe, *Epochen der Völkerrechtsgeschichte* (Baden Baden, 1984), 300–22.

NAVAL POWER AND CONTROL OF THE SEA IN THE BALTIC IN THE SIXTEENTH CENTURY

Jan Glete*

Why did the two Nordic kingdoms of Denmark-Norway and Sweden become important naval powers in the sixteenth century? And why did the sea power of the German Hanse that had dominated the Baltic for hundreds of years evaporate in this century? Which incentives stimulated Nordic rulers to buy and build specialised warships, arm them with modern heavy guns and create the infrastructures with dockyards, seamen, officers and skilled artisans which were necessary to make naval forces operationally useful? Was it urgent requirements during wars or ambitious long-term policies that were decisive?[1]

The transformation of the political power structure in the Baltic region in the first half of the sixteenth century was rapid and radical. In the late Middle Ages, the Baltic had been a part of Europe where power had been strongly connected with trade and the control of markets. The importance of the Hanse is the most obvious example. The role of territorial states in Baltic power politics had been limited in comparison to the resources of the societies. The Nordic and Polish-Lithuanian kings, the north German princes and the Teutonic Orders which controlled Estonia, Livonia, Courland and Prussia had had limited possibilities to mobilise the resources of their territories. With large merchantmen and concentrated financial resources, autonomous cities and mercantile interests could exercise a political influence out of proportion to their resources in an area where maritime lines of communication were very important for bulk trade, trade in valuable commodities and the transfer of military resources between strategically important areas.

The development of two centralised Nordic territorial states with permanent navies changed this situation radically. Denmark-Norway and Sweden not only gained full and undisputed control of their own territories but also began to pursue imperial policies in the Baltic region, actions that were based on their increasing superiority at sea. In the seventeenth century, these ambitions culminated in a Swedish–Danish struggle about hegemony in the Baltic and the creation of a Swedish empire. From the fifteenth century the Danish kings also

---

* The research for this paper has received support from the Bank of Sweden Tercentenary Foundation.
[1] For a detailed bibliography, see J. Glete, *Warfare at Sea, 1500–1650: Maritime Conflicts and the Transformation of Europe* (London, 2000), 112–130.

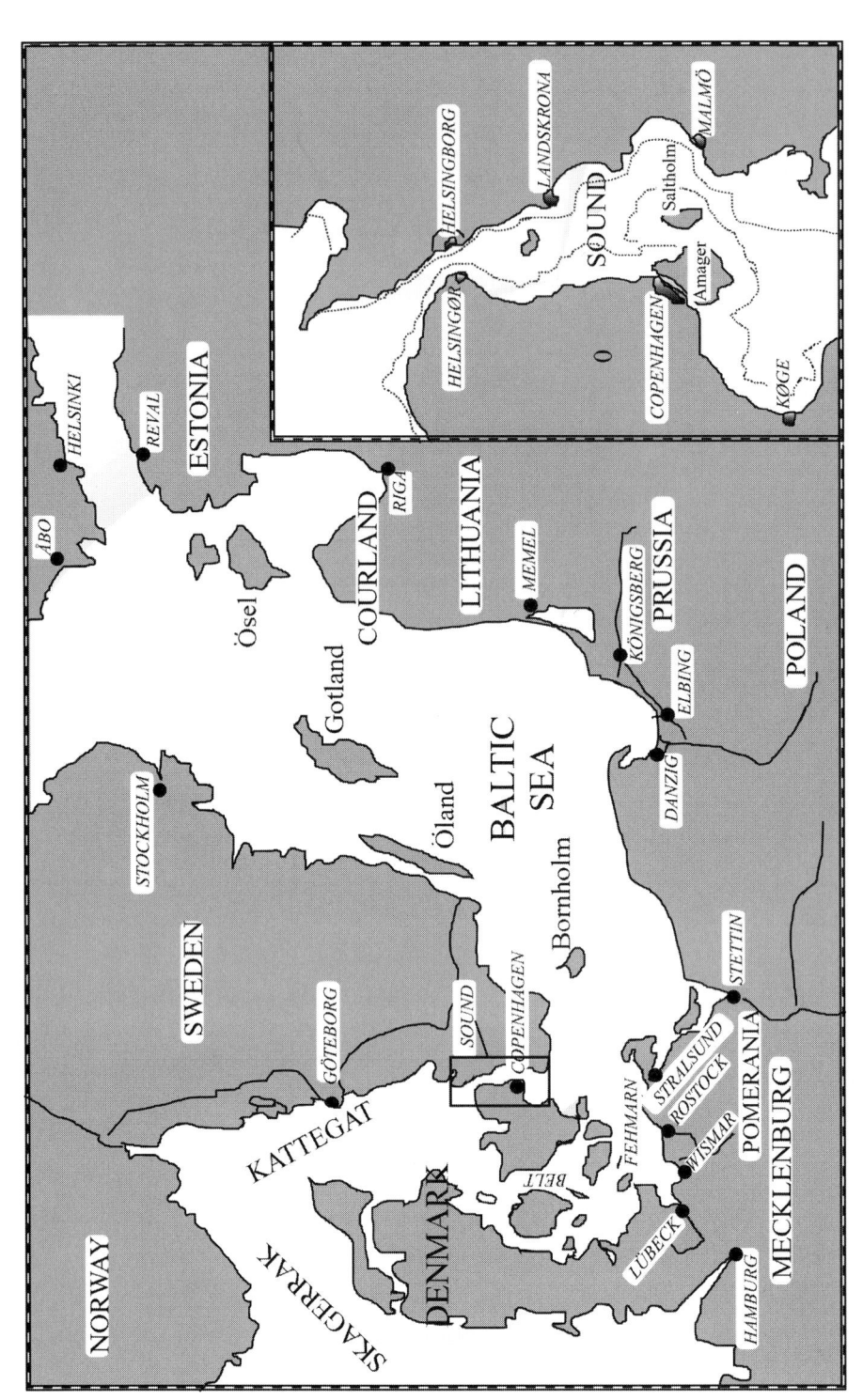

Map 1. The Baltic Region

used their position at the Sound to raise custom duties on foreign shipping. From the mid-sixteenth century the Swedish kings began to show an interest in raising similar customs in the northern and eastern Baltic, a policy that during the Thirty Years War was extended to the southern Baltic. The purpose that legitimated these duties was that they were used to finance protection of shipping through the Baltic. But the origins of the two Nordic navies had nothing to do with expansionism outside their own territories and only indirectly with trade protection. The driving force was primarily state building efforts by ambitious rulers who used innovations in gunnery and shipbuilding to create new instruments of power. Their main ambition was to gain control over Nordic territories but these territories were to a very large extent connected with each other and with the rest of Europe by sea. Control of the sea lines of communication made it possible to transfer military power from one area to another, to sustain fortresses and cities under siege and to enforce or break trade blockades. Control of the sea also meant control of the supply routes between the Nordic territories and the cities and territories in other parts of the Baltic. In the late Middle Ages, alliances between mercantile cities and territorial rulers around the Baltic and various contesting factions in the Nordic countries had been important in power struggles over Nordic territories. With efficient naval power, rulers in the Nordic countries might cut off contacts between their territories and the rest of Europe, thus facilitating the stabilisation of their domestic power.

The importance of control of the sea for maritime cities and mercantile interests is easy to understand and its role for the Baltic Hanse city does not need any explanation. But why were the Nordic states both vulnerable to and dependent on sea power? Geography is the obvious answer but the military and political implications of sixteenth-century Nordic geography and national borders need some explanation. Denmark was composed of Jutland, the south-western tip of the Scandinavian peninsula (the provinces of Skåne, Halland and Blekinge which since 1645/58 have been Swedish) and the large islands between these two peninsulas: Själland (Zealand) and Fyn. The island of Gotland also belonged to Denmark. This geographical configuration made the Danish kingdom dependent on sea lines of communication. Denmark was also strategically situated at the straits, which connected the Baltic Sea with the North Sea, a position that might be exploited in European politics if Denmark developed as a naval power. The population of Norway lived in scattered settlements and towns along the coast. This mountainous country was easy to defend against land attacks from Sweden but, as the sea often was the only practical connection between the inhabited areas, Norway could be controlled from the sea. In early modern Europe, Denmark and Norway were the countries that were most dependent on the sea for their survival in wartime. If an enemy gained control of the sea the land forces could not be concentrated and the enemy could defeat these forces when they were separated.[2] Sweden in the sixteenth century was

---

[2] Great Britain is dependent on sea power but as England, Scotland and Wales form one large and populous island, Britain does not rely on the sea to concentrate its domestic

composed of most of what today is Sweden, except its southern part and the west coast which belonged to Denmark and Norway. Only the estuary of the Göta älv (where Gothenburg is situated today) provided Sweden with a western port. Finland was an integrated part of the Swedish kingdom. Sweden was more continental than Denmark and Norway but it was also vulnerable to sea power. The sea connected Sweden and Finland and nearly all important towns were accessible from the sea. In contrast, the land frontiers with Denmark, Norway and Russia were covered with deep forests with few roads. It was difficult to launch large-scale attacks on land in both directions. War experiences showed that a power that controlled the Baltic Sea could blockade Sweden, invade it from the sea and maintain garrisons in strategic towns along the coast. Much of Sweden's foreign trade was dependent on shipping and in a war with Denmark-Norway only the sea remained as a connection with the rest of Europe.

Geography made control of the sea into one precondition for effective control of the territories that made up the three Nordic kingdoms. The other precondition for territorial control was cooperation from the local elites. The Nordic kingdoms were fairly typical of medieval European societies with only a rudimentary central administration, elected kings,[3] strong aristocratic councils and a Church in which aristocratic families had great influence. Sweden and to an even greater extent Norway were, however, special as large parts of the countries had no local nobility. In these areas, the elites were peasants and to some extent burghers and priests. In earlier periods, peasant communities along the coasts had provided the early Nordic states with a militia type of force at sea with small oared warships, the *leding* (Danish), *ledung* (Swedish) or *leidang* (Norwegian). Already before the fifteenth century these forces had become obsolete and the duty to serve was largely replaced with taxes. Nordic sea power, in this century, mainly consisted of ships provided by kings, aristocrats, bishops and cities. Most of these were small and inferior to the numerous large merchantmen the German trading cities could arm in wartime. Denmark with its rich aristocrats, more urbanised economy and royal customs duties on foreign shipping in the Sound was the Nordic country best situated to act as a sea power of this type. Up to the 1520s this is visible in the attempts to create a Nordic union based on Danish sea power. From that decade, Swedish territorial resources were mobilised and organised for the creation of effective sea power, a development that changed the power structure within the Nordic countries.

From the late fourteenth century the three Nordic kingdoms formed a union. It was effective up to 1448 but from then it began to disintegrate, primarily because of different ambitions and strategies among the elite groups. The Danish aristocracy preferred to elect kings from the German Oldenburg dynasty

resources for defence. Denmark and Norway formed a state that could be cut into isolated sections by superior sea power.

[3] Constitutionally Norway was a hereditary monarchy but from the fifteenth century the king chosen by the Danish Council became in practice the king in Norway too. Norway was formally integrated with Denmark into one kingdom in 1536. The Oldenburg kings were also hereditary dukes in Holstein, a part of the German Empire.

while the Swedish Council was split into factions that either supported the Oldenburgs or preferred to rule Sweden on their own, with or without a nominal king. In the last decades of the fifteenth century the Oldenburg Hans (1481–1513) methodically accumulated power to himself in Denmark and Norway. He was one of the creators of the European new monarchies – stronger and more centralised states where the rulers claimed a monopoly of violence. He was also one of the pioneers in creating permanent sailing navies as instruments of state power. In 1497 King Hans was able to take control of Sweden with a combination of armed force on land and sea and negotiations with the Swedish Council. But soon after, in 1501, a faction of the Swedish aristocracy rebelled against him.

The final phase of disintegration of the Nordic union began. That process also saw the birth of two permanent navies. After 1501, Hans retained control over the Baltic Sea with his navy, which he used for a trade blockade of Sweden as well as support of Swedish castles in his possession and attacks on Swedish towns and coasts. It was in the decades around 1500 that the Danish-Norwegian navy developed into a strong and permanent force armed with heavy guns. In the early decades of the sixteenth century king Hans built a few of the largest warships in the world: *Engelen* (built *c.*1509–10) and *Maria* (*c.*1512–14).[4] The most important driving force behind this major effort to create a navy was the power struggle over Sweden. The ships owned by the king were still supplemented by privately owned ships during major operations but Danish and Norwegian sea power increasingly became dominated by ships, guns and men directly controlled by the ruler. The customs paid by the rapidly increasing foreign shipping in the Sound went to the royal treasury and the king could use the money to maintain a navy of his own. This royal navy was also common to both Denmark and Norway, an important step towards an organisational merger of state power within the Nordic union.

Swedish naval power up to 1520 was of a much smaller magnitude and could not offer serious resistance in the northern Baltic. A small but concentrated force might sometimes successfully attack single Danish cruisers but it could not break the blockade. Some of the Swedish aristocrats who ruled the country and controlled the crown domains and the major seaside castles owned ships but these forces could only be regarded as the embryo of a navy. Sweden mainly fought the war with the peasant militia, a force that was fairly efficient in territorial defence. The resources to build and maintain a substantial navy were not available as Sweden lacked shipping and the central government was financially weak. But it was not only Sweden that was hit by the Danish blockade. In 1509

---

[4] Their size was probably around 1500 to 2000 tonnes displacement, N. M. Probst, 'Hovedskibet Maria 1514–1525. Ett rekonstruktionsforsög', *Marinehistorisk tidsskrift*, 23, no. 2, 1990. *Engelen* was loaned to Christian II's brother-in-law Charles (V) as his flagship when he sailed to his new kingdoms in Spain in 1517. The great ship made an impression in Spain but it was accidentally burnt at Santander in 1518, C. Fernandez Duro, *Armada espanola*, vol. I (Madrid, 1895, 1972), 123–6.

Lübeck went to war against Denmark, followed by the smaller Hanse cities of Rostock, Wismar and Stralsund. They were dissatisfied with the king's policy of reducing their trading privileges in Denmark and Norway and supporting Dutch trade with the Baltic. They were also hurt by the Danish blockade of Sweden, which was one of their key areas for trade.

The German Hanse cities were soon to prove that the old rulers of the Baltic Sea were still powerful. Lübeck sent a fleet to Stockholm, which broke the Danish blockade on trade, and during 1510–11 Denmark's and Lübeck's fleets operated against each other. The Danish fleet could no longer support the Oldenburg strongholds in Sweden and in 1510 the Swedes retook the castle in Kalmar and the island of Öland. During 1511 the Danish and Lübeck fleets fought a major fleet action, mainly with guns, off Bornholm. It ended with a draw but soon after Lübeck's fleet was able to destroy much of a large Dutch convoy that the Danish fleet in vain sought to protect. The naval operations in this war were attempts to gain control of the sea lines of communication for strategic purposes. When peace was concluded in 1512 king Hans had to give up the attempt to reconquer Sweden, but the Hanse had to cease the attempts to exclude the Dutch from the Baltic. Danish sea power kept the Sound open while Hanse sea power had forced the Danes out of Sweden. King Hans's son, Christian II (1513–23), developed his father's policy with radical ideas. He hoped to gain Sweden, create a centralised-union monarchy, found a trading company based in Copenhagen and Stockholm in order to control trade between the Baltic and Western Europe and eliminate the Hanse as a strong economic and political power. Christian married a sister of Charles V, king of Spain, German emperor and ruler of the Netherlands, a dynastic alliance that also created bonds of interest between Denmark and the rising mercantile centre in Western Europe. A strong navy with large ships armed with heavy guns and an increased Sound toll were cornerstones of this policy of maritime empire-building. In the early 1520s Christian had a royal navy of at least thirty ships. The size of many of these ships is only vaguely known but the total displacement was probably somewhere between 7000 and 10,000 tons. It was one of Europe's largest sailing navies.[5]

Christian II used his fleet to make amphibious attacks against Stockholm in 1517 and 1518 but his army was defeated on land. During the winter of 1520 a large Danish mercenary army was able to penetrate central Sweden, and during the summer Christian arrived at Stockholm with his main fleet in order to take control of the country. Sweden had to accept him as king but the army was too

---

[5] The English royal navy in 1520 was of about 14,000 tons, while the French navy was of around 10,000 to 15,000 tons of sailing warships and a small galley force of around 2000 tons. It is impossible even to guess at the size of the important Portuguese navy. Spain had at this time only a small galley force while Venice had a galley navy of around 25,000 tons. The Ottoman navy may have been of the same magnitude. Jan Glete, *Warfare at Sea*, 188–9.

expensive to maintain and already in 1521 rebellious Swedes under the young aristocrat Gustav Vasa were in control of most of the country. With his navy, Christian could keep Stockholm and other fortified coastal places and he could blockade Sweden and deny it import of essential products such as salt. The king could also regain control over Finland with sea-borne forces. Again, the essentially maritime character of Danish power became visible. Gustav Vasa realised that he had to acquire armed force at sea which could break the blockade and isolate the towns under Christian's control. Otherwise the rebellion might be suppressed. In 1522 Gustav Vasa bought a fleet of at least eleven armed merchantmen in Lübeck and Stralsund, a force that also brought mercenary soldiers and weapons to Sweden. Lübeck merchants with interest in the Swedish trade provided the necessary credits to the Swedish rebels in the hope that they would be paid from future taxes and by trading privileges. Lübeck and other Hanse cities soon joined Sweden and the allied fleets began to assert control over the Baltic. In late 1522 they stopped a Danish attempt to supply Stockholm with provisions for the winter. It might have been expected that the main Danish fleet would attempt to bring aid to Stockholm the following spring. Surprisingly, it was instead used to bring Christian II to the Netherlands. His regime in Denmark had become increasingly insecure and in early 1523 the Danish nobility sided with Lübeck under the leadership of his uncle Frederik (I) who was elected king of Denmark. In 1523 Gustav Vasa was elected king of Sweden. The war continued against Christian II's forces and the allied Hanse and (largely German-manned) Swedish fleets could blockade Stockholm, Copenhagen and other fortified towns into surrender. German mercantile sea power had proved decisive in the Nordic power struggle. Lübeck could reassert its position as the leading Baltic entrepôt by new trade privileges in the Nordic countries as rewards for its financial, naval and military help to the two victors.

The positions of both Frederik and Gustav as rulers were initially insecure. Christian II was expected to launch a counter-attack from the Netherlands with the help of his Habsburg relatives. In the Baltic, his admiral Sören Norby fought a skilful rearguard action on land and at sea until 1526. There were also domestic oppositions in the Nordic countries. Gustav again decided on a bold policy to strengthen his position. One cornerstone in this was a Lutheran reformation of the Church in 1527, which gave him control of extensive economic resources. He used these to build large warships armed with heavy guns and to employ a small but professional army. The largest unit of his navy was the great ship *Stora Kravelen* (possibly around 1700 tons) built around 1530. These forces were controlled by the king, not by nobles or peasant communities, and they were politically and militarily suitable for rapid strikes against domestic and foreign enemies or alliances between them. Frederik I had similar ambitions in Denmark but his position was weaker. He never gained full control over Norway and the navy did not recover from its near destruction during the civil war. A few major ships of which *Michael* (probably around 1000–1500 tons) was the largest were however owned by the king in the early 1530s.

Christian II did finally sail to Norway with a Habsburg-sponsored army in

1531, but he was met by resistance from Sweden on land and by a Danish-Lübeck fleet and was finally taken prisoner. When Frederik I died in 1533, the councils of Denmark and Norway did not wish to elect his eldest son Duke Christian (III) of Holstein as king, partly because he was a Lutheran. In 1534 a civil war started in Denmark. Lübeck intervened on the side of Duke Christian's enemies and they took control of Copenhagen and the Danish royal fleet. This was part of a radical programme where the old Hanse city tried to close the Sound to the Dutch and regain favourable trading privileges in Scandinavia.

King Gustav of Sweden had by 1533 broken with his old allies in Lübeck and he regarded developments in Denmark as a serious threat to his own regime. He had many opponents in his own country and if Lübeck was successful in Denmark that city might infiltrate Sweden too. He chose to support Christian III in the Danish civil war and used his new armed forces for mobile and offensive warfare of a type which Swedish rulers had been unable to undertake for generations. The army intervened in eastern Denmark and in spring 1535 his new fleet was sent to the southern Baltic. It joined ships sent by Prussia and Christian III, although most of these were small vessels or armed merchantmen. A major part of the Swedish army sailed with this fleet. The allies first drove away Lübeck's main fleet (including the largest Danish ships) at Bornholm in a gunfire battle on 9 June, and then destroyed or captured another enemy fleet which controlled the Danish straits. The allies were now in control of the sea lines of communication in the Baltic, the island of Själland (Zealand) could be invaded and the allied army and fleet surrounded Copenhagen and Malmö. Lübeck was forced to conclude peace and its role as a power on the same level as the two Nordic kingdoms with ambitions to intervene in their domestic politics was finished. With control of the sea, Christian III could gain full control over Denmark and enforce a Lutheran reformation as well as a more centralised form of government. During 1536 he sent a fleet with an army to Norway, which brought that country and its church under his control. A Habsburg attempt to send a fleet of Dutch armed merchantmen to Denmark or Norway in order to support his opponents and liberate Christian II failed. Dutch mercantile interests were reluctant to start a conflict with the power that controlled the Sound and the Danish-Norwegian navy had by 1536 again reached such strength that it was a powerful deterrent force.

The end of the great power struggle did not mean that the two Scandinavian kingdoms which had emerged out of the union reduced their navies. On the contrary they strengthened them with several new warships built in the late 1530s and the 1540s. As permanent navies were something new and unusual in Europe this was a sign that organised Nordic sea power had become a part of a new type of state. It was a state in which the kings controlled armed forces of their own in order to protect the country and enforce a monopoly of violence. In Denmark-Norway the navy and the artillery (largely intended for the navy) were the only permanent armed forces while the Vasa kings in Sweden also created a militia army under their control. From 1540 Sweden began to create a substantial galley fleet that by 1560 had twenty-six large and small units.[6] This was partly due to its usefulness in archipelagos but it may also have reflected lessons of war with sailing warships that still had rather limited capability.[7] The existence of a Swedish army made it possible to use soldiers as oarsmen and the galleys also gave the new army an amphibious capability.

Why did the Scandinavian kings expend so much effort and money on their navies in a period of peace? The explanation must be sought in their experiences from the long period of struggle for control over territories. Both the Oldenburg and Vasa rulers had seen that naval power might be of decisive importance in such power struggles. Their use of such power had been of fundamental importance for their success and they must have realised that they had to own modern gun-armed warships if this success was to be lasting. With such warships, Nordic rulers had gained considerable political leverage against potential competitors, a leverage that had not existed before the late fifteenth century. First, kings became efficient protectors of their territories against sea-borne invasions and blockades that might cut off the supply of essential products, such as salt. This made it easier for them to raise taxes to pay for this protection. Second, the numerous domestic opponents to the rulers could no longer easily communicate with groups on the other side of the Baltic who wished to interfere in Nordic politics in order to promote trade or dynastic interests. Control of the Baltic Sea with royal warships was thus an important precondition for undisturbed state formation and centralisation of power in Denmark-Norway and Sweden. The central political role of the two royal navies is visible in the fact that the ships, the guns and the dockyard facilities were concentrated in the capital cities and located as close to royal castles as possible. From 1536 to 1544 both kings were on their guard against Habsburg attempts to bring Christian II or his relatives back to power.[8] Both were usurpers and both had also taken the fateful step of breaking relations with the Catholic Church in order to gain control of the economic and political power of the Church. They were aware that those foreign enemies and internal opponents to their regimes might use any sign of weakness as in invitation to reverse the decisions reached by 1536. They were also suspicious of each other but the threat from the Habsburgs forced Sweden and Denmark-Norway to form an alliance in 1541. The royal navies were useful for the maintenance of internal security, the upkeep of law and order on the sea and as deterrents against foreign powers. Both kings sent out their

---

6   Most of these were of a smaller type than the normal Mediterranean *galea* with three men to each oar. They were probably comparable to the Mediterranean *galeota* type with two men to each oar, J. Glete, 'Svenska örlogsfartyg 1521–1560', *Forum Navale*, nos 30–31 (1976–77).
7   On experiences with galleys and sailing warships in western Europe up to 1560, see Glete, *Warfare at Sea*, 137–44. See also N. A. M. Rodger, 'The Development of Broadside Gunnery, 1450–1650', *Mariner's Mirror*, 82 (1996), 301–24.
8   On Swedish trade and foreign policy see S. Lundkvist, *Gustav Vasa och Europa: Svensk handels- och utrikespolitik, 1534–1557* (Uppsala, 1960). On Nordic foreign policy see G. Landberg, *De nordiska rikena under Brömsebroförbundet* (Uppsala, 1925), maritime and naval aspects, 72–89.

small ships to be on guard against foreign threats, suppress piracy, protect trade to their own ports and enforce trade regulations. Especially Denmark began to assert a conscious *dominium* policy in which the Danish king asserted that the southern Baltic Sea, the Kattegat and Skagerrak, were Danish streams in which he had a monopoly of violence at sea. This *dominium* meant that Danish warships should protect foreign ships, which had to pay for this protection, when they passed the Sound.

Both navies also had to fight short wars in this period. The unsettled relations with the Habsburgs caused both Nordic states to ally themselves with France. When France and the Habsburg powers went to war in 1542 Denmark-Norway became actively involved. The Sound was closed to Habsburg, that is mainly Dutch, shipping and Danish, French and Scottish ships cruised in the North Sea searching for merchantmen from the Netherlands and Spain. In 1543 the Danish fleet was concentrated for an assault on Walcheren, the centre of Dutch sea power. Unexpectedly severe summer gales brought that attempt to an end. In 1544 Christian III and Charles V made peace and in practice Sweden also ceased to be a potential Habsburg enemy when the Habsburgs accepted that Christian II was no longer king in the three Nordic realms. All major European powers had now accepted the two Nordic kingdoms, their new regimes and their break with the Catholic Church. Their ability to effectively manifest their strength and determination at sea had been important in this process of stabilisation and international recognition. Sweden gradually turned its interest eastward to the security problems along the border with Russia, the increasing trade passing through the Gulf of Finland and the growing political crisis in the eastern Baltic, for centuries ruled by the Teutonic Order of Knights. This area provided both risks and opportunities and for more than a century it would remain a tempting area for ambitious Swedish empire-builders in search of territories and the diversion of the rich Russian trade to Swedish-controlled ports.[9] The result was first that these territories were consolidated into a Swedish empire that in the early eighteenth century was to be conquered by Russia. The beginning was more inconspicuous. Swedish warships began to patrol the Gulf of Finland and King Gustav tried to use them to favour trade through his ports, Viborg (Viipuri) and Helsingfors (Helsinki). The latter town was founded in 1550 as a rival to the old entrepôt, Reval (Tallinn), in Estonia.

During 1554/55 Gustav had to face a rising crisis along the Russian border and in 1555 he mobilised the army and the galley fleet and sent them to Finland. After a failed attempt to take a Russian fortress at the river Neva with an amphibious attack the Swedish forces were used defensively until peace was concluded in 1557. The war was inconclusive, but Sweden's new armed forces

---

[9] A. Attman, *The Struggle for Baltic Markets: Powers in Conflict, 1558–1618* (Gothenburg, 1979); S. Troebst, *Handelskontrolle, Derivation, Eindämmerung: Schwedische Moskaupolitik, 1617–1661* (Wiesbaden, 1997). There is a long scholarly debate about the ultimate motives for Swedish imperial expansion. Here it is enough to say that both territorial expansion and the control of trade were motives.

had shown mobility and a degree of readiness that may have encouraged the young Vasa princes, Erik and Johan, both future kings, to think in terms of imperial expansion in the East, even against opponents with inherently much larger resources.[10]

In 1558 Russia took the important port of Narva in eastern Estonia. Denmark took control of the large island of Ösel (Saaremaa) and some territories in western Estonia, thus extending its maritime empire close to the Gulf of Finland and the Bay of Riga, two main outlets for Russian and Lithuanian trade. In 1561 Poland-Lithuania became protector of Livonia and Sweden of most of Estonia. Sweden immediately began to use naval power to regulate trade in the Gulf of Finland in the interest of the Crown of Sweden and its new subjects in the city of Reval (Tallinn). Swedish warships blockaded Narva, an action that severely hit the interests of Lübeck, which still controlled much of the trade in valuable commodities in the Baltic. In a few years four powers had appeared as protectors of the territories and cities which up to then had been controlled or protected by the Teutonic Order. In the power vacuum left when the Order dissolved, the territorial states took control and began to levy taxes and customs in order to pay for the protection.

The new protection-sellers immediately ran into a conflict over how the market for protection should be shared. Denmark and Poland became allied against Sweden in Estonia and Denmark also formed an alliance with Lübeck in order to secure trade against Swedish interference. Furthermore, Denmark and Sweden began to raise old disputes from the union period. Russia and Sweden attempted to maintain an uneasy friendship based on a common antagonism against Poland. In this situation control of the Baltic Sea became an issue of decisive importance. The trade which flowed through the Baltic – naval stores, Russian luxury products and Polish grain to the west, cloth, wine, salt and various manufactured products from Western Europe to the east – was very valuable in proportion to the resources of the sparsely populated countries of northern Europe. It was tempting to profit from this trade by selling protection, in the form of taxes and custom duties, for trade or shipping. Traditionally, the autonomous Hanse cities had organised trade, shipping and protection on their own, a mercantile sea power strategy centred on large armed merchantmen. But in the Baltic, protection of sea-borne trade was now ultimately dependent on organised Nordic naval power.

Furthermore, Danish and Swedish imperial aspirations in the eastern Baltic required naval power in order to secure military communications across the sea. From 1558 the Swedish navy was rapidly strengthened by a programme of new construction of large warships and mass production of efficient but expensive copper guns. Domestic resources of timber, copper and high-quality iron and many years of peacetime hoarding of silver made this programme feasible. From

---

[10] A detailed study of this war is A. Viljanti, *Gustav Vasa ryska krig, 1554–1557*, 2 vols (Stockholm, 1957).

1560 to 1563 no less than seven ships from about 600 to 1800 tons as well as several smaller warships were launched. The new king, Erik XIV (1560–8), followed an offensive maritime strategy aiming at control over the Baltic Sea. Denmark-Norway under its new king Frederik II (1559–88) also increased its navy and the old system where small ships were armed by cities was largely replaced by taxes that could support a centralised royal navy. This state, which lacked domestic resources of copper, was less well provided with modern copper artillery. From 1563 to 1570 Sweden fought a major war with Denmark-Norway and Lübeck at sea and with Denmark-Norway and Poland-Lithuania on land.[11] The Nordic Seven Years War was the first modern war at sea in Europe where sailing gun-armed battle fleets repeatedly fought for command of the sea. From 1563 to 1566 no less than seven major battles were fought.

Contrary to what happened in earlier wars in the Baltic the main fleets were no longer used for power-projection operations. The fleets were no longer sent to Stockholm or Copenhagen with a major army in order to assault the city from both land and sea. The size of the armies had increased to tens of thousands, which made it impossible to concentrate a main army on a fleet. Furthermore, the principal armament of the navies was now guns, not infantry weapons, and this made it impossible to gain command of the sea with only a superior army on board the ships of a fleet. Gun-armed fleets had to gain command before an army could be sent to a decisive area of operation or a fleet could provide an advancing army with logistical support.

These preconditions were never fulfilled in this war. The Danish army did once, in the winter of 1567–8, advance far into Sweden but at that time the Danish-Lübeck fleet was too diminished to provide logistical support and to enforce a blockade that might have decided the war. On the other hand, Swedish success at sea could not be used for an invasion of Denmark as the Swedish army was too occupied with defensive warfare along the border between Sweden and Denmark-Norway. This army was never able to penetrate deep into Skåne where it might have joined with the navy in attacks on the centre of Danish power around the Sound. Furthermore, in earlier wars maritime power projection against the enemy capital had been co-ordinated with political contacts with opposition groups within the elite. Such contacts were no longer possible, a sign that the two Nordic kingdoms definitely had become politically separated.

Two concentrated battle fleets at sea were the main forces that fought the war. Lübeck sent its main fleet to join the Danish-Norwegian fleet, and the allies were under the command of a Danish admiral. The two opposing fleets had to a

---

[11] The latest study of this war is F. P. Jensen, *Danmarks konflikt med Sverige, 1563–1570* (Copenhagen, 1982). On the war in the eastern Baltic, see S. Arnell, *Bidrag till belysning av den baltiska fronten under det nordiska sjuårskriget 1563–1570* (Stockholm, 1977). For more details about the naval operations and the literature about these, see Glete, *Warfare at Sea*, 120–4.

large extent the same strategic aims. They intended to enforce a blockade on the enemy, secure trade to their own ports, destroy enemy trade and protect the sea-lanes, which were essential for communication within the states. The Swedish fleet also raised customs from neutral shipping and sold licences to trade. Both fleets raided coasts and cooperated with the army in some types of operations. Lübeck was the power that had the largest merchant fleet to protect, but as the city now fought as a junior partner to Denmark-Norway it was no longer able to direct its fleet in the interest of its trade. The allied battle fleet never seriously attempted to break the Swedish blockade of Narva, which would have been desirable for Lübeck. Primarily this fleet fought for control of the southern Baltic Sea, a Danish interest that Lübeck could support. The Swedish fleet fought in order to maintain essential Swedish trade with neutral ports in northern Germany, to destroy Lübeck's trade and to damage Denmark and its *dominium* in the southern Baltic as much as possible.

The war started with an encounter at sea in spring 1563. A Danish fleet demanded that a Swedish fleet should pay respect to the Danish king. This was refused and in the battle, the First Battle of Bornholm on 30 May, the Danish flagship and two other ships were captured. Denmark-Norway and Lübeck formed a large fleet mainly composed of armed merchantmen, which sailed to the northern Baltic in the autumn. The Swedish fleet attempted to fight it in a battle on 11 September but had to withdraw to the archipelago around Stockholm. Early the following year an increased Swedish fleet sailed southward with orders to break the blockade. This ended with a Swedish defeat in the first battle of Öland on 30–1 May 1564. The Swedish fleet was, however, quickly sent to sea again and had the fortune of finding and capturing a richly laden Lübeck convoy which was sailing in the belief that the sea was secured for the allies. From 11 to 15 August the two fleets fought a stand-off gunfire battle, the Second Battle of Öland, which ended with the Danish fleet losing three ships, which by mistake had sailed into the Swedish fleet during the night.

In spring 1565 an expanded Swedish fleet was able to take control of the southern Baltic Sea and destroy an allied cruiser squadron. The allied fleet made two attempts to force the Swedes to leave the area. The first battle, at Bukow on 4 June, was a draw, and the second, the Second Battle of Bornholm on 7 July, was a hard-fought Swedish victory. In the following year, the Swedish fleet again took control of the Baltic. The allied powers had strengthened their fleets and in the Third Battle of Öland on 26 July 1566 they again attempted to defeat the Swedish fleet. This action ended in a draw but soon after a large part of the allied fleet was destroyed in a sudden summer gale off Visby. This ended the struggle for command of the Baltic, although it was only in 1567 and 1570 that the Swedish fleet was sent out in full strength in order to assert command of the sea. Both sides were by now exhausted by the war efforts and Sweden went through a political crisis and a brief civil war in 1567–8 when Johan III (1568–92) deposed his brother Erik XIV. Erik had been an energetic and innovative organiser of the war efforts and his naval policy was highly successful but his mental stability was gradually undermined until he lost control of domestic politics. Peace was concluded in late 1570. Denmark gained some real advantages out of the peace but Lübeck only gained advantages on paper. After the peace was concluded Sweden continued to harass Lübeck shipping in the Gulf of Finland and Denmark had lost interest in supporting its former ally. Danish imperial ambitions in the eastern Baltic ceased when it became obvious that they meant war with Russia. Sweden on the other hand chose to fight Russia in a war that lasted until 1595.

During the northern Seven Years War the Swedes and the allied fleet originally attempted to fight with widely different tactics. The allies attempted to board the Swedish ships and fight with infantry weapons. The Swedish fleet with its high proportion of purpose-built warships manoeuvred to avoid that and fought with guns, mainly modern copper guns that could be fired with large powder charges. The Danish fleet was mainly armed with wrought-iron breech-loaders, which could only be fired with small powder-charges and had less effect on major ships. During the war the allies gradually renewed their armament, the Danes especially by purchase of English cast-iron guns, which were the only guns that could be acquired quickly. The contending navies also made large investments in purpose-built warships, even ships of about 2000 tons displacement or more. During the 1560s they grew to be the largest sailing fleets in Europe and they were visible proof that sailing warships were viable instruments of modern sea power. In the same period, the Mediterranean galley fleets reached their apogee as fighting forces.

During the last battle in 1566 both fleets deliberately fought with guns. By then, experience from several battles had shown that gunfire could prevent boarding and even sink ships and that purpose-built warships were far superior to armed merchantmen due to their armament, speed, weatherliness and ability to resist gunfire. Tactically the navies developed new ideas. From 1564 the Danish-Lübeck fleet was divided into groups of three ships, one large and two smaller. The fleet was intended to form a wedge when it attacked from a windward position and line ahead for mutual support when it was attacked in a leeward position. The Swedish fleet also used three-ship formations but here the tactical idea seems to have been that the major ships should form line abreast or line ahead, each with two smaller ships in a second line, ready to support the major units when they became engaged with the enemy.

Technology, tactics and practical implementation of theories and lessons from earlier battles interacted as never before since the introduction of gunpowder in warfare between sailing ships. The least dramatic, but probably very important, lessons were logistical and organisational. Both sides had attempted to keep their fleets at sea from spring to autumn. Earlier naval operations had often been concentrated in confined waters such as the Danish straits and the Swedish archipelago where the role of the weather in the outcome was much smaller. The new type of naval operations required large-scale preparations during the winter and a well-planned supply of food and spare parts during operations that lasted seven to eight months. Ships damaged in combat and by heavy weather had to be repaired quickly and seamen and soldiers had to be found continuously to replace losses. Many officers were initially inexperienced in sea service and they had to learn how to solve these problems on a routine basis without immediately returning to the main bases in Stockholm, Copenhagen and Lübeck, which often were at a distance from the critical area of operation.

The interaction between state formation, technology and naval and military organisation was also obvious. It was an initial Swedish advantage in modern gunnery and purpose-built warships that enabled that country to break the blockade which otherwise might have caused an early defeat. As the allies must have had an advantage in the number of experienced seamen – Lübeck was still a major shipping city – the Swedish advantage in technology was even more important as it neutralised this inferiority. The fact that Sweden, the power with the least developed maritime economy, was able to resist and defeat an alliance of the two powers which since the fifteenth century had fought over naval hegemony in the Baltic shows that the organisational power of the state had become decisive in naval warfare.

The development of Nordic naval power and the growth of two centralised territorial states in northern Europe were two sides of the same coin. Gun-armed purpose-built warships were a new technology that gave the kings a new instrument of power against various threats to their position. Such ships could cut the lines of communication between external and internal enemies, break blockades, project military power and protect trade. The new technology gave a plausible argument for the development of permanent royal navies, which had to be supported by increased taxes, custom duties and the accumulated wealth of the church. Warships armed with guns gave rulers a new political leverage both within their own countries and in the Baltic. Copenhagen and Stockholm turned into centres of empires or potential empires.

Why were the Hanse cities, still the leading shipping and trading centres in the Baltic, unable to respond? The decline of armed merchantmen as potential warships is one technical explanation that must be taken seriously. It was not the whole explanation, however. The cities had always been small compared to the territorial states. They had, however, had strong incentives to fight in order to protect and promote the trade they lived on. The territorial rulers on the southern and eastern sides of the Baltic were much less dependent on the sea than the Nordic rulers and they showed little interest in developing sea power. When the Nordic states began to assert control and even a *dominium maris Baltici*, German and Polish territorial interests hardly responded with a naval policy of their own.

The Hanse cities were not interested in an increased dependence on their nominal territorial lords and did not ask them for help at sea. No German or Polish state-building of the Nordic type occurred and the cities were usually relatively satisfied with a situation where the Nordic fleets guaranteed law and order in the Baltic. Only Lübeck, the informal capital of the Hanse, tried to resist, but its strength was too limited to stem the rising wave of Nordic state formation. The Baltic became a normally peaceful sea where foreign ships could sail unharmed and unarmed as long as they paid for the protection enforced by the Nordic kings.

Table I. The structure of the Nordic navies, 1530–70

	1530	1540	1550	1560	1565	1570
Denmark-Norway						
Sailing warships						
1501–2200	–	–	–	–	–	2
1001–1500	1	1	2	1	2	–
501–1000	1	3	3	3	6	7
100–500	2	8/10	8/10	20	23	22
Total	4	12/14	13/15	24	31	31
Galleys 100 and above	–	–	–	–	1	4/5
Sweden						
Sailing warships						
1501–2200	1	1	1	–	–	1
1001–1500	–	–	–	2	2	3
501–1000	1	3	2	3	8	10
100–500	5	11	9	14	38	28
Total	7	15	12	19	48	42
Galleys 100 and above	–	2	17	21	9	1

Number of warships, divided in size groups. The size is displacement in tons, calculated by the author. Warships smaller than 100 tons, transports and royal merchantmen are not included. The figures are approximate, especially for Denmark-Norway 1530–50. Sources: J. Glete, *Navies and Nations*, 607, and information about the Danish-Norwegian navy from Niels M. Probst.

Table II. The size of the Nordic and English navies

	1520	1530	1540	1550	1560	1565	1570
Denmark-Norway	7/10	2/3	5/7	6/8	8	13	16
Sweden	1	3/4	7	7	9	18	21
England	14	7	7	17	14	15	14

Total displacement of the navies in thousand tons

Sources: J. Glete, *Navies and Nations*, 549, 607; J. Glete, *Warfare at Sea*, 188–9 and information from Niels M. Probst

THE NEW ATLANTIC:
NAVAL WARFARE IN THE SIXTEENTH CENTURY

N. A. M. Rodger

It has long been customary to regard naval warfare as the business of navies, and it usually still is. This creates an obvious problem, for navies, as the word is generally understood today, are instruments of the state; permanent fleets of warships, manned by professional officers and men, supported by an elaborate infrastructure and maintained from the revenues of central government. These are the normal instruments of naval warfare in the modern world, and it is easy to assume that they are the natural if not the only ones. Yet even a superficial knowledge of European history will show that navies in this sense were unusual if not unknown before the Renaissance. Byzantium and Venice have some claims to have possessed navies in something like the modern form, at some periods, but medieval naval warfare was generally conducted without navies. Historians have been reluctant to confront the fact. In the British case, Sir William Laid Clowes in the 1890s began his history of the Royal Navy in the third century BC, though he believed that the Navy, as an institution, had been founded in the sixteenth century AD.[1] Even a modern publisher might hesitate at so wide a discrepancy between title and contents, yet a century after Laird Clowes, the *Oxford Illustrated History of the Royal Navy*[2] adopts the same approach on a slightly more modest scale, beginning eight hundred years before the foundation of the Royal Navy. The basic confusion arises from a refusal to acknowledge that navies, in our modern sense of the word, are a modern creation, a product of the early modern and modern state. Naval warfare existed long before navies, but it took other institutional forms.

We may distinguish at least six different forms of naval organisation that existed in Europe alone at various times before the seventeenth century: (1) Requisitioning, (2) Ship Musters, (3) Chartered Squadrons, (4) Local Navies, (5) Feudal Navies, and (6) Private Forces.

1. Requisitioning. The simplest of all forms of naval organisation, this called for the prince to use his authority to call up unmodified (and usually unpaid) merchant ships for war service. Once assembled, fleets of this sort were used

---

[1] *The Royal Navy: A History from the Earliest Times to the Present*, 7 vols. (London, 1897–1903).
[2] Ed. J. R. Hill (Oxford, 1995).

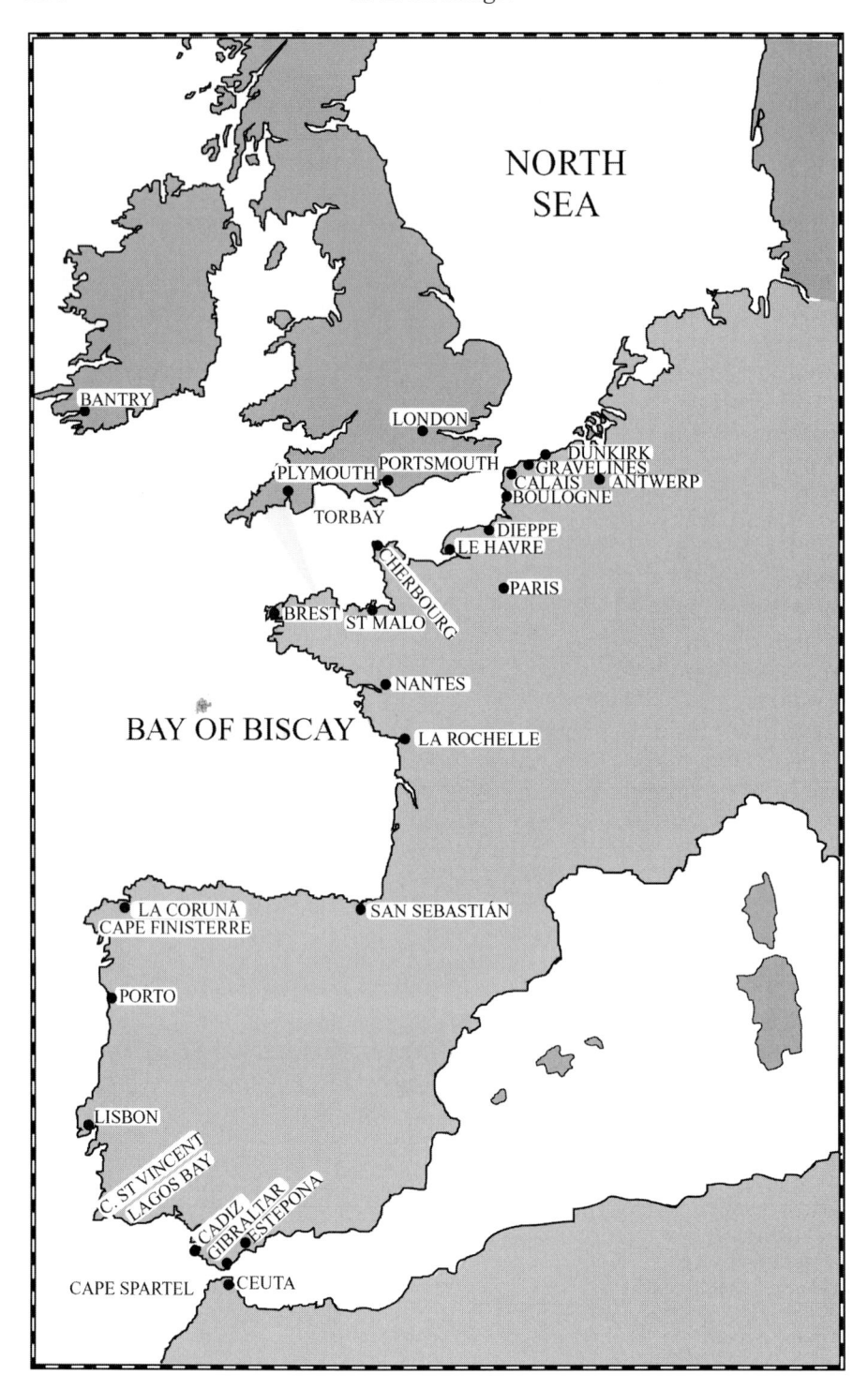

Map 1. The European Atlantic Coast

mainly to transport troops overseas, but the ships might also be fitted as 'warships', with 'castles' or fighting platforms, or simply by adding a number of soldiers to the usual crew. The system was incapable of providing any specialised warships, and it was extremely slow and cumbersome to operate, but it cost the prince very little and laid all the burden of naval war on his ship-owning subjects. This was the method by which medieval English kings assembled the large fleets that they needed to carry English armies overseas to France, Flanders, Scotland, Ireland and Wales.[3]

2. Ship Musters. In some countries, notably in Scandinavia but also in England before the Norman Conquest and in parts of the Celtic world, law or custom laid an obligation on coastal districts to build and man one or more warships each, available for national service in specified circumstances and for a fixed period. It is unclear to what extent, and when, the Scandinavian *leidang* existed as an operational force rather than a legal fiction, but the English equivalent certainly functioned in the tenth and eleventh centuries. Such a system was capable of providing a large national fleet of warships at no direct cost to the Crown, and with no known central organisation.[4]

3. Chartered Squadrons. Warships might be owned by private entrepreneurs who chartered their squadrons to the Crown, in some cases contracting to build as well as operate them. By this method the Crown subcontracted the organisational, and many of the operational requirements of naval warfare, retaining only the financial obligation to pay for them. Mediterranean galley fleets were often made up partly or wholly of such private squadrons, and Spain applied the same method to obtain the bulk of its naval forces in the Atlantic in the sixteenth century. The Genoese and Ragusans were noted specialists in this business, while Basque contractors built and owned much of the Spanish Atlantic fleet.[5]

4. Local Navies. Another approach to sea power was to create squadrons on the basis of local rather than national government. Provinces or individual seaports might organise their own forces, paid from their own revenues, to protect their

---

[3] N. A. M. Rodger, *The Safeguard of the Sea: A Naval History of Britain, Volume I: 660–1649* (London, 1997), 117–30, deals with the organisation of these English fleets.

[4] Rodger, *Safeguard of the Sea*, 23–7; Hans Kuhn, *Das altnordische Seekriegswesen*, ed. Sigrid Engeler and Dietrich Hofmann (Heidelberg, 1991), 54–87; Lucien Musset, 'Problèmes militaires du monde scandinave (VIIe–XIIe siècles)', in *Ordinamenti militari in Occidente nell'alto medievo* (Spoleto, 1968), 229–91, at 279–84; Niels Lund, 'The Armies of Swein Forkbeard and Cnut: *leding* or *lið*?', *Anglo-Saxon England*, 15 (1986), 105–18; Hugh Marwick, 'Naval Defence in Norse Scotland', *Scottish Historical Review*, 28 (1949), 1–11; John Bannerman, *Studies in the History of Dalriada* (Edinburgh, 1974), 140–1.

[5] Kenneth R. Andrews, *The Spanish Caribbean: Trade and Plunder 1530–1630* (New Haven, 1978), 90–4; Huguette and Pierre Chaunu, *Séville et l'Atlantique (1504–1650)*, 8 vols in 11 (Paris, 1955–9), VIII, i, 255–7; Francisco-Felipe Olesa Muñido, *La organización naval de los estados Mediterráneos y en especial de España durante los siglos XVI y XVII*, 2 vols (Madrid, 1968), I, 463–88; I. A. A. Thompson, *War and Government in Habsburg Spain 1560–1620* (London, 1976), 164–204 and 267–73; J. F. Guilmartin, *Gunpowder and Galleys: Changing Technology and Mediterranean Warfare at Sea in the Sixteenth Century* (Cambridge, 1974), 26–34.

own interests. Depending on the power of the centre, these might also be combined on occasion to form a national fleet. Renaissance Spain again is an outstanding example of this approach: it had at least eight navies operational at one time or another. The galleys of Castile were paid for from Castilian revenues, and the galleys of Aragon from Aragonese revenues; the ships of the *Guarda de Indias* were provided by the *Casa de Contratación* of Seville and paid for by the *avería* charged to the merchantmen which sailed under their convoy; the *Armada de Flandes* in the North Sea, the *Armada de Barlovento* in the Caribbean and the *Armada del Mar del Sur* in the Pacific were paid for by the local authorities. Only the Portuguese royal galleons (acquired by conquest in 1580) and the *Armada del Mar Océano* could be regarded as elements of a national fleet, albeit the latter was largely provided by contractors.[6] The Dutch adopted the same approach with greater success. Five provincial admiralties (nominally federal institutions but in practice dominated by local interests) each maintained a fleet and a naval establishment from their own taxation. Two great joint-stock companies, the East and West India Companies, each financed substantial naval forces from their shareholders' capital. Six individual seaports provided municipal navies (the '*directieschepen*') to protect their own shipping. All of these forces could coalesce in wartime to make up a national fleet, but not until 1653 did the Dutch Republic possess any ships that had been directly paid for out of central-government revenues and were unequivocally the property of the Republic, and not until 1795 did it have a single national naval organisation.[7]

5. Feudal Navies. It was possible for the military obligations of feudal or quasi-feudal systems to be discharged by naval service. In such a system landholders built and manned warships, which they were obliged to put to sea at their lord's command under specified conditions. Feudal naval service of this nature existed in Norman Sicily, and in the West Highlands and Western Isles of Scotland it provided the fleets that preserved into the seventeenth century the naval architecture and fighting traditions of the Viking Age.[8]

6. Private Forces. In the majority of countries private ship-owners built or used ships for warlike purposes on their own account. This might be done in wartime, and the ships might be combined with forces raised by other methods, but it was very often done in peacetime. To understand this to modern eyes anomalous or improper situation we need to discuss the objectives of medieval and Renaissance naval warfare.

Just as the forms of naval warfare have been confused, so also have been the

---

[6] Ricardo Cerezo Martínez, *Las Armadas de Felipe II* (Madrid, 1988); José Luis Casada Soto, *Los barcos españoles del siglo XVI y la Gran Armada de 1588* (Madrid, 1988), 25–34.

[7] J. R. Bruijn, *Varend Verleden: De Nederlandse Oorlogsvloot in de 17de en 18de eeuw* (Amsterdam, 1998).

[8] D. P. Waley, ' "Combined Operations" in Sicily, A.D. 1060–78', *Papers of the British School at Rome*, 22 (1954), 118–25; Alexander Grant, 'Scotland's "Celtic Fringe" in the Late Middle Ages: The Macdonald Lords of the Isles and the Kingdom of Scotland', in *The British Isles 1100–1500: Comparisons, Contrasts and Connections*, ed. R. R. Davies (Edinburgh, 1988), 118–41.

functions. A modern navy is an instrument of the state, and in peace or war, it is employed about the purposes of the state. Modern navies therefore are political animals, and their objects are naturally and properly understood in political terms, as they have been by theorists from Mahan to our own times. Medieval and Renaissance sea power, however, was often private rather than public, and served commercial rather than political ends. Even the public, political objectives of naval warfare were not usually those about which naval theorists since Mahan have built their analyses. The concept of 'command of the sea' had been known in the classical world (the Greek is θαλασσωκρατος) and, consequently, it was known to educated medieval writers, but it was not often of practical relevance to the naval warfare of their time. Some medieval examples can be found of maritime warfare as it has been understood in the modern era: the wars of the Venetians and Genoese, fought for the control of the trade routes on which the belligerents depended for their prosperity, can be plausibly seen in quasi-Mahanian terms as a struggle for command of the sea.[9] To some extent the Baltic naval wars of the mid-sixteenth century could be fitted into the same mould.[10] This is unusual, however, anywhere in European naval warfare before the seventeenth century.

Most medieval naval warfare fell into one of two broad categories, which we may call public and private, or military and commercial. Public, military naval warfare was auxiliary to the operations of armies on land. The function of the ships was to transport the troops to the theatre of war, or to support their operations. This was the most important duty of galleys and other oared warships, which were essentially short-range instruments of amphibious warfare. Even when they did fight one another, they did so in a military fashion, commanded by soldiers, using military tactics. The prestige of the galley, which rose in the seventeenth century to be the supreme symbol of royal power even as it declined into insignificance as a practical warship, derived from its intimate association with armies, and consequently with princes.[11] Sailing ships did not have this connection or this status, but they too were frequently employed in this sort of warfare, both in the Mediterranean and in northern waters. This public, military, sea warfare, being an aspect of the warfare of armies and princes, was normally conducted at times of public, declared war between kingdoms.

Private or commercial naval warfare, on the other hand, was a normal aspect of the use of the sea at all times. The objective of the private ship-owner was business, but few if any medieval ship-owners could expect to make money without being willing to fight for it. Modern historians often present an implicitly dualist contrast between the peaceful trader and the aggressive pirate, but in

---

[9] John E. Dotson, 'Naval Strategy in the First Genoese–Venetian War, 1257–1270', *American Neptune*, 46 (1986), 84–90.
[10] Jan Glete, *Warfare at Sea, 1500–1650: Maritime Conflicts and the Transformation of Europe* (London, 2000), 133–44.
[11] Marc Vigié, 'Galères et "Sea-power" en France au XVIIe siècle', *Revue historique des armées*, 182 (1991), 45–56.

medieval reality the two were usually the same. In northern waters the sea was often seen as a debatable land lying beyond the frontiers of settled society, where no sovereign could impose his peace, and no court had jurisdiction. Though at various periods English and French kings claimed some jurisdiction over the sea or those who used it, the claim was difficult or impossible to make good.[12] Robbery under arms was a normal aspect of sea-borne trade. All merchant ships went armed, and were prepared to gain a good cargo by paying for it or not, as opportunity might offer. There were no non-combatants at sea. Even in periods of profound peace, ships of rival nations, or simply rival ports, frequently attacked one another. For English ships, it appears to have been almost a reflex action to attack all foreigners; in the case of the Cinque Ports, to attack other English ships as well.[13] The English were the most notorious pirates of northern Europe, but all ships, of all nations, had to be prepared to fight on occasion.

Insofar as any legal cover was necessary for this private naval warfare, it could be found in the doctrine of reprisals. In such attacks the crews of the victims were usually murdered, but if the shipmaster or ship-owner survived, it was open to him to seek legal redress in the courts of the nation or seaport from which his attackers came. Such a suit was usually a civil action for the recovery of losses, not a criminal prosecution for assault or murder. In English law piracy was not even recognised as a crime until 1536, and English courts intervened, if at all, only to moderate a settlement between disputants whom they regarded as being essentially on the same footing. It was rare in any country for courts to treat suits between foreigners and locals with impartiality. The aggrieved ship-owner who had failed to gain legal redress, however, like the merchant or traveller who had been robbed by bandits ashore, could appeal to his own sovereign to grant him a letter of reprisal under marcher law, a *lettre de merk* in French, which authorised him to seize goods up to the value of his losses from the fellow-countrymen or fellow-citizens of those who had robbed him. Reprisals under marcher law were by definition available only in time of peace; they assumed, however unrealistically, that the attack had been improper and that foreign courts were open to a suit for redress. Reprisals might be a diplomatic weapon in a time of tension between princes, but there was no reason in theory or practice why they could not coexist with peace and good international relations. Kings were not necessarily much interested in the private misfortunes of their trading subjects. Then as now, legal disputes between persons of different nationality did not oblige their governments to go to war on their behalf. Reprisals allowed a legal dispute to issue in private war, but this private war remained private, not public.[14]

---

[12] Rodger, *Safeguard of the Sea*, 78–9.
[13] N. A. M. Rodger, 'The Naval Service of the Cinque Ports', *English Historical Review*, 111 (1996), 636–51, at 646–7.
[14] D. A. Gardiner, 'The History of Belligerent Rights on the High Seas in the Fourteenth Century', *Law Quarterly Review*, 48 (1932), 521–46. René de Mas Latrie, 'Du droit de

In the Mediterranean world there existed from the sixteenth to the nineteenth centuries a different system of private naval war, the *corsa* of the North African Regencies. Often misrepresented by English-speaking historians as 'Barbary piracy', their naval warfare was by no means piratical either in its legal status or its structure. The three Regencies of Tunis, Tripoli and Algiers engaged in open, public war against some Christian powers, and observed treaties of peace with others, generally with a more scrupulous regard for their obligations than the Christian powers showed in return. It was necessary for them to maintain permanent war against at least some of the trading nations of the Mediterranean for political rather than economic reasons. The Turkish Janissary garrisons of these quasi-independent states, nominally subject to the Ottoman Empire, were the leading factor in their internal politics, accustomed to make and unmake (meaning murder) the local rulers with uncomfortable frequency. The *corsa* provided a harmless and profitable outlet for their energies, which kept them out of mischief at home. Thus the naval warfare of the Barbary States, though declared public war, was largely or entirely conducted by private interests. It was a permanent necessity generated by the internal political structure of the Regencies, not a temporary response to external threats or opportunities. Moreover it differed from other private naval warfare in that the principal profit came not from ships or goods but people. Slaving, in turn, required and depended on extensive trade between enemies, for only poor and friendless slaves were retained in the labour force. The best profits were made by selling slaves for ransom, or trading them for Muslims enslaved by the Christian counter-*corsa* practised by the Knights of Malta, the Knights of St Stephen and other Christian navies. This traffic was made possible by slave markets on both sides of the Mediterranean, linked by extensive commercial and diplomatic contacts. The *corsa* differed from the naval traditions of the northern Europeans, but it had a similar effect in generating a system of warfare that blended symbiotically with trade. Though native to the Mediterranean, it was extended to the eastern Atlantic and even the Channel in the late sixteenth century, mainly by the Algerines.[15]

The *corsa* of the Regencies should in turn be distinguished from the activities

---

marque ou droit de représailles au Moyen Âge', *Bibliothèque de l'École des chartes*, 27 (1866), 529–77, and 29 (1868), 294–347 and 612–35; Marie-Claire Chavarot, 'La Pratique des lettres de marque d'après les arrêts du Parlement (XIIIe–debut XVe siècle)', *Bibliothèque de l'École des chartes*, 149 (1981), 51–89; Pierre Chaplais, 'Règlement des conflits internationaux franco-anglais au XIVe siècle (1293–1377)', *Le Moyen Age*, 57 (1951), 259–302; Florence E. Dyer, 'Reprisals in the Sixteenth Century', *Mariner's Mirror*, 21 (1935), 187–97; *Documents Relating to Law and Custom of the Sea*. Navy Records Society 49 and 50, ed. R. G. Marsden (1915–16), I, 119–24.

[15] Sir Godfrey Fisher, *Barbary Legend: War, Trade and Piracy in North Africa 1415–1830* (Oxford, 1957); Peter Earle, *Corsairs of Malta and Barbary* (London, 1970); J. de Courcy Ireland, 'The Corsairs of North Africa', *Mariner's Mirror*, 62 (1976), 271–83; *El comerç alternatiu: corsarisme i contraban (ss. XV–XVIII)*, ed. Gonçal López Nadal (Palma de Mallorca, 1990).

of Salee and other Moroccan Atlantic ports. They were not subject to the Sultan, nor affected by the same internal political pressure, but for long periods under weak or non-existent political control by the Moroccan emperor, and heirs to a private war against Spain and Portugal in particular. The style and legal status of this warfare fell midway between the *corsa* of the Mediterranean and the traditional private war of northern waters, while the cruising range of the Saletines reached far into both seas.[16]

Private, commercial war was fought by individuals for financial profit, not by states for political objectives. Medieval and Renaissance princes might find themselves in either category. Often they made war for identifiably political objectives, usually the conquest of territory, and their accompanying naval operations, if any, fell into the public, military category. But in political theory a Renaissance prince was simply an exceptionally great nobleman who was expected to support his state from his own revenues. Like his subjects, he badly needed to make money, and like them, he might engage in private, commercial war. Even at times of open war between princes, private operations might take place alongside public ones. The Anglo-Spanish War of 1585–1603, which was never formally declared on either side, was waged from the point of view of English law as a campaign of reprisals, in which Queen Elizabeth participated as an aggrieved party like her subjects. Though her primary objective (survival) was unequivocally political, she had an urgent need to make money to finance the war.

The legal regime of reprisals has been easily and frequently confused with the quite different system of privateering, as developed in English law in the mid-seventeenth century.[17] A privateer was a privately owned warship licensed in time of open war to attack the shipping of the public enemy.[18] As the name implies, a privateer was the private exception to what had become the public rule: it was inherent in the concept of privateering that ships not owned by the state might not legitimately engage in warfare, even in wartime, without licence. Warfare had become an exclusive activity of state; a formal, public undertaking entered into by a prince for a limited period, and concluded with proper ceremony. Privateering belonged to an entirely different legal and strategic system that evolved during the seventeenth century. There could be no privateering in the Elizabethan age or earlier, because there was no private exception; private, commercial warfare was the normal form of warfare in the open sea. Unfortu-

---

[16] Roger Coindreau, *Les Corsaires de Salé* (Paris, 1948).

[17] But English law was slow in this respect. The Flemish or Dutch *kaperbrief*, for example, provided for privateering roughly in the modern sense from the late fifteenth century: Louis Sicking, *Zeemacht en Onmacht: Maritieme politiek in de Nederlanden 1488–1558* (Amsterdam, 1998), 214–21; C. G. Roelofsen, 'Grotius and the International Politics of the Seventeenth Century', in *Hugo Grotius and International Relations*, ed. H. Bull, B. Kingsbury and A. Roberts (Oxford, 1990), 95–131; L. H. J. Sicking, 'Recht aan zee. De afhandeling van prijszaken na het bestand van Bomy en de Vrede van Nice met Frankrijk (1537–1538)', *Stichting tot uitgaaf der bronnen van het Oud-Vaterlandse Recht: verslagen en mededelingen*, n.s. 10 (1999), 163–80. I am indebted to Dr Sicking for a copy of this article.

[18] David J. Starkey, *British Privateering Enterprise in the Eighteenth Century* (Exeter, 1990), 19–34.

nately the English jurists who devised the concept of privateering used the old term to name their new licences: they called them 'letters of marque'. It cannot be too strongly emphasised that the *'lettre de merk'* and the 'letter of marque' were entirely different things. However often we may speak or write of 'Elizabethan privateers', the term is strictly anachronistic; there were no privateers in the sixteenth century.

In this and other aspects, however, this was a period of transition, in which the naval traditions of the Middle Ages developed and combined to create new forms of warfare at sea. It was a period of rapid technical change, in which ideas and terminology were in a state of flux. Contemporaries reached into the past in search of words and ideas with which to make sense of their situation, with limited success. Later historians attempted, and sometimes still attempt, to force the sixteenth century into the framework so familiar from the eighteenth.

Moreover the problem was not simply one of rapid change over time, reflected in anachronistic words and concepts. Geography was changing as well as technology. As Spain and Portugal expanded from the Mediterranean to the 'Mediterranean Atlantic' and thence to the transatlantic world, they carried the language and ideas of the Mediterranean into a different geographical and political situation. There in due course they came into collision with French, English and Dutch seamen who themselves were venturing into a new geographical space, a new legal and political context, armed with attitudes and concepts derived from the naval warfare of late medieval northern Europe. At the same time the *corsa* of the North African Regencies, and the raids of Salee, extended from the Mediterranean to cover most of the Atlantic world, and in the early seventeenth century blended with the quite different private warfare of the English to create a unique, and for a while uniquely effective, hybrid form of naval warfare. Thus words and ideas borrowed from the past were mixed with words and ideas borrowed from other cultures, all subjected to extensive mistranslation by contemporaries, and extensive misconstruction by later historians.

In the sixteenth century, the Atlantic, the Mediterranean and northern Europe collided. The northerners brought the private, commercial style of war, combined with the new three-masted ship rig to give an instrument of much greater range and power than had been available to private owners before. The Mediterranean powers, above all Spain, brought the public, military tradition of naval warfare. They also attempted to apply the legal regime of the Mediterranean to the Atlantic. Where seafaring was seasonal and coastal, the passage of ships could be controlled and taxed in much the same way as the passage of merchants was controlled and taxed ashore. Coastal fortresses such as Monaco, Villafranca, Gibraltar, Piombino, Amalfi, Messina, Durazzo, Cerigo, Monemvasia, Rhodes and hundreds of others divided the sea into jurisdictions like the land.[19] Whereas the northern seas were effectively lawless, the southern seas were subject to local and national government.

---

[19] Fernand Braudel, *The Mediterranean and the Mediterranean World in the Age of Philip II*, 2 vols, trans. Siân Reynolds (London, 1972), I, 103–8.

This legal tradition was completely disconnected from the geographical and technical realities of the Atlantic. For a time Spaniards and Portuguese were the only deep-sea navigators in the world and their new empires were protected by distance, but by the 1540s French and Scottish ships were already crossing the Atlantic, followed a generation later by the English, and later the Dutch. There was no possible physical barrier that could prevent foreigners penetrating into the waters from which they were excluded by Spanish and Portuguese law. Spain did not simply reserve her colonial trade to her own shipping, as other colonial powers were to do; she pretended to forbid all foreign presence, even under pain of death. Moreover Spain's object was not to preserve a flourishing commerce in her own hands, as the Dutch and English were to do. The Spanish colonial system was not directed to promoting or preserving any sort of trade; it was designed solely to protect the flow of bullion. It served the private interests of the monarch, not the public interest of his people. Trade was permitted to use the convoys to reach the ports which they served, but almost nothing was done for the rest of the Spanish empire. Many Spanish colonial ports had in practice no legal means of exporting or importing anything. As the official convoy system declined, even the major ports ceased to have any legal trade. In 1707, the newly appointed Viceroy of Peru reported that it was more than ten years since his government (the whole of Spanish South America) had had any official trading contact with Spain.[20] This was an anti-colonial policy. The object was to preserve the Empire intact from the taint of foreign contact at any price. The Spanish government was even prepared to destroy and depopulate a colony (the northern part of Hispaniola in 1604) rather than see its people profit in any way from foreign contact.[21] The policy can perhaps best be understood in terms of the drive for *limpieza de sangre*, 'purity of blood', which marked Spain's internal policies in this era. The effect of the law was to criminalise all foreign activity or presence. Until 1670 Spain explicitly denied that any of her treaties with foreign powers had force west of the Azores or south of the Tropic of Capricorn. As a consequence there was literally 'no peace beyond the line', and no restraint on the activities of foreigners whom Spain had made outlaws.[22] By attempting to apply an inappropriate and unenforceable legal system to its overseas empire, the Spanish Crown contributed powerfully to justify and perpetuate a style of mingled war and trade in which violence, or the threat of violence, was always present. Thus, the medieval northern form of private, commercial warfare was artificially preserved long after it had disappeared from European waters. The raiders of the sixteenth century, and the buccaneers of the seventeenth, were not simply the offspring of Spanish colonial policy, but that policy acted to promote and prolong their activities, and to prevent them settling into

---

[20] Henry Kamen, *The War of Succession in Spain 1700–15* (London, 1969), 145.
[21] Andrews, *The Spanish Caribbean*, 208–10; K. R. Andrews, *Elizabethan Privateering: English Privateering during the Spanish War, 1585–1603* (Cambridge, 1964), 183–4.
[22] A. P. Thornton, *West-India Policy under the Restoration* (Oxford, 1956), 76–7, 87, 97–101 and 122–3.

peaceful channels.[23] In particular it gave the English, later British and Dutch, governments powerful and plausibly legitimate reasons for supporting violence, which they would otherwise have cooperated to suppress. This issue brought Britain and Spain to war as late as 1739, more than a century after the English government had turned against all other forms of piracy.

While Spain carried the public, military tradition of naval warfare from the medieval Mediterranean to the sixteenth-century Atlantic, the Barbary 'pirates' spread their tradition of private, commercial war. Both the Regencies and the Moroccan ports were affected in the late sixteenth century by northern European influence. Christian renegades who had 'turned Turk' helped the Muslim fleets to adopt sailing ships in place of galleys, greatly increasing their cruising range and putting both coasts of the North Atlantic at risk of slave raids virtually from the Equator to the Arctic. Next, some northern pirates, chiefly English, started to operate out of Muslim ports, with the agreement of the local authorities. This movement reached its apogee after the Anglo-Spanish peace of 1603, and the accession of James VI and I the same year, which turned adrift many ships and men, especially in the West Country, who had been employed in raiding the Spanish Empire, and gradually made English ports less comfortable bases for private war. For about fifteen years Moroccan ports, especially Mamora and Sallee, became the winter bases of English raiders who in summer worked from West Country or Irish ports, and who combined the attack on Spanish ports and shipping to which they had long been accustomed with the slave-raiding they learnt from the *corsa*.[24] The most famous of these pirates was the lexicographer Sir Henry Manwaring. A maker of dictionaries, but by no means a harmless drudge, Sir Henry was in his day the most feared man in the North Atlantic.[25]

Thus the naval warfare of northern Europe and the Atlantic in the sixteenth century was shaped by the collision and mingling of public and private naval warfare in both their northern and southern versions. This alone would have been sufficient to generate a great deal of novelty and confusion, but there were several other new factors affecting, and changing, the nature of naval war. First among these was the fracture of the Christian world, and the civil wars that followed in several European states. Religion, which had always been a factor in the naval warfare of the Mediterranean, now influenced war at sea in northern waters as well. In particular there was in practice, though not in theological principle, a powerful connection between Calvinism and private naval war. The French Atlantic and Channel ports, especially Dieppe and La Rochelle, were

---

[23] Andrews, *The Spanish Caribbean*, 74–80 and 208–22; R. H. Boulind, 'The Strength and Weakness of Spanish Control of the Caribbean, 1520–1650: The Case for the *Armada de Barlovento*' (Ph.D. dissertation, University of Cambridge, 1965), 61–5 and 405–10.

[24] C. M. Senior, *A Nation of Pirates: English Piracy in Its Heyday* (Newton Abbot, 1976); D. D. Hebb, *Piracy and the English Government, 1616–1642* (Aldershot, 1994); Christopher Lloyd, *English Corsairs on the Barbary Coast* (London, 1981).

[25] *The Life and Works of Sir Henry Mainwaring*. Navy Records Society 54 and 56, ed. G. E. Manwaring and W. G. Perrin (1920–2).

both Huguenot strongholds and the centres of a school of navigators, pilots and cartographers who were the first Christians outside Iberia to learn the skills necessary for oceanic naval warfare. Joined at an early stage by Scottish ships and navigators, these men expressed their religious sympathies and professional skills by mounting the first raids on the Spanish Empire. When the Wars of Religion broke out in France, the Protestant cause was heavily supported by the profits of private war conducted under the cover of letters of reprisal issued by Huguenot leaders like Condé and Coligny (as Admiral of France). By the 1560s the English, especially the West Countrymen, were keen participants in this war, sailing under French letters of reprisal, and learning the professional skills of their new allies.[26] A generation later the Dutch in turn attached themselves to the Calvinist International, sailing out of English ports under letters of reprisal issued by the Prince of Orange, and learning from the English the techniques of navigation which they themselves had but lately acquired. The break-up of kingdoms and empires multiplied the number of leaders willing, indeed desperate, to finance their war-effort and assure their survival by issuing letters of reprisal. The legal mechanism itself was easily flexible enough to accommodate itself to civil war and rebellion, while religious hatred endowed it with renewed moral legitimacy. The experiment of 'general reprisals' under proclamation, which permitted any ship to make any prizes of a named enemy without any restriction or supervision, was tried by the English three times, in 1544, 1557 and 1563,[27] but it proved unsatisfactory: indiscriminate, uncontrollable, and barely distinguishable from a public declaration of war, it carried heavy diplomatic and commercial penalties. The ambiguity, flexibility and profitability of private war much better suited the situation of the English, Huguenots and Dutch.

Overlaying all these changes in the motives and contexts of naval warfare were developments in ships and weapons. The forms of naval warfare, both in northern waters and in the Mediterranean, had remained more or less stable for several centuries, and were not essentially changed by the introduction of 'man-killing' guns in the fourteenth century. So long as all fighting was hand to hand, the size of sailing ships gave them an overwhelming advantage over galleys, with their exposed crews and low freeboard. As a result the two types did not often face one another in action, but fulfilled distinct roles in different forms of naval warfare. The galley was the instrument of coastal operations, raids and landings. Wherever shallow draught was essential and short range no obstacle, galleys were the natural choice. For long passages in the open sea, for carrying men and goods in quantity, and for fighting other ships, sailing ships, and above all the great carracks developed in the fifteenth century, were essential. When a ship fought at sea, the first necessity was to gain the weather gage,

---

[26] Martine Acerra and Guy Martinière, eds, *Coligny, les protestants et la mer* (Paris, 1997); N. A. M. Rodger, 'The Myth of Seapower in English Politics, 1568–1815' (forthcoming); Brian Dietz, 'The Huguenot and English Corsairs during the Third Civil War in France, 1568 to 1570', *Proceedings of the Huguenot Society*, 19 (1952–58), 278–94.
[27] Marsden, *Law and Custom of the Sea*, I, 155–8, 162–5 and 174.

from which position she bore up to attack. All available missile weapons, including guns, were fired as the two ships closed, and as they grappled together the issue was settled by hand-to-hand fighting.[28]

I have argued elsewhere that the adoption of the heavy gun by galleys about the beginning of the sixteenth century caused a crisis in naval warfare. By allowing galleys to engage and even sink ships outside small-arms range, it rendered them obsolete, without providing any effective alternative. The challenge for ship designers was now to devise an effective counter to the galley. The problem was much more acute in northern waters, for the limited range and sea-keeping capacity of the galley were much more serious disadvantages in these open seas. Moreover the adoption of the heavy gun pushed galleys to adopt the *a scaloccio* oaring system, which further reduced their speed and range, while increasing the demand for oarsmen which the northern powers (with no tradition of the *corsa* and no slave markets) found it impossible to meet.[29] Those who had very lately developed the three-masted ship rig, who had experience of the novel combination of power and manoeuvrability which it provided, were not prepared to abandon it in favour of oars. Their requirement was to combine two apparently incompatible novelties: the ahead-firing heavy gun which gave the galley its uncontestable military superiority, and the new ship rig whose speed and power made ocean passages possible. They were not looking for just any method of mounting heavy guns in a sailing ship, but one in particular. By the early years of the sixteenth century if not before, ships already carried stern-firing heavy guns in their gunrooms, and were beginning to mount some lighter pieces below decks on the broadside. But there was no method of attacking the enemy while sailing astern or sideways. Moreover contemporaries wanted to sink ships, as galleys could, by firing at the waterline, and at the very short fighting ranges of the period this required the gun itself to be mounted low.[30]

I believe that the solution to this problem was the development, apparently between the 1530s and 1550s, of the galleon. The essence of the galleon seems to have been the bow and lines of a galley, grafted onto the stern and hull structure of a ship, giving the characteristic crescent shape of the true galleon. This preserved and indeed improved the speed and endurance of the ship rig, while mounting a heavy armament of ahead-firing guns. The galleon could beat the galley at her own game, without sacrificing the capacity to make long sea passages at high speed. How and where the galleon first emerged is as yet obscure. It may have been in England, Scotland, Portugal, Denmark, Venice, Genoa or elsewhere. What is reasonably clear is that the new type was rapidly

---

[28] N. A. M. Rodger, 'The Development of Broadside Gunnery, 1450–1650', *Mariner's Mirror*, 82 (1996), 301–24, at 302.
[29] Francisco-Felipe Olesa Muñido, *La galera en la navegación y el combate*, 2 vols (Madrid, 1971). Mauro Bondioli, René Burlet and André Zysberg, 'Oar Mechanics and Oar Power in Medieval and Later Galleys', in *The Age of the Galley: Mediterranean Oared Vessels since Pre-Classical Times*, ed. John Morrison (London, 1995), 172–205.
[30] Rodger, 'Broadside Gunnery', 303.

adopted by the Huguenots and the English, and formed a key element in their style of private, commercial warfare. These fast warships with their heavy armament, fine lines but limited stowage were designed to overwhelm the defences of individual merchantmen, convoys, and coastal forts, while avoiding close action with powerful forces. They suited those who penetrated the Spanish Empire to conduct raids or illegal trade, not those who sustained distant colonies and oceanic commerce themselves. They were better adapted to disrupting command of the sea than to gaining or keeping it. Though they were in structural terms the first true sailing warships and the ancestors of the eighteenth-century ship of the line, in function they were the last and most effective exponents of medieval private, commercial war.[31]

For these and other reasons the type, though successful, was also transitional. Though Huguenot sea power disappeared, the English and Dutch prospered by naval war against Spain. Soon they themselves were possessors, with rich home and colonial trades to conduct and protect, with waters of their own from which they aspired to exclude foreign traders. First the Dutch and then the English ceased to sponsor and began to suppress the private warfare of their subjects. In England the old style of warfare was briefly revived during the Civil Wars, partly because the Protestant radicals who created the English Republic warmly embraced the ideology of their Elizabethan predecessors. By the 1660s, however, the sixteenth-century style of naval warfare, the tactics and ship designs associated with it, were extinct everywhere except in the Caribbean. Only the word 'galleon' survived to be used with ever-decreasing precision down to our own day.

This has been the fate the naval warfare of the period as a whole; that is, to be dressed in clothes of the wrong period. Treating peace and war as mutually exclusive and coterminous categories, historians have described naval warfare in 'peacetime' as piracy, and private men-of-war in 'wartime' as 'privateers'. In reality war and peace were blended in various ways which have no modern parallels, and for which modern languages provide an inadequate vocabulary. There was, for example, and to an extent there still is a meaningless controversy as to whether Sir Francis Drake was or was not a 'pirate'.[32] This arose from the discomfort of Victorian popular writers like Charles Kingsley and Sir Henry Newbolt at the suggestion that their model of manly Christian heroism might have been a common criminal. It was an entirely bogus controversy, setting a figure who never existed against anachronistic legal and moral criteria, and it rested on mistranslation, the assumption that Drake's Spanish contemporaries had accused him of being a pirate, whereas they usually used the word *corsario*, not *pirata*. *Corsario* itself, of course, is a borrowing from another context, but it

---

[31] Ibid., 305–6; and Rodger, 'Guns and Sails in the First Phase of English Colonization, 1500–1650', in *The Oxford History of the British Empire, Volume I: The Origins of Empire*, ed. Nicholas Canny (Oxford, 1998), 79–98, at 82–8 and 96–87.
[32] It has been revived by Drake's latest biographer: Harry Kelsey, *Sir Francis Drake: The Queen's Pirate* (New Haven, 1998).

is an intelligent adaptation of a word that does convey much of the style of warfare Drake undertook. Unfortunately the English word 'corsair' is now so encrusted with spurious Byronic romanticism that it is probably irrecoverable for any serious purpose. Moreover English historians have long been accustomed to echo the error of the Frenchmen who first applied the phrase *guerre de course* to the very different legal and strategic situation of seventeenth and eighteenth-century privateering – and thus made it harder to describe the *corsa* itself with any clarity.

Thus the limitations of language continue to baffle our attempts to understand the sixteenth century at sea, and it continues to be treated as a sort of historical junk-room from which historians may borrow all sorts of scraps to construct ambitious intellectual edifices. It has long been customary to see the period through eighteenth-century spectacles. Indeed it is often analysed in terms of categories which themselves are anachronistic constructs developed in the late nineteenth century in order to understand the eighteenth. In recent years attempts have been made to discover the line of battle in the sixteenth century and even earlier, generally by reading any use of the word 'line' (not even 'line ahead') to mean 'line of battle', in one case with the help of terminology apparently borrowed from fighter-aircraft tactics.[33] This ruthless perversion of language and confusion of ideas makes it impossible to speak or write clearly about a period of rapid change to which many of our natural modern assumptions are inapplicable. No prince or state then possessed or claimed any monopoly on the use of force, which remained a normal means of settling all sorts of private as well as public disputes. The distinction between sailing warships and merchantmen was only beginning to emerge, because, under sail at least, war and trade were still usually combined. None of these circumstances can easily be accommodated to our preconceptions or our terminology. We shall never understand this period until we cease to stage it in modern dress.

---

[33] William Maltby, 'Politics, Professionalism, and the Evolution of Sailing-Ship Tactics, 1650–1714', in John A. Lynn, ed., *Tools of War: Instruments, Ideas and Institutions of Warfare, 1445–1871* (Urbana, Illinois, 1990), 53–73; Rodger, 'Broadside Gunnery', 301–2.

CONCLUSION

TOWARD A HISTORY OF MEDIEVAL SEA POWER

Richard W. Unger

THE papers in this volume address again and again the problem of writing a history of navies, of naval power, of violence at sea in medieval Europe. The idea that there should be such a history is not an old one. In the Middle Ages very few people took up the issue. Typically historians in the last two centuries have ignored the Middle Ages in histories of sea power. While recently there is more recognition of the years between the fall of the Roman Empire and the seventeenth century in works on naval history the period still receives cursory treatment. The handbook for courses in naval history by Clark Reynolds is an excellent example of both the recognition of the Middle Ages as a time when naval power could be an issue and the relative insignificance of the topic compared to the years from the seventeenth century on.[1] Some historians of the Middle Ages have long argued for an important role for the sea in the cultural and economic changes of the period.[2] Such studies have had little impact on the discussion of naval history and also limited effect on the general discussion of the history of medieval Europe.

The goal of this volume is not to carry out the all too normal task of historians of filling in a gap left by earlier research and writing. Presumably, though, it does serve to illustrate many of the facets of what is a varied and complex evolution that was intimately related to many other developments in medieval and Renaissance Europe. The goal of the volume is even more ambitious. The intention is to offer not just observations but also to create a theory of medieval naval power which would explain why what happened did in fact happen. The theoretical discussion of naval warfare is still struggling with the modern period but it has proved to be totally inadequate to date in dealing with the period before 1650. It has long been obvious that the critical parameters, the

---

[1] Clark G. Reynolds, *Navies in History* (Annapolis, 1998); George Modelski and William R. Thompson, *Seapower in Global Politics, 1494–1993* (London, 1988); James Cable, *The Political Influence of Naval Force in History* (London, 1998).
[2] The most famous case is Henri Pirenne, *Mohammed and Charlemagne* (New York, 1937). More recently Archibald R. Lewis, *Naval Power and Trade in the Mediterranean A.D. 500–1100* (Princeton, 1951), and Archibald R. Lewis, *The Northern Seas, Shipping and Commerce in Northern Europe A.D. 300–1100* (Princeton, 1958). See also Archibald R. Lewis and Timothy J. Runyan, *European Naval and Maritime History, 300–1500* (Bloomington, 1985).

central issues in the discussion identified by modern historians simply do not apply in anything other than a very haphazard way to the Middle Ages. That theoretical gap was the one this volume set out to fill. By no means is the task completed but perhaps in the varied studies covering naval action from the Byzantine Empire and its confrontations with Muslim and Scandinavian naval forces to the battles for Baltic supremacy among Lübeck, Denmark-Norway and Sweden the volume does offer some progress toward the goal of identifying the critical features in the foundation of European sea power.

Many of the authors indicate why the Middle Ages, and for that matter the Renaissance, has not received the same consideration as other periods in naval and maritime history. The authors, in exploring different times and places, allow the chronological developments in navies to unfold. They also allow the significant geographical differences within Europe to unfold. It comes as no surprise that there was a great difference in what happened in the evolution of violence at sea between southern and northern European waters and then Atlantic waters. The basin of the Mediterranean Sea and the littoral of the North and Baltic Seas saw almost no maritime contact in the early Middle Ages. Only in the thirteenth century did the two regions begin to see ships and people moving back and forth. The examples are few but they became increasingly common from the thirteenth century on.[3] For the Middle Ages and the Renaissance the South was also more 'advanced' than northern Europe, that is in economic terms but also in many facets of public life. The character and nature of trade was different in the two large regions of Europe in terms of geography, value, volume and was also different over time as evolution took different paths. Technology and, critical for naval history, the technology of shipbuilding and ship design was another vector which distinguished the two large regions of maritime Europe through much of the period, the distinction changing dramatically and at varying rates over time.

Political differences among jurisdictions were critical for the existence and character of navies. Navies are above all political institutions. It is necessary to distinguish between naval force, the use of violence at sea, and naval power, something sought and practised by political units to achieve political goals. Navies cannot exist without some political institutions, and not just to sanction them but to support them, legitimise them and integrate them into policy creation and execution. Politics then is another force identified by the authors which in the Middle Ages and the Renaissance shaped navies and the use of

---

[3] For example, it appears that the first Catalans were not living in the Low Countries until the end of the thirteenth century. But in the fourteenth and fifteenth centuries direct trade between Barcelona and Flanders became more frequent and more important to the economies of both regions. Antonio de Capmany y de Monpalau, *Memorias históricas sobre la marina, commercio y artes de la antiqua ciudad de Barcelona*, ed. E. Giralt y Reventós and C. Batlle y Gallart (Barcelona, 1961), 317–23, 760. Archibald R. Lewis, 'Northern European Sea Power and the Straits of Gibraltar, 1031–1350 A.D.', in William C. Jordan *et al.*, eds, *Order and Innovation in the Middle Ages: Essays in Honor of Joseph R. Strayer* (Princeton, 1976), 139–64.

violence at sea. Along with politics came ideas about naval force which influenced its character. Ideas about navies and violence on the water is probably the least discussed aspect of navies but potentially one of the most productive. The need to dominate the sea became a common feature of European government policy in the eighteenth and nineteenth centuries. The language policy makers used was classical and so it is not surprising that the first discussion of power at sea and over the sea appears in the Renaissance. But that language presumably had some reflection in reality or, at the very least, the language used by policy makers influenced the reality of naval policy. Either way or both ways the conception and the form in which the idea was articulated made a difference to the evolution of European naval forces.

There is a great deal, factual and theoretical, packed by the authors into the papers in this volume. Their variety in approach as well as in topics make it impossible to summarise all their findings or even to place all the information into one grand structure. It is feasible, though, to suggest a broad outline of what happened in the light of what the various contributors describe. Equally it is feasible to identify features of the histories they report which proved to be most critical to the emergence of modern navies and have given form to the treatment of the Middle Ages in general works on naval history.

Periodisation, the delineation of different blocks of times which have common features and the identification of points in time when dramatic changes occurred, is almost invariably a boring topic, one of those tasks where value is not to be found in the process of getting the result but in the result. Still the separation of the past into periods is necessary in order to have a framework for the discussion of any topic. That is even more true for the study of the history of medieval sea power since it has, at least until now, lacked an organising principle. Certainly for a long time the end point has been clear. In the mid-seventeenth century there emerged something like modern navies deployed to rule the waves. The mid-seventeenth century is precisely the point at which Alfred Thayer Mahan chose to start his own examination of the history of sea power. By then there were national navies. There is little question that something new existed by the second half of the seventeenth century, that there had been a break with the past, but the identification of that break makes even more pressing the need to ask where that break came from and how the world of sea power was different after around 1650 from the world before that date.

If the end point is known then where to start the study of medieval sea power is much more difficult to decide. There are signs that in the tenth century there was a significant change or at least signs of change in how Europeans acted on the sea. It was in the tenth century that an expansion of trade had already begun from a few ports on the Italian peninsula, exploiting connections with Muslim ports to the south and east. By the tenth century Scandinavian sailors were making long-distance voyages across the North Atlantic and going south, even on one or two occasions penetrating the Mediterranean. Those men, some of whom came to be called Vikings, did have trouble differentiating between peace and war, between trading and raiding. They took advantage of circumstances and sought gain in the most practical way. There are indications, however, that certain lines were being drawn, that sailors were expected to indicate in advance if they were interested in peaceful exchange or simple theft. One continuing feature which would dominate travel on the sea in the Middle Ages and the Renaissance was precisely that inability to distinguish between peace and war and, along with that confusion, sustained efforts to establish a legal basis for whatever distinction there was. In the tenth century naval action was amphibious and more generally was always tied to action on land. Byzantine naval forces, the best organised and supported of early medieval Europe, still invariably had as their purpose control of objectives on land rather than trying to control maritime space. The amphibious nature of naval action would prove a persistent feature of the entire period from the tenth well into the seventeenth century. From Scandinavia to the eastern Mediterranean actions in the high Middle Ages would almost invariably have been ones where armed ships were used in conjunction with land force, to support them and to supply them.

Europe, as it went through a long process of defining itself, developed its first frontiers, and they were on the water. The western Mediterranean became the contested boundary for Latin Christendom and it was along that border that Europeans began to expand. They pushed, by force, their frontier outward by attacks on Muslims. The Crusades starting at the end of the eleventh century were the culmination on a grand scale of the long-term development of a frontier and then the manipulation of that frontier through violence but also through commerce and cultural exchange.[4] The expansion of Europe which began in the eleventh century began on the sea. That would be the case as much or more in the Renaissance when the expansion went on throughout the globe and the frontier became the shores of all the lands in the world.

In the eleventh century there were as yet no navies nor were there ideas expressed of keeping the seas. Still there had been some significant movement in practice beyond what had existed in the early Middle Ages and indeed what had existed since the last century of effective rule by the Roman Empire in the West. The one place that there were some residual features of Roman naval practice was in the surviving portion of the Empire in the Greek East. The Byzantine navy was the exception to the complete breakdown of naval forces in the early Middle Ages. The long-term struggle against Muslim forces and Muslim states on land and sea had forced on the Byzantines the maintenance of standing fleets and all the apparatus of administration and finding funding which that implied. By no means was Byzantine policy consistent. Naval forces waxed and waned in favour and importance in the Empire. They were, as with all other maritime forces of the day, designed to support land forces. They also offered an example of how to organise navies for Western Europe and especially for Italian port

---

[4] On the frontier in the history of medieval Europe see Robert Bartlett, *The Making of Europe: Conquest, Colonization, and Cultural Change, 950–1350* (London, 1993). See also Robert I. Burns, 'Significance of the Frontier in the Middle Ages', in Robert Bartlett and Angus MacKay, eds, *Medieval Frontier Societies* (Oxford, 1989), 307–30.

towns. They became a model for the use and administration of force at sea. In the hands of those Italian towns the shape and form of naval forces changed dramatically and that set the stage for the next phase in the development of European navies starting in the thirteenth century.

While it was in those Italian towns that the most obvious changes in naval forces took place there were new forms and practices in northern Europe as well, so the years from around 1200 to around 1300 deserve recognition as a time of significant change in the history of navies. It was the merchant republics like Pisa, Genoa and especially Venice which established more enduring methods of visiting violence at sea and of doing so as part of a coherent if not always consistent policy. They also put in place ways of regulating, controlling and taxing trade so that commerce would be part of those same policies. The towns established bases at home but also, through alliance or possession, bases at various points around the Mediterranean. The governments of the towns supported directly and indirectly fleets of galleys which were to fight protracted wars in order to control shipping. Naval forces fought battles and wars over control of strategic points, sites that had to be controlled in order to have command over trade routes.[5] Those were places which fit well the criteria laid down by Mahan for such critical places. But many of the major narrows of the Mediterranean and the other seas of the basin were wide so the policy of those towns could at best only be partially successful. Improvements in navigation toward the end of the thirteenth century allowing for a longer sailing season and use of more routes also mitigated the advantages of being in command of specific sites. Control of strategic harbours could, however, be highly effective since the warships of the day, galleys, needed harbours for refuge in bad weather and sites for resupply. By the fourteenth century controlling trade to starve out opponents or at the least to strangle their sources of funding for naval forces was part of both strategic and tactical thinking in places like Genoa and Venice. The perception expressed some centuries later by Mahan that 'Money, credit, is the life of war; lessen it, and vigor flags; destroy it and resistance dies',[6] was one already appreciated by the late thirteenth century. In the North there was an interest in having naval bases as well. The kings of Denmark had already started that practice in the twelfth century at least and the king of France set up a base at Rouen in 1294 in clear imitation of Italian precedent. There were differences between the two regions. In northern European waters the wars were more ones of supply, that is to maintain fleets so that they could transport and maintain troops on land. In southern waters concern was as much or more with commerce and strategic points.

In both parts of Europe gradually structures emerged to deal with the chronic

---

[5] See for example John Dotson, 'Naval Strategy in the First Genoese–Venetian War, 1257–1270', *The American Neptune*, 46 (1986), 85–6.
[6] Alfred T. Mahan, 'Sea Power and Its Relation to the War of 1812', in Allan Westcott, ed., *Mahan on Naval Warfare, Selections from the Writings of Read Admiral Alfred T Mahan* (Boston, 1942), 92.

problem of what to do in peacetime when naval forces quite naturally contracted but still had to be kept at some level of readiness for the next inevitable conflict. In the North royal governments shifted fighting ships back and forth from naval to commercial use. In the South governments established permanent shipyards with continuing personnel and storage for ships, equipment and spare parts. The Arsenal in Venice, started as early as 1104 but subject to massive expansion over subsequent centuries, was followed by similar institutions in Barcelona and later in Tortosa, Valencia and other sites.[7] In both parts of Europe governments used entrepreneurs, private ship-owners, to supply warships. The practice was more transparent and also on a larger scale in the South. Private individuals were willing to raise naval forces, always for a fee of course. Such practices were possible because of the rising volume of long-distance trade by sea. The naval power of a town or king or duke came to depend on the shipping in the jurisdiction, on the maritime potential and the access the government had to that potential. Private shippers owned the vessels and they put those ships at the disposal of the state. The private owners took on the risk and sunk costs of building ships and keeping them at sea in exchange for payments from governments for use of the ships in wartime as well as for the potential of gaining privileges and political influence in their towns or kingdoms. Entrepreneurial warfare would prove to be a common feature of naval force at sea in Europe from the thirteenth down well into the seventeenth century. It would even be true outside Europe, Spain for example leasing armed merchantmen for protecting trade to the New World as late as the 1570s.

In the North as well as the South governments and individuals used reprisal virtually all of the time against enemies, real, imagined, past, potential. Allowing reprisal was a way for governments to diffuse any opposition that might develop at home. Promoting reprisal was a way for governments to carry out belligerent acts without expenditure and without suffering through some general conflict. Reprisals were a way to make enemies, present or future, at the least uncomfortable. The fact that all governments allowed reprisal as a normal form of redress for any earlier insult meant that there was invariably reason to continue with the practice. There was always an aggrieved party. By the late thirteenth century feudal monarchs in northern Europe and Iberia, acting with the powers of an emperor in their own lands, made claims of rights to violence everywhere and that included at sea.[8] Solidifying their power they tried to regulate maritime trade and to control violence along their coasts. That meant reprisal and indeed all use of force at sea became more and more frequently something done with the approval and support of the government.

There are, then, broadly three periods in the history of medieval sea power.

---

[7] Frederic C. Lane, *Venice, a Maritime Republic* (Baltimore, 1973), 14, 163–4. Gervasio de Artiñano y de Galdàcano, *La arquitectura naval Española (en Madera)* (Madrid, 1920), 18. Antonio de Capmany y de Monpalau, *Memorias históricas*, I, 45–50.
[8] See Fredric L. Cheyette, 'The Sovereign and the Pirates, 1332', *Speculum*, 45 (1970), 40–68.

The first, from the late tenth into the thirteenth century, was dominated by the use of militias and by the independent action of locally important figures and individual traders and ship-owners. The term feudal is used inaccurately and indiscriminately but warfare at sea in the period had some similarities to its organisation on land, an organisation that is often typified as feudal. The second period, from the thirteenth through to the mid-seventeenth century, was dominated by growing government interest in control of specific sites and control of violence at sea along with the use of privately owned ships for acts of war. It was a golden age for entrepreneurial navies. There was a critical era of transformation in the Renaissance as the second period ended. That explains the concentration of historians on the sixteenth century in discussions of naval power. It was a period of great success for Europeans at sea around the world. It was also a period when something like modern navies began to take shape. There were in the sixteenth century signs of naval warfare as it would be for many years after. It was in the Baltic in the late sixteenth century that state-owned navies with government employees fought each other over domination of the sea.

It was not only practice at sea and organisation of naval forces on land that changed in the late Renaissance. At the same time the language of government changed. The passing comment in the late fourteenth century about the kings of England being *roys des mer* is seen to be anachronistic, something of the moment with no effect on policy and not reflecting the goals or understanding of the king or government of the day. As to monarchs in England before the sixteenth century, 'There is no sign in the policy of the early kings of any perception of the value of a navy as a militant instrument like an army, or any sense of the importance of a real continuity in its maintenance and use'.[9] A contemporary Catalan chronicler did also speak about his king needing to rule the sea.[10] Not long after that in the 1430s, an English government bureaucrat wrote a long poem about the need to defend the island kingdom on the seas. In the *Libelle of Engliyshe Polycye* the author used the phrase 'We be maysters of the narowe see', meaning the Channel. The words were a reflection of recent success in the Hundred Years War, success which proved ephemeral. It was also not a novel claim but rather another honorific and one claimed not incidentally by the king of France as well.[11] Thinking about navies and lobbying governments to establish navies was part a long process, one already begun by the early fifteenth century. The discussion in those years did not go far.

It was in the mid-sixteenth century that a senior official in the Low Countries recommended that his ruler, Charles V, gain domination of the sea as the proper

---

[9] Michael Oppenheim, *A History of the Administration of the Royal Navy* (London, 1896), 6.
[10] Felipe Fernnández-Armesto, 'Naval Warfare after the Viking Age c.1100–1500', in Maurice Keen, ed., *Medieval Warfare, A History* (Oxford, 1999), 242–3.
[11] *The Libelle of Englyshe Polycye: A Poem on the Use of Sea-Power, 1436*, ed. Sir George Warner (Oxford, 1926); Michael Oppenheim, *A History of the Administration of the Royal Navy* (London, 1896), 6.

goal of government policy on trade, shipping and commerce. The author, Cornelis de Schepper, was asked to draft a statement about what the government should do in the face of a threatened French invasion, that in February 1552. His memorandum described what would be the strategic thinking about naval activity in the Low Countries for four hundred years. He urged the maintenance of warships to serve for convoy duty but also that they should be the agents to make Emperor Charles V 'master of the sea'.[12] De Schepper was a humanist with the advantage of a classical education and so a knowledge of and facility with language to express the novel concept. He was also an old soldier who perhaps brought ideas of territorial domination from land warfare to bear on matters to do with the sea. His thoughts and his expression of them were also very much the product of new possibilities created in the sixteenth century, of changing forms of government. His ideas about maritime strategy were closely linked with ideas about the sovereign's honour, status, place and position in the world. The government of Charles V like many before his thought in those terms. Though the representatives of the emperor in Brussels may not have believed in the necessity of holding the sea a certain notion of sea power did come to play a role in their strategic thinking. Two significant changes occurred to make it possible for de Schepper to write the way he did. One was the classical revival typical of the Renaissance, that is a return to the language of Greece and Rome. The other was a change in the character of governments, that is the emergence of what have been called the new monarchies. In Scandinavia in the five decades after de Schepper wrote ambitious rulers used fleets as instruments of state-building. The kings set up something novel – permanent navies – which they controlled in order to protect their own kingdoms and also in order to maintain order and their own power at home. While it may not have been possible in the late sixteenth century for one king or emperor or state to dominate the sea still there existed the signs of thinking and talking about doing just that.

There was not just talk about dominion over the oceans of the world. The sixteenth century also gave graphic representation of that dominion. European expansion gave birth in the sixteenth century to schools of cartography which produced elaborate and luxuriously decorated maps of the world, maps as works of art and not for practical use. The maps and charts were weighted with political intent. A Portuguese school of cartography was not surprisingly the first to embark on the path of producing such showpieces, works to show the successful voyages of discovery and so the accomplishments of the kingdom of Portugal. Colonialism and the domination of other parts of the world started for Europeans with domination of the sea and the maps show precisely that ability of people to do what they liked. Cartographers decorated their maps with ships at sea.[13] The vessels do more than fill empty space. They depict the technological

[12] J. C. M. Warnsinck, 'De memorie van Cornelis de Schepper van den 12-den Februari 1552 over de verdediging van Holland, Zeeland en Vlaanderen, in den oorlog tegen Frankrijk', in *Historische opstellen aangeboden aan J. Huizinga* (Haarlem, 1948), 249, 265–8.
[13] For example Huntington Library, Medieval and Renaissance Manuscripts, HM 29, 45.

advances of the types of vessels that Europeans used to trade around the globe. Caravels for example turn up thirty-two times on Portuguese charts and maps from 1500 to 1621.[14] In one case the artist shows the same ship making a voyage to Lisbon from India in different postures as it takes advantage of the prevailing winds.[15] Such illustrations serve as invaluable evidence for the history of ship design. The purpose of the cartographers and their patrons was different, however. They saw those ships as signs of the domination of the sea.

The emergence of navies and the strategic use of naval power along with the novel understanding of domination of the sea were an integral part of the economic and political development of medieval and Renaissance Europe. That is certainly no surprise but medieval sea power changed in character and conception and took the form it did because of specific influences in medieval and Renaissance Europe. The development of naval force relied heavily on the evolution of trade and of technology. That too is no surprise in broad general terms but the changes in commerce and technology in their detail gave precise form to sea power. Navies without states were certainly impossible but medieval Europeans demonstrated that states without navies were possible. A number of Italian port towns, some prominent centres of maritime trade, hardly had a standing navy. Genoa is probably the best example. In the fourteenth and fifteenth centuries Genoa had many features of other Renaissance states but relied on non-government sources for most of the vessels deployed in naval conflicts. Certainly the Genoese knew that the fleet was an important element of their power and prosperity. The idea of having a standing navy for defence and action on the high seas was floated in the first decade of the fifteenth century but nothing came of the proposal. It would not be until 1559 that Genoa took steps to establish some permanent form of naval administration to organise a state fleet. Venice with state-owned ships, with space leased to shippers in peace time, and its own government shipyard had something similar to a modern or rather early modern navy. But a pattern like that at Genoa with a combination of state and privately financed warships was more common in both southern and northern Europe before the seventeenth century.

The reason for the choices states made was simple. Navies were very expensive. The ship was the largest unit of investment apart from land in premodern Europe. But in addition to the expensive ships there were crews, equipment and all the supplies that were needed to keep the men and ships at sea and battle ready. States needed extensive financial resources to support any naval forces, even those they did not own and only hired for the duration of open warfare.

More completely, Armando Cortesão and Avelino Teixeira da Mota, *Portugaliae Monumenta Carthographica* (Lisbon, 1960), I, plates 17–19, 59–68, 75–8.
[14] Henrique Quirino da Fonseca, *A caravela portuguesa e a prioridade téchnica das navegaçoes henriquinas*, 2nd edn with commentary by Joao da Gama Pimental Barata (Lisbon, 1973), II, 13–19.
[15] Armando Cortesão and Avelino Teixeira da Mota, *Portugaliae Monumenta Carthographica* (Lisbon, 1960), I, plate 40.

Renaissance princes starting in Italy and then throughout Europe devoted themselves to finding money. Governments were typified by an acquisitive fiscalism, seeking any and all sources of income and exploiting in any way they could developing international financial structures to raise masses of funds. There were many examples and they only increased over time. Some predated the Renaissance and many were connected to expanding maritime potential. For example, King Ferdinand of Portugal in the fourteenth century gave subsidies for the construction of bigger ships and offered tax relief for acquisition of shipbuilding materials so that he could increase his income from duties on goods entering his kingdom in Portuguese bottoms. Contemporaries recognised both the importance and the fiscal goal at the centre of the entire scheme.[16] The reliance on deficit financing, with the hope that various taxes would somehow eventually generate the income to pay off debts, did not always work, as the history of Spanish naval efforts in the sixteenth century showed. The expenses incurred to pursue an aggressive foreign policy proved too much for the government and bankruptcies became an almost regular occurrence. Navies as institutions with even temporary existence depended entirely on the ability of governments to raise the necessary and sizeable funds. Prosperous Italian towns of the thirteenth century with access to much more funding than their predecessors or other contemporary jurisdictions still had trouble in getting their fleets fitted out and deployed at sea year after year. The naval wars they fought often ended not in victory for one side or the other but in fiscal exhaustion.

In order to generate the income to pay for a fleet, governments had to have a stream of trade to tax. Income from trade was a necessary precursor for the creation of naval forces, something implied by Mahan's own analysis of naval strategy. It is highly doubtful that an economy based on agriculture alone could have supplied the money needed to support naval forces and certainly not from the thirteenth century on. What is more, without sea-borne trade to protect and promote there was little point in public authorities supporting naval forces. The interest in developing naval forces of whatever type and in using force at sea was a product of the growth in sea-borne trade of the years after the tenth century. The influence of that expansion in trade became even greater after the thirteenth century as the total value of commerce increased and, with the growth in exchange of bulk goods especially in northern Europe, the total volume of trade rose sharply. The greater interest in having naval forces was generated in part because trade created growth in income for individuals and, through customs duties and taxes, growth in income for governments. It was in part because trade created a growth in piracy, in theft at sea, and so generated a need for protection for shipping in some form. It was in part because trade in many political jurisdictions created a powerful political faction which wanted and demanded protection for their trade. It was in part because trade created the raw materials, the personnel and vessels, needed for deploying naval forces. The

[16] Edgar Prestage, *The Chronicles of Fernão Lopes and Gomes Eannes de Zurara with Translated Extracts and Seven Illustrations* (Watford, 1928), 23–9.

presence of those necessary components of naval power was something surveyed and recorded by, for example, the English Crown in the late sixteenth century in order to know exactly what the maritime potential of the kingdom was and how great a force the kingdom might be able to muster when war came.[17] It was not just the value but also the character of trade that influenced when naval forces emerged and in what form. In the South virtually all developments came earlier than in the North. In the South galleys were the principal weapons at sea and control of specific strategic points, especially critical ports, was the basis for the navies that existed. Galleys were not used exclusively in the Mediterranean. Oared vessels were part of naval forces in the Atlantic in the Middle Ages and in the Caribbean and the Indian Ocean in the sixteenth century as European naval forces extended their reach. But it was in the Mediterranean through the sixteenth century that galley fleets were part of all naval forces and remained essential weapons for fighting either on the sea or in support of troops on land. In the North, trade in bulk goods dominated, especially after the thirteenth century. Violent confrontations by government-sponsored and government-controlled fleets tended to be less frequent in the North and those battles were typically dominated by sailing ships. That is not to say there were no small actions and no amphibious operations. They were, however, less common in the North than in the South. In the North fishers were among those commonly attacked in small actions and they looked to governments for protection. They became vocal supporters of naval forces, pressing for the manning and maintenance of armed ships. In yielding to those demands governments established navies at the very least on a temporary but over time more often on something like a permanent basis. The calls from fishers, most notably in the Low Countries, were inspired by technical changes in the catching and treating of fish in the fourteenth and fifteenth centuries.[18]

Technical change was another driving force that shaped the character and timing of the creation of naval forces. It was not just the evolution of warships and of guns on board them that influenced the choices of governments. Certainly advances made in the design and in the reliability of those two were absolutely critical to the development of naval forces. But advances in the design of merchant ships, the character of the best ships for moving the goods that could pay the freight, determined not only the need for naval forces but also their nature. The evolution of ship design in southern and northern Europe from the thirteenth century, changes in the way rowers sat in galleys in the Mediterranean to the fifteenth-century adoption of the full-rigged ship with shell-first construction in the North, left an obvious imprint on the evolution of

---

[17] Huntington Library, manuscript HM 30661 is a survey of all ships that might be used for defence from around 1630. It followed a number of earlier similar surveys. See Richard W. Unger, 'The Tonnage of Europe's Merchant Fleets 1300–1800', *The American Neptune*, 52 (Fall, 1992), 253–4.

[18] Richard W. Unger, 'The Netherlands Herring Fishery in the Late Middle Ages: The False Legend of William Beukels of Biervliet', *Viator*, 9 (1978), 335–56.

trade and on the character of fighting ships.[19] The influence was reciprocal. Over time the need for naval forces to protect merchant ships and fulfil government policy goals drove technical changes in fighting ships while effective fighting ships made it possible to change and improve the design of merchant vessels. While that mutual influence was more obvious in Renaissance Europe, again a critical period in the history of sea power, such stimulation of innovation existed throughout the years from the tenth century on. The impact of guns on the development of naval forces is probably overrated. The effects of using gunpowder weapons on board ship did not come immediately. There was a slow evolution in their effectiveness, a result of the slow evolution in their reliability, accuracy and cost. Again it was in the Renaissance that guns were to have their greatest influence. By the late sixteenth century guns were inexpensive enough and effective enough and there were enough ships designed to carry them that they could and did decide contests at sea. The introduction of gunpowder weapons very late in the thirteenth century marks one break in the history of medieval sea power and their improvement to the point of being the decisive factor in naval battles in the late Renaissance marks a second break, and also marks the beginning of the modern era of naval history.

It was not just developments in the technology of fighting and trading ships which influenced the evolution of sea power. Developments in related technologies also in a number of cases had significant influence. Improved methods in catching and curing herring at sea in the fourteenth century had a direct and long-term impact on the need for deploying naval forces to protect vulnerable sailors and their vessels. The ability to use ships of different designs and the ability to move goods economically always depended on the design and efficiency of harbour facilities. And commerce could not have functioned or expanded without improvements in the organisation of trade and in the transfer of funds over long distances so goods could flow. Navies were the product of trade, of government action and of technical change, which meant that each in different ways played a role in how force could be and was used at sea in the Middle Ages.

Theorists of naval power, of whom Alfred Thayer Mahan has for over a century been the leading figure, have ignored the Middle Ages. It appears that he and others like him were right to do so. The history of sea power in the Middle Ages and the early Renaissance was unique, very different from what was to follow. The patterns, ideas and actions of other times and places did not apply or applied only sporadically and only under certain specific circumstances. It has been wrong to try to force the era between the fall of Rome and the Anglo-Dutch Wars of the seventeenth century into the same mould as the centuries before and after.[20] It is absolutely necessary to understand navies, naval power, the use of force at sea in the intervening period on their own terms

---

[19] For a general if somewhat out-dated overview see Richard W. Unger, *The Ship in the Medieval Economy, 600–1600* (London and Montreal, 1980).
[20] For an effort somewhat along those lines see Richard W. Unger, 'Alfred Thayer Mahan,

in the context of the commerce, technology and political structures of the period. Navies after the sixteenth century would be standing forces with administration, a more-or-less permanent officer corps and shipyards, that is arsenals. Some of those elements turned up here and there before 1650 but it was only in the seventeenth century that they all came together. It was the politics, economics and technology along with the common understanding of the nature of the universe which created a different approach to the sea and questions about it, different from such views at any other time. The period from the tenth through to the sixteenth century deserves examination for that reason alone, that is its uniqueness. It is an artefact, which when compared to other times and places illustrates the forces that go into generating the types of naval forces that do prevail at any time and any place. Medieval and Renaissance maritime history is also important for what it shows about the centuries that followed. It was in those years before 1650 that the origins of modern navies are to be found. The history of sea power in the era offers a graphic example of how and why modern states emerged. No navies in the modern sense could exist without governments to create them and pay for them to continue. No modern states, at least in the form they emerged, could exist without the need to generate effective naval forces. The kingdoms of Scandinavia in the sixteenth century again offer an excellent but by no means exclusive example. The examination of sea power in the Middle Ages and Renaissance is also a process of finding when and where and why Europe changed to having competing naval forces that would claim and effectively establish dominion over the seas of the world.

The contributions to this volume, separately or taken as a whole, do not solve all the problems to do with the study of naval power before 1650. The collection should be taken as much as a guide to ignorance and where knowledge needs to expand, as a summation of the answers. With any luck it also serves as a guide to what is known at this stage in the exploration of the topic. The different authors demonstrate beyond doubt the importance of technology to this discussion. They also, either overtly and more often covertly, deal with the relationship of the changing character of government to the character of armed force at sea. The volume in the end does point to the need to understand that naval history is not just the nuts and bolts of ships and guns or the development of government departments. The volume suggests the importance of how people of the time comprehended naval power and the ways they expressed that comprehension in the language of government documents and resolutions. Their language shaped and formed the evolution of naval forces in all their aspects from the design of ships to the foundation of naval bases and to the establishment of government offices and officers. Language had its role alongside the many other pressures that joined together to create the world of European navies, navies that became a feature of what has come to be called the modern world.

Ship Design, and the Evolution of Sea Power in the Late Middle Ages', *The International History Review*, 19, 3 (August, 1997), 505–21.

INDEX

Absolon, bishop of Roskilde 29
Abū Dīnār 96
Accounts 54, 55, 58–60, 69, 70, 76
  See also Economics and Finance
Acre 120–3, 147, 154, 156
Administration 10, 253–4, 261
  in Byzantine Empire 83
  in Catalonia and Aragon 107–8, 110, 113
  in Cordoba 105
  in Denmark 225
  in England 63–4, 74
  in France, 63–4, 141
  in Genoa 123, 135, 139–45
  in Habsburg Netherlands 201–2
  Militia 25, 233–6
  Muslim 105, 108
  in Portugal 109
  Scandinavian *leding/ledung/leidang system* 29–34, 35, 46, 48–50, 235
  in Spain 105, 107–10, 115, 118
  in Sweden 230–1
  in Tuscany 172
  in Venice 155–62
  types of in the sixteenth century 233–6
Admiral 63, 63, 83, 103, 105, 108, 110, 175, 201–2
Adriatic Sea 123, 126–8, 135, 152–5
Adurnus Raphael 149
Advocatus Leonellus 147
Advoctus Petrus 147
Aegean Sea 83, 98, 104, 135, 152, 154, 160, 182
Africa 60
  Barbary coast and states 142, 145, 160, 163, 179–81, 195, 239, 241, 243
  West 196
Aigues Mortes 161–2
Albania 155, 157
Albenga 146
Alexandria 146, 157–8, 161
Alfonso III, king of Portugal 106
Alfonso V, king of Aragon 111, 141
Alfonso X, king of Castile 108
Algarve 106
Algeciras 105

Algiers 171, 180, 202, 239
Almeida, A. A. Marques de 192
Almeria 106
Almohads 105
Almoravids 105
Alva, duke of 213
Amalfi 151, 241
America 60, 92, 113, 242
American Historical Association xiii, 67
Amphibious operations *see* Operations
Ancona 147
Anderson, Per Kohrtz 42
Andronicus V 130
Anthony Roll 189
Antwerp 54, 200–1
Anund, king 28
archaeology, underwater xiii, 37, 40, 41, 46, 58
Arab *see* Muslim fleets
Aragon 105–6, 109–12, 116, 128, 130, 163, 236
Aragona Appiano, Alfonso 176 n. 22
Aragona Appiano, Iacopo VI 172, 176, 178
Arba 155
Arguim 196
Armenia 124–5, 127
Arnemuiden 200, 202, 206, 213
Arsenal
  of Barcelona 254
  of Candia 155
  of Crete 162
  of Genoa 138, 140, 143–5
  of the Peloponnese 161
  of Pisa 172 n. 5, 176
  of Tortosa, 254
  of Valencia 254
  of Venice 153–5, 171, 254
Artillery *see under* Weapons
Asiento 176–8
Atlantic Ocean 113, 117, 148, 156, 197, 259
Attaleia 83
Auria, Aitonus de 148
Auria, Gaspar de 148
Auria, Lamba de 148

264   *Index*

Auria, Lucianus de   149
Auria, Odoardus de   148
Auria, Paganinus de   149
Auria, Petrus de   149
Auria, Philipus de   149
Auria, Tediscus de   148
Auriae, Conradus   148
Auriae, Obertinus   147
Auriae, Petrus   146
Auriae, Polinus   147
Auriae, Thedisius   148
Austria, Don Juan of   178–80
Azores   196, 242

Bahia   196
Baker, Geoffrey le   65
Balard, Michel   viii, 137–49
Baldwin II, emperor   122
Balearic Islands   106
Baltic Sea   201, 214, 217–32, 250
Banco di San Giorgi   139, 141
Barbary coast and states *see under* Africa
Barcelona   108, 110, 250 n. 3
Bardas Phōkas   96
Bardas Sklēros   96
Barsi, Jacopo   155
Bases   11, 135, 190, 191, 193, 253
    See also Ports
Basil I   83
Basil II   83, 85
Basil Hexamilitēs   96, 100
Basil the Parakoimōmenos   84
Basil the Patrician   84
Bastia   170
Basque region   106, 169
Battle
  map locations of   116, 132
  names of
    Acre (1257)   132
    Acre (1258)   132
    Alghero (1353)   129, 132
    Armada (1588)   114
    Attaleia (790)   96
    Battle of the Masts (655)   96, 103
    Beversholdsveld (1382)   54
    Bona (1607)   182
    Bornholm (1535)   224
    Bornholm I (1563)   229
    Bornholm II (1565)   229
    Bosporus (1352)   129
    Carlo Zeni (1379)   132
    Carlo Zenno (1380)   132
    Cape Anzio (1378)   131–2
    Cape Chelidonia (96)   96
    Castro   132
    Chef de Caux (1417)   71
    Chioggia (1380)   132
    Chios (911)   96
    Coron (1293)   132
    Curzola (1298)   127, 132
    Cyprus (963)   96
    Djerba (1560)   113
    Durazzo (1264)   132
    l'Espagnols sur mer (1350)   56, 58, 109
    Gibraltar (1476)   111
    Great Fleet (1295)   132
    Gulf of Corinth (879)   96
    Harfleur (1416)   71, 78
    Lajazzo (1294)   132
    Lemnos (921–2)   96
    Lepanto (1571)   62, 113, 145, 178
    La Rochelle (1372)   65, 109
    Meloria (1284)   124, 128, 132, 135
    Messina (901)   96
    Milazzo (888)   96
    Naples (1284)   100 n.34
    Öland I (May 1564)   229
    Öland II (Aug 1564)   229
    Öland III (1566)   229
    Phoenix (655)   100
    Pola (1379)   131–2
    Porto Longo (1354)   130, 132
    Prevesa (1538)   113, 171
    Punto Stilo (880)   96
    St Thomas Day (905)   96
    Settepozzi (1263)   132
    Sluis (1340)   65
    Straits of Messina (965)   96
    Syracuse (827–8)   96
    Syracuse (859)   96
    Thasos (839)   96
    Trapani (1266)   122, 134
    Tripoli (975)   96
    Tripoli (998)   96
    Tunis (1535)   113
    Tyre (1257)   132
    Winchelsea (1350)   65
    Zonchio (1499)   162, 164
    See also Operations, battle
Baugh, Daniel A.   9
Bayeux tapestry   26
Bayerische Staatsbibliotek   85
Bayonne   60
Bengal, Bay of   196
Beirut   142, 146, 157
Bergen   41, 43
Bernotti, Admiral Romeo   14

Index

Biblioteca Ambrosiana, Milan 84
Biblioteca Medicea Laurenziana 85
Bill, Jan viii, 35–50, 71
Bisagno river 140
Biscay, Bay of 60, 105, 108–9
Black Death 75–76, 125, 128
Black Sea 122, 128, 143, 157
Black Prince *see* Edward of Woodstock
Blockade *see under* Operations
Bodilsen, Peder 33–4
Boletus, Ansaldus 146
Būne (Al Anabas) 182
Bonifacio 147
Booth, Ken 15
Borbonius, Lanfancus 147
Borborino, Lanfanco 122
Bordeaux 75–6
Bornholm 218, 222, 224
Boucicault, Marshal 141–3
Bragança, D. Alvaro de 192
Brasil 115, 196
Braudel, Fernand 17, 152
Brindisi 155
Brittany 75
Bruges 58
Buccaneers 242–3
Buccanigra, Egidius 149
Buccanigra, Marinus 147
Bueil, Jean de 57
Bueil, Pierre de 58
Bulgarian Empire 83
Bureaucracy *see* Administration
Burgundy 54, 201
Burgundy, Anthony of 213
Burgundy, Maximilian of 209–10
Byzantine Empire 73–104, 119, 127–8, 152–3, 250, 252

Cable, Sir James 15
Cabral, Pedro Álvarez 193
Cadiz 105, 115
Caffa 127, 143
Calais 66
Callwell, Colonel Charles 13
Camilla, Franciscus de 147
Camilla, Octobonus de, 146
Campofregoso, Pietro di 130, 140
Campofregoso, Tommasino di 141
Candia 155
Cannon *see under* Weapons
Canute the Great 26, 27
Cape Verde 196
Caribbean Sea 114, 236, 259
Carrara, Francesco 130

Cartography 215–16, 256–7
Casa de Contratacíon 236
Castex, Raoul, admiral 14
Castles *see under* Ship, design of
Castile 105–6, 108–12, 116, 149, 236
Castro 128
Catalonia and Catalans 60, 105, 107, 115, 120, 123, 129–30, 139, 145, 148, 151, 169, 250 n.3, 255
Cattaneo, Damiano 130, 140
Cattaneus, Damianus 149
Cattaro 155
Centurionus, Iohannes 149
Cephalonia 164
Cerigo 241
Ceuta 106, 146, 151
Chacuni, Francesco 155
Channel 64–6, 109, 115, 160, 206, 209
Charlemagne 25, 26
Charles of Anjou 123
Charles the Bald 27, 28
Charles V, emperor 113, 169, 172–3, 202, 208, 210–11, 221–2, 226, 255
Charles VII, king of France 58
Charles VIII, king of France 138, 143, 163
Chersōn 104
China 196
Chioggia 131–33
Chios 94, 139–40, 149
Chivalry 57
Christian II, king of Denmark 222–3, 225
Christian III, king of Denmark 224, 226
Christiana 94
Cigala, Ianotus 148
Cilicia 151
Cinque Ports 238
Cleves, Philip of, admiral-general of the Netherlands 203, 214
Clowes, William Laird 233
Coastal patrol *see under* Operations
Cock, Hieronimus, 215–16
Cog *see under* Vessel types
Colomb, Sir Philip, vice-admiral 5, 13
Columbus, Christopher 63, 188, 194
Command 10
  of the sea, 13, 237
  See also Control
Comnena, Anna 58
Compera Magna Venetorum 140
Compofregosa, Domenico, doge of Venice 131, 142
Concini, Batolomeo 173
Conservatore del mare 142

266   Index

Constans II, emperor   96, 100, 103
Constantine Condomytēs   96
Constantine VII Poryphyrogennētos   85
Constantinople   83, 87, 94, 95, 121–2, 128, 146–7, 149, 154, 179, 202
Contamine, Philippe   56
Control   13, 98, 104, 190, 207–9, 211–12, 214–15, 219, 222, 237, 253
Convoy *see under* Operations, trade protection
Copenhagen   46, 47, 223–4, 231
Copper   227–8, 230
Corbett, Sir Julian   13
Cordoba, caliphate of   105
Corfu   155
Cornaro, Giorgio, bishop of Treviso   174
Coron   152
Corsa and Corsairs   xv, 18, 110, 142, 145, 171, 181, 184, 196, 209, 236–41, 243, 246–7
See also Privateering
Corsica   124, 128, 142
Cosimo I de' Medici   169–78, 185
Cosimo II de' Medici   182
Costa, Leonor Freire   192–3
Crews *see* Manning
Courland   217
Crete   83, 85, 87, 89, 92, 95, 96, 98, 99, 146, 152, 154–5, 183
Crusader States   120, 154
Crusades
  Baltic   29
  First   55, 63, 119–20, 151, 252
  Second   95
  Fourth   152–3
  of Louis IX   146–7
Cycles in history   189–91
Cyprus   83, 124–5, 134, 140–3, 147, 149, 177, 182

Dain, Alphonse   84, 85
Dalmatia   104, 127, 154–5, 157, 164
Damietta   146
Dancing   55, 58
Dandolo, Andrea   127
Dandolo, Enrico, doge of Venice   153
Dandolo, Jacopo   122
Danube River   95
David, William G.   7
De Cerimoniis   85, 88
Defence   10, 16, 49, 50, 64–5, 104, 141, 190, 215
Dendrochronology, dating by, 41, 46

Denmark
  Medieval   25–34
  under Oldenberg dynasty   204, 206, 220–1, 225
  thirteenth-fourteenth century   35–51
  underwater archaeology in   39–41
  in the sixteenth century   217–32, 245, 249
Dieppe   243
Diet *see* Victualling
Diplomacy   15
Dockyards *see under* Shipbuilding, yards
Domingues, Francisco Content   viii, xiv, 187–97
Doria, Andrea   143–4
Doria, Gian Andrea   181
Doria, Lamba   127
Doria, Oberto   123–4
Doria, Paganino   129–30, 140, 144
Dotson, John   viii, 119–35
Doumerc, Bernard   viii, 151–65
Dover, 66
  Strait of   206
Drake, Sir Francis   246–7
Drums   58
Durazzo   241
Dutch Republic, (Republic of the United Provinces)   113, 115, 117–18, 187–8, 201, 216, 236, 243

East India Company, Dutch (VOC)   214, 236
Ecology   18
Economic warfare   16, 121
  See also under Operations, commerce raiding
Economics and finance, 8–10, 48, 50–51, 59, 74, 75, 107–10, 112–13, 118, 121, 138–45, 152, 156–60, 162, 173, 178, 183, 190, 205–6, 208–9, 211, 215, 221, 225, 227, 236, 250 n.3, 254, 261
  See also Accounts
Education and training   175 n. 16
Edward I, king of England   70, 77
Edward III, king of England   53, 56, 58, 64, 65, 75
Edward of Woodstock, the 'Black Prince'   55, 58
Elba   123, 172–3
Eleonora, queen of France   211
Embronus, Petrus   147
Engelsborg   36

England 26, 53–67, 69–79, 113–15, 117–18, 156, 169, 187–8, 191, 204, 219–20 n. 1, 243, 245
Environment 18
Erik XIV, king of Sweden 227–9
Erik Menved, king of Denmark 46, 48–51
Estonia 217–18, 226–7
Euboea 152
Eustatios Argyros 100

Facio, Clemens de 149
Famagusta 141, 181, 185
Farinha, Dias 196
Ferdinand, king of Portugal 258
Ferdinando I, grand duke of Tuscany 180–2, 185
Ferdinando II, grand duke of Tuscany 182–4
Fernando III, king of Castile 108
Fieschi, Luigi 131
Finance *see* Economics and Finance
Finland 223
Fishing 259
Fiske, Bradley, rear-admiral 13
Flags and pennants, 55–6, 64
Flanders *see* Netherlands
Fleets 11, 12
  size of war fleets 75, 125–8, 138, 145–9, 163, 204, 209, 222 n. 4
  size of merchant fleets 201
Flisco, Ludovicus de 149
Florence 85, 124, 135, 169–85
Folgietta, Paolo 144
Fondaçao Oriente xiv, xvi
Fonseca, Henrique Quirino da 191, 194
Food *see* Victuals and Victualling
Fournoi 94
France and French fleets 31, 63–5, 69, 74, 79, 109, 115–16, 118, 145, 148, 163, 169, 180, 183–4, 188, 204, 206, 209–10, 235
Francesco I, grand duke of Tuscany 178–80
Frederick I, emperor 152
Frederik I, king of Denmark 223–4
Frederik II, king of Denmark 228
Friel, Ian viii–ix, 69–9
Froissart, Jean 55, 56–7
Fulk d'Anou 26

Galicia 106
Galinara 146
Galley *see under* Vessel types
Gama, Vasco da 112, 193
Gascony 53, 66
Gemignani, Marco ix, 169–85

Genoa and Genoese ships 60, 64, 65, 71, 78, 90, 94, 95, 105–6, 108–10, 116, 151, 235, 253, 257
  in the thirteenth and fourteenth centuries 119–35, 154
  in the fifteenth and sixteenth centuries 137–49, 245
  in the seventeenth century 183
Geographical factors 10, 11, 108, 115, 118, 124, 132, 219–20, 241, 250
Gerold the Steward 26
Ghent 54
Gibraltar, Strait and Rock of 108, 111, 169, 196, 241
Giffard, Walter 26
Gigala, Nicola 147
Giustiniani, Fabrizio 143
Glete, Jan ix, 112, 207, 217–32
Gloucester 70
Goa 112, 192, 196
Goano, Petrus de 148
Godfred 25–6
Golwitz 49
Gothenberg (Göteborg) 220
Gotland 218–19
Gotti, Alessandro de 155
Granellus, Georgius 149
Grassi, Christoforo 144–5
Great Yarmouth 59
Gregory XIII, pope 178–80
Greenland 61
Grenada 177
Grillo, Simon 122–3, 125, 134, 147
Grillus, Accelinus 148
Grimaldi, Antonio 129, 148
Grimaldi, Gaspar de 148
Grimaldis, Luchetus de 147
Grimaldo, Petrinus de 147
Grimani, Antonio 164
Guadalquivir river 106
Guarco, Isnardus de 149
Guarco, Nicolo, doge of Venice 131
Guercius, Fulco 146
Guercius, Simon 147
Guerre de course *see* Privateering; Corsairs; *and under* Operations, commerce raiding
Guilmartin, John F., Jr 17, 207
Gunpowder and Guns *see under* Weapons
Gun carriages 73, 117–18
Gun ports *see under* Ship, design of
Gunners 73
Gustav I Vasa, king of Sweden 223–4, 226

Index

Hans, king of Denmark   36, 221–2
Hanseatic League   xv, 17, 46, 47, 49, 50, 217, 222–3, 231
Harwich   65
Hattendorf, John B.   ix, xiii–xv, 1–22, 197
Hawley, John, of Dartmouth   77
Hebrides   61
Hedeby   47
Heeres, Jacques   137–8
Helsingborg   47, 218
Helsingfors (Helsinki)   218, 226
Henry, count of Malta   146
Henry II, king of England   57
Henry IV, king of England   70, 72, 77–8
Henry IV, king of France   180
Henry V, king of England   66, 71, 73–4, 75–8
Henry VII, king of England   73
Henry VIII, king of England   189, 204, 208
Heraldry   55–6
Hesychios of Alexandria   84
Himerios   92, 96
Himmelev   44, 45
Hjelm   48
Holy League   177, 179
Horik   25–6
Horses   47, 53, 54, 59, 95
Houts, Elizabeth van   26
Howard, Sir John   72, 73
Hugh, count of Avranches   26
Hugh of Montfort   26
Huizinga, Johan   57
Hungarians and Hungary   130–1, 154
Hyth   59
Hvide family   49

Iacharia, Benedictus   147–8
Iconography *see under* Ship, illustrations and iconography of
Igor   95
India   192–3, 196
Indian Ocean   60, 112, 117, 195–6, 259
Inghirami, Iacopo, admiral   181 n. 48
Innocent X, pope   183
Insignia *see* Heraldry; Flags and Pennants
Intelligence   66, 99
Ionian Sea   97
Ios   94
Ipswich   59, 62
Ireland   61, 70, 235, 243
Iron   227, 230
Istria   130–1, 154

Jaime I, king of Catalonia   63

James VI and I, king of Scotland and England, 243
Janus, king of Cyprus   141
Japan   196
Jaroslav   95
Jersey, island of   109
Jerusalem   154
   See also Crusader States
Johan III, king of Sweden   227, 229
John, king of England   70, 74, 77
John Cantacuzene, emperor   128
John Echimos   96
Joseph Bringas   87
Jouvencel, Le   57
Julius Pollux   84

Kalmar   222
Karpathos   98
Kattegat   218, 226
Kibyrrhaiōtai   96, 100, 103
Kings Lynn   70
Kingsley, Charles, 246
Knights   55–6
   See also Orders
Knud the Holy, king of Denmark   28, 31, 33
Knud VI, king of Denmark   29, 34
Kuscadasi   94

Lajazzo   151
Lam, Erik   33–4
Lane, Frederic   128
Language and expression   55–7
Lannoye, Philip of   213
Lateran Council, Second (1119)   58
Laughton, Sir John Knox   5, 12
Law
   and the sea   64, 238, 240–2
   Codes
      Jutland   30, 32, 48
      Norway   32–3
      Scandinavian   25, 29–34
      Siete Partidas   110
      Skåne   30, 48
      Sweden   31
Leipzig University Library   85
Leghorn   169–72, 175, 180, 183–4
Leo VI, emperor   84–5, 97, 99, 101–2
Leo of Tripoli   96, 100
Lercarius, Nicola   146
Lercarius, Ugo   146
Lesina   155
Letter of Marque   241
Lettre de Merk   238, 241

Index

Levanto, Iacobus de   146
Libelle of Englyshe Polycye   66, 208, 255
Lighthouses   209
Liguria   131, 142, 145
Limited warfare, 13
Lines of communication *see* Routes at sea
Lions, Gulf of   177
Lisbon   105–6, 109, 112, 196
Lithuania   217–18, 227
Livonia   50, 217, 227
Livorno *see* Leghorn
Logistics   59, 191, 230
   See also Victualling
Lopez, Robert S.   137
Louis III of Duras   142
Louis IX, king of France   123, 146–7
Lübeck   27, 50, 222–4, 227, 231, 249
Lucca   124, 135
Luce, Stephen B., rear-admiral   5, 12, 21
Lund, Niels   ix, 25–34
Lusignans, kingdom of the   141. *See also* Peter II of Lusignan

Macao   196
Macedonia   83
Machiavelli, Nicolò   173
Machiavelli, Piero   173, 176
McNeill, John R.   18
Madeira   197
Magistrate delle galee   144
Magnerri, Nicolaus   149
Mahan, Alfred Thayer, rear-admiral
   his work and influence   1–22, 119
   analysis and interpretation   2, 6–12
   relevance or non-relevance to the medieval period   5, 18–21, 66–67, 104, 118, 187, 189, 193, 197, 199, 207–9, 212, 236, 251, 253, 258, 260–1
Majorca   180
Malacca   112
Malaga   176
Mälaren, Lake   39
Mallonus, Paschetus   147
Mallorca   106–7
Malocellus, Carbonus   146
Malocellus, Iacobus   146
Malonus, Guglielmus   146
Malonus, N.   146
Malonus, Octobonus   146
Malta, knights of, *see under* Order, St John of Jerusalem
Malvasia (Monemvasia)   122
Mamlukes   142

Mamora   243
Manning
   in Byzantium   86, 95–7
   in England   59, 71
   in Genoa   126 n. 24, 138, 141
   in Iberia   107, 110–11, 114
   in Scandinavia   29–34, 50–1
   in Venice   128, 155, 160, 162, 164, 171
Manwaring, Sir Henry   243
Maona   142
   of Chios   140, 143
   Vecchia di Cipro   140–1
Marchioni, D. Álvaro de   192
Maremma coast   172
Margaret, Queen   49–51
Mari, Enricus de   147
Mari, Gando de   127
Mari, Ivanesius de   149
Marini, Franciscus de   148
Marinis, Octobonus de   148
Marseilles   161–2, 176
Maruffus, Matheus   149
Maruffus, Nicolaus   149
Mary of Hungary, regent of the Netherlands   202, 209, 211
Massa   147
Masts   45, 60, 61, 69, 72, 78, 193–5
   See also Rigs
Matilda, queen   26
Maurice   84
Mazarin, cardinal   183
Mecklenburg   49, 218
Medici family   169–85
Medici, Francesco, prince   178
Medici, Giulio de'   175
Medici, Marie de'   180
Medici, Pietro de'   178
Medici, Tommaso de', admiral   179–80
Medina Sidonia   105
Melcomb, Dorset   59
Menon, Raja   16
Messina   181, 241
Messina, strait of   126
Michael II, emperor   96
Michael Palaeologus   121
Milan   84, 128, 131, 133–4, 145, 163
Military Revolution   10, 57, 67
Militia *see under* Administration
Mina (Elmina)   196
Modelski, George   187–93, 196
Modena   182
Modon   152, 164
Molo   140
Monaco   127, 184, 241

Monemvasia   241
Montaldo, Leonardo   142
Morea   122
Morosini, Albertino   124
Morosini, Giacomo, 'el zio'   155
Mott, Lawrence V.   x, 105–18
Mozambique   192
Munich   85
Muritius, Thomas   149
Music   55, 58
Muslim fleets   96, 99, 104, 105, 107, 116, 180–1, 184, 243, 250

Næstved   33, 48
Naples   111, 163, 169, 183
Narva   227, 229
Naser   96–7
Nation-building   15
Nauplia   155
Naval Architecture *see under* Ship, design of
Navarino   178
Navies, standing   204–5, 209–11, 231, 236, 252
   types of in the sixteenth century   233–6
Navigation, knowledge of   64, 175
Naxos   92, 94, 152
Negroponte   122, 128–9, 154
Netherlands   114, 156, 163, 177, 196, 235, 250 n.3
   Habsburg   199–216
   Map of   200
   See also Dutch Republic
Newbolt, Sir Henry   246
Nicholas, abbot of St Ouen   26
Niels, brother of Knud the Holy   32
Nigro, Luchinus de   148
Nigro, Sologrus de   148
Nikephōros Ouranos   84, 85, 97, 99, 100
Nikētas Ooryphas   96
Nikētas Magistros   92
Nizza Marittima   146
Nocera   142
Norby, Sören, admiral   223
Normandy   69, 70, 75
Normans   105, 151, 236
North Sea   66, 201, 209, 236, 250
Norway   27, 29, 41, 46, 47, 220 n. 2
Novi   133

Oarsmen and oarage systems   86–93, 225, 245, 259
Odo, bishop of Bayeux   26
Offensive stance   16, 49, 79, 209, 212
Officium Balie Marittime   141

Officium Gazarie   141
Officium Guerre Venetorum   140
Officium Maris   141
Officium super gubernatione Darsine Communis Janue et armamentorum gallearum   143
Oissel island   27
Öland   218, 222
Oleg of Kiev   95
Oltremare   120 n. 4, 121–2, 134, 146–7
Operations
   types of
      ambushes   100
      amphibious   16, 47, 55, 181–2, 185, 222, 225–6, 237, 244, 252
      anti-pirate/corsair   49, 109, 160, 163, 184, 209–10, 239
      battle   11, 13, 46, 56, 96, 99, 109, 111, 113, 116, 128, 132, 134–5, 199
      blockade   47, 63, 106, 109, 125, 134, 199, 221–2, 227, 229
      coastal patrol   33, 142, 160, 194, 196, 209, 244
      commerce raiding   74, 109, 124–5, 135, 160, 214, 247
      commerce protection   45, 66, 75, 114, 143, 145, 155, 160–1, 184, 194, 209, 211, 226–7, 242
      raids   16, 45, 46, 47, 65, 122–3, 132, 244
      sentry   142–4
      supply   47, 122, 145, 253
      transporting troops   45, 46, 53, 63, 99, 122, 202, 244, 253
      See also Offense; Defence, Shipping, merchant
Oran   176
Orbetello   173
Order
   of the Knights of Alcantara   174
   of Calatrava   174
   of Christ   174
   of St Iacopo of the Sword, 174
   of St John of Jerusalem (Malta)   xv, 161, 181 n. 47, 239
   of St Stephen, 173–85, 239
   Teutonic, 217, 226–7
Ordo galearum armatarum (1321)   156
Organization *see* Administration
Orwell   59
Ösel (Saaremaa) island   218, 227
Otranto, Straits of   98

Index

Ottoman Empire 113–14, 116–17, 135, 145, 154, 181, 182, 239

Pacific Ocean 236
Padua 130
Pago 155
Panzanus, Bonifacius 146
Papacy and Papal States 113, 121–2, 142, 145, 147, 163, 169, 178–9, 184
Parker, Geoffrey 207
Parma 182
Paros 92
Pasajes 115
Patzinak 83
Pedersen, Ole Crumlin 71
Pedro IV, king of Aragon 110, 128
Peñon de Velez 176
Pera 122, 125, 127–9, 135, 143
Pereira, Moacyr Soares 192
Persian Gulf 62, 196
Peter II of Lusignan, king of Jerusalem and Cyprus, 130–1, 140
Petrarco, Nicolinus de 148
Philippe de Poitiers, lord of La Ferte 58
Philip of Monfort, lord of Tyre and king of Armenia 120–1
Philip II, king of Spain 114, 172–3, 176–7, 179, 204, 208, 215
Philip III, king of Spain 115, 180
Philip IV, king of Spain 183–4
Phillips, Carl Rahn 18
Philothenes 103
Phygela 94
Pietrasanta 161
Pilots 59
Piombino 170, 172–3, 241
Piombino Channel 183
Pirates and piracy 49, 65, 77, 105–6, 109–10, 113–14, 156, 163, 209–10, 237–9, 243, 246
Pisa 95, 119–21, 123–4, 130, 135, 146–8, 151, 169–72, 174, 177–8, 253
Pisani, Niccolo 129
Pisani, Vettor 131, 133
Pius IV, pope 173–4
Pius V, pope 177
Plymouth 53, 65
Po River 152
Podebusk, Henning 49
Podestat of Genoa 146–7
Poland-Lithuania 217, 227, 231
Pomegues island 176
Poole 109

Pope *see* Papacy *and* names of individual popes
Porcellus, Franeschinus 148
Pore 154
Port'Ercole 170, 173
Portoferraio 170, 172–4
Porto Pisano 169–70
Ports 51, 53, 59, 94, 114, 152–4, 191
    See also Bases
Portugal 72, 75, 106, 108, 111–13, 115–16, 118, 187–97, 206, 240–2, 245
    and Aviz dynasty 204
Position *see* Geographical factors
Príncipe 196
Privateering 66, 160, 171, 236–41
    anachronistic use of term 240–1
    See also Corsairs *and under* Operations, commerce raiding
Procida, strait of 170
Provence 123, 142, 161
Provisions *see* Victualling
Prussia 49, 75, 217–18, 224
Pryor, John H. x, 83–104
Position *see* Geographical position
Puglia 55
Pula 54

Quarto, Simon de 49

Ragusa 235
Raiding expeditions *see under* Operations
Recco 140–1, 144
Recruiting *see* Manning
Red Sea 62, 196
Remigius, almoner of Fecamp and bishop of Lincoln 26
Reprisal, letters of 238, 244
Resources 11
Reval (Tallinin) 218, 226–7
Reynolds, Clark G. 14, 16, 249
Rhodes 83, 98, 148, 162, 241
Ribnitz 49
Richard I, king of England 70
Richard II, king of England 78
Richmond, Admiral Sir Herbert 14
Riga 218, 227
Rigs
    types of sailing 78, 111, 194–5, 210, 245
    lateen 72, 193
Riviera 140–1, 144, 146–8
Robert, count of Eu 26
Robert of Anjou 28

Robert the Frisian, count of Flanders 28
Rodger, N. A. M.   x, 71, 110, 233–47
Roger, count of Mortain   26
Roger of Beaumont   26
Roger of Lauria   100 n.34
Roger of Montgomery   26
Romania   125, 127, 129, 146–9, 154
Rōmanos I Lekapēnos   103
Rome   146
    Roman Empire   252
Rosinski, Herbert   2 n. 7, 14
Roskilde   33
Rossermini, Simone   178–9 n.35
Rosso della Turca   122
Rostock   49, 222
Rouen   27, 74
Routes at sea   10, 11, 65, 87, 94, 132, 145, 156–7, 160–1, 163, 190, 192–3, 196, 214, 219, 222, 224, 237, 253
Rudder   61–3, 69
Rügen, Arkona   33
Runyan, Timothy J.   x, 43, 53–67
Russia   95, 104, 188, 220, 226–7
Rye   59

Sails *see* Masts; Rigs
St Ansgar, life of   28
St Antony the Younger   96
St Bertin, Annals of   27
St-Maur-des-Fossés   27
St Olav   39
St Stephan, pope and martyr   174
    See also under Order, St Stephan
Salee   240–1, 243
Salle, Antoine de la   56
Salmon, duke of Brittany   28
Salvago, António   192
Samos   83, 94, 104
Sancho IV, king of Castile   109
Sandwich   53
Santiago de Compostella, bishop of   105
Sanudo, Marino   127, 159
São Tomé   196
Sardinia   120, 124, 127–8, 130, 142, 147
Sarzano   140
Savona   140–1, 144, 146
Saxo Grammaticus   29, 33, 45–6
Schepper, Cornelis de   203–4, 206, 209, 211, 213, 215, 256
Scotland   64, 65, 69, 74, 79, 235–6, 242, 245
Sebenico   155
Seine river   27, 28
Senarega, Matteo, doge of Genoa   139
Sernigi, Girolamo   192

Sestri Levante   140–1, 144
Settepozzi (Spetsai)   122
Seville   105, 108–9
Ships
    Cruising range of   92–5
    Design of   60–1, 72, 117, 152, 158, 188, 193–5, 245–6, 250, 257
        Castles on ships   40, 44, 45–6, 69, 71, 75, 101, 106, 112, 193, 235, 259
        Gun ports and rooms   72, 79, 203, 210
    Illustrations and iconography of   37–9, 44, 45,55, 60, 62, 71
    Inventory of   73
    Names of
        All Hallows Cog   73
        Bremen Cog   39, 42, 62
        Capitana   176
        Cog John   75
        La Cordeliere   73
        Craacher   77
        Dieulabenie   78
        Dragon   207
        Eagle   207
        Edward   72
        Edward Howard   73
        Engelen   221
        Esprivier   207
        Falcon [1]   204
        Falcon [2]   207
        Fiorenza   175–6, 178
        Flying Deer   207
        Flying Griffen   207
        Fortuna   178–9
        Fox of Dieppe   207
        Galley of Flanders   158
        George Howard   73
        Goat   207
        Golden Lion   207
        Grace Dieu   72, 78
        Grace de Dieu   76
        Helgeandsholmen V   38
        Holigost   73, 78
        Jesus   77, 78
        Jonas   207
        Kollerup cog   41–2
        Lupa   175
        Maria   221
        Martin Garsia   73
        Mary   207
        Mary of the Tower   73
        Mary Rose   58
        Michael   223

Index

Nossa Senhora Aununciada 192
Olympias 88
Ox 39
Pisana 171
Raven 207
Regent 73, 74, 78
Regina 176
Roaring Lion 207
Roskilde 6, 46
Salvator 207
Santa Maria 63
Sea Knight 207
Skanör *cog* 39
Snake 39
Sovereign 73
Stora Kravelen 223
Swallow 207
Trinity 78
Sizes of 37, 46, 47, 50, 71, 78, 137–8, 230. See also Tonnage
Speed of 92
Types of *see* Vessels
Shipbuilding 77, 138, 153, 219, 250
 techniques of 38, 40–2, 56, 60, 72, 77, 158
 carvel-built 193
 clinker-built 37, 43, 61, 69, 70, 77, 106
 cog tradition 38, 42, 44
 shell-first construction 61
 yards 36, 74, 225, 257
Shipping, merchant 8, 17, 47, 61, 62, 66, 75, 114, 128, 134, 137–8, 145, 152, 155, 158, 162, 184, 189, 195, 199, 204, 212, 214, 226–7, 253
Sicily 90, 107, 126–7, 145, 151, 181, 236
Sicking, Louis x, 197, 199–216
Sidroc, earl 28
Siena 172–4
Signaling 64, 65, 98
Silva e Meneses, D. Diogo da, king's tutor and count of Portalegre 192
Skaggerak 218, 226
Skamstrup 39
Skrøbelev 44, 45
Slave trade 239
Slesvig 49
Slesvig, duke of 34
Slien 49
Sluis 200
Smyrna 149
Soldanus, Ansaldus 146
Sound, The 201, 212, 218, 220, 222, 226, 228
Southampton 53, 65

Spain (after 1479) 113, 143, 145, 171, 176, 179, 181, 183–5, 187 n. 4, 188, 204, 211, 215–16, 221n.3, 235, 240–2, 254
 See also Aragon; Castile; Portugal
Spezia, La 170
Spies *see* Intelligence
Spinola, Oberto 123
Spinola, Tomaso 127
Spinula, Lanfrancus 146
Spinula, Neapolionus 148
Spinula, Nicolaus 146
Split 155
Starr, Chester 207
State formation 231
Steering devices *see* Rudder
Stella, Giorgio 129, 139
Stockholm 39, 218, 222–3, 231
Stralsund 49, 50, 222–3
Strategy, 10, 64, 65, 66, 97–103, 119, 121, 123, 132, 134, 185, 215, 227
Struppa, Aron de 149
Sumida, Jon Tetsuro 2 n. 7, 7–8
Superiority 11, 79, 99
Supplies *see* Logistics; Victualling
Susa 180
Syria 142
Syrianos Magistros 98, 100
Sweden 27, 28, 47, 49
 in the sixteenth century 217–32, 250
 under Vasa dynasty 204, 206, 223–32
Swein Forkbeard 26, 27
Syria 121

Tabour 58
Tacitus 25
Tactics 64, 65, 70, 74, 79, 97–103, 112, 122, 230, 244–7
 Taktikon Beneševic 104
 Taktikon Uspenskij 103
Talamone 173
Tarifa 108
Tarsos 96, 100
Taxes *see* Economics and Finance
Technology xii, 4, 57, 61 n. 31, 69–79, 134, 185, 231, 241, 250
Telo, António José 190
Tenedos 130, 133
Texel 200
Theophilos, emperor 96
Thēra 94
Thessalonikē 100
Thomas the Slav 95, 96
Thompson, William R. 187–93, 196

Thorkel the Tall 27, 28
Thoukydidēs, 84
Tiberios II 103
Tiepolo, Lorenzo, doge of Venice 120, 154
Timber, for shipbuilding 43, 46, 138, 153, 162, 177, 227
Toledo, Don Garcia de 176–7
Tonnage 60, 70, 76, 138, 221 n.3, 223, 230, 232
   See also under Ship, sizes of
Tortosa 176
Tracy, James D. 207–8, 212
Trade *see* Shipping, merchant
Trapini 146
Trau 155
Treaties
   Cateau-Cambrésis (1559) 206
   Nymphaeum (1261) 121
   Spain and Tuscany (1557) 173
   Tordesillas (1494) 216 n. 53
   Turin (1381) 133
Trevisan, Marco 164
Treviso 174
Tripoli 147, 149, 239
Trumpet 58
Tunis and Tunisia 96, 97, 123, 147, 149, 161, 202, 239
Turcha, Rubeus de 146–7
Tuscany 124, 169–85
Tyre 120–2, 147
Tyrrhenian Sea 119, 123, 135, 169–70, 172, 182–4

Ultremare *see* Oltremare
Unger, Richard, W. x, xiii–xv, 21, 119 n. 1, 197, 207, 249–61
Uniforms 56
United Provinces of the Netherlands see *Dutch Republic*
United States of America 187–8
Urban II, pope 122
Urban VI, pope 142
Urban VIII, pope 182

Valdemar I the Great 28, 29, 46, 47
Valdemar II the Victorious 25, 34
Valdemar IV Atterdag 47, 49
Valencia 106–7, 110
Valente, Giovanni, doge of Genoa 140
Veere 200, 202, 204–6, 210, 213
Vegitius xiv, xv n.3
Venice, 58, 60, 95, 116, 143, 145
   in the thirteenth and fourteenth centuries 119–35, 147–8, 152–3
   in the fifteenth century 154–65
   in the sixteenth and seventeenth centuries 179, 182–3, 245
Ventimiglia 146
Ventus, Otto 147
Ventus, Ugo 147
Vessel types
   Arab 62–3
   Ballinger 60, 69, 70–2, 77
   Barache 138
   Barge 59, 60, 69, 70–1, 73, 77
   Barcha 147; bark, 69, 77
   Bireme 85, 124–5, 134
   Boat 60
   Brigantine 138, 143
   Bucius 146
   Busse 59, 60
   Carabela 111
   Caravel 72, 112, 192, 194–5
   Carrack 71–2, 77–8, 112, 117, 244, 257
   Chelandion 89, 94–5
   Cocha 72
   Cogge/cog 37, 39–42, 44–8, 50, 59, 60, 62, 63, 71, 109, 111
   Crayer 60
   Dogger 60
   Drakkar/dragon ship 45, 70
   Dromon 85–103
   Egyptian funerary boats 62
   Flune 60
   Fuste 138
   Gabot 60
   Galleas 141, 178–9
   Galleon 112, 114, 117, 179, 192–5, 245–6
   Galioni 138, 147–8
   Galley 37, 47, 50, 59, 60, 65, 69, 70, 84, 86, 106, 109, 111, 113, 122, 138, 141, 143, 145–9, 152, 155, 157–8, 160–85, 225, 237, 244–5, 259
   Holc/hulk 37, 59, 60, 203
   Huisser 141
   Liburna 40, 45
   Ligna 146
   Lodship 60
   Longship 45, 47
   Nao 111, 192–5
   Navi 37, 122, 138, 141, 146–7, 157, 171
   Nef 60, 109, 111
   Parau 192
   Saette 138–9

Sagitteae 146–7
Scandinavian warships 35–51, 236
Schep/ship 37, 60, 78, 111
Skute 37
Snekke 37
Spinace 59, 60
Tampions 73
Tarida 146
Tarite 60
Triēreis 84, 91, 97
Trireme 124–5, 134
See also Shipping, merchant *and under* Ship, names of
Viborg (Viipuri) 226
Vicomes, Belmustus 146
Victuals and Victualling 49, 53–5, 87–92, 99
Vignoso, Simone 139–40, 149
Vikings 25–50
See also Normans
Villafranca 241
Villani, Giovanni 60
Visby 229
Visconti, Bernabò 131
Visconti, Giovanni, archbishop of Milan 130
Visconti, Matteo 128
Vital, Laurent 208
Vitalie brothers 49, 50
Vivaldo, Ugolinus de 148
Volta, Iohanes Rubeus de 146
Voyages, length of 87

Walcheren island 202, 205–6, 213, 226
Waldemar *see* Valdemar
Wales 69, 79, 235
Walsingham 109
Wars
    American Civil War (1861–65) 5
    Anglo-Dutch 3, 197, 260
    Anglo-French naval wars (1689–1815) 4, 5, 8
    Anglo-Spanish (1585–1603) 240
    The Barbarini (1640–4) 182–3
    Bosphorus (1350–5) 140
    Candia (1645) 182
    Carthaginian 16
    Castilian-Aragonese (1357) 109
    Chioggia (1372) 130, 139, 156
    Crete (1645) 183
    Curzola (1294–97) 124–6, 128, 134
    Dutch Revolt 213
    First War of Castro (1640–4) 182–3
    French-Habsburg (1521–1559) 202

    Graeco-Persian (fifth century BC) 16
    Hundred Years' War (1337–1453) 54–67, 79, 109, 208, 255
    Morea 185
    Nordic Seven Years' (1563–1760) 228–30
    Portuguese-Castilian 196
    Punic 16
    of Religion 243–4
    Russo-Japanese War 5
    San Saba (1257) 120–2
    Second World War 14
    Sicilian Vespers (1282–1302) 110
    Spanish-American War (1898) 5
    Thirty Years' (1618–1648) 115, 183, 219
    Turko-Iranian (16th–18th centuries) 16
    Venetian-Genoese (1379) 133, 156
    See also Crusades
Water supply 87–92, 99
Weapons
    Arbalest 54
    Bombard 73, 111, 133
    bow and arrow 53, 65, 102
    bow-ballistae 102
    caltrops 102
    catapult 46, 47, 54
    cannon 50, 54, 71, 73, 78, 111, 113, 117, 133–4, 195, 203, 205, 210, 214, 219, 221–2, 230, 244–5, 260
    chanber 73
    crane 103
    Crossbow 47, 58, 65, 175 n.16
    Grappling 102, 245
    Greek fire 54, 95, 97, 97 n.28, 101–2
    Gunpowder 54, 58, 64, 66, 78, 111, 133, 195, 261
    Hakbush 73
    Javelin 102
    Musket 73
    Ram 97
    Ribald 57
    Rocks 102–3
    Serpentines 73
    Spur 97
    Werke 47
    See also Gunners; Gun Carriages
Weather 98, 129, 176–7
Wegener, Wolfgang, vice-admrial 13
Weland 27, 28
Wends 28, 33
William, count of Evreux 26
William the conqueror, duke of Normandy 26, 33

William fitz Osborn 26
William, John 77
Winchester 27, 62
Wismar 49, 222
Wood *see* Timber
Wylie, Joseph C., rear-admiral, 16

Zaccaria, Benedetto, admiral 109, 124, 135
Zacharias, Martinus 149
Zara 155, 163
Zeno, Carlo 131–3

The Battle of Hastings: Sources and Interpretations
edited and introduced by Stephen Morillo

Infantry Warfare in the Early Fourteenth Century:
Discipline, Tactics, and Technology
Kelly DeVries

The Art of Warfare in Western Europe during
the Middle Ages, from the Eighth Century to 1340 (second edition)
J. F. Verbruggen

Knights and Peasants:
The Hundred Years War in the French Countryside
Nicholas Wright

Society at War:
The Experience of England and France during the Hundred Years War
edited by Christopher Allmand

The Circle of War in the Middle Ages:
Essays on Medieval Military and Naval History
edited by Donald J. Kagay and L. J. Andrew Villalon

The Anglo-Scots Wars, 1513–1550: A Military History
Gervase Phillips

The Norwegian Invasion of England in 1066
Kelly DeVries

The Wars of Edward III: Sources and Interpretations
edited and introduced by Clifford J. Rogers

War Cruel and Sharp:
English Strategy under Edward III, 1327–1360
Clifford J. Rogers

The Normans and their Adversaries at War:
Essays in Memory of C. Warren Hollister
edited by Richard P. Abels and Bernard S. Bachrach

The Battle of the Golden Spurs (Courtrai, 11 July 1302)
A Contribution to the History of Flanders' War of Liberation
J.F. Verbruggen